New St. Joseph

Handbook for Proclaimers of the Word

LITURGICAL YEAR A

2002

By

Rev. Jude Winkler, OFM Conv.

WITH THE "NEW AMERICAN BIBLE" TEXT
FROM THE REVISED SUNDAY LECTIONARY

CATHOLIC BOOK PUBLISHING CO.
New Jersey

Concordat cum originali:
Reverend James P. Moroney
Executive Director, Secretariat for the Liturgy
National Conference of Catholic Bishops

ACKNOWLEDGMENTS

(T-84)

CONTENTS

SEASON OF ADVENT

December 2, 2001
First Sunday of Advent 10
December 8, 2001
The Immaculate Conception.........................14
December 9, 2001
Second Sunday of Advent.............................18
December 16, 2001
Third Sunday of Advent 23
December 23, 2001
Fourth Sunday of Advent 27

SEASON OF CHRISTMAS

December 25, 2001
Christmas—At the Vigil Mass 30
December 25, 2001
Christmas—Mass at Midnight......................36
December 25, 2001
Christmas—Mass at Dawn 40
December 25, 2001
Christmas—Mass During the Day 43
December 30, 2001
The Holy Family..49
January 1, 2002
Mary, the Mother of God.............................54
January 6, 2002
The Epiphany of the Lord 57
January 13, 2002
The Baptism of the Lord 61

ORDINARY TIME

January 20, 2002
Second Sunday in Ordinary Time 64
January 27, 2002
Third Sunday in Ordinary Time...................67
February 3, 2002
Fourth Sunday in Ordinary Time.................72
February 10, 2002
Fifth Sunday in Ordinary Time 76

SEASON OF LENT

February 13, 2002
Ash Wednesday 79

February 17, 2002
First Sunday of Lent 83
February 24, 2002
Second Sunday of Lent 89
March 3, 2002
Third Sunday of Lent...................................92
March 10, 2002
Fourth Sunday of Lent.................................100
March 17, 2002
Fifth Sunday of Lent 108
March 24, 2002
Palm Sunday of the Lord's Passion 116
March 28, 2002
Chrism Mass...135

EASTER TRIDUUM AND SEASON OF EASTER

March 28, 2002
Holy Thursday—Evening Mass
of the Lord's Supper 138
March 29, 2002
Good Friday of the Lord's Passion.............143
March 30, 2002
The Easter Vigil...156
March 31, 2002
Easter Sunday 183
April 7, 2002
Second Sunday of Easter 188
April 14, 2002
Third Sunday of Easter 193
April 21, 2002
Fourth Sunday of Easter 199
April 28, 2002
Fifth Sunday of Easter 204
May 5, 2002
Sixth Sunday of Easter................................209
May 09, 2002
The Ascension of the Lord 213
May 12, 2002
Seventh Sunday of Easter...........................217

CONTENTS

May 19, 2002
Pentecost Sunday, At the Vigil Mass 221
May 19, 2002
Pentecost Sunday, Mass During
the Day 229

ORDINARY TIME

May 26, 2002
The Most Holy Trinity................................234
June 2, 2002
The Most Holy Body and
Blood of Christ 237
June 9, 2002
Tenth Sunday in Ordinary Time 243
June 16, 2002
Eleventh Sunday in Ordinary Time............247
June 23, 2002
Twelfth Sunday in Ordinary Time 251
June 30, 2002
Thirteenth Sunday in Ordinary Time.........255
July 7, 2002
Fourteenth Sunday in Ordinary Time 259
July 14, 2002
Fifteenth Sunday in Ordinary Time............263
July 21, 2002
Sixteenth Sunday in Ordinary Time 269
July 28, 2002
Seventeenth Sunday in Ordinary
Time...274
August 4, 2002
Eighteenth Sunday in Ordinary
Time...279
August 11, 2002
Nineteenth Sunday in Ordinary
Time...283
August 15, 2002
The Assumption, At the Vigil Mass 287
August 15, 2002
The Assumption, Mass During the Day 290
August 18, 2002
Twentieth Sunday in Ordinary Time 294

August 25, 2002
Twenty-First Sunday in Ordinary Time......298
September 1, 2002
Twenty-Second Sunday in Ordinary
Time...301
September 8, 2002
Twenty-Third Sunday in Ordinary Time 304
September 15, 2002
Twenty-Fourth Sunday in Ordinary
Time...307
September 22, 2002
Twenty-Fifth Sunday in Ordinary Time 312
September 29, 2002
Twenty-Sixth Sunday in Ordinary Time ...316
October 6, 2002
Twenty-Seventh Sunday in Ordinary
Time...321
October 13, 2002
Twenty-Eighth Sunday in Ordinary
Time...326
October 20, 2002
Twenty-Ninth Sunday in Ordinary Time....331
October 27, 2002
Thirtieth Sunday in Ordinary Time............334
November 1, 2002
All Saints..338
November 3, 2002
Thirty-First Sunday in Ordinary Time 342
November 10, 2002
Thirty-Second Sunday in Ordinary
Time...346
November 17, 2002
Thirty-Third Sunday in Ordinary Time......350
November 24, 2002
Christ the King 355

APPENDICES

1: The Books of the Bible Read in the
   Three-Year Cycle...............................360
2: The Responsorial Psalm 382
3: Glossary and Pronunciation Guide........385
4: Index of Biblical Texts 397

INTRODUCTION

THE WORD OF GOD

"The word of God is alive and active, sharper than a two-edged sword, able to separate soul and spirit, bone and marrow, discerning the thoughts and intentions of the heart" (Hebrews 4:12).

With these words, the author of the Letter to the Hebrews speaks of the power of the word of God. It has a profound effect both upon creation and upon our hearts. It was by the word that God created the heavens and the earth. The word is effective, for in Hebrew theology the word makes present and real the things that it proclaims. Thus, God speaks, and those things come into existence. God even shares the power of the word with us, for he commands Adam to name the animals he had created. By naming the animals, Adam is given dominion over all of creation.

The word is the communication of God's will. He reveals his word to the prophets who then proclaim it to the people of Israel. He gives his law that teaches us how to walk in God's ways. (Remember, the ten commandments are also called the "decalogue," which means the "ten words"). He sends wisdom to reveal his mysteries to his beloved chosen people. Wisdom instructs the foolish and brings them to the path of righteousness.

In the New Testament, we hear that the word of God is Jesus, the Son of God. The word of God existed in the beginning. It was communicated to God's people, Israel, throughout their history. Then, in the fullness of time, it was made flesh and dwelt among us.

Jesus proclaimed the word of God in word and deed to those who would listen and change their hearts. He promised the gift of the Holy Spirit so that the community could remember what he had done and understand what it all meant.

As the community of believers grew and matured, it realized that it needed to preserve their words about Jesus. Members of the community wrote Letters, Gospels, collections of stories, and even prophetic revelations so that they would know the life and teaching of Jesus and also what those things meant for their daily lives.

MINISTERS OF THE WORD

The Church affirmed that this word (the New Testament) and the word of revelation known as the Hebrew Scriptures (the Old Testament) were inspired by the Holy Spirit. She entrusted that word to the community. Some in the community were called to copy and preserve the word, others to study it, others to proclaim it liturgically, others to preach on how to apply it to their lives, etc.

As lectors, you share in the tradition of proclaiming the word to the community. This is not a responsibility to be taken lightly. God has called you to this mission. The Spirit has given you the gift of being able to present the word to the community and, even more important, the gift of being able to discern its meaning for yourself.

GIFT OF THE SPIRIT

Saint Paul speaks about how the Spirit gives these gifts to members of the community. These gifts are called charisms. Everyone has received gifts from the Lord that were given for the good of that community. Not all the gifts are the same. Not everyone has received the same gift. This is important, for it means that we need everyone and their gifts to make the community complete. If we do not allow certain members of the community to share their gifts, we will be subtly rejecting the gifts that the Spirit of God has given to us, and we will be lacking something that we need to grow in the Spirit.

Your call to be a lector in the community is not your own choice, nor is it the choice of the pastor or committee that invited you to read at Mass. Rather, it is the Spirit who has called you. The Holy Spirit worked in and through various means (the pastor, the committee, the hunger in your own heart that made you volunteer for service, etc.) to bring you to this ministry.

Now, you must discern how to respond in the best manner possible to that call. It is not enough to say that if the Spirit called you, the Spirit will provide what is needed. As with all gifts of the Spirit, we must work to perform our ministry well. We are, as Saint Paul says in the First Letter to the Thessalonians, God's coworkers. While this is God's work, he has entrusted it to us. It has been said that we must do everything as if it depended upon us, realizing that it all depends upon the Lord.

This preparation involves working on the technique of presentation, but also working on our own hearts so that the things that we proclaim are proclaimed with a profound faith.

PREPARING THE READING

A first logical step in preparing for this service is to read and reread the text that we are going to proclaim. It is not enough to show up in the sacristy a few minutes before the Mass and read over the text once or twice. Preferably, we should have read it early in the week and often during the week.

This text should be read aloud. It might seem a bit embarrassing to read it out loud to ourselves, but it is essential. There are words and phrases that might appear to present no difficulty when we are reading them silently but that end up being much more difficult when we read them out loud.

We must check out the pronunciation of difficult words (especially unusual names). A Pronunciation Guide will be found on pages 385-396 to help you in this task.

If you do not know the meaning of certain words, it is always advisable to do a bit of research in a dictionary or some other source book.

Some of the liturgical texts that you will read are rather short and difficult to understand if you do not know their context. Thus, it might be a good idea to go to the Bible and read at least the entire chapter in which your reading occurs.

A good amount of information has been provided in this handbook so that you might understand better what you are reading (both alongside of the readings and in the appendices at the end of the handbook). If those are not enough, you could check in your parish library or with your liturgy committee or lector coordinator for recommendations for other resources. It might even be a good project to study at least one book of the Bible each year as part of your study preparations for your ministry. Adult education classes are also a good aid to one's own personal growth.

PHYSICAL CONSIDERATIONS

There are also a number of physical considerations in your presentations.

Know when you are supposed to read. Check the schedule and be responsible in either being there when you are assigned or in arranging for a substitute when you cannot be present (each parish has a different way of arranging for substitute readers).

Dress appropriately. You should be drawing attention to the word of God and not to yourself. You should dress in a simple and yet respectful manner, which shows that you recognize the dignity of that which you are doing.

Walk to the lectern with a dignified, deliberate pace. Do not run. Do not walk so slowly that people feel uncomfortable. In theory, only one thing should be happening in the liturgy at a time. Thus, the lector should approach the lectern after the Opening Prayer and not during it (unless you have been instructed by the coordinator of lectors to do otherwise).

Know which year you are reading. If your Sunday Lectionary has A, B, and C readings or your Weekday Lectionary has year 1 and 2 readings, you should know which year it is.

Know your microphone system. Each system is different. Each microphone has an optimal distance and direction from which you should read. Some systems have cut offs that will block the sound if you are too loud. Others are temperamental. Before you ever read for Mass, make sure that you have tried out the system. This should be done at a time when it will not disturb people who are trying to pray in Church, e.g., immediately before Mass.

Read questions as questions. Read phrases that end with exclamation points with emphasis. Know the mood of the reading. If the author is being dramatic, the reading should have a bit of drama. Try not to be monotonous in your reading.

Be careful with certain sounds when you read. The letters "S" and "P" can be picked up by the sound system as a hissing or an explosive sound.

Do not make gestures that render you the center of attention. Your hands, in fact, should be placed where they will not distract. If you are nervous, you might hold on to the sides of the lectern.

Read from the Lectionary. There is a certain dignity to that which you are doing. You should not be reading from a missalette or from this handbook. If you have prepared the reading from one of these other sources, check out where the reading is on the page of the Lectionary so that you will not have to search for it when you stand up to read.

Do not read too fast or too slow. Make sure you pause when you reach the end of a phrase (this is much easier now that the Lectionary has divided the reading into sense lines). Read slowly enough that you communicate the dignity of the occasion, without becoming overly dramatic. If the reading is a hymn, read it as such (i.e., poetry is always read in a more dramatic manner than simple narratives).

Try to look up during the reading. When you first start reading, this might be both difficult and a bit artificial. But it is always good to keep eye contact with the audience.

Know whether you will be reading the Responsorial Psalm or whether it will be sung. It is not a good idea to arrive at the psalm and then glance at the organist with a quizzical look on your face.

A few people have the habit of memorizing the reading and then proclaiming it without reading it. While that is admirable from a certain point of view, it is also very distracting. People almost always are more attentive to the reader's remarkable memory than to what is actually being read.

If you make a mistake, do not become nervous or feel anxious. If you judge it appropriate, simply reread the phrase correctly. If needed, you could make a comment that lets the community know that you have made a mistake (e.g., "I'm sorry, I started the wrong reading").

This ministry is so important to the faith life of the community that it is essential for its ministers to have a sense of humility. Ask for your friends or family members to give you an occasional honest critique on your reading style. If you are not reading well, admit it and seek help. If, after having sought help, you still cannot read well, it is important to be humble enough to admit it and suggest to your community that it might be better for you to serve it in some other ministry.

GOD'S WORD AND OUR HEARTS

Having spoken about a number of the physical considerations in reading for the liturgy, we now must speak about some of the questions of the Spirit.

We have to allow God's word to speak to us. If we are not listening to God's word at the deepest part of our heart, then those who are listening to us will perceive that we are reading and not proclaiming. They will understand without our ever saying it that we really do not believe what we are proclaiming.

This means that we must pray God's word. We have to ask ourselves what this word means for us today. We have to allow the Spirit of God to make it real and alive. Just as the Spirit inspired the sacred authors to write these texts in the first place, so now that same Spirit breathes into our hearts so that we can make the word of God alive again for ourselves and our community.

We have to place our own experiences in the context of the word. It is a wonderful thing if we find ourselves asking, "what does God's word say to me in these circumstances?" God's word is not a history book about things long since dead, it is a presentation of salvation history that is still alive and vitally important today.

Every reading and every Gospel should in some way call us to conversion. If after preparing the readings for a Sunday, you cannot say that the readings are calling you to change even one thing in your life, you have probably missed the point. It is not a bad idea to ask what you would preach about the reading if you had the opportunity. (Some parishes, in fact, have preparation meetings in which parishioners suggest to the preachers what might be said that weekend).

Become that which you read. Your actions on a daily basis will proclaim loud and clear whether what you are proclaiming on Sunday are "just words" or whether they are words that are like a two-edged sword. People do look at what you are doing outside of the church, and they are either edified or scandalized by whether you are living the word of God or in some way denying it.

Finally, if possible, arrive in church well before the beginning of the Mass so that you can pray to the Spirit to guide you in your ministry that day.

May God bless you in your ministry.

Shalom,

Fr. Jude Winkler, OFM Conv.

A LECTOR'S PRAYER

EVERLASTING Father
in the beginning your Word brought forth life
and called us into being.

In the fullness of time,
Jesus, your Son, the Word became flesh.

In the synagogue at Nazareth
and on the hills of Galilee,
he taught the good news of salvation,
the Gospel of life and of truth.

In an act of everlasting love
he opened his arms on the cross
and by his death destroyed all death,
leading us to everlasting life.

Lord, open my lips,
that my mouth may declare your praise.
Open my heart,
that I may proclaim the Word made flesh.
Strengthen my mind,
that I may live the holy words I speak.

For your Word is all holy and all true
and lives in glory with you and the Holy Spirit,
one God, forever and ever. Amen.

December 2, 2001

FIRST SUNDAY OF ADVENT

Lect. No. 1 **FIRST READING: Isaiah 2:1-5**

The Lord will gather all nations into the eternal peace of the kingdom of God.

In this First Reading we hear a prophecy that is found both in Isaiah and in Micah. It speaks of the LORD's blessing that would accompany the future judgment that the LORD would deliver upon Israel and her enemies.

Typical of prophecies written during this period, the blessing would be centered upon Mount Zion, the mountain upon which the temple was built. Even though the mountain was not the highest mountain, it would certainly be given a special prestige in the coming era.

The coming judgment would not be one of war and destruction. Rather, it would establish justice throughout the world so profound that the weapons of war could be destroyed for they would never be needed again.

While this era certainly began with the birth of Jesus that we are now awaiting with hope and expectation, it will only fully be realized when Jesus returns in glory at the end of time.

A reading from the Book of the Prophet Isaiah

This is what Isaiah, son of Amoz,
    saw concerning Judah and Jerusalem.
  In days to come,
the mountain of the LORD's house
    shall be established as the highest mountain
    and raised above the hills.
All nations shall stream toward it;
    many peoples shall come and say:
"Come, let us climb the LORD's mountain,
    to the house of the God of Jacob,
that he may instruct us in his ways,
    and we may walk in his paths."
For from Zion shall go forth instruction,
    and the word of the LORD from Jerusalem.
He shall judge between the nations,
    and impose terms on many peoples.
They shall beat their swords into plowshares
    and their spears into pruning hooks;
one nation shall not raise the sword against another,
    nor shall they train for war again.
O house of Jacob, come,
    let us walk in the light of the LORD!

The word of the Lord.

Lect. No. 1

RESPONSORIAL PSALM: Ps 122:1-2, 3-4, 4-5, 6-7, 8-9

Psalm 122 was written as a pilgrimage psalm to celebrate one's journey to the temple in Jerusalem.

The city of Jerusalem and the temple represent God's blessing upon Israel, for it is there that God's people can encounter and worship their LORD.

The unity and order of the city are a symbol of the ability to live a well-ordered life, one that will receive God's blessing.

The people of Israel would be given the privilege of sharing in God's judgment upon the nations of the earth. They have this special honor for they are a chosen people, a people of the covenant.

The ultimate promise and reward of the covenant is Peace, Shalom. The Biblical concept of peace goes far beyond an absence of war. It is a peace so profound that it affects even nature.

For Christians, Jerusalem is a symbol both of life in the Church and of life in the heavenly Jerusalem where all of the promises that God has made us will be fulfilled. We begin to live Christ's peace here on earth, but we can only hope to find eternal peace with our Lord in heaven.

℟. **Let us go rejoicing to the house of the Lord.**

I rejoiced because they said to me,
    "We will go up to the house of the LORD."
And now we have set foot
    within your gates, O Jerusalem.

℟. **Let us go rejoicing to the house of the Lord.**

Jerusalem, built as a city
    with compact unity.
To it the tribes go up,
    the tribes of the LORD.

℟. **Let us go rejoicing to the house of the Lord.**

According to the decree for Israel,
    to give thanks to the name of the LORD.
In it are set up judgment seats,
    seats for the house of David.

℟. **Let us go rejoicing to the house of the Lord.**

Pray for the peace of Jerusalem!
    May those who love you prosper!
May peace be within your walls,
    prosperity in your buildings.

℟. **Let us go rejoicing to the house of the Lord.**

Because of my brothers and friends
    I will say, "Peace be within you!"
Because of the house of the LORD, our God,
    I will pray for your good.

℟. **Let us go rejoicing to the house of the Lord.**

Lect. No. 1

SECOND READING: Romans 13:11-14

Our salvation is nearer.

Saint Paul speaks to the Romans about how they must live virtuous lives. He uses apocalyptic language to remind us that we are living in the end times. This is no time to be lukewarm.

This does not mean that the world is coming to an end immediately. It simply means that we do not know when the end of the world (or, at the very least, the end of our world) will occur.

Paul closes by reminding us that we have already made our choice—we have chosen to live for and in Jesus. This means that our everyday decisions must reflect the decision that we have already professed.

A reading from the Letter of Saint Paul
to the Romans

Brothers and sisters:
  You know the time;
  it is the hour now for you to awake from sleep.
For our salvation is nearer now than when we first
    believed;
  the night is advanced, the day is at hand.
Let us then throw off the works of darkness
  and put on the armor of light;
  let us conduct ourselves properly as in the day,
  not in orgies and drunkenness,
  not in promiscuity and lust,
  not in rivalry and jealousy.
But put on the Lord Jesus Christ,
  and make no provision for the desires of the flesh.

The word of the Lord.

Lect. No. 1

ALLELUIA: cf. Psalm 85:8

We await the birth of Jesus in Bethlehem and his return in glory at the end of time: This is our salvation.

℟. **Alleluia, alleluia.**

Show us, Lord, your love;
and grant us your salvation.

℟. **Alleluia, alleluia.**

Lect.
No. 1

GOSPEL: Matthew 24:37-44

Stay awake, that you may be prepared!

The Gospel continues the theme of the return of Jesus in glory at the end of time.

In the earliest days of the Church, emphasis was placed upon the idea that the end of the world was at hand. The reason for this was the fact that Jesus had risen from the dead. In Old Testament times, the resurrection of the dead was considered to be a sign of the Day of the Lord. Jesus' resurrection was understood to be a fulfillment of that expectation.

As time went on and Jesus still did not return in glory, Christians began to speak about his expected coming in terms of not knowing when it would occur.

They spoke of the return of the Lord as something that would happen at an unexpected time, arriving like a thief in the night.

For us, the important thing to remember is that we simply do not know how much time we will have. Therefore, we must always be prepared. We must live today as if it were the last day of our lives.

A reading from the holy Gospel according to Matthew

Jesus said to his disciples:
"As it was in the days of Noah,
   so it will be at the coming of the Son of Man.
In those days before the flood,
   they were eating and drinking,
   marrying and giving in marriage,
   up to the day that Noah entered the ark.
They did not know until the flood came and carried
      them all away.
So will it be also at the coming of the Son of Man.
Two men will be out in the field;
   one will be taken, and one will be left.
Two women will be grinding at the mill;
   one will be taken, and one will be left.
Therefore, stay awake!
For you do not know on which day your Lord will
      come.
Be sure of this: if the master of the house
      had known the hour of night when the thief was
         coming,
   he would have stayed awake
   and not let his house be broken into.
So too, you also must be prepared,
   for at an hour you do not expect, the Son of Man
      will come."

The Gospel of the Lord.

December 8, 2001

THE IMMACULATE CONCEPTION OF THE BLESSED VIRGIN MARY

Lect. No. 689 | **FIRST READING: Genesis 3:9-15, 20**

I will put enmity between your offspring and hers.

On this feast of the Immaculate Conception, we read about the entrance of sin into the world and the punishment that we received because of it.

The first effect of sin is alienation: from God, from each other, and even from nature.

Before they sinned, Adam and Eve had been naked, but they felt no shame. They had been living in a state of pure innocence. After their sin they felt only shame. They hid themselves and ran away from God, the one who loved them most. They blamed each other and the snake for their fall.

God punished the man, the woman, and the snake. The man's punishment, which we do not hear in this passage, was to work hard for a living but never receive a just recompense. The woman suffers childbirth pains. The snake loses its legs and crawls on its belly.

We also hear that the woman and her offspring will live in perpetual enmity with the serpent and his offspring. We hear that Satan would torment humanity,

A reading from the Book of Genesis

After the man, Adam, had eaten of the tree,
the LORD God called to the man and asked him,
"Where are you?"
He answered, "I heard you in the garden;
but I was afraid, because I was naked,
so I hid myself."
Then he asked, "Who told you that you were naked?
You have eaten, then,
from the tree of which I had forbidden you to eat!"
The man replied, "The woman whom you put here
with me—
she gave me fruit from the tree, and so I ate it."
The LORD God then asked the woman,
"Why did you do such a thing?"
The woman answered, "The serpent tricked me into
it, so I ate it."

Then the LORD God said to the serpent:
"Because you have done this, you shall be banned
from all the animals
and from all the wild creatures;
on your belly shall you crawl,
and dirt shall you eat
all the days of your life.
I will put enmity between you and the woman,
and between your offspring and hers;
he will strike at your head,
while you strike at his heel."

but Jesus, born of an immaculate mother, would deliver us from our slavery to sin.

The man called his wife Eve,
    because she became the mother of all the living.

The word of the Lord.

Lect. No. 689

RESPONSORIAL PSALM: Ps 98:1, 2-3, 3-4 (℟.: 1a)

As we meditate upon the meaning of this feast, that God prepared the Blessed Virgin Mary in a miraculous way to be the mother of his Son, we are filled with gratitude and wonder. We break into song to celebrate God's goodness.

"The LORD has made his salvation known." There are two understandings of salvation in the New Testament. In Saint Paul's understanding, we will be saved in the final judgment at the end of time. Jesus will intercede for us so that we might obtain the fullness of God's mercy.

According to Saint Luke, salvation is something that we already experience here upon the earth. When we encounter Jesus, we realize that he has come into our lives with great signs of mercy and love. We already experience that here and now. Our lives have meaning because Jesus is a part of them.

℟. **Sing to the Lord a new song, for he has done marvelous deeds.**

Sing to the LORD a new song,
    for he has done wondrous deeds;
his right hand has won victory for him,
    his holy arm.

℟. **Sing to the Lord a new song, for he has done marvelous deeds.**

The LORD has made his salvation known:
    in the sight of the nations he has revealed his justice.
He has remembered his kindness and his faithfulness
    toward the house of Israel.

℟. **Sing to the Lord a new song, for he has done marvelous deeds.**

All the ends of the earth have seen
    the salvation by our God.
Sing joyfully to the LORD, all you lands;
    break into song; sing praise.

℟. **Sing to the Lord a new song, for he has done marvelous deeds.**

Lect. No. 689

SECOND READING: Ephesians 1:3-6, 11-12

He chose us in Christ before the foundation of the world.

This reading is a hymn of praise to celebrate the fact that we were chosen by our Lord for salvation before the foundation of the world. This is the proper idea of predestination, that God has always called us to participate in his life.

A reading from the Letter of Saint Paul
    to the Ephesians

Brothers and sisters:
Blessed be the God and Father of our Lord Jesus Christ,

Predestination does not mean that we must do something, it means that we have the freedom to do it. We always have the possibility to say no, but why would we want to?

The extent of God's favor is expressed in the fact that we have been adopted to be God's children. We have become his chosen ones, his beloved.

It is Jesus who, through his death and resurrection, made all of this possible. He is our brother, and God is our "Abba," Father.

Our only possible response to this miracle is gratitude and praise. We live to praise the Lord.

Lect.
No. 689

We praise Mary with the words the archangel Gabriel used when he came to give her the glorious message that she was to be the Mother of God and blessed among all women.

Lect.
No. 689

The annunciation is patterned after many of the annunciation stories found in the Old Testament. It is also a loose parallel to the annunciation of John the Baptist. While John's birth is great, that of Jesus is even greater. John's mother and father were elderly; Jesus' mother was a virgin.

who has blessed us in Christ
with every spiritual blessing in the heavens,
as he chose us in him, before the foundation of
the world,
to be holy and without blemish before him.
In love he destined us for adoption to himself
through Jesus Christ,
in accord with the favor of his will,
for the praise of the glory of his grace
that he granted us in the beloved.

In him we were also chosen,
destined in accord with the purpose of the One
who accomplishes all things according to the intention of his will,
so that we might exist for the praise of his glory,
we who first hoped in Christ.

The word of the Lord.

ALLELUIA: cf. Luke 1:28

℟. **Alleluia, alleluia.**

Hail, Mary, full of grace, the Lord is with you;
blessed are you among women.

℟. **Alleluia, alleluia.**

GOSPEL: Luke 1:26-38

Hail, full of grace! The Lord is with you.

A reading from the holy Gospel according to Luke

The angel Gabriel was sent from God
to a town of Galilee called Nazareth,
to a virgin betrothed to a man named Joseph,
of the house of David,
and the virgin's name was Mary.
And coming to her, he said,
"Hail, full of grace! The Lord is with you."

The archangel Gabriel greets Mary by stating, "Hail, full of grace!" This greeting is actually an important scriptural proof for the dogma of the Immaculate Conception.

The phrase, "full of grace" is in the perfect tense in the original Greek version of this gospel. The perfect was used for things that began in the past and were still true in the present, such as saying that the flowers bloomed yesterday and were still in bloom today.

Mary was already full of grace even before the angel arrived. She had been protected from the effects of the original sin.

This is why Mary could respond with so much generosity to the invitation of the Lord. Those of us who have been wounded by sin tend to be selfish. Mary, on the other hand, was able to think in terms of service and vulnerability. She pronounced herself the handmaid of the Lord.

The birth came about through the intervention of the Holy Spirit who overshadowed her, even as the cloud had overshadowed the Ark of the Covenant in the Old Testament.

But she was greatly troubled at what was said
    and pondered what sort of greeting this might be.
Then the angel said to her,
    "Do not be afraid, Mary,
    for you have found favor with God.
Behold, you will conceive in your womb and bear a son,
    and you shall name him Jesus.
He will be great and will be called Son of the Most High,
    and the Lord God will give him the throne of David his father,
    and he will rule over the house of Jacob forever,
    and of his kingdom there will be no end."
But Mary said to the angel,
    "How can this be,
    since I have no relations with a man?"
And the angel said to her in reply,
    "The Holy Spirit will come upon you,
    and the power of the Most High will overshadow you.
Therefore the child to be born
    will be called holy, the Son of God.
And behold, Elizabeth, your relative,
    has also conceived a son in her old age,
    and this is the sixth month for her who was called barren;
    for nothing will be impossible for God."
Mary said, "Behold, I am the handmaid of the Lord.
May it be done to me according to your word."
Then the angel departed from her.

The Gospel of the Lord.

December 9, 2001

SECOND SUNDAY OF ADVENT

Lect. No. 4   **FIRST READING: Isaiah 11:1-10**

He shall judge the poor with justice.

The Advent theme changes this week. The first week emphasized the return of Jesus in glory at the end of time. The readings this week speak of the need for conversion in order to meet the Messiah whom God is sending into the world.

Isaiah, like many of the prophets of his day, became disillusioned with the failure of the kings of Judah to do the will of the LORD. He longed for the coming of a Messiah (Anointed One) who would truly live God's call to righteousness.

This Messiah would have the spirit of the LORD, a spirit of wisdom and understanding, counsel and strength, knowledge and fear of the LORD. This is the scripture passage that outlines the seven gifts of the Holy Spirit.

The Messiah of God would institute a period of profound justice and peace.

The peace the Messiah would bring would be so all-encompassing that it would affect even nature. Animals that were known to be enemies would live in peace. Nature would experience the innocence of its early days (before the first sin).

A reading from the Book of the Prophet Isaiah

On that day, a shoot shall sprout from the stump of Jesse,
    and from his roots a bud shall blossom.
The spirit of the LORD shall rest upon him:
    a spirit of wisdom and of understanding,
a spirit of counsel and of strength,
    a spirit of knowledge and of fear of the LORD,
    and his delight shall be the fear of the LORD.
Not by appearance shall he judge,
    nor by hearsay shall he decide,
but he shall judge the poor with justice,
    and decide aright for the land's afflicted.
He shall strike the ruthless with the rod of his mouth,
    and with the breath of his lips he shall slay the wicked.
Justice shall be the band around his waist,
    and faithfulness a belt upon his hips.
Then the wolf shall be a guest of the lamb,
    and the leopard shall lie down with the kid;
the calf and the young lion shall browse together,
    with a little child to guide them.
The cow and the bear shall be neighbors,
    together their young shall rest;
    the lion shall eat hay like the ox.
The baby shall play by the cobra's den,
    and the child lay his hand on the adder's lair.
There shall be no harm or ruin on all my holy mountain;

His word, which is symbolized by the phrases "rod of his mouth" and "breath of his lips," would establish God's righteousness upon the earth, a righteousness so exceptional that even the Gentiles would seek the LORD (for the LORD is the God of all nations).

for the earth shall be filled with knowledge of the
    LORD,
    as water covers the sea.
On that day, the root of Jesse,
    set up as a signal for the nations,
the Gentiles shall seek out,
    for his dwelling shall be glorious.

The word of the Lord.

Lect. No. 4 **RESPONSORIAL PSALM: Ps 72:1-2, 7-8, 12-13,17 (℟.: cf. 7)**

Psalm 72 presents an idealized portrait of the king of the Jewish people. He was to be a representative of the LORD upon the earth.

One of his most important functions was to be the guarantor of justice in the land. How could he possibly represent the LORD as his viceroy upon the earth if he did not govern the land with righteousness?

The measure of true justice in the land was how well he treated those who were without political or economic power. The assumption was that the rich could buy justice, but the poor did not have a way to obtain justice except by seeking the assistance of the king,

Christians have that same duty today. We are representatives of Jesus, called to establish his justice upon the earth. That commitment has to be lived in the way we treat each other in our families, at work, in social gathering, etc.

℟. **Justice shall flourish in his time, and fullness of peace forever.**

O God, with your judgment endow the king,
    and with your justice, the king's son;
he shall govern your people with justice
    and your afflicted ones with judgment.

℟. **Justice shall flourish in his time, and fullness of peace forever.**

Justice shall flower in his days,
    and profound peace, till the moon be no more.
May he rule from sea to sea,
    and from the River to the ends of the earth.

℟. **Justice shall flourish in his time, and fullness of peace forever.**

For he shall rescue the poor when he cries out,
    and the afflicted when he has no one to help him.
He shall have pity for the lowly and the poor;
    the lives of the poor he shall save.

℟. **Justice shall flourish in his time, and fullness of peace forever.**

May his name be blessed forever;
    as long as the sun his name shall remain.

Furthermore, our commitment to justice is measured by how the least powerful in our society are treated. The elderly, unborn, foreigners, mentally ill, etc. are all in need of our protection.

In him shall all the tribes of the earth be blessed;
all the nations shall proclaim his happiness.

℟. **Justice shall flourish in his time, and fullness of peace forever.**

Lect.
No. 4

SECOND READING: Romans 15:4-9

Christ saves everyone.

This reading comes from the end of the Letter to the Romans. Typical of Paul's letters, this one concludes with a series of instructions on what it means to live a Christian life.

The point strongly emphasized in this passage is that our Christian calling should lead us to live at peace with each other.

The source of that unity is our common calling in Christ Jesus. Advent is a good time to remember this fact and to make peace with others.

The distinctions that formerly separated us, e.g., Jews and Gentiles, are no longer barriers to our unity.

This ideal can never be fully realized until we allow our thoughts to be those of Christ. We have to remember how God has blessed us by choosing us and giving us his grace. We must treat others as we have been treated.

Prejudice and judgmentalism only create divisions that ultimately hinder gospel harmony.

A reading from the Letter of Saint Paul
to the Romans

Brothers and sisters:
Whatever was written previously was written for our instruction,
that by endurance and by the encouragement of the Scriptures
we might have hope.
May the God of endurance and encouragement
grant you to think in harmony with one another,
in keeping with Christ Jesus,
that with one accord you may with one voice
glorify the God and Father of our Lord Jesus Christ.

Welcome one another, then, as Christ welcomed you,
for the glory of God.
For I say that Christ became a minister of the circumcised
to show God's truthfulness,
to confirm the promises to the patriarchs,
but so that the Gentiles might glorify God for his mercy.
As it is written:
*Therefore, I will praise you among the Gentiles
and sing praises to your name.*

The word of the Lord.

Lect.
No. 4

Our preparation for Christmas starts with a conversion of our hearts. We have to make the crooked ways straight.

Lect.
No. 4

ALLELUIA: Luke 3:4, 6

℟. **Alleluia, alleluia.**

Prepare the way of the Lord, make straight his paths:
all flesh shall see the salvation of God.

℟. **Alleluia, alleluia.**

GOSPEL: Matthew 3:1-12

Repent, for the kingdom of heaven is at hand!

A reading from the holy Gospel according
to Matthew

This account emphasizes John the Baptist's role in preparing Israel for the Day of the Lord, the arrival of the Messiah of Yahweh. John is presented as a new Elijah, he who would make straight the paths for the Lord.

We are given the impression of a great number of people who travel down to the Jordan River to hear his preaching and to be baptized with his baptism of repentance. They have come to turn from their sins and to turn back to the Lord.

Not all of those who come to the Jordan, however, are there for the proper reasons. The Pharisees and the Sadducees, the leaders of the Jewish people, are berated by John. He calls them a brood of vipers.

One must remember that the serpent was a symbol for the power of Satan, so John is implying that their presence is not one of conversion and preparation for the kingdom of God, but rather to do the work of Satan.

John the Baptist appeared, preaching in the desert of Judea
and saying, "Repent, for the kingdom of heaven is at hand!"
It was of him that the prophet Isaiah had spoken when he said:

A voice of one crying out in the desert,
Prepare the way of the Lord,
make straight his paths.

John wore clothing made of camel's hair
and had a leather belt around his waist.
His food was locusts and wild honey.
At that time Jerusalem, all Judea,
and the whole region around the Jordan
were going out to him
and were being baptized by him in the Jordan River
as they acknowledged their sins.

When he saw many of the Pharisees and Sadducees coming to his baptism, he said to them, "You brood of vipers!
Who warned you to flee from the coming wrath?
Produce good fruit as evidence of your repentance.

John warns the leaders of the Jews that they should not presume upon the mercy of God just because they are the chosen people, for God could easily reject them and choose another people. This warning is just as valid for Christians lest we presume upon God's mercy and judge ourselves to be superior to others.

Finally, this passage distinguishes between John's baptism, which produces a remission of sin, and Christian baptism, which remits sin and also creates a special relationship with God through the action of the Holy Spirit. Through our Christian baptism we become children of God and brothers and sisters of Jesus.

And do not presume to say to yourselves,
  'We have Abraham as our father.'
For I tell you,
  God can raise up children to Abraham from these
    stones.
Even now the ax lies at the root of the trees.
Therefore every tree that does not bear good fruit
  will be cut down and thrown into the fire.
I am baptizing you with water, for repentance,
  but the one who is coming after me is mightier
    than I.
I am not worthy to carry his sandals.
He will baptize you with the Holy Spirit and fire.
His winnowing fan is in his hand.
He will clear his threshing floor
  and gather his wheat into his barn,
  but the chaff he will burn with unquenchable
    fire."

The Gospel of the Lord.

| Lect. No. 7 | **FIRST READING: Isaiah 35:1-6a, 10** |

God himself will come to save us.

This passage from the Prophet Isaiah speaks of the restoration that God will work in the land.

There is a tremendous sense of joy and expectation in this and the other readings for this Third Sunday of Advent.

Everything and everyone that suffered up to now will be vindicated and will become fruitful. God will work wonders in our land.

All of those situations that imprisoned us, or left us with a sense of inadequacy, will be abolished. We will be made whole again.

While this Old Testament reading was intended to be understood in a physical sense, through Jesus we understand the call to joy and gladness in a spiritual sense as well.

Among those things that most imprison and alienate us are our own sin and selfishness. The Messiah, Jesus born into our world, liberates us from that prison by bringing us forgiveness of sin and an invitation into the life and the love of God. We can live in the freedom of God's children.

A reading from the Book of the Prophet Isaiah

The desert and the parched land will exult;
    the steppe will rejoice and bloom.
They will bloom with abundant flowers,
    and rejoice with joyful song.
The glory of Lebanon will be given to them,
    the splendor of Carmel and Sharon;
they will see the glory of the LORD,
    the splendor of our God.
Strengthen the hands that are feeble,
    make firm the knees that are weak,
say to those whose hearts are frightened:
    Be strong, fear not!
Here is your God,
    he comes with vindication;
with divine recompense
    he comes to save you.
Then will the eyes of the blind be opened,
    the ears of the deaf be cleared;
then will the lame leap like a stag,
    then the tongue of the mute will sing.

Those whom the LORD has ransomed will return
    and enter Zion singing,
    crowned with everlasting joy;
they will meet with joy and gladness,
    sorrow and mourning will flee.

The word of the Lord.

| Lect. No. 7 | **RESPONSORIAL PSALM: Ps 146:6-7, 8-9, 9-10 (℟.: cf. Isaiah 35:4)** |

This psalm is a hymn of praise for all of the glorious ways that God intervenes in our life to deliver us from those things that oppress us.

God is the Creator and Lord over all, the Sustainer and Provider, the Righteous One who disperses justice to both the godly and the wicked, and the great King who reigns forever.

God is not only faithful with those who deserve it; he also reaches out to those who most need his help.

As is often the case in Old Testament writings, those most in need are represented by the widow and the orphan, the blind and the lame.

The wicked, on the other hand, have no standing before God. While they might seem almighty upon the earth, yet God easily thwarts them.

This is an important reminder of the power of God's mercy and compassion and the total powerlessness of the forces of evil.

℟. **Lord, come and save us.**
or:

℟. **Alleluia.**

The LORD God keeps faith forever,
   secures justice for the oppressed,
   gives food to the hungry.
The LORD sets captives free.

℟. **Lord, come and save us.**
or:

℟. **Alleluia.**

The LORD gives sight to the blind;
   the LORD raises up those who were bowed down.
The LORD loves the just;
   the LORD protects strangers.

℟. **Lord, come and save us.**
or:

℟. **Alleluia.**

The fatherless and the widow he sustains,
   but the way of the wicked he thwarts.
The LORD shall reign forever;
   your God, O Zion, through all generations.

℟. **Lord, come and save us.**
or:

℟. **Alleluia.**

| Lect. No. 7 | **SECOND READING: James 5:7-10** |

Make your hearts firm, because the coming of the Lord is at hand.

This reading from the Letter of James strongly emphasizes the need for patience. The time is at hand. There is no need to judge others beforehand. The Day of the Lord is already dawning.

A reading from the Letter of Saint James

Be patient, brothers and sisters,
   until the coming of the Lord.
See how the farmer waits for the precious fruit of
   the earth,

Obviously this reading has been chosen to speak of the nearness of the feast for which we are preparing, Christmas.

Yet there is also value in this reading at a different level of understanding, for it gives us perspective concerning the things of the Lord. Often we get so caught up with preoccupations and worries that we lose perspective and become anxious. This reading reminds us that the Lord will take care of everything. We only have to place our trust in him.

being patient with it
until it receives the early and the late rains.
You too must be patient.
Make your hearts firm,
because the coming of the Lord is at hand.
Do not complain, brothers and sisters, about one another,
that you may not be judged.
Behold, the Judge is standing before the gates.
Take as an example of hardship and patience, brothers and sisters,
the prophets who spoke in the name of the Lord.

The word of the Lord.

Lect. No. 7

ALLELUIA: Isaiah 61:1 (cited in Luke 4:18)

In our Alleluia Verse we celebrate the coming of the anointed one: The Messiah. Jesus comes to set us free from all that enslaves us.

℟. **Alleluia, alleluia.**

The Spirit of the Lord is upon me,
because he has anointed me
to bring glad tidings to the poor.

℟. **Alleluia, alleluia.**

Lect. No. 7

GOSPEL: Matthew 11:2-11

Are you the one who is to come or should we look for another?

In this Gospel, we hear an episode that ties the ministry of John the Baptist to that of Jesus.

John had already been arrested for his adherence to the truth. He sent his disciples to inquire of Jesus whether he was the one who was expected. It is not really clear whether John is doing this for his own knowledge or to give the disciples the opportunity of witnessing Jesus' ministry for themselves (possi-

A reading from the holy Gospel according to Matthew

When John the Baptist heard in prison of the works of the Christ,
he sent his disciples to Jesus with this question,
"Are you the one who is to come,
or should we look for another?"
Jesus said to them in reply,
"Go and tell John what you hear and see:
the blind regain their sight,
the lame walk,

bly as a way of inviting them to follow Jesus now that his own end was at hand).

Jesus responds not so much with words as with actions.

Jesus then speaks of John the Baptist. Certainly John proved to be a prophet of God.

He did not have to dress in elegant clothes to prove himself, for he gave powerful testimony to the truth of his message. Therefore, he is to be considered a great witness to God's faithfulness to his covenant.

Yet, compared with John the Baptist, the smallest in the kingdom of heaven is greater than he. This is not said to denigrate John, but to show the glory to which we are called.

This passage points out how much greater Jesus is than John, but also how much greater his invitation is to us. While John's invitation was to turn from sin, Jesus' invitation is to experience the very life of God.

lepers are cleansed,
the deaf hear,
the dead are raised,
and the poor have the good news proclaimed to them.
And blessed is the one who takes no offense at me."

As they were going off,
Jesus began to speak to the crowds about John,
"What did you go out to the desert to see?
A reed swayed by the wind?
Then what did you go out to see?
Someone dressed in fine clothing?
Those who wear fine clothing are in royal palaces.
Then why did you go out? To see a prophet?
Yes, I tell you, and more than a prophet.
This is the one about whom it is written:
Behold, I am sending my messenger ahead of you;
he will prepare your way before you.
Amen, I say to you,
among those born of women
there has been none greater than John the Baptist;
yet the least in the kingdom of heaven is greater than he."

The Gospel of the Lord.

FOURTH SUNDAY OF ADVENT

Lect. No. 10 **FIRST READING: Isaiah 7:10-14**

Behold, the virgin shall conceive.

Isaiah offers the king a sign from God. The king refuses to "put the LORD to the test." He does not want a sign, lest it be given and he be forced to trust in the LORD. He would rather depend upon his own strength.

The prophet promises a sign anyway. A "young maiden" would bear a child named Emmanuel. Originally, this was a child who would be given a symbolic name to remind the king that the LORD was near, but when the word for "young maiden" was translated from Hebrew into Greek, it was rendered "virgin," foretelling the virginal birth of Jesus.

A reading from the Book of the Prophet Isaiah

The LORD spoke to Ahaz, saying:
Ask for a sign from the LORD, your God;
  let it be deep as the netherworld, or high as the
    sky!
But Ahaz answered,
  "I will not ask! I will not tempt the Lord!"
Then Isaiah said:
  Listen, O house of David!
Is it not enough for you to weary people,
  must you also weary my God?
Therefore the LORD himself will give you this sign:
  the virgin shall conceive, and bear a son,
  and shall name him Emmanuel.

The word of the Lord.

Lect. No. 10 **RESPONSORIAL PSALM: Ps 24:1-2, 3-4, 5-6 (℟.: 7c and 10b)**

Psalm 24 was most probably used during processions to the temple.

The first part of the psalm praises God as the God of creation.

The second part of the psalm asks who, then, can stand before such a mighty God? Who could possibly be worthy of such a great honor? The answer is that only the person who has kept the law of the LORD would dare enter into the presence of God.

℟. **Let the Lord enter; he is king of glory.**

The LORD'S are the earth and its fullness;
  the world and those who dwell in it.
For he founded it upon the seas
  and established it upon the rivers.

℟. **Let the Lord enter; he is king of glory.**

Who can ascend the mountain of the LORD?
  or who may stand in his holy place?
One whose hands are sinless, whose heart is clean,
  who desires not what is vain.

The intention of this psalm is not to exclude people who are sinners but yet might be ready to convert; it is to speak of the fact that we must live a virtuous life if we expect to live in the Lord. We have to live our Christian commitment with consistency.

℟. **Let the Lord enter; he is king of glory.**

He shall receive a blessing from the Lord,
a reward from God his savior.
Such is the race that seeks for him,
that seeks the face of the God of Jacob.

℟. **Let the Lord enter; he is king of glory.**

Lect. No. 10

SECOND READING: Romans 1:1-7

Jesus Christ, descended from David, is the Son of God.

Saint Paul writes this letter to a community that he did not establish nor had even visited. Thus, he tries to express his deep theology in every phrase of the letter, even this introductory greeting.

He speaks of Jesus being the fulfillment of the promises made by Yahweh to the Jewish people. The Christian community in Rome had a strong Jewish-Christian faction and Paul wanted to speak to them in language that they could appreciate.

Thus Paul speaks of how the prophets spoke of Jesus and how David was his ancestor according to the flesh.

We hear that Jesus is established Son of God in power through the resurrection. This does not mean that he became the Son of God at that moment, but only that what was always true throughout eternity was then publicly manifested in the resurrection.

A reading from the beginning of the
Letter of Saint Paul to the Romans

Paul, a slave of Christ Jesus,
called to be an apostle and set apart for the gospel of God,
which he promised previously through the prophets in the holy Scriptures,
the gospel about his Son, descended from David according to the flesh,
but established as Son of God in power
according to the Spirit of holiness
through resurrection from the dead, Jesus Christ our Lord.
Through him we have received the grace of apostleship,
to bring about the obedience of faith,
for the sake of his name, among all the Gentiles,
among whom are you also, who are called to belong to Jesus Christ;
to all the beloved of God in Rome, called to be holy.
Grace to you and peace from God our Father
and the Lord Jesus Christ.

The word of the Lord.

Lect. No. 10

This promise is fulfilled in the birth of Jesus at Bethlehem, for he is truly God's presence in our midst.

Lect. No. 10

The Gospel of Matthew does not have an annunciation scene, but in this passage one can see that Mary's conception of the child is brought about through a special intervention of the Holy Spirit.

Throughout the infancy stories in Matthew, Joseph receives revelations from the Lord in dreams, for he is named after Joseph the Patriarch, the great dreamer of the Old Testament.

Both Matthew and Luke insist that Mary was a virgin when her child was born. Mary and Joseph were betrothed, formally engaged but not yet living together as husband and wife.

We see Matthew quote the prophecy from Isaiah that we heard in the First Reading. This is typical of Matthew, for he wants to show that Jesus is the fulfillment of all of the promises that God had made to Israel in the old covenant.

Finally, like Luke, Matthew tells us that Jesus' name (a form of the name Joshua) is given in a revelation. His name and his destiny are to be the savior of his people.

ALLELUIA: Matthew 1:23

℞. **Alleluia, alleluia.**

The virgin shall conceive, and bear a son,
and they shall name him Emmanuel.

℞. **Alleluia, alleluia.**

GOSPEL: Matthew 1:18-24

Jesus will be born of Mary, the betrothed of Joseph, a son of David.

A reading from the holy Gospel according to Matthew

This is how the birth of Jesus Christ came about.
When his mother Mary was betrothed to Joseph,
    but before they lived together,
    she was found with child through the Holy Spirit.
Joseph her husband, since he was a righteous man,
    yet unwilling to expose her to shame,
    decided to divorce her quietly.
Such was his intention when, behold,
    the angel of the Lord appeared to him in a dream
        and said,
    "Joseph, son of David,
    do not be afraid to take Mary your wife into your
        home.
For it is through the Holy Spirit
    that this child has been conceived in her.
She will bear a son and you are to name him Jesus,
    because he will save his people from their sins."
All this took place to fulfill what the Lord had said
        through the prophet:
    Behold, the virgin shall conceive and bear a son,
    and they shall name him Emmanuel,
    which means "God is with us."
When Joseph awoke,
    he did as the angel of the Lord had commanded him
and took his wife into his home.

The Gospel of the Lord.

THE NATIVITY OF THE LORD (CHRISTMAS)

AT THE VIGIL MASS

Lect. No. 13

FIRST READING: Isaiah 62:1-5

The Lord delights in you.

This prophecy speaks of the restoration of the people of Israel. They had suffered terribly during the years of exile and during the difficult years when they first came back from exile. They wondered whether God had forgotten them or possibly was still angry at them.

This reading makes it clear that this is not God's attitude. Using matrimonial symbolism, the prophet speaks of the remarkable restoration that will occur.

The LORD would espouse his people. They would be given a new name that expresses the delight of the LORD. This reading is filled with a sense of joy and new possibilities. The promise that it expresses was fulfilled when God established a new covenant with his chosen people.

The hymn is written with parallelism, saying the same thing a second time with slightly different words.

A reading from the Book of the Prophet Isaiah

For Zion's sake I will not be silent,
for Jerusalem's sake I will not be quiet,
until her vindication shines forth like the dawn
and her victory like a burning torch.

Nations shall behold your vindication,
and all the kings your glory;
you shall be called by a new name
pronounced by the mouth of the LORD.
You shall be a glorious crown in the hand of the LORD,
a royal diadem held by your God.
No more shall people call you "Forsaken,"
or your land "Desolate,"
but you shall be called "My Delight,"
and your land "Espoused."
For the LORD delights in you
and makes your land his spouse.
As a young man marries a virgin,
your Builder shall marry you;
and as a bridegroom rejoices in his bride
so shall your God rejoice in you.

The word of the Lord.

Lect. No. 13 — RESPONSORIAL PSALM: Ps 89:4-5, 16-17, 27, 29 (R⁄.: 2a)

The psalm celebrates the covenant that God has made with his people as well as with the great King David. God would always remain faithful to his covenant. Even if we were to sin against God's goodness, God would not abandon his promises. We never have to worry about God hiding his face or forgetting us, for we will walk in the light of his countenance.

The only possible response to this remarkable generosity is great joy. We are filled with awe at the goodness of God.

We are also filled with confidence, for we know that God will always defend us against our enemies. Thus, we can call God, "my father, my God, the rock, my savior."

R⁄. **Forever I will sing the goodness of the Lord.**

I have made a covenant with my chosen one,
    I have sworn to David my servant:
forever will I confirm your posterity
    and establish your throne for all generations.

R⁄. **Forever I will sing the goodness of the Lord.**

Blessed the people who know the joyful shout;
    in the light of your countenance, O LORD, they walk.
At your name they rejoice all the day,
    and through your justice they are exalted.

R⁄. **Forever I will sing the goodness of the Lord.**

He shall say of me, "You are my father,
    my God, the rock, my savior."
Forever I will maintain my kindness toward him,
    and my covenant with him stands firm.

R⁄. **Forever I will sing the goodness of the Lord.**

Lect. No. 13 — SECOND READING: Acts 13:16-17, 22-25

Paul bears witness to Christ, the Son of David.

This speech presents a form of the early "kerygma," the things that Saint Paul would preach when he first entered a new city.

This kerygma is very Jewish in tone for Paul is speaking in a synagogue. He wants to present the message in such a way that they could understand who Jesus was and what he meant for them.

Notice that two kings are mentioned in the course of the speech: Saul and David. This is actually a subtle threat to the community.

A reading from the Acts of the Apostles

When Paul reached Antioch in Pisidia and entered the synagogue,
    he stood up, motioned with his hand, and said,
    "Fellow Israelites and you others who are God-fearing, listen.
The God of this people Israel chose our ancestors
    and exalted the people during their sojourn in the land of Egypt.
With uplifted arm he led them out of it.
Then he removed Saul and raised up David as king;
    of him he testified,
    'I have found David, son of Jesse, a man after my own heart;

Saul had been chosen by the LORD to be king, but he displeased the LORD and was rejected. God then chose David to be the new king of Israel.

Paul was warning the community that the same could happen to them. They, too, considered themselves to be the chosen, but if they did not accept his message, they, too, could be rejected. Their only recourse was to accept Jesus as their Messiah and to be baptized.

Lect.
No. 13

The birth of the child at Bethlehem destroys the promise of darkness and restores the world to life. He is Prince of Peace and King of Kings.

Lect.
No. 13

Matthew presents an extensive genealogy to show that Jesus is a true son of David, son of Abraham. This would show that Jesus is the fulfillment of God's promise to his people.

Abraham was the founder of the Jewish people. By tracing Jesus' genealogy back to Abraham, he is showing that Jesus is the Messiah whom Yahweh had sent to his chosen people.

he will carry out my every wish.'
From this man's descendants God, according to his
promise,
has brought to Israel a savior, Jesus.
John heralded his coming by proclaiming a baptism
of repentance
to all the people of Israel;
and as John was completing his course, he would
say,
'What do you suppose that I am? I am not he.
Behold, one is coming after me;
I am not worthy to unfasten the sandals of his
feet.'"

The word of the Lord.

ALLELUIA

℟. **Alleluia, alleluia.**

Tomorrow the wickedness of the earth will be destroyed:
the Savior of the world will reign over us.

℟. **Alleluia, alleluia.**

GOSPEL: A Longer Form: Matthew 1:1-25

The genealogy of Jesus Christ, the Son of David.

A reading from the beginning of the
holy Gospel according to Matthew

The book of the genealogy of Jesus Christ,
the son of David, the son of Abraham.

Abraham became the father of Isaac,
Isaac the father of Jacob,
Jacob the father of Judah and his brothers.
Judah became the father of Perez and Zerah,
whose mother was Tamar.
Perez became the father of Hezron,
Hezron the father of Ram,

David was the great king of Israel and model of what the Messiah should be. Jesus was a true son of David, and he would inherit his eternal throne.

The list of ancestors of Jesus is a bit unhistorical. Matthew tries to make three sets of fourteen names each. The middle set of names skips a few generations in order to make the list add up to fourteen names.

The number fourteen is important for that is the symbolic number for the name David. By producing three lists of fourteen, Matthew is saying that Jesus is three times more important than David. Hebrew had no superlative degree, so saying a word three times in a row was their way of expressing that idea (e.g., holy, holy, holy means the holiest). Jesus was three times "David," and he was therefore the "Davidest."

There are a number of women mentioned in the list. This is unusual. Normally genealogies only had names of men. Furthermore, the women mentioned had unusual pasts. One was an adulteress, one a foreigner, one committed incest, and one was a prostitute. Matthew was trying to say that God had worked in most unusual ways throughout history. He had chosen most unexpected people to be instruments of his will. This was also true of the fifth woman on his list, a poor virgin named Mary.

After the genealogy, we hear about the birth of Jesus.

Ram the father of Amminadab.
Amminadab became the father of Nahshon,
  Nahshon the father of Salmon,
  Salmon the father of Boaz,
  whose mother was Rahab.
Boaz became the father of Obed,
  whose mother was Ruth.
Obed became the father of Jesse,
  Jesse the father of David the king.

David became the father of Solomon,
  whose mother had been the wife of Uriah.
Solomon became the father of Rehoboam,
  Rehoboam the father of Abijah,
  Abijah the father of Asaph.
Asaph became the father of Jehoshaphat,
  Jehoshaphat the father of Joram,
  Joram the father of Uzziah.
Uzziah became the father of Jotham,
  Jotham the father of Ahaz,
  Ahaz the father of Hezekiah.
Hezekiah became the father of Manasseh,
  Manasseh the father of Amos,
  Amos the father of Josiah.
Josiah became the father of Jechoniah and his brothers
  at the time of the Babylonian exile.

After the Babylonian exile,
  Jechoniah became the father of Shealtiel,
  Shealtiel the father of Zerubbabel,
  Zerubbabel the father of Abiud.
Abiud became the father of Eliakim,
  Eliakim the father of Azor,
  Azor the father of Zadok.
Zadok became the father of Achim,
  Achim the father of Eliud,
  Eliud the father of Eleazar.
Eleazar became the father of Matthan,
  Matthan the father of Jacob,

Mary and Joseph were betrothed. This means that they were engaged but not yet living together.

We hear that the child was conceived through the action of the Holy Spirit.

The phrase about Joseph being a righteous man is not clear. A truly righteous man (in the Jewish definition) would have had Mary killed. Matthew might have meant to say that although he was righteous, he decided to divorce her. Whatever Matthew might have meant, he probably wants to show Joseph as a truly righteous man (one who exhibits the traits of New Testament righteousness).

Joseph is warned in a dream to accept Mary and her child. Joseph is named after Joseph the Patriarch, the dreamer of the Old Testament, so like him he received his revelations through dreams.

Matthew also shows how Jesus fulfills all of the predictions about the Messiah contained in the law and the prophets. Jesus is Emmanuel, a name that means God is with us.

The passage ends with us hearing that Joseph had no relations with his wife before the child was born. This does not mean that they had relations after, only that there could be absolutely no doubt that the child was the Son of God. Catholic tradition holds that Mary remained a virgin throughout her life.

Jacob the father of Joseph, the husband of Mary.
Of her was born Jesus who is called the Christ.

Thus the total number of generations
    from Abraham to David
    is fourteen generations;
    from David to the Babylonian exile,
    fourteen generations;
    from the Babylonian exile to the Christ,
    fourteen generations.

Now this is how the birth of Jesus Christ came about.
When his mother Mary was betrothed to Joseph,
    but before they lived together,
    she was found with child through the Holy Spirit.
Joseph her husband, since he was a righteous man,
    yet unwilling to expose her to shame,
    decided to divorce her quietly.
Such was his intention when, behold,
    the angel of the Lord appeared to him in a dream
        and said,
    "Joseph, son of David,
    do not be afraid to take Mary your wife into your
        home.
For it is through the Holy Spirit
    that this child has been conceived in her.
She will bear a son and you are to name him Jesus,
    because he will save his people from their sins."
All this took place to fulfill
    what the Lord had said through the prophet:
        Behold, the virgin shall conceive and bear a son,
            and they shall name him Emmanuel,
    which means "God is with us."
When Joseph awoke,
    he did as the angel of the Lord had commanded him
    and took his wife into his home.
He had no relations with her until she bore a son,
    and he named him Jesus.

The Gospel of the Lord.

Lect.
No. 13

GOSPEL: B Shorter Form: Matthew 1:18-25

Mary will give birth to a son, and you are to name him Jesus.

We hear that the child was conceived through the action of the Holy Spirit.

The phrase about Joseph being a righteous man is not clear. A truly righteous man (in the Jewish definition) would have had Mary killed. Matthew might have meant to say that although he was righteous, he decided to divorce her. Whatever Matthew might have meant, he probably wants to show Joseph as a truly righteous man (one who exhibits the traits of New Testament righteousness).

Joseph is warned in a dream to accept Mary and her child. Joseph is named after Joseph the Patriarch, the dreamer of the Old Testament, so like him he received his revelations through dreams.

Matthew also shows how Jesus fulfills all of the predictions about the Messiah contained in the law and the prophets. Jesus is Emmanuel, a name that means God is with us.

The passage ends with us hearing that Joseph had no relations with his wife before the child was born. This does not mean that they had relations after, only that there could be absolutely no doubt that the child was the Son of God. Catholic tradition holds that Mary remained a virgin throughout her life.

A reading from the holy Gospel according to Matthew

This is how the birth of Jesus Christ came about.
When his mother Mary was betrothed to Joseph,
but before they lived together,
she was found with child through the Holy Spirit.
Joseph her husband, since he was a righteous man,
yet unwilling to expose her to shame,
decided to divorce her quietly.
Such was his intention when, behold,
the angel of the Lord appeared to him in a dream
and said,
"Joseph, son of David,
do not be afraid to take Mary your wife into your
home.
For it is through the Holy Spirit
that this child has been conceived in her.
She will bear a son and you are to name him Jesus,
because he will save his people from their sins."
All this took place to fulfill
what the Lord had said through the prophet:
Behold, the virgin shall conceive and bear a son,
and they shall name him Emmanuel,
which means "God is with us."
When Joseph awoke,
he did as the angel of the Lord had commanded
him
and took his wife into his home.
He had no relations with her until she bore a son,
and he named him Jesus.

The Gospel of the Lord.

December 25, 2001

THE NATIVITY OF THE LORD (CHRISTMAS)

MASS AT MIDNIGHT

Lect. No. 14

FIRST READING: Isaiah 9:1-6

A son is given us.

This passage is taken from a series of prophecies about the Messiah. Isaiah had long hoped that the kings of Israel would reform and prove to be faithful to their anointing. They all disappointed him, however, and Isaiah realized that things would change only if God sent a chosen one. This could not only be a messiah, it would have to be the Messiah.

This Messiah would change the world. The Israelites who were enslaved and burdened would be liberated. They had lived in gloom, but they would see a great light. They had been filled with sadness and confusion, but now they would be filled with joy.

The Messiah would have a series of symbolic names that would describe him. This was typical of ancient kings who would receive a series of symbolic names when they were enthroned.

He would be called Wonder-Counselor, God-Hero, Father-Forever, and Prince of Peace. He would inherit David's throne and reign forever. His reign would be marked by justice and peace.

A reading from the Book of the Prophet Isaiah

The people who walked in darkness
 have seen a great light;
upon those who dwelt in the land of gloom
 a light has shone.
You have brought them abundant joy
 and great rejoicing,
as they rejoice before you as at the harvest,
 as people make merry when dividing spoils.
For the yoke that burdened them,
 the pole on their shoulder,
and the rod of their taskmaster
 you have smashed, as on the day of Midian.
For every boot that tramped in battle,
 every cloak rolled in blood,
 will be burned as fuel for flames.
For a child is born to us, a son is given us;
 upon his shoulder dominion rests.
They name him Wonder–Counselor, God–Hero,
 Father–Forever, Prince of Peace.
His dominion is vast
 and forever peaceful,
from David's throne, and over his kingdom,
 which he confirms and sustains
by judgment and justice,
 both now and forever.
The zeal of the LORD of hosts will do this!

The word of the Lord.

Lect. No. 14 | **RESPONSORIAL PSALM: Ps 96:1-2, 2-3, 11-12, 13 (℟.: Luke 2:11)**

This hymn of praise invites us to sing a new song. There are two words for new in ancient languages. One word means that which is not old, the other means that which is radically new.

We are celebrating something radically new, an intervention of God in our history that makes all previous interventions seem insignificant. God becomes incarnate and thus fills this created world with his majesty.

The only possible response to this wondrous situation is to be filled with praise and awe. We even invite creation to praise God. Saint Paul tells us how creation was imprisoned in futility by our sin. Jesus now liberates it by becoming a creature. He restores creation to what God meant it to be when it was first created. Thus, the world and everyone who is in it should raise their voices to praise the Lord.

℟. **Today is born our Savior, Christ the Lord.**

Sing to the LORD a new song;
 sing to the LORD, all you lands.
Sing to the LORD; bless his name.

℟. **Today is born our Savior, Christ the Lord.**

Announce his salvation, day after day.
 Tell his glory among the nations;
 among all peoples, his wondrous deeds.

℟. **Today is born our Savior, Christ the Lord.**

Let the heavens be glad and the earth rejoice;
 let the sea and what fills it resound;
 let the plains be joyful and all that is in them!
Then shall all the trees of the forest exult.

℟. **Today is born our Savior, Christ the Lord.**

They shall exult before the LORD, for he comes;
 for he comes to rule the earth.
He shall rule the world with justice
 and the peoples with his constancy.

℟. **Today is born our Savior, Christ the Lord.**

Lect. No. 14 | ## SECOND READING: Titus 2:11-14

The grace of God has appeared to all.

The second reading reminds us that the birth of Jesus is not just a time to rejoice, it is also a time to call us to account.

Jesus is born into our world in order to sanctify and call us to live a righteous life. Therefore, we must reject those things that separate us from God's love.

A reading from the Letter of Saint Paul to Titus

Beloved:
 The grace of God has appeared, saving all
 and training us to reject godless ways and worldly desires
 and to live temperately, justly, and devoutly in this age,
 as we await the blessed hope,

We also recall in this reading that while we celebrate the first coming of Jesus into the world, we also are preparing for his return in glory at the end of time. This, too, is a joyous expectation, for we do not fear the return of the Lord. Our prayer is *Maranatha,* "Come, Lord Jesus."

the appearance of the glory of our great God
and savior Jesus Christ,
who gave himself for us to deliver us from all law-
    lessness
and to cleanse for himself a people as his own,
eager to do what is good.

The word of the Lord.

Lect.
No. 14

ALLELUIA: Luke 2:10-11

Today we celebrate the birth of our Savior. We are filled with a profound sense of joy. That for which we waited so long has arrived.

℟. **Alleluia, alleluia.**

I proclaim to you good news of great joy:
today a Savior is born for us,
Christ the Lord.

℟. **Alleluia, alleluia.**

Lect.
No. 14

GOSPEL: Luke 2:1-14

Today a Savior has been born for you.

Luke includes many of his major themes in his account of the birth of Jesus.

He starts his account by placing the birth in context of world history by reciting the names of kings and governors. By mentioning that the great Caesar Augustus called a worldwide census, Luke is reminding us that the child being born in a small village at the corner of the Roman empire would transform the entire world. We see this implicit prophecy fulfilled at the end of Acts when the gospel is proclaimed in Rome.

A reading from the holy Gospel according to Luke

In those days a decree went out from Caesar Au-
    gustus
    that the whole world should be enrolled.
This was the first enrollment,
    when Quirinius was governor of Syria.
So all went to be enrolled, each to his own town.
And Joseph too went up from Galilee from the town
    of Nazareth
    to Judea, to the city of David that is called Bethle-
      hem,
    because he was of the house and family of David,
    to be enrolled with Mary, his betrothed, who was
      with child.
While they were there,
    the time came for her to have her child,

Certain of the details in this account are exactly the same as in Matthew's version of the story. Those common details have a high level of credibility. In both accounts, the mother is Mary, a virgin betrothed to a man named Joseph. The child's name was Jesus, a name revealed by God. The child was conceived through the power of the Holy Spirit. Jesus was born in Bethlehem and grew up in Nazareth. When one considers how many of the central details are in agreement, it is astounding. Some of the secondary details, e.g., whether shepherds or magi visit the baby, etc. are secondary.

The story emphasizes the poverty of the holy family. The child is born in a cave and laid in a manger, for there was no room in the inn.

The first people in Luke to visit baby Jesus were the shepherds. In the time of Jesus, shepherds were considered to be untrustworthy and their work made them ceremonially unclean. They were social outcasts. The message Luke is presenting is that God sent the message of salvation first to those who most needed it.

and she gave birth to her firstborn son.
She wrapped him in swaddling clothes and laid him
    in a manger,
    because there was no room for them in the inn.

Now there were shepherds in that region living in
    the fields
    and keeping the night watch over their flock.
The angel of the Lord appeared to them
    and the glory of the Lord shone around them,
    and they were struck with great fear.
The angel said to them,
    "Do not be afraid;
    for behold, I proclaim to you good news of great
      joy
    that will be for all the people.
For today in the city of David
    a savior has been born for you who is Christ and
      Lord.
And this will be a sign for you:
    you will find an infant wrapped in swaddling
      clothes
    and lying in a manger."
And suddenly there was a multitude of the heavenly
    host with the angel,
    praising God and saying:
      "Glory to God in the highest
        and on earth peace to those on whom his
        favor rests."

The Gospel of the Lord.

December 25, 2001
THE NATIVITY OF THE LORD (CHRISTMAS)
MASS AT DAWN

Lect. No. 15

FIRST READING: Isaiah 62:11-12

Behold, your Savior comes!

The First Reading this morning celebrates the promise of salvation given to the community of Israel. It is a proclamation that should reach to the ends of the earth. They saw Israel's pain when she was punished, and now they must witness her restoration.

Israel will be a holy people. The word "holy" means that they are set apart for a sacred purpose, to proclaim the goodness of the LORD. They are also redeemed, bought back from slavery.

A reading from the Book of the Prophet Isaiah

See, the LORD proclaims
to the ends of the earth:
say to daughter Zion,
   your savior comes!
Here is his reward with him,
   his recompense before him.
They shall be called the holy people,
   the redeemed of the LORD,
and you shall be called "Frequented,"
   a city that is not forsaken.

The word of the Lord.

Lect. No. 15

RESPONSORIAL PSALM: Ps 97:1, 6, 11-12

Psalm 97 is an exuberant song of joy for the salvation that the LORD is accomplishing upon the earth.

When the psalmist speaks of the heavens and the earth rejoicing, he is using a typical Hebrew symbolism. By citing the two extremes, he means that everything in between is also involved in this act of praise.

We are filled with joy, for once we were in the darkness and now we have seen the light: once we were imprisoned in sin and now we are free.

℞. **A light will shine on us this day: the Lord is born for us.**

The LORD is king; let the earth rejoice;
   let the many islands be glad.
The heavens proclaim his justice,
   and all peoples see his glory.

℞. **A light will shine on us this day: the Lord is born for us.**

Light dawns for the just;
   and gladness, for the upright of heart.
Be glad in the LORD, you just,
   and give thanks to his holy name.

℞. **A light will shine on us this day: the Lord is born for us.**

Lect.
No. 15

SECOND READING: Titus 3:4-7

Because of his mercy, he saved us.

This morning we celebrate new birth, that of the babe of Bethlehem and also our own re-birth through the sacrament of Baptism. Both of these births are signs of incredible mercy. We have not earned God's love; it is a gracious gift.

Justified by God's grace, we hear that we have become heirs in hope of eternal life. This means that God has estab-lished a relationship of peace with us through the death and resurrection of his son, Jesus. Now we can live in hope, for if God would allow his son to die for us, certainly he will call us into his glory.

A reading from the Letter of Saint Paul to Titus

Beloved:
When the kindness and generous love
    of God our savior appeared,
not because of any righteous deeds we had done
    but because of his mercy,
he saved us through the bath of rebirth
    and renewal by the Holy Spirit,
whom he richly poured out on us
    through Jesus Christ our savior,
so that we might be justified by his grace
    and become heirs in hope of eternal life.

The word of the Lord.

Lect.
No. 15

ALLELUIA: Luke 2:14

We join the angels as they proclaim the glory of God to celebrate the birth of his Son in Bethlehem. This favor is ex-tended to all God's children upon the earth.

℟. **Alleluia, alleluia.**

Glory to God in the highest,
and on earth peace to those
on whom his favor rests.

℟. **Alleluia, alleluia.**

Lect.
No. 15

GOSPEL: Luke 2:15-20

The shepherds found Mary and Joseph and the infant.

This is the account of the shepherds who visit the baby and his parents. Everything in the account is filled with wonder and joy.

The last thing that the Holy Family would have expected is for shepherds to arrive in order to pay homage. Shepherds in the time of the birth of Jesus were feared and avoided. They were regarded as untrustworthy and their work made them ceremonially unclean. They were social outcasts. Yet they pay homage to the newborn king of the Jews and give praise and glory to God for his wondrous deeds.

Mary ponders these things in her heart. In Biblical symbolism, the heart is the organ of thinking, not feeling. (One feels with one's guts or stomach according to the Bible.) Thus, Mary is wondering about the meaning of the things that were happening.

A reading from the holy Gospel according to Luke

When the angels went away from them to heaven,
the shepherds said to one another,
"Let us go, then, to Bethlehem
to see this thing that has taken place,
which the Lord has made known to us."
So they went in haste and found Mary and Joseph,
and the infant lying in the manger.
When they saw this,
they made known the message
that had been told them about this child.
All who heard it were amazed
by what had been told them by the shepherds.
And Mary kept all these things,
reflecting on them in her heart.
Then the shepherds returned,
glorifying and praising God
for all they had heard and seen,
just as it had been told to them.

The Gospel of the Lord.

THE NATIVITY OF THE LORD (CHRISTMAS)

MASS DURING THE DAY

Lect. No. 16

FIRST READING: Isaiah 52:7-10

All the ends of the earth will behold the salvation of our God.

In this First Reading we hear of how the LORD comforts his people. This is, in fact, the major theme of this section of the Book of the Prophet Isaiah. It begins, "Comfort, be comforted my people" (Isaiah 40:1).

We also hear that it is the LORD himself who will comfort his people. Throughout these chapters the LORD insists that he will intervene himself. We hear phrases like "I will rescue," "I will redeem," "I will create," etc. This is fulfilled in the birth of the babe of Bethlehem, for the child is God among us.

The prophet struggles to find words appropriate for this announcement. It is glad tidings, an announcement of peace, good news.

A reading from the Book of the Prophet Isaiah

How beautiful upon the mountains
are the feet of him who brings glad tidings,
announcing peace, bearing good news,
announcing salvation, and saying to Zion,
"Your God is King!"

Hark! Your sentinels raise a cry,
together they shout for joy,
for they see directly, before their eyes,
the LORD restoring Zion.
Break out together in song,
O ruins of Jerusalem!
For the LORD comforts his people,
he redeems Jerusalem.
The LORD has bared his holy arm
in the sight of all the nations;
all the ends of the earth will behold
the salvation of our God.

The word of the Lord.

Lect. No. 16

RESPONSORIAL PSALM: Ps 98:1, 2-3, 3-4, 5-6.(℟.: 3c)

This entire psalm is a hymn of praise for the wondrous deeds that God has done for his chosen people.

Normally when the people of Israel praised God for acts of

℟. **All the ends of the earth have seen the saving power of God.**

Sing to the LORD a new song,
for he has done wondrous deeds;
his right hand has won victory for him,
his holy arm.

salvation, it was a remembrance of the Exodus experience.

This psalm, however, seems to have been written later, and probably refers to the salvation that the LORD worked through the second exodus, the return of the Israelites from Babylon.

Yet, there is also a third application, that of the birth of Jesus, whose very name means "Yahweh saves."

The psalmist praises the LORD by singing a new song. There are two forms of the word new in Biblical languages. One word simply means that it is not old. The other word means that it is radically new.

The salvation of the LORD would be for all the nations of the earth. It was no longer restricted to one people or one time.

The psalmist calls upon the community to use every musical instrument to praise the LORD. As we sing our Christmas carols, we join centuries of Christians and choirs of angels in praising God.

℟. **All the ends of the earth have seen the saving power of God.**

The LORD has made his salvation known:
in the sight of the nations he has revealed his justice.
He has remembered his kindness and his faithfulness
toward the house of Israel.

℟. **All the ends of the earth have seen the saving power of God.**

All the ends of the earth have seen
the salvation by our God.
Sing joyfully to the LORD, all you lands;
break into song; sing praise.

℟. **All the ends of the earth have seen the saving power of God.**

Sing praise to the LORD with the harp,
with the harp and melodious song.
With trumpets and the sound of the horn
sing joyfully before the King, the LORD.

℟. **All the ends of the earth have seen the saving power of God.**

Lect. No. 16

SECOND READING: Hebrews 1:1-6

God has spoken to us through the Son.

The author of the Letter to the Hebrews combines Jewish learning and Greek philosophy to proclaim Jesus as our High Priest.

He speaks of how God revealed his word through the prophets of old. This was a wonderful gift, but the prophets could never fully communicate God's

A reading from the beginning of the Letter to the Hebrews

Brothers and sisters:
In times past, God spoke in partial and various ways
to our ancestors through the prophets;
in these last days, he has spoken to us through the Son,
whom he made heir of all things

word in human words. Human words always fall short. That is why there had to be many prophets, because none was ever fully successful in revealing God's word to his people.

This is why God chose to send his own Son. Jesus, the only-begotten Son of God, is the Word of God, the perfect expression of who God is and what he asks of us.

The last part of this reading tries to establish Jesus as superior to the angels. In Greek philosophy, totally spiritual beings were superior to material beings. Angels are totally spiritual beings. Jesus took on our flesh, so some wondered if angels were superior to him. Our author argues that Jesus is the Son of God and above every angel.

and through whom he created the universe,
> who is the refulgence of his glory, the very imprint of his being,
and who sustains all things by his mighty word.
When he had accomplished purification from sins,
> he took his seat at the right hand of the Majesty on high,
as far superior to the angels
as the name he has inherited is more excellent than theirs.

For to which of the angels did God ever say:
> *You are my son; this day I have begotten you?*

Or again:
> *I will be a father to him, and he shall be a son to me?*

And again, when he leads the firstborn into the world, he says:
> *Let all the angels of God worship him.*

The word of the Lord.

Lect.
No. 16

As the Lord Jesus comes to proclaim his gospel to us, we rise to greet him and adore him as the light of the world.

ALLELUIA

℟. **Alleluia, alleluia.**

A holy day has dawned upon us.
Come, you nations, and adore the Lord.
For today a great light has come upon the earth.

℟. **Alleluia, alleluia.**

GOSPEL: 🅰 Longer Form: John 1:1-18

The Word became flesh and made his dwelling among us.

The Prologue of the Gospel of John presents Jesus as the Word of God. The author of this hymn is presenting Jesus as wisdom incarnate. This was a way of saying that even before Jesus was born in the flesh in Bethlehem, he already existed. Our author is saying that although the Old Testament authors did not know it, they were actually writing about Jesus whenever they wrote about Wisdom.

John the Baptist was a witness to the fact that Jesus is the Son of God. Unlike the other gospels where John the Baptist is constantly calling people to conversion, in the Gospel of John he continuously gives witness to the identity of Jesus. He proclaims that Jesus is the Messiah and that he is not.

When this hymn speaks about the Word being in the world and the world not knowing it, it is not speaking about the rejection of Jesus. It is speaking about Israel's rejection of all of the prophets whom Yahweh sent to call her to conversion.

In verse 14 we begin to speak about Jesus incarnate. We hear that the Word became flesh. This means that God did not consider our material world to be evil, but rather decided to join us and thus bless and consecrate this created world.

A reading from the holy Gospel according to John

In the beginning was the Word,
and the Word was with God,
and the Word was God.
He was in the beginning with God.
All things came to be through him,
and without him nothing came to be.
What came to be through him was life,
and this life was the light of the human race;
the light shines in the darkness,
and the darkness has not overcome it.

A man named John was sent from God.
He came for testimony, to testify to the light,
so that all might believe through him.
He was not the light,
but came to testify to the light.
The true light, which enlightens everyone,
was coming into the world.

He was in the world,
and the world came to be through him,
but the world did not know him.
He came to what was his own,
but his own people did not accept him.

But to those who did accept him
he gave power to become children of God,
to those who believe in his name,
who were born not by natural generation
nor by human choice nor by a man's decision
but of God.

And the Word became flesh
and made his dwelling among us,
and we saw his glory,

We hear that Jesus is full of grace and truth. These two words are actually Old Testament ideas: that God loves us with a covenant love and God is always faithful. Jesus is God's love and faithfulness incarnate.

Jesus is the only Son of God. In the Old Testament, "the son of God" was often a synonym for hero. But to be the only Son of God is to be the eternally begotten Son of God.

Finally, we hear that Jesus reveals who God is. As the wisdom of God, Jesus can fill us with knowledge of God. We cannot hope to understand who God is except through Jesus' revelation.

the glory as of the Father's only Son,
    full of grace and truth.

John testified to him and cried out, saying,
    "This was he of whom I said,
    'The one who is coming after me ranks ahead of
      me
    because he existed before me.' "
From his fullness we have all received,
    grace in place of grace,
    because while the law was given through Moses,
    grace and truth came through Jesus Christ.
No one has ever seen God.
The only Son, God, who is at the Father's side,
    has revealed him.

The Gospel of the Lord.

| Lect.
No. 16 |

GOSPEL: B Shorter Form: John 1:1-5, 9-14

The Word became flesh and made his dwelling among us.

The Prologue of the Gospel of John presents Jesus as the Word of God. The author of this hymn is presenting Jesus as wisdom incarnate. This was a way of saying that even before Jesus was born in the flesh in Bethlehem, he already existed. Our author is saying that although the Old Testament authors did not know it, they were actually writing about Jesus whenever they wrote about Wisdom.

When this hymn speaks about the Word being in the world and the world not knowing it, it is not speaking about the rejection of Jesus. It is speaking about Israel's rejection of all of the prophets whom Yahweh sent to call her to con-

A reading from the holy Gospel according
to John

In the beginning was the Word,
    and the Word was with God,
    and the Word was God.
He was in the beginning with God.
All things came to be through him,
    and without him nothing came to be.
What came to be through him was life,
    and this life was the light of the human race;
the light shines in the darkness,
    and the darkness has not overcome it.
The true light, which enlightens everyone,
    was coming into the world.

He was in the world,
    and the world came to be through him,
    but the world did not know him.

In verse 14 we begin to speak about Jesus incarnate. We hear that the Word became flesh. This means that God did not consider our material world to be evil, but rather decided to join us and thus bless and consecrate this created world.

We hear that Jesus is full of grace and truth. These two words are actually Old Testament ideas: that God loves us with a covenant love and God is always faithful. Jesus is God's love and faithfulness incarnate.

Jesus is the only Son of God. In the old Testament, "the son of God" was often a synonym for hero. But to be the only Son of God is to be the eternally begotten Son of God.

He came to what was his own,
but his own people did not accept him.

But to those who did accept him
he gave power to become children of God,
to those who believe in his name,
who were born not by natural generation
nor by human choice nor by a man's decision
but of God.

And the Word became flesh
and made his dwelling among us,
and we saw his glory,
the glory as of the Father's only Son,
full of grace and truth.

The Gospel of the Lord.

THE HOLY FAMILY OF JESUS, MARY, AND JOSEPH

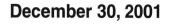

| Lect. No. 17 | **FIRST READING: Sirach 3:2-7, 12-14** |

Those who fear the Lord honor their parents.

The Book of Sirach was written late in the Old Testament period when Jewish society was strongly influenced by Greek culture.

A Greek ideal was to live an ordered life that would give public witness to the values that were the core of one's beliefs.

The author of this book combined this ideal with the traditional respect for parents and the family found in faith. Together they produce this beautiful appeal for a family life in which one's parents are treated with great respect.

Although this portrait is idealized, it also shows signs of realism. It acknowledges that the situation might arise in which one's parents are no longer mentally alert. Nevertheless, care for parents is a sacred responsibility.

A reading from the Book of Sirach

God sets a father in honor over his children;
    a mother's authority he confirms over her sons.
Whoever honors his father atones for sins,
    and preserves himself from them.
When he prays, he is heard;
    he stores up riches who reveres his mother.
Whoever honors his father is gladdened by children,
    and, when he prays, is heard.
Whoever reveres his father will live a long life;
    he who obeys his father brings comfort to his mother.

My son, take care of your father when he is old;
    grieve him not as long as he lives.
Even if his mind fail, be considerate of him;
    revile him not all the days of his life;
kindness to a father will not be forgotten,
    firmly planted against the debt of your sins
    —a house raised in justice to you.

The word of the Lord.

| Lect. No. 17 | **RESPONSORIAL PSALM: Ps 128:1-2, 3, 4-5 (℟.: cf. 1)** |

Like the First Reading, Psalm 128 is taken from the Wisdom tradition of Old Testament literature. Wisdom literature answered the question, "How can we live a good and virtuous life?"

℟. **Blessed are those who fear the Lord and walk in his ways.**

Blessed is everyone who fears the LORD,
    who walks in his ways!

This psalm responds that one must fear the LORD. This expression is often misunderstood. People sometimes think that we must be afraid that God will judge us as worthy of punishment.

Fear of the LORD is really a profound sense of reverence and awe when one considers the greatness of God. We are creatures, while God is the creator of all. We cannot even begin to understand the wonder of God's majesty.

If we have this attitude toward God, our everyday lives will reflect it and we will observe his law. Then our families will be blessed, for our life-styles will be respectful and gracious. We will not be selfish and egocentric.

For you shall eat the fruit of your handiwork;
   blessed shall you be, and favored.

R⸔. **Blessed are those who fear the Lord and walk in his ways.**

Your wife shall be like a fruitful vine
   in the recesses of your home;
your children like olive plants
   around your table.

R⸔. **Blessed are those who fear the Lord and walk in his ways.**

Behold, thus is the man blessed
   who fears the LORD.
The LORD bless you from Zion:
   may you see the prosperity of Jerusalem
   all the days of your life.

R⸔. **Blessed are those who fear the Lord and walk in his ways.**

| Lect. No. 17 | **SECOND READING:** 🅐 **Longer Form: Colossians 3:12-21** |

Family life in the Lord.

The first part of this reading exhorts the community to a life of virtue. Early Christians felt that it was essential for them to live at peace with one another so that pagans could see how virtuous their calling was and might be led to conversion. This is why they were to live in compassion, kindness, humility, gentleness, and patience, etc. Christ was to guide their hearts.

This ideal is just as important today. Often one hears of people who go to Mass but do not live their faith on an everyday basis, especially in the way they treat their own family.

A reading from the Letter of Saint Paul to the Colossians

Brothers and sisters:
   Put on, as God's chosen ones, holy and beloved,
   heartfelt compassion, kindness, humility, gentleness, and patience,
   bearing with one another and forgiving one another,
   if one has a grievance against another;
   as the Lord has forgiven you, so must you also do.
And over all these put on love,
   that is, the bond of perfection.
And let the peace of Christ control your hearts,
   the peace into which you were also called in one body.

We cannot hope to live our Christian calling if we are not filled with a sense of gratitude. It is the virtue that reminds us how much we depend upon the Lord. This reading encourages expressions of gratitude toward the Lord for all that we have received.

The latter part of the reading exhorts family members to live the relationships that the community felt were established by God.

Notice, though, rather than emphasizing the control of one member over another, the letter emphasizes the mutual responsibilities of one family member toward the others.

And be thankful.
Let the word of Christ dwell in you richly,
    as in all wisdom you teach and admonish one another,
    singing psalms, hymns, and spiritual songs
    with gratitude in your hearts to God.
And whatever you do, in word or in deed,
    do everything in the name of the Lord Jesus,
    giving thanks to God the Father through him.

Wives, be subordinate to your husbands,
    as is proper in the Lord.
Husbands, love your wives,
    and avoid any bitterness toward them.
Children, obey your parents in everything,
    for this is pleasing to the Lord.
Fathers, do not provoke your children,
    so they may not become discouraged.

The word of the Lord.

Lect. No. 17

SECOND READING: B Shorter Form: Colossians 3:12-17

Family life in the Lord.

The first part of this reading exhorts the community to a life of virtue. Early Christians felt that it was essential for them to live at peace with one another so that pagans could see how virtuous their calling was and might be led to conversion. This is why they were to live in compassion, kindness, humility, gentleness, and patience, etc. Christ was to guide their hearts.

This ideal is just as important today. Often one hears of people who go to Mass but do not live their faith on an everyday basis, especially in the way they treat their own family.

A reading from the Letter of Saint Paul
to the Colossians

Brothers and sisters:
    Put on, as God's chosen ones, holy and beloved,
    heartfelt compassion, kindness, humility, gentleness, and patience,
    bearing with one another and forgiving one another,
    if one has a grievance against another;
    as the Lord has forgiven you, so must you also do.
And over all these put on love,
    that is, the bond of perfection.
And let the peace of Christ control your hearts,
    the peace into which you were also called in one body.

We cannot hope to live our Christian calling if we are not filled with a sense of gratitude. It is the virtue that reminds us how much we depend upon the Lord. None of us is truly self-sufficient. This reading encourages expressions of gratitude toward the Lord for all that we have received.

And be thankful.
Let the word of Christ dwell in you richly,
    as in all wisdom you teach and admonish one an-
        other,
    singing psalms, hymns, and spiritual songs
    with gratitude in your hearts to God.
And whatever you do, in word or in deed,
    do everything in the name of the Lord Jesus,
    giving thanks to God the Father through him.

The word of the Lord.

| Lect. |
| No. 17 |

ALLELUIA: Colossians 3:15a, 16a

The only way that our families can be peace-filled is by making Christ the center of our lives.

℟. **Alleluia, alleluia.**

Let the peace of Christ control your hearts;
let the word of Christ dwell in you richly.

℟. **Alleluia, alleluia.**

| Lect. |
| No. 17 |

GOSPEL: Matthew: 2:13-15, 19-23

Take the child and his mother, and flee into Egypt.

In this episode, we see how God protects the Holy Family from persecution by the evil King Herod. We know from history that Herod was an especially cruel and paranoid king. It would have been entirely within his character for him to kill any rival to the throne.

The Holy Family is led by Joseph to exile in Egypt. He knew that there was an extensive Jewish population in northern Egypt. Therefore, it would have been logical for the Holy Family to flee there.

A reading from the holy Gospel according
to Matthew

When the magi had departed, behold,
    the angel of the Lord appeared to Joseph in a
        dream and said,
    "Rise, take the child and his mother, flee to Egypt,
    and stay there until I tell you.
Herod is going to search for the child to destroy
    him."
Joseph rose and took the child and his mother by
    night
    and departed for Egypt.
He stayed there until the death of Herod,
    that what the Lord had said through the prophet
        might be fulfilled,

Once again Matthew shows us how Jesus fulfills everything that was predicted by the prophets concerning the Messiah.

Herod the Great died in 4 B.C. (Jesus was probably born around 6 B.C.—the monk who invented our calendar intended Jesus to be born in the year zero but made a miscalculation).

We know that Herod's son Archelaus was, if possible, even more cruel than his father. He was deposed by the Romans for that tendency in 6 A.D.

Note that in the Gospel of Matthew it appears as if the Holy Family does not live in Nazareth until after the exile in Egypt (unlike Luke's version, which has the Holy Family begin their story in Nazareth).

Out of Egypt I called my son.

When Herod had died, behold,
  the angel of the Lord appeared in a dream
  to Joseph in Egypt and said,
  "Rise, take the child and his mother and go to the
    land of Israel,
  for those who sought the child's life are dead."
He rose, took the child and his mother,
  and went to the land of Israel.
But when he heard that Archelaus was ruling over
    Judea
  in place of his father Herod,
  he was afraid to go back there.
And because he had been warned in a dream,
  he departed for the region of Galilee.
He went and dwelt in a town called Nazareth,
  so that what had been spoken through the
    prophets might be fulfilled,
  He shall be called a Nazorean.

The Gospel of the Lord.

January 1, 2002

THE OCTAVE DAY OF CHRISTMAS

SOLEMNITY OF THE BLESSED VIRGIN MARY, THE MOTHER OF GOD

Lect. No. 18

FIRST READING: Numbers 6:22-27

They shall invoke my name upon the Israelites, and I will bless them.

The First Reading for this feast records the blessing that the LORD gave to Moses that he was to invoke over the people of Israel.

It is the presence of God in our lives that is the true definition of blessing. Our lives, in fact, only have meaning inasmuch as we make God the center.

This blessing is also called the blessing of Saint Francis, for he recommended this greeting to his followers.

A reading from the Book of Numbers

The LORD said to Moses:
"Speak to Aaron and his sons and tell them:
This is how you shall bless the Israelites.
Say to them:
The LORD bless you and keep you!
The LORD let his face shine upon you, and be gracious to you!
The LORD look upon you kindly and give you peace!
So shall they invoke my name upon the Israelites, and I will bless them."

The word of the Lord.

Lect. No. 18

RESPONSORIAL PSALM: Ps 67:2-3, 5, 6, 8 (℟.: 2a)

The psalm continues the theme that the only true blessing is that which is found in the presence of the LORD. God is the source of mercy. God is the source of our salvation.

We should remember that there are two meanings for the word salvation.

Saint Paul always speaks about salvation as what will

℟. **May God bless us in his mercy.**

May God have pity on us and bless us;
   may he let his face shine upon us.
So may your way be known upon earth;
   among all nations, your salvation.

℟. **May God bless us in his mercy.**

May the nations be glad and exult
   because you rule the peoples in equity;
   the nations on the earth you guide.

happen to us when God welcomes us into heaven.

Saint Luke speaks about salvation as something that is already happening to us now. The minute we make Jesus a part of our lives, we are already experiencing the joys of heaven here upon the earth.

Lect. No. 18

There are two words for time in Greek. One word simply means the passing of one minute to the next. The other, that which Saint Paul uses here, signifies time that is sacred time.

This is the first reference in Scripture to the birth of Jesus (written over a decade before the first gospel).

God sends the Holy Spirit into our hearts so that we can know how much God loves us. This means that when we ask ourselves what we would most like to hear God tell us, the answer is not so much ours as that of the Spirit speaking in our hearts.

Lect. No. 18

Jesus is the Word of God that reveals to us the mystery of God's love for us. He is the revelation of who God is and what God wills for us.

R̸. **May God bless us in his mercy.**

May the peoples praise you, O God;
    may all the peoples praise you!
May God bless us,
    and may all the ends of the earth fear him!

R̸. **May God bless us in his mercy.**

SECOND READING: Galatians 4:4-7

God sent his Son, born of a woman.

A reading from the Letter of Saint Paul
to the Galatians

Brothers and sisters:
When the fullness of time had come, God sent his Son,
    born of a woman, born under the law,
    to ransom those under the law,
    so that we might receive adoption as sons.
As proof that you are sons,
    God sent the Spirit of his Son into our hearts,
    crying out, "Abba, Father!"
So you are no longer a slave but a son,
    and if a son then also an heir, through God.

The word of the Lord.

ALLELUIA: Hebrews 1:1-2

R̸. **Alleluia, alleluia.**

In the past God spoke to our ancestors through the
    prophets;
in these last days, he has spoken to us through the
    Son.

R̸. **Alleluia, alleluia.**

Lect.
No. 18

GOSPEL: Luke 2:16-21

They found Mary and Joseph and the infant.
When the eight days were completed, he was named Jesus.

This passage from the Gospel of Luke tells some of the wondrous events that accompanied the birth of Jesus. Note especially that Mary pondered all of these things in her heart. In Biblical symbolism, the heart is where one thinks. Thus, Mary is pictured as wondering what the meaning of all these things could be.

It is also important to remember that shepherds were not considered to be reputable people. They were social outcasts, thieves and worse. The message of salvation was given first of all to those who most needed it.

Mary and Joseph, being good Jews, fulfill all of the prescriptions of the law by circumcising Jesus eight days after he was born and giving him the name that had been revealed to them by the archangel Gabriel.

A reading from the holy Gospel according to Luke

The shepherds went in haste to Bethlehem and found Mary and Joseph,
and the infant lying in the manger.
When they saw this,
they made known the message
that had been told them about this child.
All who heard it were amazed
by what had been told them by the shepherds.
And Mary kept all these things,
reflecting on them in her heart.
Then the shepherds returned,
glorifying and praising God
for all they had heard and seen,
just as it had been told to them.
When eight days were completed for his circumcision,
he was named Jesus, the name given him by the angel
before he was conceived in the womb.

The Gospel of the Lord.

THE EPIPHANY OF THE LORD

Lect. No. 20

FIRST READING: Isaiah 60:1-6

The glory of the Lord shines upon you.

This part of the Book of the Prophet Isaiah was written shortly after the Jews returned from exile in Babylon (c. 539 B.C.).

In the previous part of the Book of Isaiah, we had heard of how Yahweh would restore the fortune of his beloved people. Thus, when the Persian emperor Cyrus allowed the Jewish people to return to their homeland, they were exultant. Yet, when they arrived home, all they found was devastation.

In this part of Isaiah, we hear that God would still fulfill the promises found in Second-Isaiah (chs. 40—55).

The glory of God would be upon Israel to such an extent that even the Gentile peoples would come in pilgrimage to Jerusalem to pay homage to the LORD. No longer would the pagans carry the Israelites off into exile. Now the pagans would bring their riches to give glory to the God of Israel.

A reading from the Book of the Prophet Isaiah

Rise up in splendor, Jerusalem! Your light has come,
    the glory of the LORD shines upon you.
See, darkness covers the earth,
    and thick clouds cover the peoples;
but upon you the LORD shines,
    and over you appears his glory.
Nations shall walk by your light,
    and kings by your shining radiance.
Raise your eyes and look about;
    they all gather and come to you:
your sons come from afar,
    and your daughters in the arms of their nurses.

Then you shall be radiant at what you see,
    your heart shall throb and overflow,
for the riches of the sea shall be emptied out before
        you,
    the wealth of nations shall be brought to you.
Caravans of camels shall fill you,
    dromedaries from Midian and Ephah;
all from Sheba shall come
    bearing gold and frankincense,
    and proclaiming the praises of the LORD.

The word of the Lord.

Lect. No. 20 — RESPONSORIAL PSALM: Ps 72:1-2, 7-8, 10-11, 12-13 (℟.: cf. 11)

Psalm 72 gives a description of the perfect king of Israel. He would be someone who was filled with wisdom like Solomon, as well as a great warrior who could enlarge the boundaries of Israel from sea to sea, an accomplishment of David, and someone who guaranteed justice in the land, especially to the poor.

As with the First Reading, we hear that even Gentile kings would recognize the splendor of that king's reign and come to pay him homage.

None of the kings of Israel could fulfill all of these expectations. Every time that the prophets spoke of a king whom they hoped would finally do the will of the LORD, they ended up being disillusioned. Thus, they began to speak about an anointed one in the future who would be unlike all of the other kings of Israel.

The arrival of the Magi to pay homage to baby Jesus, the Messiah of the LORD who would inaugurate the reign of God, was the fulfillment of this prophecy.

℟. **Lord, every nation on earth will adore you.**

O God, with your judgment endow the king,
    and with your justice, the king's son;
he shall govern your people with justice
    and your afflicted ones with judgment.

℟. **Lord, every nation on earth will adore you.**

Justice shall flower in his days,
    and profound peace, till the moon be no more.
May he rule from sea to sea,
    and from the River to the ends of the earth.

℟. **Lord, every nation on earth will adore you.**

The kings of Tarshish and the Isles shall offer gifts;
    the kings of Arabia and Seba shall bring tribute.
All kings shall pay him homage,
    all nations shall serve him.

℟. **Lord, every nation on earth will adore you.**

For he shall rescue the poor when he cries out,
    and the afflicted when he has no one to help him.
He shall have pity for the lowly and the poor;
    the lives of the poor he shall save.

℟. **Lord, every nation on earth will adore you.**

Lect. No. 20 — SECOND READING: Ephesians 3:2-3a, 5-6

Now it has been revealed that the Gentiles are coheirs of the promise.

In the Old Covenant, only the Jewish people received the promise. They were the chosen people and heirs of the promises that God had made to the patriarchs and the prophets of Israel.

A reading from the Letter of Saint Paul
to the Ephesians

Brothers and sisters:
You have heard of the stewardship of God's grace
that was given to me for your benefit,

In the New Covenant all peoples will participate in the grace of the Lord. There will be no distinction between Jew and Greek, slave or free, male or female. They all are chosen by the Lord. All will participate in the promise of the Gospel. They all are part of the body of Christ, which is the Church. This is the mystery of salvation: the bounty of God's love for all people.

namely, that the mystery was made known to me
  by revelation.
It was not made known to people in other generations
  as it has now been revealed
  to his holy apostles and prophets by the Spirit:
  that the Gentiles are coheirs, members of the
    same body,
  and copartners in the promise in Christ Jesus
    through the gospel.

The word of the Lord.

| Lect. |
| No. 20 |

ALLELUIA: Matthew 2:2

℟. **Alleluia, alleluia.**

We saw his star at its rising
and have come to do him homage.

℟. **Alleluia, alleluia.**

Like the Magi, we too have seen signs of Jesus' birth for us. Come, let us adore him.

| Lect. |
| No. 20 |

GOSPEL: Matthew 2:1-12

We saw his star at its rising and have come to do him homage.

The feast of the Epiphany celebrates the arrival of the Magi to pay homage to baby Jesus. Epiphany means manifestation, for we are commemorating the day when the glory of God's Messiah was made manifest to the pagans (in the person of the Magi).

Magi were astrologers. They were not kings (although that title is often used for them) nor does it say that there were three (that is the number of gifts). The account speaks of them coming from the east (possibly Persia or Babylon).

A reading from the holy Gospel according
to Matthew

When Jesus was born in Bethlehem of Judea,
  in the days of King Herod,
  behold, magi from the east arrived in Jerusalem,
    saying,
  "Where is the newborn king of the Jews?
We saw his star at its rising
  and have come to do him homage."
When King Herod heard this,
  he was greatly troubled,
  and all Jerusalem with him.
Assembling all the chief priests and the scribes of
  the people,

It is possible that the star that they saw was the elision of three planets, Mars, Jupiter, and Saturn, which occurred around 7 B.C. The technical name for this type of elision is syzygy.

The Magi would naturally have gone to Jerusalem to inquire about the birth of a Jewish king. Herod intends to use them to murder what he considers to be a rival to his throne. From many sources we know that Herod was a murderous paranoid when it came to his throne. He murdered a wife, three sons, and a brother-in-law, who was the high priest.

Jewish scholars use a passage taken from Micah to determine that the Messiah was to be born in Bethlehem. This is typical of Matthew who always shows how Jesus fulfills the law and the prophets.

The Magi bring gold, frankincense, and myrrh. They would have brought these products because they were easy to carry and valuable. Later authors found symbolic meaning in these gifts. They spoke of gold as a gift one would give a king, frankincense as an incense one would burn to honor a god, and myrrh as an ointment used in burials, foretelling how Jesus would save us.

he inquired of them where the Christ was to be born.

They said to him, "In Bethlehem of Judea,
for thus it has been written through the prophet:
And you, Bethlehem, land of Judah,
are by no means least among the rulers of Judah;
since from you shall come a ruler,
who is to shepherd my people Israel."
Then Herod called the magi secretly
and ascertained from them the time of the star's appearance.
He sent them to Bethlehem and said,
"Go and search diligently for the child.
When you have found him, bring me word,
that I too may go and do him homage."
After their audience with the king they set out.
And behold, the star that they had seen at its rising preceded them,
until it came and stopped over the place where the child was.
They were overjoyed at seeing the star,
and on entering the house
they saw the child with Mary his mother.
They prostrated themselves and did him homage.
Then they opened their treasures
and offered him gifts of gold, frankincense, and myrrh.
And having been warned in a dream not to return to Herod,
they departed for their country by another way.

The Gospel of the Lord.

January 13, 2002

THE BAPTISM OF THE LORD

(First Sunday in Ordinary Time)

Lect. No. 21 | **FIRST READING: Isaiah 42:1-4, 6-7**

Behold my servant with whom I am well pleased.

This is the first of four hymns in Isaiah that speak about a mysterious figure called the Suffering Servant of Yahweh (the LORD). They are scattered throughout the second part of the Book of the Prophet Isaiah.

In this hymn we hear that the Servant is a chosen one of the LORD. He is called a "beloved" (even as Jesus is called "beloved" during his baptism).

The Servant was to be a gentle figure who would bring justice to the entire world (and not just to the people of Israel).

Throughout the Old Testament it is never quite clear who this Servant was supposed to be. Some suggested that it was the nation of Israel, others that it was one of the prophets.

Jesus applied this prophecy to himself wherever he spoke about his mission, especially his suffering and death on the cross.

A reading from the Book of the Prophet Isaiah

Thus says the LORD:
 Here is my servant whom I uphold,
  my chosen one with whom I am pleased,
upon whom I have put my spirit;
  he shall bring forth justice to the nations,
not crying out, not shouting,
  not making his voice heard in the street.
A bruised reed he shall not break,
  and a smoldering wick he shall not quench,
until he establishes justice on the earth;
  the coastlands will wait for his teaching.

I, the LORD, have called you for the victory of justice,
  I have grasped you by the hand;
I formed you, and set you
  as a covenant of the people,
  a light for the nations,
to open the eyes of the blind,
  to bring out prisoners from confinement,
  and from the dungeon, those who live in darkness.

The word of the Lord.

Lect.
No. 21
RESPONSORIAL PSALM: Ps 29:1-2, 3-4, 3, 9-10 (℟.: 11b)

This psalm is an ancient hymn to Yahweh. It was probably originally a Canaanite hymn to Baal, the god of the storms. The phrase, "voice of the LORD," is actually a Hebrew phrase for thunder.

At some point a Jewish theologian replaced the name Baal with the name of the Israelite God, Yahweh (transcribed here as LORD). This was an act of faith, for this person was proclaiming that Yahweh was the true source of fertility and life for the land.

The same Jewish author then tied this psalm more closely to the Jewish faith by speaking of the temple of the LORD (referring to the temple in Jerusalem).

℟. **The Lord will bless his people with peace.**

Give to the LORD, you sons of God,
  give to the LORD glory and praise,
give to the LORD the glory due his name;
  adore the LORD in holy attire.

℟. **The Lord will bless his people with peace.**

The voice of the LORD is over the waters,
  the LORD, over vast waters.
The voice of the LORD is mighty;
  the voice of the LORD is majestic.

℟. **The Lord will bless his people with peace.**

The God of glory thunders,
  and in his temple all say, "Glory!"
The LORD is enthroned above the flood;
  the LORD is enthroned as king forever.

℟. **The Lord will bless his people with peace.**

Lect.
No. 21
SECOND READING: Acts 10:34-38

God anointed him with the Holy Spirit.

Immediately before this passage from the Acts of the Apostles, we hear how Saint Peter was invited to the house of Cornelius, a Roman pagan who wanted to become a Christian. He was a God-fearer, a pagan who sympathized with Jewish ways.

In Peter's address we hear how the Holy Spirit gave a sign to the early Christian community that both Jew and Gentile are being invited into the life of the Lord, for the Holy Spirit descended upon Cornelius even before he was baptized.

In the discourse, Peter mentions two baptisms. The first is

A reading from the Acts of the Apostles

Peter proceeded to speak to those gathered
  in the house of Cornelius, saying:
"In truth, I see that God shows no partiality.
Rather, in every nation whoever fears him and acts
    uprightly
  is acceptable to him.
You know the word that he sent to the Israelites
  as he proclaimed peace through Jesus Christ, who
    is Lord of all,
  what has happened all over Judea,
  beginning in Galilee after the baptism
  that John preached,
  how God anointed Jesus of Nazareth
  with the Holy Spirit and power.

that given by John the Baptist. It was a baptism of conversion. The second baptism is that given by Jesus. It was a baptism of both conversion and the reception of the Holy Spirit.

Lect. No. 21

Today, as we celebrate the feast of the Baptism of Jesus, we are remembering that Jesus is not simply a person who is being baptized by John the Baptist, he is also the only-begotten Son of God.

Lect. No. 21

The baptism of Jesus helps us to understand the difference between the baptism of John the Baptist and Christian baptism. While John's is one of conversion, Jesus' baptism brings about both conversion and an invitation into the life of the Trinity.

Matthew, typically, also adds the idea that Jesus must fulfill everything that was expected of him.

The Holy Spirit appears in the form of a dove because the dove is a symbol of love in the Old Testament. The Holy Spirit is the love between the Father and the Son. The Spirit is also their love for us.

God breathes his Spirit into our hearts so that we might know that we are his beloved children.

He went about doing good
    and healing all those oppressed by the devil,
    for God was with him."

The word of the Lord.

ALLELUIA: cf. Mark 9:7

℟. **Alleluia, alleluia.**

The heavens were opened and the voice of the
    Father thundered:
This is my beloved Son, listen to him.

℟. **Alleluia, alleluia.**

GOSPEL: Matthew 3:13-17

After Jesus was baptized, he saw the Spirit of God coming upon him.

A reading from the holy Gospel according
to Matthew

Jesus came from Galilee to John at the Jordan
    to be baptized by him.
John tried to prevent him, saying,
    "I need to be baptized by you,
    and yet you are coming to me?"
Jesus said to him in reply,
    "Allow it now, for thus it is fitting for us
    to fulfill all righteousness."
Then he allowed him.
After Jesus was baptized,
    he came up from the water and behold,
    the heavens were opened for him,
    and he saw the Spirit of God descending like a
      dove
    and coming upon him.
And a voice came from the heavens, saying,
    "This is my beloved Son, with whom I am well
      pleased."

The Gospel of the Lord.

January 20, 2002

SECOND SUNDAY IN ORDINARY TIME

Lect. No. 64   **FIRST READING: Isaiah 49:3, 5-6**

I will make you a light to the nations,
that my salvation may reach to the ends of the earth.

This Sunday's First Reading, like last Sunday's, is one of the hymns of the Suffering Servant of Yahweh.

Like last week's, this one emphasizes the fact that this unidentified figure has been chosen and sent not just to address the needs of Israel. He also has a mission to the nations. This term, "the nations," is the phrase used by the Jews for the pagans who surrounded and so often threatened them.

He is to be a light to the nations, a title that Jesus would fulfill when he proclaimed himself to be the light of the world.

A reading from the Book of the Prophet Isaiah

The LORD said to me: You are my servant,
   Israel, through whom I show my glory.
Now the LORD has spoken
   who formed me as his servant from the womb,
that Jacob may be brought back to him
   and Israel gathered to him;
and I am made glorious in the sight of the LORD,
   and my God is now my strength!
It is too little, the LORD says, for you to be my servant,
   to raise up the tribes of Jacob,
   and restore the survivors of Israel;
I will make you a light to the nations,
   that my salvation may reach to the ends of the earth.

The word of the Lord.

Lect. No. 64   **RESPONSORIAL PSALM: Ps 40:2, 4, 7-8, 8-9, 10 (℟.: 8a and 9a)**

Psalm 40 is used in a biographical manner so that it might be applied to Jesus' ministry. He is the servant who is called to do the Father's will. It is he who would announce "God's justice in the vast assembly."

By praying this psalm, however, we are also promising to participate in the mission of Jesus.

℟. **Here am I, Lord; I come to do your will.**

I have waited, waited for the LORD,
   and he stooped toward me and heard my cry.
And he put a new song into my mouth,
   a hymn to our God.

℟. **Here am I, Lord; I come to do your will.**

Sacrifice or offering you wished not,
   but ears open to obedience you gave me.

Our mission is not to offer up sin-offerings or holocausts. We cannot think in terms of doing what we want and then later trying to placate God. Rather, we have to place ourselves totally at the service of our Lord's mission. This is the only thing that will bring us true joy.

We do not know where that commitment will carry us. Yet we must, like young Samuel, be ready to respond, "Here am I, Lord, I come to do your will."

Holocausts or sin–offerings you sought not;
  then said I, "Behold I come."

℞. **Here am I, Lord; I come to do your will.**

"In the written scroll it is prescribed for me,
to do your will, O my God, is my delight,
  and your law is within my heart!"

℞. **Here am I, Lord; I come to do your will.**

I announced your justice in the vast assembly;
  I did not restrain my lips, as you, O LORD, know.

℞. **Here am I, Lord; I come to do your will.**

Lect.
No. 64

SECOND READING: 1 Corinthians 1:1-3

Grace to you and peace from God our Father and the Lord Jesus Christ.

The beginning of Saint Paul's letters often give us an indication of the problem with which he is dealing. In these verses we see a continuous repetition of the words "Lord Jesus Christ."

The Corinthian community overemphasized the role of the Holy Spirit in their lives. They all but denied the importance of Jesus. By referring to Jesus over and over again, Paul is reminding the community that Jesus is the source and the goal of who and what they are.

A reading from the beginning of the
first Letter of Saint Paul to the Corinthians

Paul, called to be an apostle of Christ Jesus by the
  will of God,
  and Sosthenes our brother,
  to the church of God that is in Corinth,
  to you who have been sanctified in Christ Jesus,
    called to be holy,
  with all those everywhere who call upon the name
    of our Lord Jesus Christ, their Lord and ours.
Grace to you and peace from God our Father
  and the Lord Jesus Christ.

The word of the Lord.

Lect.
No. 64

ALLELUIA: John 1:14a, 12a

We celebrate the birth of Jesus. He has made his dwelling among us and has called us to be children of God.

℞. **Alleluia, alleluia.**

The Word of God became flesh and dwelt among us.
To those who accepted him,
  he gave power to become children of God.

℞. **Alleluia, alleluia.**

Lect.
No. 64

GOSPEL: John 1:29-34

Behold, the Lamb of God who takes away the sin of the world.

John the Baptist identified Jesus as the Lamb of God. This is a word play, for the word in Aramaic for "lamb" is almost the same as the word for "servant." Jesus is both the servant of God foretold in the prophet Isaiah and the lamb whose sacrifice would obtain forgiveness of our sins.

In the Gospel of John the Spirit descends and remains upon Jesus in the form of a dove. Jesus, throughout his ministry, possesses the anointing of the Spirit of God.

We hear that Jesus existed before John the Baptist. This confirms what we heard in the prologue to this gospel, that Jesus already existed "in the beginning."

In the Gospel of John, John the Baptist does not emphasize the call to repentance. He gives witness to the fact that Jesus is the Son of God. His role, like our own, is to bring people to Jesus.

A reading from the holy Gospel according to John

John the Baptist saw Jesus coming toward him and said,
   "Behold, the Lamb of God, who takes away the sin of the world.
He is the one of whom I said,
   'A man is coming after me who ranks ahead of me because he existed before me.'
I did not know him,
   but the reason why I came baptizing with water was that he might be made known to Israel."
John testified further, saying,
   "I saw the Spirit come down like a dove from heaven
   and remain upon him.
I did not know him,
   but the one who sent me to baptize with water told me,
   'On whomever you see the Spirit come down and remain,
   he is the one who will baptize with the Holy Spirit.'
Now I have seen and testified that he is the Son of God."

The Gospel of the Lord.

January 27, 2002

THIRD SUNDAY IN ORDINARY TIME

FIRST READING: Isaiah 8:23—9:3

In Galilee of the Gentiles, the people have seen a great light.

The northern areas of Israel were often considered contaminated by influences of the pagans who lived there. For good reason, the territory of Zebulun and Naphtali, the tribes that lived in the north, was considered to be the district of the Gentiles.

The Prophet Isaiah uses the symbolic images of light and darkness to express the present gloomy situation in which these territories find themselves and the future hope of restoration. The LORD would call them from darkness and gloom to see a great light.

It was only the LORD who could bring about this reversal of fortune. As he had saved his people from the hands of their enemies in the past, so he would save the peoples of the north. The LORD would fill this people with great joy.

A reading from the Book of the Prophet Isaiah

First the LORD degraded the land of Zebulun
and the land of Naphtali;
but in the end he has glorified the seaward road,
the land west of the Jordan,
the District of the Gentiles.

Anguish has taken wing, dispelled is darkness:
    for there is no gloom where but now there was
        distress.
The people who walked in darkness
    have seen a great light;
upon those who dwelt in the land of gloom
    a light has shone.
You have brought them abundant joy
    and great rejoicing,
as they rejoice before you as at the harvest,
    as people make merry when dividing spoils.
For the yoke that burdened them,
    the pole on their shoulder,
and the rod of their taskmaster
    you have smashed, as on the day of Midian.

The word of the Lord.

RESPONSORIAL PSALM: Ps 27:1, 4, 13-14 (℟.: 1a)

The theme of light and salvation continues in the Responsorial Psalm.

This is a psalm of trust in which one places oneself in the hands of a loving God.

℟. **The Lord is my light and my salvation.**

The LORD is my light and my salvation;
    whom should I fear?
The LORD is my life's refuge;
    of whom should I be afraid?

This God will not only rescue us from every danger, he will also respond to the deepest needs of our heart. This is why the psalmist speaks of longing to spend time with the LORD in the temple.

The temple is the place where the LORD dwelt upon the earth (or at the very least where one could be in contact with the LORD). In our case, we could speak of encountering God in the sacraments, in prayer, etc.

This psalm can be a tremendous act of faith, especially when we want to believe these words but are not sure we can.

R⁓. **The Lord is my light and my salvation.**

One thing I ask of the LORD;
    this I seek:
to dwell in the house of the LORD
    all the days of my life,
that I may gaze on the loveliness of the LORD
    and contemplate his temple.

R⁓. **The Lord is my light and my salvation.**

I believe that I shall see the bounty of the LORD
    in the land of the living.
Wait for the LORD with courage;
    be stouthearted, and wait for the LORD.

R⁓. **The Lord is my light and my salvation.**

Lect. No. 67

SECOND READING: 1 Corinthians 1:10-13, 17

That all of you may agree in what you say, and that there be
no divisions among you.

Saint Paul addresses a difficult situation that had arisen in the community at Corinth. They were new Christians, and they were not yet mature in the faith.

A sense of factionalism had arisen within the community. One group militated against the other.

They all claimed to be faithful Christians, even citing one or another of the apostles as their authority, but they were betraying the gospel through the things they said and did against each other.

Paul closes this section by distinguishing between the wisdom of the world and the wisdom of the Lord. He is subtly

A reading from the first Letter of Saint Paul
to the Corinthians

I urge you, brothers and sisters, in the name of our
    Lord Jesus Christ,
    that all of you agree in what you say,
    and that there be no divisions among you,
    but that you be united in the same mind and in
        the same purpose.
For it has been reported to me about you, my brothers and sisters,
    by Chloe's people, that there are rivalries among
        you.
I mean that each of you is saying,
    "I belong to Paul," or "I belong to Apollos,"
    or "I belong to Cephas," or "I belong to Christ."
Is Christ divided?
Was Paul crucified for you?
Or were you baptized in the name of Paul?

accusing the Corinthians of living in a worldly manner for they are only concerned with their own profit. The wisdom of the cross is one of service and sacrifice, not trying to make oneself more important than others.

For Christ did not send me to baptize but to preach the gospel,
and not with the wisdom of human eloquence,
so that the cross of Christ might not be emptied of its meaning.

The word of the Lord.

Lect. No. 67

ALLELUIA: cf. Matthew 4:23

Jesus proclaimed the dawning of God's reign upon the earth. He would heal bodies and hearts wounded by sin.

℟. **Alleluia, alleluia.**

Jesus proclaimed the Gospel of the kingdom
and cured every disease among the people.

℟. **Alleluia, alleluia.**

Lect. No. 67

GOSPEL: A Longer Form: Matthew 4:12-23

Jesus went to Capernaum, so that what had been said through Isaiah might be fulfilled.

Matthew quotes from Isaiah (the passage that we read in the First Reading) to show how Jesus fulfills this prophecy.

The Jewish people in the time of Jesus considered the people of Galilee to be corrupted by Gentile ways and also to be a bit unsophisticated. It was unthinkable for the Jewish leaders in Jerusalem to even consider the possibility that the Messiah would come from Galilee.

Matthew must thus show that this was not only possible, it was actually foretold. He consistently tries to show that Jesus is the fulfillment of everything written in the law and the prophets.

A reading from the holy Gospel according to Matthew

When Jesus heard that John had been arrested, he withdrew to Galilee.
He left Nazareth and went to live in Capernaum by the sea,
in the region of Zebulun and Naphtali,
that what had been said through Isaiah the prophet
might be fulfilled:
  Land of Zebulun and land of Naphtali,
    the way to the sea, beyond the Jordan,
    Galilee of the Gentiles,
  the people who sit in darkness have seen a great light,
  on those dwelling in a land overshadowed by death
    light has arisen.

Jesus preaches that we must turn away from sin in order to embrace the kingdom of God. The kingdom of God is not a place; it is experienced when we make God the center of our lives.

The second half of this passage presents the call of the first apostles. The details are fairly consistent throughout the gospels.

Peter and Andrew, James and John are presented as two sets of brothers who were fishermen. The call to discipleship involves leaving everything one has and marching off into unknown.

The connection between the brothers' occupation and their call to ministry (to become fishers of men) is important, for God asks us to use our talents and experience to serve others.

As Jesus proclaimed the kingdom of God, he also healed those who suffered from any disease. This was a sign that heaven was already dawning upon the earth (in the person of Jesus).

From that time on, Jesus began to preach and say,
  "Repent, for the kingdom of heaven is at hand."

As he was walking by the Sea of Galilee, he saw two brothers,
  Simon who is called Peter, and his brother Andrew,
  casting a net into the sea; they were fishermen.
He said to them,
  "Come after me, and I will make you fishers of men."
At once they left their nets and followed him.
He walked along from there and saw two other brothers,
  James, the son of Zebedee, and his brother John.
They were in a boat, with their father Zebedee, mending their nets.
He called them, and immediately they left their boat and their father
  and followed him.

He went around all of Galilee,
  teaching in their synagogues, proclaiming the gospel of the kingdom,
  and curing every disease and illness among the people.

The Gospel of the Lord.

Lect. No. 67

GOSPEL: B Shorter Form: Matthew 4:12-17

Jesus went to Capernaum, so that what had been said through Isaiah might be fulfilled.

Matthew quotes from Isaiah (the passage that we read in the First Reading) to show how Jesus fulfills this prophecy.

The Jewish people in the time of Jesus considered the people of Galilee to be corrupted by Gentile ways and also

A reading from the holy Gospel according to Matthew

When Jesus heard that John had been arrested, he withdrew to Galilee.
He left Nazareth and went to live in Capernaum by the sea,
  in the region of Zebulun and Naphtali,

to be a bit unsophisticated. It was unthinkable for the Jewish leaders to even consider the possibility that the Messiah would come from Galilee.

Matthew must thus show that this was not only possible but actually foretold. He consistently tries to show that Jesus is the fulfillment of everything written in the law and the prophets.

Jesus preaches that we must turn away from sin in order to embrace the kingdom of God. The kingdom of God is not a place; it is experienced when we make God the center of our lives.

that what had been said through Isaiah the prophet
might be fulfilled:
Land of Zebulun and land of Naphtali,
the way to the sea, beyond the Jordan,
Galilee of the Gentiles,
the people who sit in darkness have seen a great light,
on those dwelling in a land overshadowed by death
light has arisen.
From that time on, Jesus began to preach and say, "Repent, for the kingdom of heaven is at hand."

The Gospel of the Lord.

February 3, 2002

FOURTH SUNDAY IN ORDINARY TIME

Lect. No. 70 | **FIRST READING: Zephaniah 2:3; 3:12-13**

I will leave in your midst a people humble and lowly.

The prophecy of Zephaniah talks about the judgment that would come upon the earth. He speaks about that judgment as the Day of the LORD, which would be a day of terror and rage.

But in these verses he speaks about the "remnant" of God's faithful ones who would escape that judgment. Many of the prophets speak about a "remnant," a small number of people who remain faithful to the call of the LORD.

This "remnant" would be humble and lowly. They would not be filled with deceit. The LORD would reward them with peace. They could care for their flocks without fear.

A reading from the Book of the Prophet Zephaniah

Seek the LORD, all you humble of the earth,
who have observed his law;
seek justice, seek humility;
   perhaps you may be sheltered
   on the day of the LORD's anger.

But I will leave as a remnant in your midst
   a people humble and lowly,
who shall take refuge in the name of the LORD:
   the remnant of Israel.
They shall do no wrong
   and speak no lies;
nor shall there be found in their mouths
   a deceitful tongue;
they shall pasture and couch their flocks
   with none to disturb them.

The word of the Lord.

Lect. No. 70 | **RESPONSORIAL PSALM: Ps 146:6-7, 8-9, 9-10 (℟.: Matthew 5:3)**

This psalm expresses the trust of the psalmist in the justice and mercy of God.

It makes a distinction between those who would be blessed and those who would be cursed. God's ways are not like our ways, and God judges according to the heart, not according to human thinking.

℟. **Blessed are the poor in spirit; the kingdom of heaven is theirs!**

or:

℟. **Alleluia.**

The LORD keeps faith forever,
   secures justice for the oppressed,
   gives food to the hungry.
The LORD sets captives free.

The blessed would be the poorest of the poor. God would reach out to the oppressed, hungry, captives, etc.

While we would judge them cursed from their wretched circumstances, God considers them his chosen ones. Because their situation is desperate, they recognize their need for God to be a part of their lives.

The wicked, on the other hand, would be destroyed. It is interesting to note all of the verses that speak about the blessings God would deliver, and the one part of a verse that speaks about punishment of the wicked.

It is as if this were an afterthought. While the wicked appear to be omnipotent at times, they have no real power. In an instant, God would give them their just judgment.

℟. **Blessed are the poor in spirit; the kingdom of heaven is theirs!**

or:

℟. **Alleluia.**

The LORD gives sight to the blind;
    the LORD raises up those who were bowed down.
The LORD loves the just;
    the LORD protects strangers.

℟. **Blessed are the poor in spirit; the kingdom of heaven is theirs!**

or:

℟. **Alleluia.**

The fatherless and the widow the LORD sustains,
    but the way of the wicked he thwarts.
The LORD shall reign forever;
    your God, O Zion, through all generations. Alleluia.

℟. **Blessed are the poor in spirit; the kingdom of heaven is theirs!**

or:

℟. **Alleluia.**

Lect. No. 70

SECOND READING: 1 Corinthians 1:26-31

God chose the weak of the world.

Once again Saint Paul contrasts the wisdom of God and the wisdom of the world.

Paul speaks to the community in Corinth to remind them of their social status according to the judgments of the world. The first Christians were mostly from the lower economic classes, those who would be despised by the powers that be.

A reading from the first Letter of Saint Paul to the Corinthians

Consider your own calling, brothers and sisters. Not many of you were wise by human standards, not many were powerful, not many were of noble birth. Rather, God chose the foolish of the world to shame the wise, and God chose the weak of the world to shame the strong,

Nevertheless, God had chosen them and called them into his grace.

There is, therefore, no grounds for pride or boastfulness, for their call was from the Lord, not from their own initiative.

If we boast, it should be in the Lord. This means that we should acknowledge the Lord as the source of every blessing and praise him.

Lect. No. 70

Our Alleluia Verse calls us to rejoice in the Lord, for he is our reward in heaven and already here on earth.

Lect. No. 70

This Sunday's Gospel is the beginning of the Sermon on the Mount. Like Moses in the Old Testament, Jesus climbed a mountain in order to give the law to the new Israel.

Unlike the ten commandments, however, this new law is not a series of do's and don't's. The Beatitudes are a series of invitations to generosity and virtue. It is no longer enough to say that we did not do anything terribly wrong; we now must ask whether we have done everything that we could possibly do.

and God chose the lowly and despised of the world,

those who count for nothing,

to reduce to nothing those who are something,

so that no human being might boast before God.

It is due to him that you are in Christ Jesus,

who became for us wisdom from God,

as well as righteousness, sanctification, and redemption,

so that, as it is written,

"Whoever boasts, should boast in the Lord."

The word of the Lord.

ALLELUIA: Matthew 5:12a

℟. **Alleluia, alleluia.**

Rejoice and be glad;
your reward will be great in heaven.

℟. **Alleluia, alleluia.**

GOSPEL: Matthew 5:1-12a

Blessed are the poor in spirit.

A reading from the holy Gospel according to Matthew

When Jesus saw the crowds, he went up the mountain,

and after he had sat down, his disciples came to him.

He began to teach them, saying:

"Blessed are the poor in spirit,

for theirs is the kingdom of heaven.

Blessed are they who mourn,

for they will be comforted.

Blessed are the meek,

for they will inherit the land.

Matthew spiritualizes the Beatitudes. Whereas the beatitudes in Luke are about the poor, Matthew's are about the poor in spirit. This is typical of Matthew's gospel. It allows the Beatitudes to be applied to his community, which was suffering persecution.

The last part of the Beatitudes speaks about those who are persecuted for the sake of the kingdom.

We should not interpret this only as "red" martyrdom, the martyrdom of shedding blood. It could also be "white" martyrdom, what Saint Theresa of Lisieux calls a martyrdom of pinpricks, or everyday life. If we try to be true Christians in our families, at work, etc, we will have a price to pay.

Blessed are they who hunger and thirst for righteousness,
for they will be satisfied.
Blessed are the merciful,
for they will be shown mercy.
Blessed are the clean of heart,
for they will see God.
Blessed are the peacemakers,
for they will be called children of God.
Blessed are they who are persecuted for the sake of righteousness,
for theirs is the kingdom of heaven.
Blessed are you when they insult you and persecute you
and utter every kind of evil against you falsely because of me.
Rejoice and be glad,
for your reward will be great in heaven."

The Gospel of the Lord.

FIFTH SUNDAY IN ORDINARY TIME

Lect. No. 73

FIRST READING: Isaiah 58:7-10

Your light shall break forth like the dawn.

This reading comes from the third part of the Book of the Prophet Isaiah. It was probably written some time after the exile in Babylon (after 539 B.C.).

During the exile prophets had predicted a great restoration. But when the Israelites arrived back in Jerusalem, all they found was devastation. They wanted to know why they were still suffering.

The prophet answered that it was their fault. They were not practicing justice and caring for the poor. When they would do those things, then they could expect to receive blessings from the LORD. Then the gloom in which they were living would be filled with the LORD's light.

A reading from the Book of the Prophet Isaiah

Thus says the LORD:
  Share your bread with the hungry,
  shelter the oppressed and the homeless;
clothe the naked when you see them,
  and do not turn your back on your own.
Then your light shall break forth like the dawn,
  and your wound shall quickly be healed;
your vindication shall go before you,
  and the glory of the LORD shall be your rear guard.
Then you shall call, and the LORD will answer,
  you shall cry for help, and he will say: Here I am!
If you remove from your midst
  oppression, false accusation and malicious speech;
if you bestow your bread on the hungry
  and satisfy the afflicted;
then light shall rise for you in the darkness,
  and the gloom shall become for you like midday.

The word of the Lord.

Lect. No. 73

RESPONSORIAL PSALM: Ps 112:4-5, 6-7, 8-9 (℟.: 4a)

Psalm 112 is written in the wisdom tradition, outlining the blessings that would be showered upon the just and the punishment due to the wicked.

The just is described as being a man of God, for he exhibits many of the attributes that are normally given to God alone.

℟. **The just man is a light in darkness to the upright.**

or:

℟. **Alleluia.**

Light shines through the darkness for the upright;
  he is gracious and merciful and just.
Well for the man who is gracious and lends,
  who conducts his affairs with justice.

He is a light in the darkness, he is righteous, etc. In other words, the just person who acts in a godly manner makes present the goodness and love of God.

The just person need not fear, for God will certainly protect that person.

That does not necessarily mean that everything will always go well. But it certainly does mean that no matter what happens, God will never abandon the just. God's love is the one love in our life that never goes away or makes mistakes.

But pure justice is not enough. It is not enough just to pay one's debts and be honest. The righteous person also aids those who need assistance. The truly righteous person shares in the bounty of the LORD—with as much generosity as the LORD himself.

R⫟. **The just man is a light in darkness to the upright.**

or:

R⫟. **Alleluia.**

He shall never be moved;
  the just one shall be in everlasting remembrance.
An evil report he shall not fear;
  his heart is firm, trusting in the LORD.

R⫟. **The just man is a light in darkness to the upright.**

or:

R⫟. **Alleluia.**

His heart is steadfast; he shall not fear.
  Lavishly he gives to the poor;
his justice shall endure forever;
  his horn shall be exalted in glory.

R⫟. **The just man is a light in darkness to the upright.**

or:

R⫟. **Alleluia.**

Lect. No. 73

SECOND READING: 1 Corinthians 2:1-5

I have announced to you the mystery of Christ crucified.

As we continue to read from First Corinthians, a letter that we have been reading over the past few weeks, we hear Saint Paul contrast the wisdom of the world with the wisdom of the cross.

He had tried preaching the gospel in terms of Greek philosophy when he was in Athens. That attempt had failed; so

A reading from the first Letter of Saint Paul to the Corinthians

When I came to you, brothers and sisters, proclaiming the mystery of God,
  I did not come with sublimity of words or of wisdom.
For I resolved to know nothing while I was with you except Jesus Christ, and him crucified.
I came to you in weakness and fear and much trembling,

when he arrived in Corinth, almost immediately afterward, he did not try to preach in those terms.

Paul proclaimed the cross, and remarkably people saw the power of the Spirit in his words and turned to God.

| Lect. |
| No. 73 |

Jesus is the one true light that can guide us through the darkness. He is the path that leads to the Father.

| Lect. |
| No. 73 |

This passage taken from the Sermon on the Mount gives us two sayings that speak of the need to give witness to our beliefs.

The first saying calls Jesus' followers the "salt of the earth." Salt was an absolute necessity in a hot climate such as that of Israel. Yet, if it lost its saltiness, it would often be thrown into the street to keep the dust down.

The second saying centers on the theme of being the "light of the world." One must do good deeds and give witness to one's beliefs, but not to look good in front of others. One does this to further the cause of the kingdom.

and my message and my proclamation
were not with persuasive words of wisdom,
but with a demonstration of Spirit and power,
so that your faith might rest not on human wisdom
    dom
but on the power of God.

The word of the Lord.

ALLELUIA: John 8:12

℟. **Alleluia, alleluia.**

I am the light of the world, says the Lord;
whoever follows me will have the light of life.

℟. **Alleluia, alleluia.**

GOSPEL: Matthew 5:13-16

You are the light of the world.

A reading from the holy Gospel according
to Matthew

Jesus said to his disciples:
"You are the salt of the earth.
But if salt loses its taste, with what can it be seasoned?
    soned?
It is no longer good for anything
    but to be thrown out and trampled underfoot.
You are the light of the world.
A city set on a mountain cannot be hidden.
Nor do they light a lamp and then put it under a
    bushel basket;
    it is set on a lampstand,
    where it gives light to all in the house.
Just so, your light must shine before others,
    that they may see your good deeds
    and glorify your heavenly Father."

The Gospel of the Lord.

ASH WEDNESDAY*

These readings are found in the 1970 Lectionary, no. 220

1970
Lect.
No. 220

FIRST READING: Joel 2:12-18

Let your hearts be broken, and not your garments torn.

The First Reading gives a sense as to why we celebrate Lent each year: it is a time when we must look at our lives seriously and root out those things that keep us from loving God.

Joel speaks of God being ready to forgive us. We, however, must seek that pardon. If we are not willing to admit that we are sinners and broken, then God cannot heal us. It is not that God does not want to heal us, only that we cannot receive the healing until we open our hearts to it. God does not force his love upon us.

It is never too late to turn back to God. We must remember the story of the owner of the vineyard who rewards all of those who worked for him, even those who worked for only a very short time. Yet we cannot presume upon God's mercy. We must use this blessed time to change our ways.

The reading speaks of weeping and mourning as examples of our commitment to conversion. These were external signs of a willingness to turn from sin. Today we use ashes. They are only the external sign of what must be a serious interior disposition to turn our lives

A reading from the Book of the Prophet Joel

Even now, says the Lord,
return to me with your whole heart,
   with fasting, and weeping, and mourning;
rend your hearts, not your garments,
   and return to the Lord, your God.
For gracious and merciful is he,
   slow to anger, rich in kindness,
   and relenting in punishment.
Perhaps he will again relent
   and leave behind him a blessing,
Offerings and libations
   for the Lord, your God.

Blow the trumpet in Zion!
   proclaim a fast,
   call an assembly;
Gather the people,
   notify the congregation;
Assemble the elders,
   gather the children
   and the infants at the breast;
Let the bridegroom quit his room,
   and the bride her chamber.
Between the porch and the altar
   let the priests, the ministers of the Lord, weep,
And say, "Spare, O Lord, your people,
   and make not your heritage a reproach,
   with the nations ruling over them!
Why should they say among the peoples,
   'Where is their God?' "

around. Likewise, the fasting that we perform this Lent should be a sign of saying no to those things that are not of God and saying yes to God.

Then the LORD was stirred to concern for his land and took pity on his people.

The word of the Lord.

| 1970 |
| Lect. |
| No. 220 |

RESPONSORIAL PSALM: Ps 51:3-4, 5-6, 12-13, 14, 17 (℟.: 3)

Psalm 51 is a beautiful penitential psalm. It is dedicated to the memory of that moment when the Prophet Nathan confronted King David concerning his act of adultery with Bathsheba and his murder of Uriah the Hittite.

The psalm recognizes many of the facets of turning away from sin and back to God. It speaks of how we can only be cleansed through the intervention of God.

We recognize the fact that we are sinners and worthy of condemnation. Yet we beseech God for healing.

If God recreates us with his Spirit, we will be alive again. Our sin has made us like creatures that have lost their life, but now God has breathed his Spirit back into us. We will be filled with the joy of God, for he is the source of our life and our love and our salvation.

℟. **Be merciful, O Lord, for we have sinned.**

Have mercy on me, O God, in your goodness;
    in the greatness of your compassion wipe out my
      offense.
Thoroughly wash me from my guilt
    and of my sin cleanse me.

℟. **Be merciful, O Lord, for we have sinned.**

For I acknowledge my offense,
    and my sin is before me always:
"Against you only have I sinned,
    and done what is evil in your sight."

℟. **Be merciful, O Lord, for we have sinned.**

A clean heart create for me, O God,
    and a steadfast spirit renew within me.
Cast me not out from your presence,
    and your Holy Spirit take not from me.

℟. **Be merciful, O Lord, for we have sinned.**

Give me back the joy of your salvation,
    and a willing spirit sustain in me.
O Lord, open my lips,
    and my mouth shall proclaim your praise.

℟. **Be merciful, O Lord, for we have sinned.**

| 1970 |
| Lect. |
| No. 220 |

SECOND READING: 2 Corinthians 5:20—6:2

Be reconciled to God, now is the acceptable time.

Saint Paul speaks of being an ambassador for the message of salvation. His entire life work was to proclaim the salvation that God offers us through

A reading from the second letter of Paul
to the Corinthians

We are ambassadors for Christ,
God as it were appealing through us.

the death and resurrection of Jesus.

Now is the time to accept that salvation into our lives. The beginning of Lent is a blessed time for us to turn from our mistaken ways and find the path of truth.

This is all that God wants of us. We see this in the fact that Jesus took our human condition upon himself, even suffering and dying, although he had done nothing wrong. He became sin (adopted our sinful flesh) to set us free from our sin.

We implore you, in Christ's name:
  be reconciled to God!
For our sakes God made him who did not know sin
  to be sin,
  so that in him we might become the very holiness
  of God.

As your fellow workers we beg you
  not to receive the grace of God in vain.
For he says,
  "In an acceptable time I have heard you;
  on a day of salvation I have helped you."
Now is the acceptable time!
Now is the day of salvation!

The Word of the Lord

| 1970 |
| Lect. |
| No. 220 |

Now is the time to turn from our sin and to embrace God with all our heart. Today is the day of our salvation.

VERSE BEFORE THE GOSPEL: Psalm 95:8

If today you hear his voice,
harden not your hearts.

| 1970 |
| Lect. |
| No. 220 |

GOSPEL: Matthew 6:1-6,16-18

Your Father, who sees all that is done in secret, will reward you.

When the temple in Jerusalem was destroyed in 70 A.D., the Jewish people lost the place where they could expiate their sins. Previously, they had performed sacrifices that won them forgiveness for their sins.

Sin had brought death into their lives. The blood of their sacrifices gave them life again (for blood was a sign of life).

The people asked the rabbis what they could now do to obtain forgiveness for their sins.

A reading from the holy Gospel according
to Matthew

Jesus said to his disciples:
"Be on guard
  against performing religious acts for people to see.
Otherwise expect no recompense from your heavenly Father.
When you give alms, for example,
  do not blow a horn before you in synagogues and
  streets
  like hypocrites looking for applause.
You can be sure of this much,
  they are already repaid.

There was nowhere that they could offer sacrifices.

The rabbis answered that there were three things that brought forgiveness of sins: almsgiving, fasting, and praying.

These are the exact things that our reading asks us to do. Saint Matthew's message is that the rabbis were right, but they were wrong in the way that they did these things. They often did them to look good in front of others.

That is not the reason why we should do these things. We should do them out of a profound willingness to change our lives. They should be reflections of a change of heart. Without that, these actions are nothing more than superficial actions that do us no good.

And so today we dedicate ourselves to acts of penance. These actions are signs of our willingness to make this Lent meaningful. We commit ourselves to prayer, to acts of charity, and to acts of mortification.

These things do not have to be spectacular (in fact, it is always prudent to plan things that are reasonable lest we overcommit ourselves and lose heart after a few days). But they must be honest signs of willingness to live for and in God our Father.

In giving alms you are not to let your left hand know
     what your right hand is doing.
Keep your deeds of mercy secret,
     and your Father who sees in secret will repay you.

"When you are praying,
     do not behave like the hypocrites
     who love to stand and pray
     in synagogues or on street corners in order to be
       noticed.
I give you my word,
     they are already repaid.
Whenever you pray, go to your room,
     close your door, and pray to your Father in private.
Then your Father,
     who sees what no man sees,
     will repay you.

"When you fast,
     you are not to look glum as the hypocrites do.
They change the appearance of their faces
     so that others may see they are fasting.
I assure you, they are already repaid.
When you fast,
     see to it that you groom your hair and wash your
       face.
In that way no one can see you are fasting
     but your Father who is hidden;
     and your Father who sees what is hidden will
       repay you."

The Gospel of the Lord.

February 17, 2002

FIRST SUNDAY OF LENT

Lect.
No. 22

FIRST READING: Genesis 2:7-9; 3:1-7

The creation of our first parents, and sin.

A reading from the Book of Genesis

The LORD God formed man out of the clay of the ground
  and blew into his nostrils the breath of life,
and so man became a living being.

Then the LORD God planted a garden in Eden, in the east,
  and placed there the man whom he had formed.
Out of the ground the LORD God made various trees grow
  that were delightful to look at and good for food,
  with the tree of life in the middle of the garden
  and the tree of the knowledge of good and evil.

Now the serpent was the most cunning of all the animals
  that the LORD God had made.
The serpent asked the woman,
  "Did God really tell you not to eat
  from any of the trees in the garden?"
The woman answered the serpent:
  "We may eat of the fruit of the trees in the garden;
  it is only about the fruit of the tree
  in the middle of the garden that God said,
  'You shall not eat it or even touch it, lest you die.'"
But the serpent said to the woman:
  "You certainly will not die!
No, God knows well that the moment you eat of it
  your eyes will be opened and you will be like gods
  who know what is good and what is evil."
The woman saw that the tree was good for food,

We begin Lent by reflecting upon the creation of humanity and upon their fall into sin.

God created Adam from clay and his breath. The fact that God breathed into Adam shows that there is something of God in each one of us. We are called to share in God's life.

God cared for his creatures by placing them in the garden of Eden (a name that means paradise). He only commanded them not to eat of the fruit of the tree of good and evil. Mention of the two extremes, good and evil, shows that this is the tree of the knowledge of all things.

The serpent tempts Eve by subtly implying that God has lied to them and is trying to withhold something from them that they deserve. When the woman mentions that there is a danger of death, the snake ambiguously answers that they "certainly will not die," or, "it is not certain that they will die." The serpent never openly lies, just suggests, entices, implies.

Both Eve and Adam commit this sin. We should not blame one or the other, for they both are guilty.

Their eyes are opened, but this is not all they hoped it would be.

Before they sinned they lived in a state of innocence, as seen by the fact that they were naked but not ashamed. When they sinned, they lost something good and holy that would only be regained through the death and resurrection of Jesus.

pleasing to the eyes, and desirable for gaining wisdom.
So she took some of its fruit and ate it;
    and she also gave some to her husband, who was with her,
    and he ate it.
Then the eyes of both of them were opened,
    and they realized that they were naked;
    so they sewed fig leaves together
    and made loincloths for themselves.

The word of the Lord.

Lect. No. 22 — RESPONSORIAL PSALM: Ps 51:3-4, 5-6, 12-13, 17 (℟.: cf. 3a)

This penitential psalm recognizes our fundamental need of God's compassionate mercy, his forgiveness. We have sinned against God and our sisters and brothers. We deserve to be condemned. Yet we turn to God who gives us the possibility of a new beginning.

We must also recognize that we are fundamentally incapable of changing things. We are addicted to sin. No matter how many times we say we will never do these things again, we find ourselves doing them over and over again.

We turn to our heavenly Father to change our hearts. If we experience his incredible love, then we will have a chance to begin anew.

We ask God for a willing spirit. We have hardened our hearts and anesthetized ourselves to the pointlessness of a way of life steeped in sin. We need God to convince us that things must change.

℟. **Be merciful, O Lord, for we have sinned.**

Have mercy on me, O God, in your goodness;
    in the greatness of your compassion wipe out my offense.
Thoroughly wash me from my guilt
    and of my sin cleanse me.

℟. **Be merciful, O Lord, for we have sinned.**

For I acknowledge my offense,
    and my sin is before me always:
"Against you only have I sinned,
    and done what is evil in your sight."

℟. **Be merciful, O Lord, for we have sinned.**

A clean heart create for me, O God,
    and a steadfast spirit renew within me.
Cast me not out from your presence,
    and your Holy Spirit take not from me.

℟. **Be merciful, O Lord, for we have sinned.**

Give me back the joy of your salvation,
    and a willing spirit sustain in me.
O LORD, open my lips,
    and my mouth shall proclaim your praise.

℟. **Be merciful, O Lord, for we have sinned.**

Lect.
No. 22

SECOND READING: **A** Longer Form: Romans 5:12-19

Where sin increased, there grace increased all the more.

Saint Paul is writing this letter to a community that does not know him. He wants them to understand what he is teaching about sin and the mercy of God. Thus, he produces an elaborate argument to outline his beliefs.

Paul speaks about the effects of original sin. Adam sinned and damaged the relationship between humans and God. He brought death into the world. Paul is probably speaking about spiritual death and not physical death.

We have all shared in that original sin in two ways, through our inheritance of the hurt that Adam brought into the world and through our own sins. Once Adam sinned, it was easier for us to sin as well.

Even before we received the law on Mount Sinai, we were sinners. Although there was no law, we knew that we were sinning against God. It is even more true now that we have received the law, for now there is absolutely no excuse.

Thus, we are all worthy of condemnation, for we are all sinners. We have all called a curse down upon ourselves and are now subject to its punishments.

But while the effects were catastrophic, the effect of

A reading from the Letter of Saint Paul
to the Romans

Brothers and sisters:
Through one man sin entered the world,
and through sin, death,
and thus death came to all men, inasmuch as all sinned—
for up to the time of the law, sin was in the world,
though sin is not accounted when there is no law.
But death reigned from Adam to Moses,
even over those who did not sin
after the pattern of the trespass of Adam,
who is the type of the one who was to come.

But the gift is not like the transgression.
For if by the transgression of the one, the many died,
how much more did the grace of God
and the gracious gift of the one man Jesus Christ
overflow for the many.
And the gift is not like the result of the one who sinned.
For after one sin there was the judgment that brought condemnation;
but the gift, after many transgressions, brought acquittal.
For if, by the transgression of the one,
death came to reign through that one,
how much more will those who receive the abundance of grace
and of the gift of justification
come to reign in life through the one Jesus Christ.
In conclusion, just as through one transgression
condemnation came upon all,

Jesus' death and resurrection is even more powerful. Sin caused death, and that is just punishment. But Jesus brought life.

It is a much greater thing to bring people back to life than to kill them. Thus, what Jesus did fills us with awe.

so, through one righteous act,
acquittal and life came to all.
For just as through the disobedience of the one man
the many were made sinners,
so, through the obedience of the one,
the many will be made righteous.

The word of the Lord.

Lect. No. 22

SECOND READING: B Shorter Form: Romans 5:12, 17-19

Where sin increased, grace overflowed all the more.

Writing this letter to a community that does not know him, Paul wants them to understand what he is teaching about sin and the mercy of God. Thus, he produces an elaborate argument to outline his beliefs.

Paul speaks about the effects of original sin. Adam sinned and damaged the relationship between humans and God. He brought death into the world. Paul is probably speaking about spiritual (not physical) death.

We have all shared in that original sin in two ways, through our inheritance of the hurt that Adam brought into the world and through our own sins. Once Adam sinned, it was easier for us to sin as well.

But while the effects were catastrophic, the effect of Jesus' death and resurrection is even more powerful. Sin caused death, and that is just punishment. But Jesus brought life. It is a much greater thing to bring people back to life than to kill them. Thus, what Jesus did fills us with awe.

A reading from the Letter of Saint Paul
to the Romans

Brothers and sisters:
Through one man sin entered the world,
and through sin, death,
and thus death came to all men, inasmuch as all sinned.

For if, by the transgression of the one,
death came to reign through that one,
how much more will those who receive the abundance of grace
and of the gift of justification
come to reign in life through the one Jesus Christ.
In conclusion, just as through one transgression
condemnation came upon all,
so, through one righteous act,
acquittal and life came to all.
For just as through the disobedience of the one man
the many were made sinners,
so, through the obedience of the one,
the many will be made righteous.

The word of the Lord.

Lect. No. 22

VERSE BEFORE THE GOSPEL: Matthew 4:4b

The word of God nourishes our heart and soul and satisfies our most profound desire—for God's love.

One does not live on bread alone,
but on every word that comes forth from the mouth of God.

Lect. No. 22

GOSPEL: Matthew 4:1-11

Jesus fasted for forty days and forty nights and was tempted.

This story is material that Matthew has taken from the source named "Q," which is the material that appears in Luke and Matthew but not in Mark. (Mark only tells us that Jesus was tempted, but he does not recount what the temptations were.)

The one major difference between Luke's version and Matthew's is that Luke has the Jerusalem temptation as last (typical of Luke who emphasizes the importance of the city of Jerusalem) while Matthew has the mountain temptation as last (typical of Matthew who emphasizes mountain scenes).

Jesus is tempted to use his power in an inappropriate manner: for his own comfort and not for service. He steadfastly refuses to do this. His mission is to fulfill the Father's will and to bring us salvation.

The parapet of the temple is simply the wall of the temple. It is not a structure raised over the wall as artists sometimes picture it.

A reading from the holy Gospel according to Matthew

At that time Jesus was led by the Spirit into the desert
to be tempted by the devil.
He fasted for forty days and forty nights,
and afterwards he was hungry.
The tempter approached and said to him,
"If you are the Son of God,
command that these stones become loaves of bread."
He said in reply,
"It is written:
One does not live on bread alone,
but on every word that comes forth
from the mouth of God."

Then the devil took him to the holy city,
and made him stand on the parapet of the temple,
and said to him, "If you are the Son of God, throw yourself down.
For it is written:
He will command his angels concerning you
and with their hands they will support you,
lest you dash your foot against a stone."
Jesus answered him,
"Again it is written,
You shall not put the Lord, your God, to the test."

While the title "Son of God" in the Old Testament simply means a hero (for kings and prophets were often called sons of God), it has a different meaning here. It is coming from the mouth of Satan, a spiritual being, who recognizes that Jesus truly is the only-begotten Son of God.

Typical of Satan's temptations, this one is subtle for he makes it seem as if the choice to sin is actually a choice to do the better thing.

Then the devil took him up to a very high mountain,
and showed him all the kingdoms of the world in
their magnificence,
and he said to him, "All these I shall give to you,
if you will prostrate yourself and worship me."
At this, Jesus said to him,
"Get away, Satan!
It is written:
The Lord, your God, shall you worship
and him alone shall you serve."

Then the devil left him and, behold,
angels came and ministered to him.

The Gospel of the Lord.

SECOND SUNDAY OF LENT

Lect. No. 25

FIRST READING: Genesis 12:1-4a

The call of Abraham, the father of God's people.

A reading from the Book of Genesis

The LORD said to Abram:
"Go forth from the land of your kinsfolk
  and from your father's house to a land that I will
    show you.

"I will make of you a great nation,
    and I will bless you;
I will make your name great,
    so that you will be a blessing.
I will bless those who bless you
    and curse those who curse you.
All the communities of the earth
    shall find blessing in you."

Abram went as the LORD directed him.

The word of the Lord.

This passage from Genesis presents the call of Abraham (before his name was changed by God). God chose an individual through whom he would bring salvation to all of humanity. Abraham was to be the father of the Jewish people.

This call, though, demanded a response of faith. Abraham had to leave all that was familiar and set off to a land that he had never seen, believing that God would deliver those things he was promising.

Until the day he died, Abraham would have to continue to have faith. At his death, only the smallest part of the promise was fulfilled, and still he believed.

Lect. No. 25

RESPONSORIAL PSALM: Ps 33:4-5, 18-19, 20, 22 (℟.: 22)

Psalm 33 is a hymn of praise and trust in a God who is always faithful to his promises.

In a world filled with confusion and empty promises, God offers the one hope that will never result in disillusionment.

We call upon God as one who loves justice and that which is right. God is filled with kindness.

We have no other hope for one who can save us from our enemies. He will deliver us from

℟. **Lord, let your mercy be on us, as we place our trust in you.**

Upright is the word of the LORD,
    and all his works are trustworthy.
He loves justice and right;
    of the kindness of the LORD the earth is full.

℟. **Lord, let your mercy be on us, as we place our trust in you.**

See, the eyes of the LORD are upon those who fear
    him,
    upon those who hope for his kindness,

death and preserve us from famine. He is our help and our shield.

In the Old Testament, deliverance from death meant a physical deliverance. Throughout most of the Old Testament, people did not believe in an afterlife.

We believe that the deliverance will come not only in this world but especially in the life to come.

to deliver them from death
　and preserve them in spite of famine.

　R̸. **Lord, let your mercy be on us, as we place our trust in you.**

Our soul waits for the LORD,
　who is our help and our shield.
May your kindness, O LORD, be upon us
　who have put our hope in you.

　R̸. **Lord, let your mercy be on us, as we place our trust in you.**

Lect.
No. 25

SECOND READING: 2 Timothy 1:8b-10

God has saved us and called us to be holy.

God had a plan for our salvation, even before the creation of the world. This means that God always intended us to share in his life for all eternity. This grace is not due to anything we have done, it is due to the gratuitous love of God.

Jesus fulfilled this plan through his cross and resurrection. He has called us to a life of grace, and we must respond with a true Christian life-style. This means that we must be ready even to suffer for the gospel, for if we truly try to be Christian, there will be a price to pay.

A reading from the second Letter of Saint Paul to Timothy

Beloved:
　Bear your share of hardship for the gospel
with the strength that comes from God.

He saved us and called us to a holy life,
　not according to our works
　but according to his own design
　and the grace bestowed on us in Christ Jesus before time began,
　but now made manifest
　through the appearance of our savior Christ Jesus,
　who destroyed death and brought life and immortality
　to light through the gospel.

The word of the Lord.

Lect.
No. 25

VERSE BEFORE THE GOSPEL: cf. Matthew 17:5

We hear the Father's voice proclaim Jesus as his beloved Son. We must listen to his call.

From the shining cloud the Father's voice is heard:
This is my beloved Son, hear him.

Lect.
No. 25

GOSPEL: Matthew 17:1-9

Jesus' face shone like the sun.

The transfiguration is a pre-figuring of the glory of the resurrection. Many of the same phrases that are used in the description of Jesus and his glorified body appear in this account.

Jesus takes Peter, James, and John up the mountain. These are the three apostles who accompany Jesus whenever something important happens in the gospels.

Moses and Elijah appear to show that Jesus is the fulfillment of the prophecies about the Messiah found in the law and the prophets. These were also the two figures in the Old Testament who were prophesied to appear again at the dawning of the Day of the Lord.

The Father proclaims Jesus as his beloved Son. The apostles fall prostrate because they are in the presence of the living God.

The apostles were not to tell anything to anyone until the Son of Man had risen from the dead. It is obvious from this statement that the transfiguration occurs to prepare the apostles both for the disillusionment of the suffering and death of Jesus and for the wonder of the glory of his resurrection.

A reading from the holy Gospel according to Matthew

Jesus took Peter, James, and John his brother,
and led them up a high mountain by themselves.
And he was transfigured before them;
   his face shone like the sun
   and his clothes became white as light.
And behold, Moses and Elijah appeared to them,
   conversing with him.
Then Peter said to Jesus in reply,
   "Lord, it is good that we are here.
If you wish, I will make three tents here,
   one for you, one for Moses, and one for Elijah."
While he was still speaking, behold,
   a bright cloud cast a shadow over them,
   then from the cloud came a voice that said,
   "This is my beloved Son, with whom I am well
      pleased;
   listen to him."
When the disciples heard this, they fell prostrate
   and were very much afraid.
But Jesus came and touched them, saying,
   "Rise, and do not be afraid."
And when the disciples raised their eyes,
   they saw no one else but Jesus alone.

As they were coming down from the mountain,
   Jesus charged them,
   "Do not tell the vision to anyone
   until the Son of Man has been raised from the
      dead."

The Gospel of the Lord.

March 3, 2002

THIRD SUNDAY OF LENT

Lect. No. 28

FIRST READING: Exodus 17:3-7

Give us water, so that we may drink.

The LORD had just freed the Israelites from slavery in Egypt, intervening with powerful miracles to convince the Egyptians to let his people go, but they still grumbled against Moses and the LORD. They refused to believe that the LORD would continue to protect them and provide for their needs.

The lack of gratitude is astounding, and yet the LORD responds with another act of generosity. He provides them with water from the rock.

This was a pattern that occurred over and over again throughout the exodus experience. This is why the Israelites had to remain in the desert for forty years, to learn how to trust in the LORD.

Before we condemn the Israelites, though, it is good to admit that, in spite of all the ways we have seen God's goodness in our lives, we still doubt his presence all too often. We often hedge our bets by relying on God but also upon our own resources.

A reading from the Book of Exodus

In those days, in their thirst for water,
the people grumbled against Moses,
saying, "Why did you ever make us leave Egypt?
Was it just to have us die here of thirst
with our children and our livestock?"
So Moses cried out to the LORD,
"What shall I do with this people?
A little more and they will stone me!"
The LORD answered Moses,
"Go over there in front of the people,
along with some of the elders of Israel,
holding in your hand, as you go,
the staff with which you struck the river.
I will be standing there in front of you on the rock in
Horeb.
Strike the rock, and the water will flow from it
for the people to drink."
This Moses did, in the presence of the elders of
Israel.
The place was called Massah and Meribah,
because the Israelites quarreled there
and tested the LORD, saying,
"Is the LORD in our midst or not?"

The word of the Lord.

Lect. No. 28

RESPONSORIAL PSALM: Ps 95:1-2, 6-7, 8-9 (℟.: 8)

This is above all a hymn of praise for the LORD who is our strength and salvation. We must recognize how much we need God to be a part of our lives.

℟. **If today you hear his voice, harden not your hearts.**

Come, let us sing joyfully to the LORD;
let us acclaim the Rock of our salvation.

When we acknowledge how important God is for us, then we must fall down on our knees to worship him.

One of the goals of Lent is to do exactly this. We must discover those things that we have set at the center of our lives in the place of God and root them out. We must return God to his proper place in our lives. We must fall down on our knees in gratitude and awe.

This is why the last part of our Responsorial Psalm is a warning against arrogance and pride. We are always being tempted to self-sufficiency and the illusion that we can solve all of our problems if we just try hard enough. Only in God can we find a response to our need: only in our heavenly Father can we find peace.

Let us come into his presence with thanksgiving;
    let us joyfully sing psalms to him.

R/. **If today you hear his voice, harden not your hearts.**

Come, let us bow down in worship;
    let us kneel before the LORD who made us.
For he is our God,
    and we are the people he shepherds, the flock he guides.

R/. **If today you hear his voice, harden not your hearts.**

Oh, that today you would hear his voice:
    "Harden not your hearts as at Meribah,
    as in the day of Massah in the desert,
where your fathers tempted me;
    they tested me though they had seen my works."

R/. **If today you hear his voice, harden not your hearts.**

Lect.
No. 28

SECOND READING: Romans 5:1-2, 5-8

The love of God has been poured into our hearts through the Holy Spirit that has been given to us.

Saint Paul outlines his theology of salvation in this letter to the Christian community in Rome.

According to Paul, Christ paid the price for our redemption on the cross. When we accept the free gift of his love through our response of faith, we are justified. Justification means that we are living at peace with our God.

This gift is incredible. It was given to us not because of something that we had done, but quite the opposite. We had

A reading from the Letter of Saint Paul
to the Romans

Brothers and sisters:
    Since we have been justified by faith,
we have peace with God through our Lord Jesus Christ,
through whom we have gained access by faith
to this grace in which we stand,
and we boast in hope of the glory of God.

And hope does not disappoint,
    because the love of God has been poured out into our hearts
through the Holy Spirit who has been given to us.

sinned and rejected God's love, and God responded to that offense with a greater outpouring of love.

If God did this for us while we were sinners, then what is in store for us now that we are living at peace with him (justified). Paul marvels at the greatness of God's love and the glory into which we have been called to live for all eternity.

For Christ, while we were still helpless,
    died at the appointed time for the ungodly.
Indeed, only with difficulty does one die for a just
        person,
    though perhaps for a good person one might even
        find courage to die.
But God proves his love for us
    in that while we were still sinners Christ died for
        us.

The word of the Lord.

Lect. No. 28

VERSE BEFORE THE GOSPEL: cf. John 4:42, 15

Jesus is both the savior of the world and our own individual savior. We thirst for his love and grace, and he responds to our need with great generosity.

Lord, you are truly the Savior of the world;
    give me living water, that I may never thirst again.

Lect. No. 28

GOSPEL: ▲ Longer Form: John 4:5-42

The water that I shall give will become a spring of eternal life.

Throughout the Old Testament there are several "well" stories. In each of them, a person meets his or her spouse (e.g., Isaac, Jacob, Moses, and Ruth). The technical term for this type of pattern is "leitmotif." The differences in each of the stories gives us insights into the characters involved in these encounters.

The evangelist used the well story pattern in this account to speak of God's relationship to the Samaritans and pagans. They had not been part of the original covenant, which was a type of marriage between God and the people of Israel. God was now going to invite them into the new covenant.

A reading from the holy Gospel according to John

Jesus came to a town of Samaria called Sychar,
    near the plot of land that Jacob had given to his
        son Joseph.
Jacob's well was there.
Jesus, tired from his journey, sat down there at the
        well.
It was about noon.

A woman of Samaria came to draw water.
Jesus said to her,
    "Give me a drink."
His disciples had gone into the town to buy food.
The Samaritan woman said to him,
    "How can you, a Jew, ask me, a Samaritan
        woman, for a drink?"
—For Jews use nothing in common with Samari-
        tans.—

The Samaritan woman in this story represents the Samaritans and pagans. This is typical of John's gospel, for every time that a character is referred to by a title and not a name (e.g., man born blind, Samaritan woman), that character plays a symbolic role.

The woman goes to the well at the the sixth hour, which is noon. That is unusual, for it was too hot at that hour to go to the well for water. This woman was afraid to meet others because of her reputation, and so she avoided them by going to the well when they were not there.

Even when Jesus begins to speak to her, she is hesitant. Jesus continues to treat her with great dignity and respect— one could say with more respect than that with which she treated herself.

Jesus offers her "living water." This phrase is ambiguous for it could mean flowing water or water that gives life. She only understands flowing water.

Jesus promises that this water will become a font overflowing within her. This means that she will be filled to overflowing with God's grace and life.

The woman does not understand anything that Jesus is saying, so he instructs her to call her husband. She has had five and is now living with another man, which makes six. These husbands represent all of the gods that her people have served.

Jesus answered and said to her,
"If you knew the gift of God
and who is saying to you, 'Give me a drink,'
you would have asked him
and he would have given you living water."
The woman said to him,
"Sir, you do not even have a bucket and the cistern is deep;
where then can you get this living water?
Are you greater than our father Jacob,
who gave us this cistern and drank from it himself
with his children and his flocks?"
Jesus answered and said to her,
"Everyone who drinks this water will be thirsty again;
but whoever drinks the water I shall give will never thirst;
the water I shall give will become in him
a spring of water welling up to eternal life."
The woman said to him,
"Sir, give me this water, so that I may not be thirsty
or have to keep coming here to draw water."

Jesus said to her,
"Go call your husband and come back."
The woman answered and said to him,
"I do not have a husband."
Jesus answered her,
"You are right in saying, 'I do not have a husband.'
For you have had five husbands,
and the one you have now is not your husband.
What you have said is true."
The woman said to him,
"Sir, I can see that you are a prophet.
Our ancestors worshiped on this mountain;
but you people say that the place to worship is in Jerusalem."
Jesus said to her,

The perfect number in the Bible is seven. Jesus, by offering her water, is becoming her seventh. He is inviting the Samaritan people and the pagans into a marriage (covenant) with God. (Always remember that this is a symbolic marriage.)

The Samaritan woman asks whether Jesus might be the Messiah. The Samaritan concept of the Messiah was very different from the Jewish concept. The Jewish people expected a conquering hero, but the Samaritans expected one who would reveal the secrets of God to them. This was exactly what Jesus was doing, for he was able to reveal all of the woman's secrets.

We hear that we are to worship the Father in Spirit and in Truth. The Spirit is the Holy Spirit. and the Truth is Jesus. We worship the Father in and through Jesus and the Holy Spirit.

The woman leaves her water jar, for, as Jesus promised, his grace has become a font of living water inside of her. She proclaims her message to the people from her village. Before she avoided them (going to the well at noon to avoid speaking to them), now she shares her discovery with them and she helps to bring them to salvation.

Jesus does not need the nourishment that the disciples can offer for he is totally sustained by the Father.

"Believe me, woman, the hour is coming
　　when you will worship the Father
　　neither on this mountain nor in Jerusalem.
You people worship what you do not understand;
　　we worship what we understand,
　　because salvation is from the Jews.
But the hour is coming, and is now here,
　　when true worshipers will worship the Father in
　　　　Spirit and truth;
　　and indeed the Father seeks such people to worship him.
God is Spirit, and those who worship him
　　must worship in Spirit and truth."
The woman said to him,
　　"I know that the Messiah is coming, the one called
　　　　the Christ;
　　when he comes, he will tell us everything."
Jesus said to her,
　　"I am he, the one speaking with you."

At that moment his disciples returned,
　　and were amazed that he was talking with a
　　　　woman,
　　but still no one said, "What are you looking for?"
　　or "Why are you talking with her?"
The woman left her water jar
　　and went into the town and said to the people,
　　"Come see a man who told me everything I have
　　　　done.
Could he possibly be the Christ?"
They went out of the town and came to him.
Meanwhile, the disciples urged him, "Rabbi, eat."
But he said to them,
　　"I have food to eat of which you do not know."
So the disciples said to one another,
　　"Could someone have brought him something to
　　　　eat?"
Jesus said to them,
　　"My food is to do the will of the one who sent me

Jesus tells his disciples that the grain is already white for the harvest ("ripe" is a bit of a mistranslation). He is not pointing at the grain fields, he is pointing at the Samaritans who were coming out of the village. Samaritans wore white robes, and they were the harvest of which Jesus was speaking. The one who sowed that harvest was the Samaritan woman; now the disciples were being called to harvest what she had planted.

The Samaritans then encounter Jesus and come to a more profound faith. They no longer believe in him because of what the woman said, but because they had experienced him themselves.

This is a powerful story of conversion. A woman who previously had been filled with fear was now filled to overflowing with love.

This is also the story of a people who had searched for love in the many gods whom they worshiped, but had not found true love or peace.

Finally, this is a reminder to us. We often have our own set of gods whom we worship: work, possessions, power, etc.

and to finish his work.

Do you not say, 'In four months the harvest will be here'?

I tell you, look up and see the fields ripe for the harvest.

The reaper is already receiving payment
   and gathering crops for eternal life,
      so that the sower and reaper can rejoice together.

For here the saying is verified that 'One sows and another reaps.'

I sent you to reap what you have not worked for;
   others have done the work,
      and you are sharing the fruits of their work."

Many of the Samaritans of that town began to believe in him
   because of the word of the woman who testified,
   "He told me everything I have done."

When the Samaritans came to him,
   they invited him to stay with them;
   and he stayed there two days.

Many more began to believe in him because of his word,
   and they said to the woman,
   "We no longer believe because of your word;
   for we have heard for ourselves,
   and we know that this is truly the savior of the world."

The Gospel of the Lord.

Lect. No. 28

GOSPEL: B Shorter Form: John 4:5-15, 19b-26, 39a, 40-42

The water that I shall give will become a spring of eternal life.

Throughout the Old Testament there are several "well" stories. In each of them, a person meets his or her spouse (e.g., Isaac, Jacob, Moses, and Ruth). The technical term for

A reading from the holy Gospel according to John

Jesus came to a town of Samaria called Sychar, near the plot of land that Jacob had given to his son Joseph.

this type of pattern is "leitmotif." The differences in each of the stories gives us insights into the characters involved in these encounters.

The Samaritan woman in this story represents the Samaritans and the pagans. When Jesus begins to speak to the Samaritan woman at the well, she is hesitant. Jesus treats her with great dignity and respect—one could say with more respect than that with which she treated herself.

Jesus offers her "living water." This phrase is ambiguous for it could mean flowing water or water that gives life. She only understands flowing water.

Jesus promises that this water will become a font overflowing within her. This means that she will be filled to overflowing with God's grace and life.

The woman does not understand anything that Jesus is saying, so he instructs her to call her husband.

She has had five and is now living with another man, which makes six.

These husbands represent all of the gods that her people have served.

The perfect number in the Bible is seven. Jesus, by offering her water, is becoming her seventh.

He is inviting the Samaritan people and the pagans into a marriage (covenant) with God. (Always remember that this is a symbolic marriage).

Jacob's well was there.

Jesus, tired from his journey, sat down there at the well.

It was about noon.

A woman of Samaria came to draw water.

Jesus said to her,
  "Give me a drink."

His disciples had gone into the town to buy food.

The Samaritan woman said to him,
  "How can you, a Jew, ask me, a Samaritan woman, for a drink?"
—For Jews use nothing in common with Samaritans.—

Jesus answered and said to her,
  "If you knew the gift of God
  and who is saying to you, 'Give me a drink,'
  you would have asked him
  and he would have given you living water."

The woman said to him,
  "Sir, you do not even have a bucket and the cistern is deep;
  where then can you get this living water?

Are you greater than our father Jacob,
  who gave us this cistern and drank from it himself
  with his children and his flocks?"

Jesus answered and said to her,
  "Everyone who drinks this water will be thirsty again;
  but whoever drinks the water I shall give will never thirst;
  the water I shall give will become in him
  a spring of water welling up to eternal life."

The woman said to him,
  "Sir, give me this water, so that I may not be thirsty
  or have to keep coming here to draw water.

"I can see that you are a prophet.

The Samaritan woman asks whether Jesus might be the Messiah. The Samaritan concept of messiah was very different from the Jewish concept. The Jewish people expected a conquering hero, but the Samaritans expected one who would reveal the secrets of God to them. This was exactly what Jesus was doing, for he was able to reveal all of the woman's secrets.

We hear that we are to worship the Father in Spirit and in Truth. The Spirit is the Holy Spirit, and the Truth is Jesus. We worship the Father in and through Jesus and the Holy Spirit.

The woman leaves her water jar, for, as Jesus promised, his grace has become a font of living water inside of her. She proclaims her message to the people from her village. Before she avoided them (going to the well at noon to avoid speaking to them); now she shares her discovery with them and she helps to bring them to salvation.

The Samaritans then encounter Jesus and come to a more profound faith. They no longer believe in him because of what the woman said, but because they had experienced him themselves.

This is a reminder to us. We often have our own set of gods whom we worship: work. possessions, power, etc.

Our ancestors worshiped on this mountain;
    but you people say that the place to worship is in Jerusalem."
Jesus said to her,
    "Believe me, woman, the hour is coming
    when you will worship the Father
    neither on this mountain nor in Jerusalem.
You people worship what you do not understand;
    we worship what we understand,
    because salvation is from the Jews.
But the hour is coming, and is now here,
    when true worshipers will worship the Father in Spirit and truth;
    and indeed the Father seeks such people to worship him.
God is Spirit, and those who worship him
    must worship in Spirit and truth."
The woman said to him,
    "I know that the Messiah is coming, the one called the Christ;
    when he comes, he will tell us everything."
Jesus said to her,
    "I am he, the one who is speaking with you."

Many of the Samaritans of that town began to believe in him.
When the Samaritans came to him,
    they invited him to stay with them;
    and he stayed there two days.
Many more began to believe in him because of his word,
    and they said to the woman,
    "We no longer believe because of your word;
    for we have heard for ourselves,
    and we know that this is truly the savior of the world."

The Gospel of the Lord.

Lect. No. 31

FIRST READING:
1 Samuel 16:1b, 6-7, 10-13a

David is anointed as king of Israel.

The Israelites had asked the LORD for a king to rule over them. The LORD indicated to Samuel, the last of the judges, that Saul was to be that king. (Judges were charismatically chosen leaders who acted as king, prophet, priest, and judge.) For a while, all went well and Saul led Israel against their enemies. But Saul did what was evil in the sight of the LORD. So the LORD rejected Saul and sent Samuel to anoint another king of Israel in his place.

The LORD sent Samuel to Bethlehem, a small city in the area settled by the tribe of Judah. There Samuel spoke to Jesse and asked to see his sons. He saw one after another of the sons, and all of them seemed to be handsome and courageous. If Samuel had made the choice on appearances, he could have chosen any one of them.

But the LORD chooses according to what is in a person's heart. David was to be the new king of Israel, for he was a man according to the LORD's own heart.

Samuel anointed David, making him an anointed of the LORD. Remember, the word anointed in Hebrew is messiah. But while David was a messiah,

A reading from the first Book of Samuel

The LORD said to Samuel:
"Fill your horn with oil, and be on your way.
I am sending you to Jesse of Bethlehem,
    for I have chosen my king from among his sons."

As Jesse and his sons came to the sacrifice,
    Samuel looked at Eliab and thought,
    "Surely the LORD's anointed is here before him."
But the LORD said to Samuel:
    "Do not judge from his appearance or from his
        lofty stature,
    because I have rejected him.
Not as man sees does God see,
    because man sees the appearance
    but the LORD looks into the heart."
In the same way Jesse presented seven sons before
        Samuel,
    but Samuel said to Jesse,
    "The LORD has not chosen any one of these."
Then Samuel asked Jesse,
    "Are these all the sons you have?"
Jesse replied,
    "There is still the youngest, who is tending the
        sheep."
Samuel said to Jesse,
    "Send for him;
    we will not begin the sacrificial banquet until he
        arrives here."
Jesse sent and had the young man brought to them.

only Jesus would be the Messiah. Nevertheless, David would be regarded as the model of what the future Messiah should be. This is why the Gospel of Matthew mentions that Jesus is a son of David in its genealogy.

The Spirit of the LORD rushed upon David, even as the Spirit of the LORD would anoint Jesus to proclaim a year of favor.

He was ruddy, a youth handsome to behold
  and making a splendid appearance.
The LORD said,
  "There—anoint him, for this is the one!"
Then Samuel, with the horn of oil in hand,
  anointed David in the presence of his brothers;
  and from that day on, the spirit of the LORD
  rushed upon David.

The word of the Lord.

<table>
<tr><td>Lect.
No. 31</td></tr>
</table>

RESPONSORIAL PSALM: Ps 23:1-3a, 3b-4, 5, 6 (℟.: 1)

This psalm is a beautiful hymn of trust in the goodness of the LORD. It was probably written during the exile in Babylon when the people of Israel desperately needed the consolation of knowing that the LORD was leading them and had not forgotten or abandoned them because of their sinfulness.

Before the exile the prophets had often complained that the kings of Israel were evil shepherds who did not guide their flocks in the ways of the LORD. Now God himself would guide them.

There are several images presented in the first part of the psalm to show how God is a good shepherd. He brings the flock to verdant pastures, leads them to restful waters (remember the importance of that in an arid climate), and he leads them through dangerous places. The valley through which we are led is called the "dark valley" (more popularly known as the "valley of death"). The Hebrew meaning is a valley that is dark as death.

℟. **The Lord is my shepherd; there is nothing I shall want.**

The LORD is my shepherd; I shall not want.
  In verdant pastures he gives me repose;
beside restful waters he leads me;
  he refreshes my soul.

℟. **The Lord is my shepherd; there is nothing I shall want.**

He guides me in right paths
  for his name's sake.
Even though I walk in the dark valley
  I fear no evil; for you are at my side
with your rod and your staff
  that give me courage.

℟. **The Lord is my shepherd; there is nothing I shall want.**

You spread the table before me
  in the sight of my foes;
you anoint my head with oil;
  my cup overflows.

℟. **The Lord is my shepherd; there is nothing I shall want.**

Only goodness and kindness follow me
  all the days of my life;

His rod and staff give us comfort for while we are wandering in the dark, we can nevertheless feel his presence as he gently touches us with them.

and I shall dwell in the house of the LORD
  for years to come.

℟. **The Lord is my shepherd; there is nothing I shall want.**

Lect. No. 31

SECOND READING: Ephesians 5:8-14

Arise from the dead, and Christ will give you light.

The Second Reading develops the theme of light and darkness. These two opposites were often used as a synonym for good and evil. We must choose the good and reject evil. Otherwise, we will be children of the dark, children of the evil one.

We see this same theme developed in other places in scripture. Jesus, for example, calls himself the light of the world. He gives light to the man born blind. On the other hand, we hear that after Judas departed from the Last Supper it was dark.

One of the goals of our Lenten conversion is transparency. We should do everything in such a way that we will never be embarrassed if others see what we have done. We have to allow the light of Christ to shine through us.

A reading from the Letter of Saint Paul
to the Ephesians

Brothers and sisters:
  You were once darkness,
but now you are light in the Lord.
Live as children of light,
  for light produces every kind of goodness
  and righteousness and truth.
Try to learn what is pleasing to the Lord.
Take no part in the fruitless works of darkness;
  rather expose them, for it is shameful even to mention
  the things done by them in secret;
  but everything exposed by the light becomes visible,
for everything that becomes visible is light.
Therefore, it says:
  "Awake, O sleeper,
  and arise from the dead,
  and Christ will give you light."

The word of the Lord.

Lect. No. 31

VERSE BEFORE THE GOSPEL: John 8:12

Jesus is the light of the world. He is the source of guidance for our journey and the light toward which we all travel.

I am the light of the world, says the Lord;
  whoever follows me will have the light of life.

GOSPEL: **A** Longer Form: John 9:1-41

*The man who was blind went off and washed himself
and came back able to see.*

This story is presented at two levels of meaning. The first (superficial) level is the story of a miracle that Jesus performed during his public ministry. The second (deeper symbolic level) is a story of a community that came to faith in Jesus Christ as the light of the world.

The disciples ask whether the man born blind is a sinner or whether his parents are sinners to explain why he should have been born blind. They are using a theology in which individual maladies are the result of particular sins.

Jesus rejects their question (which was rude considering that the blind man could hear what they were saying). He speaks of God manifesting his power through him. Jesus treats the man with great respect, beginning the healing of his spirit even before he heals him physically.

Jesus uses saliva to heal the man, something that many miracle workers in his day would have done. (The Pharisees would later object for the very act of making mud was considered to be work, an act forbidden on the Sabbath.) He sends the man to wash at the pool of Siloam.

The man was immediately healed. The people who were his neighbors never really knew

A reading from the holy Gospel according to John

As Jesus passed by he saw a man blind from birth. His disciples asked him,
"Rabbi, who sinned, this man or his parents,
that he was born blind?"
Jesus answered,
"Neither he nor his parents sinned;
it is so that the works of God might be made visible through him.
We have to do the works of the one who sent me while it is day.
Night is coming when no one can work.
While I am in the world, I am the light of the world."
When he had said this, he spat on the ground
and made clay with the saliva,
and smeared the clay on his eyes, and said to him,
"Go wash in the Pool of Siloam"—which means Sent—.
So he went and washed, and came back able to see.

His neighbors and those who had seen him earlier as a beggar said,
"Isn't this the one who used to sit and beg?"
Some said, "It is,"
but others said, "No, he just looks like him."
He said, "I am."
So they said to him, "How were your eyes opened?"
He replied,
"The man called Jesus made clay and anointed my eyes
and told me, 'Go to Siloam and wash.'
So I went there and washed and was able to see."
And they said to him, "Where is he?"
He said, "I don't know."

him as a person, they only knew him as a disability. (Notice, that they do not use his name.) That is why they cannot identify him when he is healed.

The man is brought before the Pharisees. It is only then that we hear that Jesus healed the man on the Sabbath. This is intentional, for while it was not important to Jesus that it was the Sabbath, it was important to the Pharisees. They could not understand why Jesus would not wait until the next day to heal him, for it was against the law to heal him if he were not in danger of death. Jesus, on the other hand, would not make him wait even one more minute.

The fact that the man is interrogated only before the Pharisees and not before the full Sanhedrin, which was composed of both the Pharisees and the Sadducees, as one would expect, is a sign that this story has a second level, one that occurred toward the end of the century when the Sadducees had ceased to exist.

The man born blind is not given a name because he also plays a symbolic role in this gospel. He represents the members of the community of the beloved disciple that had come to believe in Jesus.

Before they converted they had been blind, for they had not known the light of the world. Jesus came into their lives, and he healed them. He brought them to faith and they were able to see the truth. But like the man born blind, they suffered for their beliefs, for they were expelled from the synagogue.

They brought the one who was once blind to the
    Pharisees.
Now Jesus had made clay and opened his eyes on a
    sabbath.
So then the Pharisees also asked him how he was
    able to see.
He said to them,
    "He put clay on my eyes, and I washed, and now I
    can see."
So some of the Pharisees said,
    "This man is not from God,
    because he does not keep the sabbath."
But others said,
    "How can a sinful man do such signs?"
And there was a division among them.
So they said to the blind man again,
    "What do you have to say about him,
    since he opened your eyes?"
He said, "He is a prophet."

Now the Jews did not believe
    that he had been blind and gained his sight
    until they summoned the parents of the one who
        had gained his sight.
They asked them,
    "Is this your son, who you say was born blind?
How does he now see?"
His parents answered and said,
    "We know that this is our son and that he was
    born blind.
We do not know how he sees now,
    nor do we know who opened his eyes.
Ask him, he is of age;
    he can speak for himself."
His parents said this because they were afraid of the
    Jews,
    for the Jews had already agreed
    that if anyone acknowledged him as the Christ,
    he would be expelled from the synagogue.

The parents of the man born blind seem to represent that part of the Christian community that denied their faith in order to remain within the synagogue. They are often called crypto-Christians, a name that means hidden Christians. They let fear guide their lives, and they thus denied the one whom they knew to be the Messiah. They are a warning to us when we subtly deny our faith by failing to give witness to who or what we are.

The man born blind humiliates the great doctors of the law with his simplicity and truth. He has no formal learning, but his wisdom is much more profound than theirs. It is the wisdom of the cross being more powerful than the wisdom of the world.

Throughout the account the man born blind has used various titles for Jesus such as "the man called Jesus," "a prophet," "a man . . . from God," etc. After he is expelled from the presence of the Pharisees (which represents the synagogue), he comes to recognize who Jesus is for him. He calls him his "Lord" and he worships him. "Lord" is a title used for Yahweh in the Old Testament. The name Yahweh was so holy that whenever one found it in Scripture, one would pronounce its substitute word, *Adonai,* which meant the "LORD." By saying that Jesus is "LORD," the author is saying that Jesus is the same thing that Yahweh is: God. Also, one only worships God; so when the man worships Jesus, he is proclaiming him as God.

It was when the man suffered and was expelled from the synagogue that he came to recognize who Jesus was for him.

For this reason his parents said,
    "He is of age; question him."

So a second time they called the man who had been blind
    and said to him, "Give God the praise!
We know that this man is a sinner."
He replied,
    "If he is a sinner, I do not know.
One thing I do know is that I was blind and now I see."
So they said to him,
    "What did he do to you?
    How did he open your eyes?"
He answered them,
    "I told you already and you did not listen.
Why do you want to hear it again?
Do you want to become his disciples, too?"
They ridiculed him and said,
    "You are that man's disciple;
    we are disciples of Moses!
We know that God spoke to Moses,
    but we do not know where this one is from."
The man answered and said to them,
    "This is what is so amazing,
    that you do not know where he is from, yet he opened my eyes.
We know that God does not listen to sinners,
    but if one is devout and does his will, he listens to him.
It is unheard of that anyone ever opened the eyes of a person born blind.
If this man were not from God,
    he would not be able to do anything."
They answered and said to him,
    "You were born totally in sin,
    and are you trying to teach us?"
Then they threw him out.

The same is often true for us, that it is in times of suffering that we finally recognize who God really is for us.

Throughout this story there has been a recurring theme of sin. The disciples thought that the man was blind as a punishment for sin. The Pharisees accused both Jesus and the man born blind of being sinners.

It is the Pharisees who are the true sinners for they had the ability to recognize who Jesus was, and they refused to see. They chose to remain in their blindness, so they were condemned to remain in the hell they had made for themselves.

Throughout this gospel we hear that Jesus has come for judgment. He does not want to condemn us. We condemn ourselves if we reject the Lord and the truth. Likewise, by choosing Jesus to be the center of our lives, we have already received our reward, for Jesus will be a part of our lives.

When Jesus heard that they had thrown him out,
he found him and said, "Do you believe in the Son of Man?"
He answered and said,
"Who is he, sir, that I may believe in him?"
Jesus said to him,
"You have seen him,
and the one speaking with you is he."
He said,
"I do believe, Lord," and he worshiped him.
Then Jesus said,
"I came into this world for judgment,
so that those who do not see might see,
and those who do see might become blind."

Some of the Pharisees who were with him heard this
and said to him, "Surely we are not also blind, are we?"
Jesus said to them,
"If you were blind, you would have no sin;
but now you are saying, 'We see,' so your sin remains."

The Gospel of the Lord.

Lect. No. 31

GOSPEL: B Shorter Form: John 9:1, 6-9, 13-17, 34-38

*The man who was blind went off and washed himself
and came back able to see.*

This story is presented at two levels of meaning. The first (superficial) level is the story of a miracle that Jesus performed during his public ministry. The second (deeper symbolic level) is a story of a community that came to faith in Jesus Christ as the light of the world.

Jesus uses saliva to heal the man born blind and sends him to wash at the pool of Siloam.

A reading from the holy Gospel according to John

As Jesus passed by he saw a man blind from birth. He spat on the ground and made clay with the saliva,
and smeared the clay on his eyes, and said to him,
"Go wash in the Pool of Siloam"—which means Sent—.
So he went and washed, and came back able to see.

His neighbors and those who had seen him earlier as a beggar said,

The man born blind is not given a name because he also plays a symbolic role in this gospel. He represents the members of the community of the beloved disciple that had come to believe in Jesus.

Before they converted they had been blind, for they had not known the light of the world. Jesus came into their lives, and he healed them. He brought them to faith and they were able to see the truth. But like the man born blind, they suffered for their beliefs, for they were expelled from the synagogue. The man born blind humiliates the great doctors of the law with his simplicity and truth. He has no formal learning, but his wisdom is much more profound than theirs. It is the wisdom of the cross being more powerful than the wisdom of the world.

Throughout the account the man born blind has used various titles for Jesus such as "the man called Jesus," "a prophet," "a man . . . from God," etc. After he is expelled from the presence of the Pharisees (which represents the synagogue), he comes to recognize who Jesus is for him. He calls him his "Lord" and he worships him. "Lord" is a title used for Yahweh in the Old Testament. The name Yahweh was so holy that whenever one found it in Scripture, one would pronounce its substitute word, *Adonai*, which meant the "Lord." By saying that Jesus is "Lord," the author is saying that Jesus is the same thing that Yahweh is: God. Furthermore, one only worships God; so when the man worships Jesus, he is proclaiming him as God.

"Isn't this the one who used to sit and beg?"
Some said, "It is,"
    but others said, "No, he just looks like him."
He said, "I am."

They brought the one who was once blind to the
    Pharisees.
Now Jesus had made clay and opened his eyes on a
    sabbath.
So then the Pharisees also asked him how he was
    able to see.
He said to them,
    "He put clay on my eyes, and I washed, and now I
    can see."
So some of the Pharisees said,
    "This man is not from God,
    because he does not keep the sabbath."
But others said,
    "How can a sinful man do such signs?"
And there was a division among them.
So they said to the blind man again,
    "What do you have to say about him,
    since he opened your eyes?"
He said, "He is a prophet."
They answered and said to him,
    "You were born totally in sin,
    and are you trying to teach us?"
Then they threw him out.

When Jesus heard that they had thrown him out,
    he found him and said, "Do you believe in the Son
    of Man?"
He answered and said,
    "Who is he, sir, that I may believe in him?"
Jesus said to him,
    "You have seen him,
    and the one speaking with you is he."
He said,
    "I do believe, Lord," and he worshiped him.

The Gospel of the Lord.

March 17, 2002

FIFTH SUNDAY OF LENT

Lect. No. 34 **FIRST READING: Ezekiel 37:12-14**

I will put my spirit in you that you may live.

This prophecy is taken from a passage that speaks about the resurrection of the dead. Ezekiel describes a plain filled with the dry bones of those who had died. He preaches to the bones and they are filled with God's breath and Spirit and brought back to life.

It appears as if Ezekiel was originally speaking about the resurrection of the nation, but his words could also be applied to the resurrection of the individual. It is the Spirit of the LORD who gives us true life, life that will never end.

A reading from the Book of the Prophet Ezekiel

Thus says the Lord GOD:
   O my people, I will open your graves
   and have you rise from them,
   and bring you back to the land of Israel.
Then you shall know that I am the LORD,
   when I open your graves and have you rise from
      them,
   O my people!
I will put my spirit in you that you may live,
   and I will settle you upon your land;
   thus you shall know that I am the LORD.
I have promised, and I will do it, says the LORD.

The word of the Lord.

Lect. No. 34 **RESPONSORIAL PSALM: Ps 130:1-2, 3-4, 5-6, 7-8 (R̸.: 7)**

Psalm 130 is an individual lament, which has certain predictable elements. It begins with an almost desperate appeal to the LORD for an intervention. Then a series of verses speak of the things tormenting the psalmist. Finally. there is a *todah*. This is a thanksgiving for the deliverance that the psalmist is sure Yahweh will deliver.

There is a sense of urgency in this psalm, as if things had gone so far that there were only moments of life left. The image of the sentinel waiting for the dawn is especially appropriate. The dark is filled with danger

R̸. **With the Lord there is mercy and fullness of redemption.**

Out of the depths I cry to you, O LORD;
   LORD, hear my voice!
Let your ears be attentive
   to my voice in supplication.

R̸. **With the Lord there is mercy and fullness of redemption.**

If you, O LORD, mark iniquities,
   LORD, who can stand?
But with you is forgiveness,
   that you may be revered.

and confusion, but with the dawn comes a restoration of hope. Throughout the Old Testament, the dawn was considered to be the hour of the day when God would intervene to save us from all of our enemies.

The psalmist readily admits that the disasters that had befallen him were probably due to his own sins. He even states that if the LORD were to mark his iniquities, he would have no chance of standing. He and Israel deserve everything that they were getting. Nevertheless. he is filled with hope that the LORD will deliver them from their dangers, for the LORD is truly merciful and gracious.

℟. **With the Lord there is mercy and fullness of redemption.**

I trust in the LORD;
    my soul trusts in his word.
More than sentinels wait for the dawn,
    let Israel wait for the LORD.

℟. **With the Lord there is mercy and fullness of redemption.**

For with the LORD is kindness
    and with him is plenteous redemption;
and he will redeem Israel
    from all their iniquities.

℟. **With the Lord there is mercy and fullness of redemption.**

| Lect. |
| No. 34 |

SECOND READING: Romans 8:8-11

The Spirit of the One who raised Jesus from the dead dwells in you.

In this passage from Saint Paul's Letter to the Romans we hear of the contrast between living according to the flesh and living according to the Spirit. In using the word flesh, Paul is not speaking about our bodies or the created world. He is speaking about that part of us which drags us down, which will lead us to sin. Saint Augustine calls this concupiscence.

The Spirit, on the other hand, is the gift of the Holy Spirit that we have received in our Baptism. We can live in the Spirit by choosing to live in God's love.

The life that we receive from the Spirit is so profound that even our mortal bodies will be filled with eternal life in the resurrection from the dead.

A reading from the Letter of Saint Paul
to the Romans

Brothers and sisters:
    Those who are in the flesh cannot please God.
But you are not in the flesh;
    on the contrary, you are in the spirit,
    if only the Spirit of God dwells in you.
Whoever does not have the Spirit of Christ does not
    belong to him.
But if Christ is in you,
    although the body is dead because of sin,
    the spirit is alive because of righteousness.
If the Spirit of the one who raised Jesus from the
    dead dwells in you,
    the one who raised Christ from the dead
    will give life to your mortal bodies also,
    through his Spirit dwelling in you.

The word of the Lord.

Lect. No. 34

VERSE BEFORE THE GOSPEL: John 11:25a, 26

Jesus is the source and the goal of our lives. Life has no meaning if it is not lived in him and for him.

I am the resurrection and the life, says the Lord; whoever believes in me will never die.

Lect. No. 34

GOSPEL: A Longer Form: John 11:1-45

I am the resurrection and the life.

Lazarus was a common name at the time of Jesus (a form of the name Eliezer, which means that "God aids") and this Lazarus should not be confused with the poor Lazarus of the parable in Luke's gospel.

Jesus stayed at the house of Lazarus and his sisters Martha and Mary during the Jewish feast days. There were so many pilgrims in Jerusalem at those times that pilgrims often stayed in the suburbs of Jerusalem. Bethany, the town where Lazarus and Mary his sister lived, was only a short distance outside of Jerusalem.

Although Mary does not anoint the feet of Jesus until chapter 12, the action is placed in the past tense. In this gospel the readers and the author already know all of the events recorded in this gospel.

It is odd that Jesus remained where he was after he had heard of the illness of his friend. It is almost as if he wanted him to die. This is only explainable if one remembers that this will be a powerful sign of God's love. In fact, it will be a sign of God's glory.

Jesus' hour of glory in this gospel is the cross and not the resurrection as one might expect. In the greatest irony of the

A reading from the holy Gospel according to John

Now a man was ill, Lazarus from Bethany,
   the village of Mary and her sister Martha.
Mary was the one who had anointed the Lord with
      perfumed oil
   and dried his feet with her hair;
   it was her brother Lazarus who was ill.
So the sisters sent word to Jesus saying,
   "Master, the one you love is ill."
When Jesus heard this he said,
   "This illness is not to end in death,
   but is for the glory of God,
   that the Son of God may be glorified through it."
Now Jesus loved Martha and her sister and
      Lazarus.
So when he heard that he was ill,
   he remained for two days in the place where he
      was.
Then after this he said to his disciples,
   "Let us go back to Judea."
The disciples said to him,
   "Rabbi, the Jews were just trying to stone you,
   and you want to go back there?"
Jesus answered,
   "Are there not twelve hours in a day?
If one walks during the day, he does not stumble,
   because he sees the light of this world.
But if one walks at night, he stumbles,
   because the light is not in him."

gospel, Jesus is put to death by the Jewish leaders specifically because he brought Lazarus back to life. The Jewish leaders wanted people to be under their control; they did not want them to be free or truly alive.

We hear that Lazarus was dead for four days already. The Jewish people believed that the soul remained in the body for the first three days after the person died. To say that someone was dead for four days was to say that they were irretrievably dead.

Martha and Mary both respond to Jesus' arrival with statements that show both a mix of annoyance at the fact that he had taken so long to get there and an expression of hope that he would still do something to help them.

Jesus responds that he is "the resurrection and the life." What is interesting about this phrase is that he is not saying that he will grant the resurrection; he is saying that he is the resurrection.

When one comes to know Jesus, one is already in some way risen. One's life is so full and profound that even if one were to die, one would continue to live in him. Eschatology speaks about the things that will occur at the end of time. This gospel has a "realized eschatology," for those things have already started to happen when Jesus came into our lives. We do not have to wait until the end of time for our eternal reward, for it has already begun here

He said this, and then told them,
    "Our friend Lazarus is asleep,
    but I am going to awaken him."
So the disciples said to him,
    "Master, if he is asleep, he will be saved."
But Jesus was talking about his death,
    while they thought that he meant ordinary sleep.
So then Jesus said to them clearly,
    "Lazarus has died.
And I am glad for you that I was not there,
    that you may believe.
Let us go to him."
So Thomas, called Didymus, said to his fellow disciples,
    "Let us also go to die with him."

When Jesus arrived, he found that Lazarus
    had already been in the tomb for four days.
Now Bethany was near Jerusalem, only about two
    miles away.
And many of the Jews had come to Martha and
    Mary
    to comfort them about their brother.
When Martha heard that Jesus was coming,
    she went to meet him;
    but Mary sat at home.
Martha said to Jesus,
    "Lord, if you had been here,
    my brother would not have died.
But even now I know that whatever you ask of God,
    God will give you."
Jesus said to her,
    "Your brother will rise."
Martha said to him,
    "I know he will rise,
    in the resurrection on the last day."
Jesus told her,
    "I am the resurrection and the life;

(although not yet in a fully realized manner).

Jesus is described as being perturbed and deeply troubled. At first we might think that he is disturbed because the Jewish people and Mary are crying (which he might have interpreted as a sign of the lack of faith in him), but he himself cries within a few minutes. It is more probable that he is angry at death itself, which has robbed him of his beloved friend. He also cries to express his grief at the death of Lazarus.

Christian hope at the death of a beloved does not mean that we have to deny our emotions. It means that we express them, but also try to maintain hope.

There are several expressions of irony throughout the story. Thomas says that the disciples should follow Jesus to die with him (when they do the exact opposite). The people watching Jesus cry ask whether he could not have saved Lazarus from death (which he, of course, could have). This is typical of the Gospel of John where we, the readers, often know more than the characters involved in the story.

Jesus proclaims a rather unusual prayer. It is almost as if it is being said for the sake of the audience so that they will know that Jesus is doing this deed of power through the intervention of the Father. Jesus does absolutely nothing in this gospel on his own. Everything he does is in obedience to the will of the Father.

whoever believes in me, even if he dies, will live,
and everyone who lives and believes in me will never die.
Do you believe this?"
She said to him, "Yes, Lord.
I have come to believe that you are the Christ, the Son of God,
the one who is coming into the world."

When she had said this,
she went and called her sister Mary secretly, saying,
"The teacher is here and is asking for you."
As soon as she heard this,
she rose quickly and went to him.
For Jesus had not yet come into the village,
but was still where Martha had met him.
So when the Jews who were with her in the house comforting her
saw Mary get up quickly and go out,
they followed her,
presuming that she was going to the tomb to weep there.
When Mary came to where Jesus was and saw him,
she fell at his feet and said to him,
"Lord, if you had been here,
my brother would not have died."
When Jesus saw her weeping and the Jews who had come with her weeping,
he became perturbed and deeply troubled, and said,
"Where have you laid him?"
They said to him, "Sir, come and see."
And Jesus wept.
So the Jews said, "See how he loved him."
But some of them said,
"Could not the one who opened the eyes of the blind man

Lazarus is not actually resurrected, he is reanimated. The difference is that Lazarus is brought back to life, but he would still have to die again some day.

Jesus, on the other hand, when he is resurrected, will never die again. He has a glorified body that is not subject to the limitations of our mortal bodies. Such is not the case with Lazarus who someday would die again.

Jesus instructs those with him to untie Lazarus. This has often been used as an image of how Jesus unbinds us from everything that imprisons us, whether it be sin or fear or the habits that leave us lonely and confused. We cannot do this by ourselves; we must seek the assistance of Jesus to set us free.

The end of the account speaks of those who had come to see Mary and Martha. The purpose is to show that this was a very public miracle and it explains why this particular miracle would be brought to the attention of the leaders of the Jews in the next verses of this story.

have done something so that this man would not have died?"

So Jesus, perturbed again, came to the tomb.
It was a cave, and a stone lay across it.
Jesus said, "Take away the stone."
Martha, the dead man's sister, said to him,
    "Lord, by now there will be a stench;
    he has been dead for four days."
Jesus said to her,
    "Did I not tell you that if you believe
    you will see the glory of God?"
So they took away the stone.
And Jesus raised his eyes and said,
    "Father, I thank you for hearing me.
I know that you always hear me;
    but because of the crowd here I have said this,
    that they may believe that you sent me."
And when he had said this,
    he cried out in a loud voice,
    "Lazarus, come out!"
The dead man came out,
    tied hand and foot with burial bands,
    and his face was wrapped in a cloth.
So Jesus said to them,
    "Untie him and let him go."

Now many of the Jews who had come to Mary
    and seen what he had done began to believe in him.

The Gospel of the Lord.

Lect. No. 34 **GOSPEL: B Shorter Form: John 11:3-7, 17, 20-27, 33b-45**

I am the resurrection and the life.

It is odd that Jesus remained where he was after he had heard of the illness of his friend Lazarus. It is almost as if he wanted him to die. This is only explainable if one remembers

A reading from the holy Gospel according to John

The sisters of Lazarus sent word to Jesus, saying, "Master, the one you love is ill."
When Jesus heard this he said,

that this will be a powerful sign of God's love. In fact, it will be a sign of God's glory.

We hear that Lazarus was dead for four days already. The Jewish people believed that the soul remained in the body for the first three days after the person died. To say that some-one was dead for four days was to say that they were irretriev-ably dead.

Martha and Mary both re-spond to Jesus' arrival with statements that show both a mix of annoyance at the fact that he had taken so long to get there and an expression of hope that he would still do something to help them.

Jesus responds that he is "the resurrection and the life." What is interesting about this phrase is that he is not saying that he will grant the resurrec-tion; he is saying that he is the resurrection.

When one comes to know Jesus, one is already in some way risen. One's life is so full and profound that even if one were to die, one would continue to live in him.

Eschatology speaks about the things that will occur at the end of time. This gospel has a "realized eschatology," for those things have already started to happen when Jesus came into our lives. We do not have to wait until the end of time for our eternal reward, for it has al-ready begun here (although not yet in a fully realized manner).

"This illness is not to end in death,
  but is for the glory of God,
  that the Son of God may be glorified through it."
Now Jesus loved Martha and her sister and
  Lazarus.
So when he heard that he was ill,
  he remained for two days in the place where he
  was.
Then after this he said to his disciples,
  "Let us go back to Judea."

When Jesus arrived, he found that Lazarus
  had already been in the tomb for four days.
When Martha heard that Jesus was coming,
  she went to meet him;
  but Mary sat at home.
Martha said to Jesus,
  "Lord, if you had been here,
  my brother would not have died.
But even now I know that whatever you ask of God,
  God will give you."
Jesus said to her,
  "Your brother will rise."
Martha said,
  "I know he will rise,
  in the resurrection on the last day."
Jesus told her,
  "I am the resurrection and the life;
  whoever believes in me, even if he dies, will live,
  and everyone who lives and believes in me will
  never die.
Do you believe this?"
She said to him, "Yes, Lord.
I have come to believe that you are the Christ, the
  Son of God,
  the one who is coming into the world."

He became perturbed and deeply troubled, and said,
  "Where have you laid him?"

Jesus is described as being perturbed and deeply troubled. At first we might think that he is disturbed because the Jewish people and Mary are crying (which he might have interpreted as a sign of the lack of faith in him), but he himself cries within a few minutes. It is more probable that he is angry at death itself, which has robbed him of his beloved friend. He also cries to express his grief at the death of Lazarus.

Christian hope at the death of a beloved does not mean that we have to deny our emotions. It means that we express them, but also try to maintain hope.

Lazarus is not actually resurrected, he is reanimated. The difference is that Lazarus is brought back to life, but he would still have to die again some day.

Jesus, on the other hand, when he is resurrected, will never die again. He has a glorified body that is not subject to the limitations of our mortal bodies. Such is not the case with Lazarus who someday would die again.

The end of the account speaks of those who had come to see Mary and Martha. The purpose is to show that this was a very public miracle and it explains why this particular miracle would be brought to the attention of the leaders of the Jews in the next verses of this story.

They said to him, "Sir, come and see."

And Jesus wept.

So the Jews said, "See how he loved him."

But some of them said,

"Could not the one who opened the eyes of the blind man

have done something so that this man would not have died?"

So Jesus, perturbed again, came to the tomb.

It was a cave, and a stone lay across it.

Jesus said, "Take away the stone."

Martha, the dead man's sister, said to him,

"Lord, by now there will be a stench;

he has been dead for four days."

Jesus said to her,

"Did I not tell you that if you believe

you will see the glory of God?"

So they took away the stone.

And Jesus raised his eyes and said,

"Father, I thank you for hearing me.

I know that you always hear me;

but because of the crowd here I have said this,

that they may believe that you sent me."

And when he had said this,

he cried out in a loud voice,

"Lazarus, come out!"

The dead man came out,

tied hand and foot with burial bands,

and his face was wrapped in a cloth.

So Jesus said to them,

"Untie him and let him go."

Now many of the Jews who had come to Mary

and seen what he had done began to believe in him.

The Gospel of the Lord.

March 24, 2002

PALM SUNDAY OF THE LORD'S PASSION

At the Procession with Palms

Lect. No. 37 **GOSPEL: Matthew 21:1-11**

Blessed is he who comes in the name of the Lord.

Unlike other Sundays, we have two Gospels on Palm Sunday, one for the procession and then a reading of the passion narrative.

Jesus enters the city riding on a donkey. This fulfills the prophecy found in the book of the Prophet Zechariah. The prophet was contrasting how various conquering kings had entered Jerusalem and how the Messiah would enter it. The worldly kings rode upon great chargers; the Messiah would enter with profound humility.

Matthew speaks of Jesus riding on both a donkey and its colt. This was a slight misunderstanding on his part of the prophecy. Zechariah speaks of a donkey, that is, a colt. Matthew thought they were two separate animals.

This passage speaks of a large crowd. The city of Jerusalem was filled to overflowing with pilgrims at Passover time. A city of about 50,000 to 60,000 was filled with another quarter of a million people. The Roman soldiers and the Jewish leaders who heard the shouts of the crowd would certainly have been concerned that a revolution was about to begin.

A reading from the holy Gospel according to Matthew

When Jesus and the disciples drew near Jerusalem and came to Bethphage on the Mount of Olives,
Jesus sent two disciples, saying to them,
"Go into the village opposite you,
and immediately you will find an ass tethered,
and a colt with her.
Untie them and bring them here to me.
And if anyone should say anything to you, reply,
    'The master has need of them.'
Then he will send them at once."
This happened so that what had been spoken
    through the prophet
might be fulfilled:
    Say to daughter Zion,
    "Behold, your king comes to you,
        meek and riding on an ass,
        and on a colt, the foal of a beast of burden."
The disciples went and did as Jesus had ordered
    them.
They brought the ass and the colt and laid their
    cloaks over them,
    and he sat upon them.
The very large crowd spread their cloaks on the road,
    while others cut branches from the trees
    and strewed them on the road.

116

Jesus is proclaimed as the Son of David for he was the fulfillment of the promises God had made to David through Nathan the Prophet that David would be the founder of an eternal dynasty.

The crowd cries out "Hosanna," which means "Yahweh, save us!" Jesus would fulfill that desire when he died on the cross only a few days later.

The crowds preceding him and those following
    kept crying out and saying:
        "Hosanna to the Son of David;
           blessed is he who comes in the name of the
              Lord;
        hosanna in the highest."
And when he entered Jerusalem
    the whole city was shaken and asked, "Who is
        this?"
And the crowds replied,
    "This is Jesus the prophet, from Nazareth in
        Galilee."

The Gospel of the Lord.

At the Mass

Lect.
No. 38

FIRST READING: Isaiah 50:4-7

My face I did not shield from buffets and spitting, knowing that I shall not be put to shame.

This reading is taken from the third song of the Suffering Servant. It speaks of the Servant as one who brings consolation to the weary, even while he is the victim of terrible suffering. We will hear in the fourth song that he suffers to bring us forgiveness of our sins.

It was never exactly clear who this figure was supposed to be during Old Testament times. Jesus, through many of the things he said, showed that he considered himself to be the fulfillment of this prophecy.

In spite of the agony of the Servant, he professes his faith in the LORD for he knew that God would deliver him from all of his distress. This deliverance was fulfilled in the resurrection of Jesus from the dead.

A reading from the Book of the Prophet Isaiah

The Lord GOD has given me
    a well-trained tongue,
that I might know how to speak to the weary
    a word that will rouse them.
Morning after morning
    he opens my ear that I may hear;
and I have not rebelled,
    have not turned back.
I gave my back to those who beat me,
    my cheeks to those who plucked my beard;
my face I did not shield
    from buffets and spitting.

The Lord GOD is my help,
    therefore I am not disgraced;
I have set my face like flint,
    knowing that I shall not be put to shame.

The word of the Lord.

Lect.
No. 38 **RESPONSORIAL PSALM: Ps 22:8-9, 17-18, 19-20, 23-24 (℟.: 2a)**

This is the psalm that Jesus quoted while he was hanging on the cross. It is a lamentation, and typical of all lamentations, it begins with an appeal, continues with a list of the sufferings that the psalmist is undergoing, and closes with a short hymn of praise in which the psalmist declares his faith in his eventual deliverance.

When Jesus quoted the first verse of this psalm, he was identifying with the psalmist's feeling of abandonment, but he was at the same time professing his faith in the fact that God would deliver him. He agreed with the sentiments found in the psalm, "I will proclaim your name to my brethren; in the midst of the assembly I will praise you."

The similarities between this psalm and what actually occurred to Jesus on the cross are astounding. It speaks of hands and feet being pierced, garments being divided, lots being cast, etc.

We can easily forget that Psalm 22 was written several hundreds of years before the time of Jesus. It fills us with a sense of awe, for here we see the Holy Spirit inspiring the psalmist in a powerful way.

℟. **My God, my God, why have you abandoned me?**

All who see me scoff at me;
   they mock me with parted lips, they wag their heads:
"He relied on the LORD; let him deliver him,
   let him rescue him, if he loves him."

℟. **My God, my God, why have you abandoned me?**

Indeed, many dogs surround me,
   a pack of evildoers closes in upon me;
they have pierced my hands and my feet;
   I can count all my bones.

℟. **My God, my God, why have you abandoned me?**

They divide my garments among them,
   and for my vesture they cast lots.
But you, O LORD, be not far from me;
   O my help, hasten to aid me.

℟. **My God, my God, why have you abandoned me?**

I will proclaim your name to my brethren;
   in the midst of the assembly I will praise you:
"You who fear the LORD, praise him;
   all you descendants of Jacob, give glory to him;
   revere him, all you descendants of Israel!"

℟. **My God, my God, why have you abandoned me?**

Lect.
No. 38

SECOND READING: Philippians 2:6-11

Christ humbled himself. Because of this God greatly exalted him.

Saint Paul presents this hymn as an example of the profound humility of Jesus. It is also a teaching about Jesus who surrendered his prerogatives as God to serve us as a human.

The phrase, "form of God," means that Jesus is God, even as God the Father is God. Yet Jesus emptied himself of his godliness. The word "empty," *kenosis* in Greek, signifies a spirituality of surrender and humility. It does not mean that he stopped being God.

The ultimate degree of humility was to be obedient to the Father, even as he died upon the cross. This humility was not a rejection of Jesus' godliness, but the fullest expression of the love of God. It is precisely for this reason that Jesus is proclaimed as Lord, a title that affirms his divinity.

A reading from the Letter of Saint Paul to the Philippians

Christ Jesus, though he was in the form of God,
did not regard equality with God
   something to be grasped.
Rather, he emptied himself,
   taking the form of a slave,
   coming in human likeness;
   and found human in appearance,
   he humbled himself,
   becoming obedient to the point of death,
   even death on a cross.
Because of this, God greatly exalted him
   and bestowed on him the name
   which is above every name,
   that at the name of Jesus
   every knee should bend,
   of those in heaven and on earth and under the
      earth,
   and every tongue confess that
Jesus Christ is Lord,
   to the glory of God the Father.

The word of the Lord.

Lect.
No. 38

VERSE BEFORE THE GOSPEL: Philippians 2:8-9

The Verse before the Gospel repeats the heart of the Philippians' hymn. It celebrates the obedience of Jesus upon the cross and his exaltation in his resurrection.

Christ became obedient to the point of death,
   even death on a cross.
Because of this, God greatly exalted him
   and bestowed on him the name which is above
      every name.

Lect.
No. 38
GOSPEL: **A** Longer Form: Matthew 26:14—27:66

The Passion of our Lord Jesus Christ.

The passion narrative from the Gospel of Matthew contains the basic information found in all of the Synoptic Gospels, but it also has nuances that are typical of this gospel. For example, the first words of this account demonstrate the guilt of the Jewish leaders in their plot to put Jesus to death.

It also tells how Jesus fulfills all of the prophecies concerning the Messiah. Here, the thirty pieces of silver recall the amount that would be paid for hurting a slave (Exodus 21:32).

The meal that Jesus eats with his apostles is the Passover meal. (in the Gospel of John, Jesus anticipates the feast by one day.)

Jesus and the twelve reclined at table, for the table was only about 18 inches high.

Jesus announces that someone would betray him, an act that is shown in all of its perfidy by the fact that the betrayer had eaten from the common food dish with Jesus (an act that normally signified communal unity).

Although the death of Jesus had been predicted and this was all in obedience to the will of God, it does not mean that the person who would betray Jesus was without guilt. Here Jesus speaks of how it would have been better if the betrayer had never been born.

The Passion of our Lord Jesus Christ according to Matthew

One of the Twelve, who was called Judas Iscariot,
    went to the chief priests and said,
    "What are you willing to give me
    if I hand him over to you?"
They paid him thirty pieces of silver,
    and from that time on he looked for an opportunity to hand him over.

On the first day of the Feast of Unleavened Bread,
    the disciples approached Jesus and said,
    "Where do you want us to prepare
    for you to eat the Passover?"
He said,
    "Go into the city to a certain man and tell him,
    'The teacher says, "My appointed time draws near;
    in your house I shall celebrate the Passover with
        my disciples."'"
The disciples then did as Jesus had ordered,
    and prepared the Passover.

When it was evening,
    he reclined at table with the Twelve.
And while they were eating, he said,
    "Amen, I say to you, one of you will betray me."
Deeply distressed at this,
    they began to say to him one after another,
    "Surely it is not I, Lord?"
He said in reply,
    "He who has dipped his hand into the dish with me
    is the one who will betray me.
The Son of Man indeed goes, as it is written of him,
    but woe to that man by whom the Son of Man is
        betrayed.
It would be better for that man if he had never been
        born."

During the Last Supper, Jesus takes bread and pronounces that it is his body. He takes wine and calls it his blood.

This account appears in the three Synoptic Gospels as well as Paul's First Letter to the Corinthians.

The "blood of the covenant" is a phrase found in the Old Testament and it recalls the fact that covenants were instituted through a sprinkling of blood upon those who were entering into the covenant.

The phrase "for many" does not mean that only certain people are invited into this new covenant. It is a Semitic phrase that means "everyone."

Passover meals normally ended with all the participants singing a "Hallel," a song of praise to the Lord.

Jesus again predicts his passion and his resurrection. In Matthew, Jesus met his apostles in Galilee after the resurrection and not in Jerusalem (as in Luke and John).

Peter tries to prove his courage in a typically impetuous manner. Jesus responds by predicting his denial.

Peter and the other disciples again profess their willingness to die with Jesus. This is tragic considering what they actually did. They could not even stay awake with him as he prayed in the garden.

Then Judas, his betrayer, said in reply,
    "Surely it is not I, Rabbi?"
He answered, "You have said so."

While they were eating,
    Jesus took bread, said the blessing,
    broke it, and giving it to his disciples said,
    "Take and eat; this is my body."
Then he took a cup, gave thanks, and gave it to
        them, saying,
    "Drink from it, all of you,
    for this is my blood of the covenant,
    which will be shed on behalf of many
    for the forgiveness of sins.
I tell you, from now on I shall not drink this fruit of
        the vine
    until the day when I drink it with you new
    in the kingdom of my Father."
Then, after singing a hymn,
    they went out to the Mount of Olives.

Then Jesus said to them,
    "This night all of you will have your faith in me
        shaken,
    for it is written:
        I will strike the shepherd,
            and the sheep of the flock will be dispersed;
    but after I have been raised up,
    I shall go before you to Galilee."
Peter said to him in reply,
    "Though all may have their faith in you shaken,
    mine will never be."
Jesus said to him,
    "Amen, I say to you,
    this very night before the cock crows,
    you will deny me three times."

Peter said to him,
    "Even though I should have to die with you,
    I will not deny you."
And all the disciples spoke likewise.

Jesus takes his disciples with him to Gethsemane, a garden on the slopes of the Mount of Olives. This mountain was always associated with the dawning of the end times in Old Testament prophecies. There he invites three of them, Peter, James, and John, to pass a vigil with him.

The depth of emotion that Jesus is feeling is obvious from the description in these verses. He says, "My soul is sorrowful even to death."

He prays to the Father that he will not have to undergo what was about to happen to him. In spite of that, he professes his willingness to do the Father's will.

This gives us a useful example as to how we should deal with the suffering of our lives. We should seek an alleviation of the pain (e.g., doctors, counselors, prayer, etc.). We should ask God to take the pain away, but, if after everything, we are still suffering, we must try to find meaning in what is happening.

The disciples fall asleep over and over again. As Jesus warns them, "The spirit is willing but the flesh is weak." This serves as a warning both to the disciples and to all of us.

Jesus does not try to avoid his fate now that it is clear that this is the Father's will.

The Jewish leaders and their forces arrive to arrest Jesus.

Then Jesus came with them to a place called Gethsemane,
and he said to his disciples,
"Sit here while I go over there and pray."
He took along Peter and the two sons of Zebedee,
and began to feel sorrow and distress.
Then he said to them,
"My soul is sorrowful even to death.
Remain here and keep watch with me."
He advanced a little and fell prostrate in prayer, saying,
"My Father, if it is possible,
let this cup pass from me;
yet, not as I will, but as you will."
When he returned to his disciples he found them asleep.
He said to Peter,
"So you could not keep watch with me for one hour?
Watch and pray that you may not undergo the test.
The spirit is willing, but the flesh is weak."
Withdrawing a second time, he prayed again,
"My Father, if it is not possible that this cup pass without my drinking it, your will be done!"
Then he returned once more and found them asleep,
for they could not keep their eyes open.
He left them and withdrew again and prayed a third time,
saying the same thing again.
Then he returned to his disciples and said to them,
"Are you still sleeping and taking your rest?
Behold, the hour is at hand
when the Son of Man is to be handed over to sinners.
Get up, let us go.
Look, my betrayer is at hand."
While he was still speaking,
Judas, one of the Twelve, arrived,

They had prepared a signal that Judas would greet Jesus with a kiss. This was a normal way to greet a friend, but in this context it reinforces the sense of Jesus being betrayed by an intimate. The signal would have been effective for it clearly pointed out the person to be seized in a dark garden.

One of those who was with Jesus (in this gospel it does not tell us which disciple) resorts to violence in an attempt to defend Jesus. Jesus rejects this alternative, for he must do the will of the Father. He tells his disciples that if he wanted to escape his fate through an intervention of violence, he could have called upon the angels and they would have defended him.

Likewise, he is indignant at the crowd that had come to arrest him by night. He had preached in the temple often and they had not opposed him there. The reason they chose the night was obvious, they were afraid of the reaction of the people who might have defended Jesus. By arresting Jesus by night, it was evident that their works were filled with darkness, for they were doing evil things.

Jesus is arrested and taken before the high priests and scribes and elders. Many believe that this was not the entire Sanhedrin, for it would have been difficult to gather them at night. It was probably a plot of some of the leaders to put Jesus, whom they considered to be a danger to the peace and their privilege, to death.

accompanied by a large crowd, with swords and clubs,
who had come from the chief priests and the elders of the people.
His betrayer had arranged a sign with them, saying,
"The man I shall kiss is the one; arrest him."
Immediately he went over to Jesus and said,
"Hail, Rabbi!" and he kissed him.
Jesus answered him,
"Friend, do what you have come for."
Then stepping forward they laid hands on Jesus and arrested him.
And behold, one of those who accompanied Jesus
put his hand to his sword, drew it,
and struck the high priest's servant, cutting off his ear.
Then Jesus said to him,
"Put your sword back into its sheath,
for all who take the sword will perish by the sword.
Do you think that I cannot call upon my Father
and he will not provide me at this moment
with more than twelve legions of angels?
But then how would the Scriptures be fulfilled
which say that it must come to pass in this way?"
At that hour Jesus said to the crowds,
"Have you come out as against a robber,
with swords and clubs to seize me?
Day after day I sat teaching in the temple area,
yet you did not arrest me.
But all this has come to pass
that the writings of the prophets may be fulfilled."
Then all the disciples left him and fled.

Those who had arrested Jesus led him away
to Caiaphas the high priest,
where the scribes and the elders were assembled.
Peter was following him at a distance
as far as the high priest's courtyard,

Yet they could not even manufacture a credible case against Jesus, for their false witnesses proved to be foolishly unbelievable.

Two men claimed that Jesus had said that he would destroy the temple and rebuild it in three days. Technically, he did say this; however, he was not talking about the Jerusalem temple but rather his body.

The high priest demanded to know if Jesus was the Christ, the Son of God. Jesus responded, "You have said so." He also states that he will be exalted in glory as the Son of Man in power. This is a fulfillment of the prophecy in Daniel that the son of man would be exalted. Jesus always used this passage and the Songs of the Suffering Servant to describe his ministry.

The high priest judges this to be an act of blasphemy and they condemn Jesus.

It is obvious from the way they speak, though, that they feel he has established too close a relationship with the Father. He has done things that only God can do (e.g., forgive sins). He has spoken of God as his "daddy" ("Abba"). He has even relativized the importance of the law and the temple. This was enough for the high priest to condemn him.

While the leaders of the Jews were condemning Jesus and humiliating him, Peter was waiting in the courtyard.

Peter had proclaimed his absolute willingness to die for Jesus rather than deny him. When the opportunity comes to give witness, he fails miserably.

and going inside he sat down with the servants to
    see the outcome.
The chief priests and the entire Sanhedrin
    kept trying to obtain false testimony against Jesus
    in order to put him to death,
but they found none,
    though many false witnesses came forward.
Finally two came forward who stated,
    "This man said, 'I can destroy the temple of God
    and within three days rebuild it.'"
The high priest rose and addressed him,
    "Have you no answer?
What are these men testifying against you?"
But Jesus was silent.
Then the high priest said to him,
    "I order you to tell us under oath before the living
      God
    whether you are the Christ, the Son of God."
Jesus said to him in reply,
    "You have said so.
But I tell you:
      From now on you will see 'the Son of Man
        seated at the right hand of the Power'
        and 'coming on the clouds of heaven.'"
Then the high priest tore his robes and said,
    "He has blasphemed!
What further need have we of witnesses?
You have now heard the blasphemy;
    what is your opinion?"
They said in reply,
    "He deserves to die!"
Then they spat in his face and struck him,
    while some slapped him, saying,
    "Prophesy for us, Christ: who is it that struck you?"

Now Peter was sitting outside in the courtyard.
One of the maids came over to him and said,
    "You too were with Jesus the Galilean."
But he denied it in front of everyone, saying,

Three times he is confronted by people who accuse him of being associated with Jesus. Once they even deduce from his accent (for people from Galilee spoke Aramaic with a particular accent) that he must be one of Jesus' followers. Yet, he vehemently denies that he even knows Jesus.

The minute that the cock crows, Peter remembers the prediction that Jesus had given and he weeps bitterly.

The leaders of the Jews take Jesus to Pilate's palace for they could not put him to death upon their own authority.

Meanwhile, Judas realized the wickedness of what he had done. He tried to return the blood money he had received, but the Jewish leaders refused to take it. In despair, he killed himself.

Even though the high priests wanted to refuse the money, they were forced into accepting it from Judas. They could not escape the guilt that they had brought upon themselves.

This is also a fulfillment text. We are told that this is the realization of what is said in Jeremiah the Prophet. The quotation is actually taken from the Book of the Prophet Zechariah (in fact, it is taken from an ancient version that is no longer extant).

The reference to Jeremiah is probably an allusion to the symbolic action that the prophet performed in which he broke a potter's flask in the field. This was, in fact, a field in which people would be buried who had no other place where they

"I do not know what you are talking about!"
As he went out to the gate, another girl saw him
    and said to those who were there,
    "This man was with Jesus the Nazarene."
Again he denied it with an oath,
    "I do not know the man!"
A little later the bystanders came over and said to
        Peter,
    "Surely you too are one of them;
    even your speech gives you away."
At that he began to curse and to swear,
    "I do not know the man."
And immediately a cock crowed.
Then Peter remembered the word that Jesus had
        spoken:
    "Before the cock crows you will deny me three
        times."
He went out and began to weep bitterly.

When it was morning,
    all the chief priests and the elders of the people
    took counsel against Jesus to put him to death.
They bound him, led him away,
    and handed him over to Pilate, the governor.

Then Judas, his betrayer, seeing that Jesus had been
        condemned,
    deeply regretted what he had done.
He returned the thirty pieces of silver
    to the chief priests and elders, saying,
    "I have sinned in betraying innocent blood."
They said,
    "What is that to us?
    Look to it yourself."
Flinging the money into the temple,
    he departed and went off and hanged himself.
The chief priests gathered up the money, but said,
    "It is not lawful to deposit this in the temple trea-
        sury,
    for it is the price of blood."

could be buried, a fulfillment of the fact that Judas' blood money would be used to buy a potter's field.

Ironically, Judas' greatest sin was not that he betrayed Jesus but that he despaired by not believing that his sin could be forgiven.

The interrogation is relatively short and Jesus gives no response to the accusations. It is almost as if he is over and above what is going on and he will not dignify the questions with an answer. The governor is filled with awe, a common response to Jesus throughout the gospel.

We hear of a custom to release a prisoner during the Passover time. Although we have no outside testimony concerning the existence of such a custom (e.g., documents), we have no reason to doubt that the evangelists were accurate in their report of this event.

Pilate invites the mob to choose between Jesus and a certain Barabbas whom this gospel describes as a notorious prisoner. In the Gospel of Mark, he is described as being a revolutionary (which probably meant that he was associated with the Zealots).

Some scholars have suggested that Barabbas' name is symbolic, for the meaning of Barabbas is "son of the father." That would mean that the people must choose between Jesus, the Son of God, and Barabbas, the son of the father.

Pilate's wife entered and spoke to him of the dream that

After consultation, they used it to buy the potter's field
as a burial place for foreigners.
That is why that field even today is called the Field of Blood.
Then was fulfilled what had been said through Jeremiah the prophet,
And they took the thirty pieces of silver,
the value of a man with a price on his head,
a price set by some of the Israelites,
and they paid it out for the potter's field
just as the Lord had commanded me.

Now Jesus stood before the governor, who questioned him,
"Are you the king of the Jews?"
Jesus said, "You say so."
And when he was accused by the chief priests and elders,
he made no answer.
Then Pilate said to him,
"Do you not hear how many things they are testifying against you?"
But he did not answer him one word,
so that the governor was greatly amazed.

Now on the occasion of the feast
the governor was accustomed to release to the crowd
one prisoner whom they wished.
And at that time they had a notorious prisoner called Barabbas.
So when they had assembled, Pilate said to them,
"Which one do you want me to release to you,
Barabbas, or Jesus called Christ?"
For he knew that it was out of envy
that they had handed him over.
While he was still seated on the bench,
his wife sent him a message,
"Have nothing to do with that righteous man.

she had concerning Jesus. This is the only gospel that speaks of this episode. It emphasizes the guilt of the Jewish people.

Both Pilate and his wife recognized the innocence of Jesus and wanted to release him, but the leaders of the people were adamant in their desire to have Jesus put to death. They even called Jesus' blood upon themselves and their children.

Pilate felt that he had no choice but to put Jesus to death, so he ordered that he be crucified. As was normal in capital cases, Jesus was handed over to the soldiers to be tortured before he was led out to be crucified. They placed a crown of thorns (probably in the form of a cap) on his head.

The soldiers also put a scarlet military cloak about Jesus. Mark had mentioned a purple cloak (the sign of royal authority). Matthew's version is actually more probable, for it is doubtful that the soldiers would have had a purple cloak at their disposition. They mocked Jesus as the "King of the Jews."

Jesus had now been condemned by his own people and by the Roman authorities. But, although he might appear to be powerless, he was invested with God's power of love and justice.

Simon the Cyrenian is forced to assist Jesus to carry the cross (most probably only the crossbar, the vertical portion was normally anchored in place). It was not unusual for

I suffered much in a dream today because of him."
The chief priests and the elders persuaded the crowds
    to ask for Barabbas but to destroy Jesus.
The governor said to them in reply,
    "Which of the two do you want me to release to you?"
They answered, "Barabbas!"
Pilate said to them,
    "Then what shall I do with Jesus called Christ?"
They all said,
    "Let him be crucified!"
But he said,
    "Why? What evil has he done?"
They only shouted the louder,
    "Let him be crucified!"
When Pilate saw that he was not succeeding at all,
    but that a riot was breaking out instead,
    he took water and washed his hands in the sight
        of the crowd,
    saying, "I am innocent of this man's blood.
Look to it yourselves."
And the whole people said in reply,
    "His blood be upon us and upon our children."
Then he released Barabbas to them,
    but after he had Jesus scourged,
    he handed him over to be crucified.

Then the soldiers of the governor took Jesus inside
        the praetorium
    and gathered the whole cohort around him.
They stripped off his clothes
    and threw a scarlet military cloak about him.
Weaving a crown out of thorns, they placed it on his
        head,
    and a reed in his right hand.
And kneeling before him, they mocked him, saying,
    "Hail, King of the Jews!"

Roman soldiers to seize work-men and force them to assist with various tasks such as this.

Golgotha was probably a used-out quarry and the stone in which the cross was placed was believed to be a stone that had a flaw (hence, the fulfill-ment of the saying that the stone rejected by the builders had become the cornerstone). Apparently, Golgotha was called the Place of the Skull be-cause its shape was in the form of a skull.

Jesus was offered wine mixed with gall. Gall was a type of narcotic to ease the pain of the prisoner, but Jesus refused to drink of it for he had prom-ised not to drink again till he was in the kingdom.

His garments were divided by lot, charges were placed over his head, and he was mocked by those who were passing by. Two revolutionaries were crucified on either side of Jesus (only in Luke do we hear of the good thief).

From noon until three "dark-ness came over the whole land." The phrase is meant to indicate something much more significant than cloud cover. It is not clear whether "the whole land" meant simply the country of Judea or possibly the entire earth.

Jesus quotes the beginning of Psalm 22 on the cross. By citing this psalm, which is a lament, he is both identifying with the feeling of being aban-

They spat upon him and took the reed
    and kept striking him on the head.
And when they had mocked him,
    they stripped him of the cloak,
    dressed him in his own clothes,
    and led him off to crucify him.

As they were going out, they met a Cyrenian named
        Simon;
    this man they pressed into service
    to carry his cross.

And when they came to a place called Golgotha
        —which means Place of the Skull—,
    they gave Jesus wine to drink mixed with gall.
But when he had tasted it, he refused to drink.
After they had crucified him,
    they divided his garments by casting lots;
    then they sat down and kept watch over him there.
And they placed over his head the written charge
        against him:
    This is Jesus, the King of the Jews.
Two revolutionaries were crucified with him,
    one on his right and the other on his left.
Those passing by reviled him, shaking their heads
        and saying,
    "You who would destroy the temple and rebuild it
        in three days,
    save yourself, if you are the Son of God,
    and come down from the cross!"
Likewise the chief priests with the scribes and el-
        ders mocked him and said,
    "He saved others; he cannot save himself.
So he is the king of Israel!
Let him come down from the cross now,
    and we will believe in him.
He trusted in God;
    let him deliver him now if he wants him.
For he said, 'I am the Son of God.'"

doned and also with the *todah* (the thanksgiving at the end of the psalm), which speaks of how the Lord would deliver him.

The crowd thinks that Jesus is calling upon Elijah because the expression "Eli" sounds like that Prophet's name.

The veil is torn from top to bottom in the sanctuary. This refers to the Holy of Holies. It had previously been divided off from the people by the veil. We were kept from contact with God. Now there was to be immediate access to the Holy One, for the gates of heaven had been opened to us through the death of Jesus.

We hear of an earthquake at the moment of Jesus' death. The creator of the world has been murdered, and so the very foundations of the earth are shaken.

We also hear about people rising from their graves. This is an apocalyptic image, for the Jewish people believed that the dead would rise from their graves on the day of the Lord. This is the only gospel that speaks of this event, and it is possibly more symbolic than historical.

The centurion professes his faith that Jesus was the Son of God. This is significant. If a Jewish person had said this, it might have meant simply that Jesus was a hero. But the centurion was a pagan. Pagans believed that gods really could have children. So when he says that Jesus was the Son of God, he is saying what we believe

The revolutionaries who were crucified with him
    also kept abusing him in the same way.

From noon onward, darkness came over the whole land
    until three in the afternoon.
And about three o'clock Jesus cried out in a loud voice,
    "Eli, Eli, lema sabachthani?"
    which means, "My God, my God, why have you forsaken me?"
Some of the bystanders who heard it said,
    "This one is calling for Elijah."
Immediately one of them ran to get a sponge;
    he soaked it in wine, and putting it on a reed,
    gave it to him to drink.
But the rest said,
    "Wait, let us see if Elijah comes to save him."
But Jesus cried out again in a loud voice,
    and gave up his spirit.

Here all kneel and pause for a short time.

And behold, the veil of the sanctuary
    was torn in two from top to bottom.
The earth quaked, rocks were split, tombs were opened,
    and the bodies of many saints who had fallen asleep were raised.
And coming forth from their tombs after his resurrection,
    they entered the holy city and appeared to many.
The centurion and the men with him who were keeping watch over Jesus
    feared greatly when they saw the earthquake
    and all that was happening, and they said,
    "Truly, this was the Son of God!"
There were many women there, looking on from a distance,
    who had followed Jesus from Galilee, ministering to him.

about Jesus being the only-begotten Son of God.

The manner in which the tomb is described makes it seem that it was a cave with a low entrance. There was a stone bed in the middle upon which the body would be laid until it decomposed. Its bones were then put in vases and the tomb was reused. Jesus' tomb was new; it had never been used.

Jesus is buried by a rich man named Joseph of Arimathea. We might consider it odd that his tomb would be so close to the place of execution, but other tombs have been found in the immediate vicinity of the place where Jesus was killed.

The Jews insist that a guard be placed at the tomb so that the disciples could not rob the body of Jesus and tell the world that Jesus had risen (for they remembered Jesus' prediction of his death and resurrection from the dead after three days).

The women remained at the tomb after Jesus' burial, so there was never a moment that the tomb was not watched and even sealed. This is Matthew's way of disproving the rumors that the leaders of the Jews had invented to deny the reality of the resurrection. The guards were bribed to give testimony that Jesus' body had been stolen.

Among them were Mary Magdalene and Mary the mother of James and Joseph, and the mother of the sons of Zebedee.

When it was evening, there came a rich man from Arimathea named Joseph, who was himself a disciple of Jesus. He went to Pilate and asked for the body of Jesus; then Pilate ordered it to be handed over. Taking the body, Joseph wrapped it in clean linen and laid it in his new tomb that he had hewn in the rock. Then he rolled a huge stone across the entrance to the tomb and departed. But Mary Magdalene and the other Mary remained sitting there, facing the tomb. The next day, the one following the day of preparation, the chief priests and the Pharisees gathered before Pilate and said, "Sir, we remember that this impostor while still alive said, 'After three days I will be raised up.' Give orders, then, that the grave be secured until the third day, lest his disciples come and steal him and say to the people, 'He has been raised from the dead.' This last imposture would be worse than the first." Pilate said to them, "The guard is yours; go, secure it as best you can." So they went and secured the tomb by fixing a seal to the stone and setting the guard.

The Gospel of the Lord.

Lect.
No. 38

GOSPEL: B Shorter Form: Matthew 27:11-54

The Passion of our Lord Jesus Christ.

The passion narrative from the Gospel of Matthew contains the basic information found in all the Synoptic Gospels, but it also has nuances that are typical of this gospel. For example, it tells how Jesus fulfills all of the prophecies concerning the Messiah.

Jesus' interrogation by Pilate is relatively short and Jesus gives no response to the accusations. It is almost as if he is over and above what is going on and he will not dignify the questions with an answer. The governor is filled with awe, a common response to Jesus throughout the gospel.

We hear of a custom to release a prisoner during the Passover time. Although we have no outside testimony concerning the existence of such a custom (e.g., documents), we have no reason to doubt that the evangelists were accurate in their report of this event.

Pilate invites the mob to choose between Jesus and a certain Barabbas whom this gospel describes as a notorious prisoner. In the Gospel of Mark, he is described as being a revolutionary (which probably meant that he was associated with the Zealots). This was Pilate's attempt to release Jesus for he knew that Jesus was innocent.

The Passion of our Lord Jesus Christ
according to Matthew

Jesus stood before the governor, Pontius Pilate,
    who questioned him,
  "Are you the king of the Jews?"
Jesus said, "You say so."
And when he was accused by the chief priests and
    elders,
  he made no answer.
Then Pilate said to him,
  "Do you not hear how many things they are testi-
    fying against you?"
But he did not answer him one word,
  so that the governor was greatly amazed.

Now on the occasion of the feast
  the governor was accustomed to release to the
    crowd
  one prisoner whom they wished.
And at that time they had a notorious prisoner
    called Barabbas.
So when they had assembled, Pilate said to them,
  "Which one do you want me to release to you,
  Barabbas, or Jesus called Christ?"
For he knew that it was out of envy
  that they had handed him over.
While he was still seated on the bench,
  his wife sent him a message,
  "Have nothing to do with that righteous man.
I suffered much in a dream today because of him."
The chief priests and the elders persuaded the
    crowds
  to ask for Barabbas but to destroy Jesus.
The governor said to them in reply,

Some scholars have suggested that Barabbas' name is symbolic, for the meaning of Barabbas is "son of the father." That would mean that the people must choose between Jesus, the Son of God, and Barabbas, the son of the father.

The leaders of the people were adamant in their desire to have Jesus put to death. They even called Jesus' blood upon themselves and their children.

Pilate felt that he had no choice but to put Jesus to death, so he ordered that he be crucified. Yet, he symbolically washed his hands to show that he was innocent of Jesus' blood.

As was normal in capital cases, Jesus was handed over to the soldiers to be tortured before he was led out to be crucified. They placed a crown of thorns (probably in the form of a cap) on his head.

The soldiers also put a scarlet military cloak about Jesus. Mark had mentioned a purple cloak (the sign of royal authority). Matthew's version is actually more probable, for it is doubtful that the soldiers would have had a purple cloak at their disposition. They mocked Jesus as the "King of the Jews."

Jesus had now been condemned by his own people and by the Roman authorities. But, although he might appear to be powerless, he was invested with God's power of love and justice.

"Which of the two do you want me to release to you?"
They answered, "Barabbas!"
Pilate said to them,
"Then what shall I do with Jesus called Christ?"
They all said,
"Let him be crucified!"
But he said,
"Why? What evil has he done?"
They only shouted the louder,
"Let him be crucified!"
When Pilate saw that he was not succeeding at all,
but that a riot was breaking out instead,
he took water and washed his hands in the sight of the crowd,
saying, "I am innocent of this man's blood.
Look to it yourselves."
And the whole people said in reply,
"His blood be upon us and upon our children."
Then he released Barabbas to them,
but after he had Jesus scourged,
he handed him over to be crucified.

Then the soldiers of the governor took Jesus inside the praetorium
and gathered the whole cohort around him.
They stripped off his clothes
and threw a scarlet military cloak about him.
Weaving a crown out of thorns, they placed it on his head,
and a reed in his right hand.
And kneeling before him, they mocked him, saying,
"Hail, King of the Jews!"
They spat upon him and took the reed
and kept striking him on the head.
And when they had mocked him,
they stripped him of the cloak,
dressed him in his own clothes,
and led him off to crucify him.

Simon the Cyrenian is forced to assist Jesus to carry the cross (most probably only the crossbar, the vertical portion was normally anchored in place). It was not unusual for Roman soldiers to seize workmen and force them to assist with various tasks such as this.

Golgotha was probably a used-out quarry and the stone in which the cross was placed was believed to be a stone that had a flaw (hence, the fulfillment of the saying that the stone rejected by the builders had become the cornerstone). It is believed that Golgotha was called the Place of the Skull because its shape was in the form of a skull.

Jesus was offered wine mixed with gall. Gall was a type of narcotic to ease the pain of the prisoner, but Jesus refused to drink of it for he had promised not to drink again till he was in the kingdom.

His garments were divided by lot, charges were placed over his head, and he was mocked by those who were passing by. Two revolutionaries were crucified on either side of Jesus (only in Luke do we hear of the good thief).

From noon until three "darkness came over the whole land." The phrase is meant to indicate something much more significant than cloud cover. It is not clear whether "the whole land" meant simply the country of Judea or possibly the entire earth.

As they were going out, they met a Cyrenian named Simon;
   this man they pressed into service
   to carry his cross.

And when they came to a place called Golgotha
   —which means Place of the Skull—,
   they gave Jesus wine to drink mixed with gall.
But when he had tasted it, he refused to drink.
After they had crucified him,
   they divided his garments by casting lots;
   then they sat down and kept watch over him there.
And they placed over his head the written charge against him:
   This is Jesus, the King of the Jews.
Two revolutionaries were crucified with him,
   one on his right and the other on his left.
Those passing by reviled him, shaking their heads and saying,
   "You who would destroy the temple and rebuild it in three days,
   save yourself, if you are the Son of God,
   and come down from the cross!"
Likewise the chief priests with the scribes and elders mocked him and said,
   "He saved others; he cannot save himself.
So he is the king of Israel!
Let him come down from the cross now,
   and we will believe in him.
He trusted in God;
   let him deliver him now if he wants him.
For he said, 'I am the Son of God.'"
The revolutionaries who were crucified with him
   also kept abusing him in the same way.

From noon onward, darkness came over the whole land
   until three in the afternoon.

Jesus quotes the beginning of Psalm 22 on the cross. By citing this psalm, which is a lament, he is both identifying with the feeling of being abandoned and also with the *todah* (the thanksgiving at the end of the psalm), which speaks of how the Lord would deliver him.

The veil is torn from top to bottom in the sanctuary. This refers to the Holy of Holies. It had previously been divided off from the people by the veil. We were kept from contact with God. Now there was to be immediate access to the Holy One, for the gates of heaven had been opened to us through the death of Jesus.

We hear of an earthquake at the moment of the death of Jesus. The creator of the world has been murdered, and so the very foundations of the earth are shaken.

We also hear about people who rise from their graves. This is an apocalyptic image, for the Jewish people believed that the dead would rise from their graves on the day of the Lord. This is the only gospel that speaks of this event, and it is possibly more symbolic than historical.

And about three o'clock Jesus cried out in a loud voice,
  "Eli, Eli, lema sabachthani?"
  which means, "My God, my God, why have you forsaken me?"
Some of the bystanders who heard it said,
  "This one is calling for Elijah."
Immediately one of them ran to get a sponge;
  he soaked it in wine, and putting it on a reed,
  gave it to him to drink.
But the rest said,
  "Wait, let us see if Elijah comes to save him."
But Jesus cried out again in a loud voice,
  and gave up his spirit.

Here all kneel and pause for a short time.

And behold, the veil of the sanctuary
  was torn in two from top to bottom.
The earth quaked, rocks were split, tombs were opened,
  and the bodies of many saints who had fallen asleep were raised.
And coming forth from their tombs after his resurrection,
  they entered the holy city and appeared to many.
The centurion and the men with him who were keeping watch over Jesus
  feared greatly when they saw the earthquake
  and all that was happening, and they said,
  "Truly, this was the Son of God!"

The Gospel of the Lord.

This passage is taken from the third part of the Book of the Prophet Isaiah, a part written by an anonymous author named Trito-Isaiah. He wrote after the exile when the people of Israel had returned from exile in Babylon.

The author speaks of an anointed one who would bring a year of favor to his people. This was to be the fulfillment of the jubilee year.

Every seven years the people did not plant crops because they wanted to show their faith in the providence of the LORD. Every seventh seven (either every forty-nine or fifty years), there was a jubilee year. Debts were forgiven, slaves were freed, properties were returned to their original owners, etc. It was to be a year of profound dedication to justice. The people were to share the providence they had received from the LORD.

The Messiah spoken of in this passage was to establish that year of favor. He was to bring consolation to a people burdened by their difficulties. He would be able to do this because he was filled with the anointing of the Spirit of the LORD (remember in Old Testament times this was considered to be an attribute of Yahweh and not a separate person).

March 28, 2002

THURSDAY OF HOLY WEEK

CHRISM MASS

Lect. No. 260

FIRST READING:

Isaiah 61:1-3ab, 6a, 8b-9

The Lord has anointed me; he has sent me to bring glad tidings to the poor and to give them oil of gladness.

A reading from the Book of the Prophet Isaiah

The spirit of the Lord GOD is upon me,
  because the LORD has anointed me;
he has sent me to bring glad tidings to the poor,
  to heal the brokenhearted,
to proclaim liberty to the captives
  and release to the prisoners,
to announce a year of favor from the LORD
  and a day of vindication by our God,
  to comfort all who mourn;
to place on those who mourn in Zion
  a diadem instead of ashes,
to give them oil of gladness in place of mourning,
  a glorious mantle instead of a listless spirit.
You yourselves shall be named priests of the LORD,
  ministers of our God you shall be called.
I will give them their recompense faithfully,
  a lasting covenant I will make with them.
Their descendants shall be renowned among the nations,
  and their offspring among the peoples;
all who see them shall acknowledge them
  as a race the LORD has blessed.

The word of the Lord.

Lect.
No. 260

RESPONSORIAL PSALM: Ps 89:21-22, 25, 27 (℟.: 2a)

At the Chrism Mass we bless the sacred oils that will be used throughout the year. This oil will be used for consecrating, anointing for healing, setting apart for God.

These passages speak of the effects of an anointing. David, the anointed of the LORD, was filled with the strength, faithfulness, and kindness of the LORD.

Anointing establishes a special relationship between us and God, who is our father, our rock, and our savior.

℟. **Forever I will sing the goodness of the Lord.**

I have found David, my servant;
  with my holy oil I have anointed him,
that my hand may be always with him,
  and that my arm may make him strong.

℟. **Forever I will sing the goodness of the Lord.**

My faithfulness and my kindness shall be with him,
  and through my name shall his horn be exalted.
"He shall cry to me, 'You are my father,
  my God, the Rock my savior.'"

℟. **Forever I will sing the goodness of the Lord.**

Lect.
No. 260

SECOND READING: Revelation 1:5-8

He has made us into a kingdom, priests for his God and Father.

The Book of Revelation is filled with liturgical hymns. This hymn lauds Jesus who is the faithful witness. The word for witness in Greek is "martureo," the source of the English word "martyr".

Jesus has granted us a royal dignity for we have become co-heirs with him of the glory of God.

We have also become priests through our baptismal anointing. We, like Jesus, offer up our sacrifice as priests. But we are also like him in that the sacrifice we offer is our own life and love, which we offer up upon the altar of the cross.

We give God all of ourselves with our hopes and disappointments, our work and leisure, even our everyday lives.

A reading from the Book of Revelation

Jesus Christ is the faithful witness,
  the firstborn of the dead and ruler of the kings of
  the earth.
To him who loves us and has freed us from our sins
  by his blood,
  who has made us into a kingdom, priests for his
  God and Father,
  to him be glory and power forever and ever.
  Amen.
  Behold, he is coming amid the clouds,
  and every eye will see him,
  even those who pierced him.
All the peoples of the earth will lament him.
  Yes. Amen.
"I am the Alpha and the Omega," says the Lord God,
  "the one who is and who was
  and who is to come, the almighty."

The word of the Lord.

Lect. No. 260 **VERSE BEFORE THE GOSPEL: Isaiah 61:1 (cited in Luke 4:18)**

This Verse before the Gospel speaks of the sacred anointing through which the Spirit of the Lord calls us to serve the poor of the Lord.

The Spirit of the Lord is upon me
for he sent me to bring glad tidings to the poor.

Lect. No. 260

GOSPEL: Luke 4:16-21

The Spirit of the Lord is upon me, because he has anointed me.

Early in his public ministry, Jesus goes into the synagogue in his home town and identifies himself as the anointed one of God.

This anointing proclaims Jesus as the fulfillment of the jubilee year of the Lord. No longer would we have to wait fifty years in order to experience God's justice. When we encounter Jesus and the love he offers, we are changed.

We can no longer treat ourselves and others as we did. We must love them with the same love as he has loved us.

As we receive the anointing of the Spirit of the Lord (using the oils blessed at this Mass), we share in Jesus' ministry to proclaim that year of favor to the world. God's Spirit empowers us to give witness to God's love.

A reading from the holy Gospel according to Luke

Jesus came to Nazareth, where he had grown up, and went according to his custom
into the synagogue on the sabbath day.
He stood up to read and was handed a scroll of the
prophet Isaiah.
He unrolled the scroll and found the passage where
it was written:
The Spirit of the Lord is upon me,
because he has anointed me
to bring glad tidings to the poor.
He has sent me to proclaim liberty to captives
and recovery of sight to the blind,
to let the oppressed go free,
and to proclaim a year acceptable to the Lord.
Rolling up the scroll, he handed it back to the attendant and sat down,
and the eyes of all in the synagogue looked intently at him.
He said to them,
"Today this Scripture passage is fulfilled in your
hearing."

The Gospel of the Lord.

March 28, 2002
HOLY THURSDAY
EVENING MASS OF THE LORD'S SUPPER

Lect. No. 39 FIRST READING: Exodus 12:1-8, 11-14

The law regarding the Passover meal.

The First Reading for Holy Thursday is a recounting of the events of the first Passover of the Exodus. Scholars now believe that the Jewish people celebrated Passover before the exodus as an agricultural feast (possibly associated with the birth of the Spring lambs). The Hebrew word for Passover, "Pesach," means leaping, probably referring to the leaping of the newborn lambs.

After the exodus, it was tied to the events that occurred in Egypt.

The month of the Passover was to be considered the first month of the year. This changed when the Israelites were in exile in Babylon. During the exile they adopted the Babylonian calendar, which marked the fall as the beginning of the year. Jewish people celebrate Rosh Hashana (New Year's Day) in September. The passing over was now understood both as the angel of death passing over Egypt and the Israelites passing over the Red Sea.

The meal was to be eaten as if they were preparing for a journey (with loins girt and sandals on their feet). They were, in fact, to relive the events every time they commemorated them.

A reading from the Book of Exodus

The LORD said to Moses and Aaron in the land of Egypt,
"This month shall stand at the head of your calendar;
you shall reckon it the first month of the year.
Tell the whole community of Israel:
On the tenth of this month every one of your families
must procure for itself a lamb, one apiece for each household.
If a family is too small for a whole lamb,
it shall join the nearest household in procuring one
and shall share in the lamb
in proportion to the number of persons who partake of it.
The lamb must be a year–old male and without blemish.
You may take it from either the sheep or the goats.
You shall keep it until the fourteenth day of this month,
and then, with the whole assembly of Israel present,
it shall be slaughtered during the evening twilight.
They shall take some of its blood
and apply it to the two doorposts and the lintel

The Israelites ate a lamb and used the blood of the lamb to mark their doorposts and lintel. This mark protected them from the depredations of the angel of death who destroyed the first born of all of the Egyptians.

It is appropriate that the doorposts should be marked with blood. In Old Testament symbolism blood signified life. The blood saved the lives of the Israelites.

The closing verses of this reading remind the Israelites that this was to be a celebration among the Jews forever, and also that it was intended to be a pilgrimage festival.

During the days of Jesus, it was believed that as many as a quarter of a million pilgrims arrived in Jerusalem to celebrate the feast.

of every house in which they partake of the lamb.
That same night they shall eat its roasted flesh
   with unleavened bread and bitter herbs.

"This is how you are to eat it:
   with your loins girt, sandals on your feet and your
      staff in hand,
   you shall eat like those who are in flight.
It is the Passover of the LORD.
For on this same night I will go through Egypt,
   striking down every firstborn of the land, both
      man and beast,
   and executing judgment on all the gods of Egypt—
      I, the LORD!
But the blood will mark the houses where you are.
Seeing the blood, I will pass over you;
   thus, when I strike the land of Egypt,
   no destructive blow will come upon you.

"This day shall be a memorial feast for you,
   which all your generations shall celebrate
   with pilgrimage to the LORD, as a perpetual insti-
      tution."

The word of the Lord.

| Lect. No. 39 |

RESPONSORIAL PSALM: Ps 116:12-13, 15-16bc, 17-18

(℟.: cf. 1 Corinthians 10:16)

Psalm 116 is a thanksgiving psalm prayed in gratitude to the LORD for a deliverance. The psalmist had been at the point of death, but the LORD had loosed his bonds (the bonds of death).

The LORD had granted him the cup of salvation (allowed him to taste the effects of the LORD's salvation). Now, he would offer him a sacrifice of thanksgiving.

℟. **Our blessing–cup is a communion with the Blood of Christ.**

How shall I make a return to the LORD
   for all the good he has done for me?
The cup of salvation I will take up,
   and I will call upon the name of the LORD.

℟. **Our blessing-cup is a communion with the Blood of Christ.**

Precious in the eyes of the LORD
   is the death of his faithful ones.

Both of these sacrificial images are appropriate for our celebration this evening. The Eucharist is both a powerful gift of salvation (celebrating the salvation offered upon the cross) and an act of thanksgiving. (The word "Eucharist" in Greek actually means to give thanks). Our only possible response to this incredible generosity is fidelity to God (we must pay our vows to him).

I am your servant, the son of your handmaid;
  you have loosed my bonds.

℞. **Our blessing-cup is a communion with the Blood of Christ.**

To you will I offer sacrifice of thanksgiving,
  and I will call upon the name of the LORD.
My vows to the LORD I will pay
  in the presence of all his people.

℞. **Our blessing-cup is a communion with the Blood of Christ.**

Lect.
No. 39

SECOND READING: 1 Corinthians 11:23-26

*For as often as you eat this bread and drink the cup,
you proclaim the death of the Lord.*

Paul wrote this account of the institution of the Eucharist to the Corinthian community because they seem to have forgotten the significance of this event. They were celebrating the Lord's Supper but not living in communion with their sisters and brothers. Some in the community had more than enough to eat when they gathered together while others were all but starving.

Paul accused them of sinning against what they were doing by not living in the same spirit as Jesus. He asked the Corinthians to examine their conscience before they received the Eucharist. They were to make sure they understood the significance of their actions.

A reading from the first Letter of Saint Paul
to the Corinthians

Brothers and sisters:
  I received from the Lord what I also handed on to you,
    that the Lord Jesus, on the night he was handed over,
  took bread, and, after he had given thanks,
    broke it and said, "This is my body that is for you.
Do this in remembrance of me."
In the same way also the cup, after supper, saying,
  "This cup is the new covenant in my blood.
Do this, as often as you drink it, in remembrance of me."
For as often as you eat this bread and drink the cup,
  you proclaim the death of the Lord until he comes.

The word of the Lord.

Lect.
No. 39

VERSE BEFORE THE GOSPEL: John 13:34

We hear a passage from the Gospel of John about loving one another. This command is the core of the sacrament we are celebrating.

I give you a new commandment, says the Lord: love one another as I have loved you.

Lect.
No. 39

GOSPEL: John 13:1-15

Jesus loved them to the end.

The account of the Last Supper found in the Gospel of John does not include an account of the institution of the Eucharist. Rather, it speaks of how Jesus washed the feet of his disciples and invited them to do the same to each other. It is not that this gospel ignores the Eucharist (quite the opposite, for it speaks of the Eucharist here, in chapter 6, and also in chapter 21).

Rather, John presents this scene to teach us the spiritual significance of the sacrament of the Eucharist. It is the sacrament through which Jesus serves us in a most profound manner, and in which he invites us to be of service to one another. This is what Jesus' ministry in this gospel is all about. He came into this world to save us.

This is why the beginning of the account mentions certain things. First of all, we hear that the feast of the Passover was near (in John the Last Supper is an anticipation of the Passover meal, for in this gospel Passover does not begin until Good Friday night).

A reading from the holy Gospel according to John

Before the feast of Passover, Jesus knew that his hour had come
   to pass from this world to the Father.
He loved his own in the world and he loved them to
   the end.
The devil had already induced Judas, son of Simon
   the Iscariot, to hand him over.
So, during supper,
   fully aware that the Father had put everything
      into his power
   and that he had come from God and was return-
      ing to God,
   he rose from supper and took off his outer gar-
      ments.
He took a towel and tied it around his waist.
Then he poured water into a basin
   and began to wash the disciples' feet
   and dry them with the towel around his waist.
He came to Simon Peter, who said to him,
   "Master, are you going to wash my feet?"
Jesus answered and said to him,
   "What I am doing, you do not understand now,
   but you will understand later."
Peter said to him, "You will never wash my feet."

We also hear that Jesus is acting in the love of the Father. Thus, his action of humility is not one performed because he did not know he is God, but rather the opposite. As we hear in the First Letter of John, God is love. Therefore, we hear of the great love he had for his disciples, a love shown in humble service.

Peter does not want his feet washed, possibly because he fears vulnerability (being served). Yet, vulnerability is an essential dimension of true love.

This chapter presents the sacrament of the Eucharist as a verb, an act of service, and an invitation to serve others. This portrayal is balanced by chapter 6 where the Eucharist is presented as a noun (the real presence of Jesus) and chapter 21, where the meal on the shore after the miraculous catch of fish has eucharistic overtones and presents the Eucharist as a call to mission (to go fishing for souls).

Jesus answered him,
   "Unless I wash you, you will have no inheritance with me."
Simon Peter said to him,
   "Master, then not only my feet, but my hands and head as well."
Jesus said to him,
   "Whoever has bathed has no need except to have his feet washed,
   for he is clean all over;
   so you are clean, but not all."
For he knew who would betray him;
   for this reason, he said, "Not all of you are clean."

So when he had washed their feet
   and put his garments back on and reclined at table again,
   he said to them, "Do you realize what I have done for you?
You call me 'teacher' and 'master,' and rightly so, for indeed I am.
If I, therefore, the master and teacher, have washed your feet,
   you ought to wash one another's feet.
I have given you a model to follow,
   so that as I have done for you, you should also do."

The Gospel of the Lord.

March 29, 2002

GOOD FRIDAY OF THE LORD'S PASSION

Lect. No. 40 **FIRST READING: Isaiah 52:13—53:12**

He himself was wounded for our sins.

(Fourth oracle of the Servant of the Lord.)

A reading from the Book of the Prophet Isaiah

This is the fourth of the songs of the Suffering Servant of Yahweh. These songs were incorporated into the second part of the Book of the Prophet Isaiah. They are attributed to an anonymous author called Second Isaiah (he prophesied during the Babylonian exile).

These songs speak about a mysterious figure who would suffer to fulfill the mission of the LORD. This mission was to bring about an era of justice and peace. This wondrous future would be given not only to the people of the nation of Israel, but also to all the nations (the Hebrew phrase for the Gentiles).

The Servant would not bring about this new dispensation through violence. He would be meek and gentle and would not crush a bruised reed .

The author of the song speaks of the awe that this figure evokes (both at his willingness to suffer and at the extent of that suffering).

It was not known in ancient times who this Servant was. Some said that it was the personification of the nation of Israel, others that it was one of the prophets (possibly Jeremiah). It was Jesus who first applied these prophecies to himself.

See, my servant shall prosper,
    he shall be raised high and greatly exalted.
Even as many were amazed at him—
    so marred was his look beyond human semblance
    and his appearance beyond that of the sons of
        man—
so shall he startle many nations,
    because of him kings shall stand speechless;
for those who have not been told shall see,
    those who have not heard shall ponder it.

Who would believe what we have heard?
    To whom has the arm of the LORD been revealed?
He grew up like a sapling before him,
    like a shoot from the parched earth;
there was in him no stately bearing to make us look
        at him,
    nor appearance that would attract us to him.
He was spurned and avoided by people,
    a man of suffering, accustomed to infirmity,
one of those from whom people hide their faces,
    spurned, and we held him in no esteem.

Yet it was our infirmities that he bore,
    our sufferings that he endured,
while we thought of him as stricken,
    as one smitten by God and afflicted.
But he was pierced for our offenses,
    crushed for our sins;

The fourth song is the most poignant in its description. It contains two elements that were not part of the theology of the era in which it was written.

First of all, it speaks about the ultimate exaltation of the Servant after he had been killed in the service of the LORD. This means his resurrection from the dead, an idea that had not yet been fully developed in the theology of Israel.

Even stranger for this era was the idea that this Servant would bear the sins of the people upon himself: expiation. The Jewish people did not believe that the suffering and death of any person could bring about good. Their Messiah was to conquer, not to be killed.

What is being described is what Saint Paul speaks of as the wisdom of God or the wisdom of the cross. In that wisdom, one must die in order to live forever.

The description of the sufferings of this servant are similar to those of Psalm 22 and are uncannily similar to what actually happened to Jesus. He was like a sheep led to the slaughter, cut off from the land of the living, buried among wrongdoers, crushed. Yet, because he was obedient to the will of the Father, he won pardon for our offenses and would be exalted in glory and proclaimed as Lord of everything that exists in heaven, on the earth, and under the earth.

upon him was the chastisement that makes us whole,
    by his stripes we were healed.
We had all gone astray like sheep,
    each following his own way;
but the LORD laid upon him
    the guilt of us all.

Though he was harshly treated, he submitted
    and opened not his mouth;
like a lamb led to the slaughter
    or a sheep before the shearers,
    he was silent and opened not his mouth.
Oppressed and condemned, he was taken away,
    and who would have thought any more of his destiny?
When he was cut off from the land of the living,
    and smitten for the sin of his people,
a grave was assigned him among the wicked
    and a burial place with evildoers,
though he had done no wrong
    nor spoken any falsehood.
But the LORD was pleased
    to crush him in infirmity.

If he gives his life as an offering for sin,
    he shall see his descendants in a long life,
    and the will of the LORD shall be accomplished
    through him.

Because of his affliction
    he shall see the light
    in fullness of days;
through his suffering, my servant shall justify many,
    and their guilt he shall bear.
Therefore I will give him his portion among the great,
    and he shall divide the spoils with the mighty,
because he surrendered himself to death
    and was counted among the wicked;
and he shall take away the sins of many,
    and win pardon for their offenses.

The word of the Lord.

Lect. No. 40

RESPONSORIAL PSALM: Ps 31:2, 6, 12-13, 15-16, 17, 25
(℞.: Luke 23:46)

Psalm 31 is a psalm of thanksgiving written by one who had been delivered from horrible life-threatening dangers. It expresses faith in the fact that God would surely provide deliverance for the LORD is truly a refuge.

It might seem odd to be reciting this psalm today, since it almost seems too positive in tone. Yet, there is a strong sense of hope in our commemoration for we are certain that the defeat on the cross will be followed by the triumph of the resurrection. This also reminds us that not all of our deliverances will be in this life. We must live in hope of a future fulfillment of God's promises in our resurrection from the dead.

Even on Good Friday Jesus expressed this same hope. He was citing Psalm 22 when he prayed, "My God, my God, why have you forsaken me?" These are the first words of this psalm of lamentation. All lamentations end with a profession of faith in God's ultimate deliverance. While Jesus was speaking of his feelings of abandonment, he was also professing his faith that the LORD, his Father, would deliver him.

℞. **Father, into your hands I commend my spirit.**

In you, O LORD, I take refuge;
  let me never be put to shame.
In your justice rescue me.
  Into your hands I commend my spirit;
you will redeem me, O LORD, O faithful God.

℞. **Father, into your hands I commend my spirit.**

For all my foes I am an object of reproach,
  a laughingstock to my neighbors, and a dread to
    my friends;
  they who see me abroad flee from me.
I am forgotten like the unremembered dead;
  I am like a dish that is broken.

℞. **Father, into your hands I commend my spirit.**

But my trust is in you, O LORD;
  I say, "You are my God.
In your hands is my destiny; rescue me
  from the clutches of my enemies and my persecu-
    tors."

℞. **Father, into your hands I commend my spirit.**

Let your face shine upon your servant;
  save me in your kindness.
Take courage and be stouthearted,
  all you who hope in the LORD.

℞. **Father, into your hands I commend my spirit.**

Lect. No. 40

SECOND READING: Hebrews 4:14-16; 5:7-9

Jesus learned obedience and became the source of salvation for all who obey him.

One of the major themes developed in the Letter to the Hebrews is that Jesus is our High Priest. Unlike the high priests of the Old Testament, Jesus was not a sinner. Being totally sinless, he therefore did not have to perform sacrifices for his own sins. His sacrifice was performed totally for our benefit.

Yet, in spite of the fact that Jesus was perfect and without sin, he nevertheless was able to empathize with us (because he shared our human condition). He was like us in all things but sin.

The second part of the reading speaks of Jesus' obedience to the will of the Father. This should not be understood as a blind obedience that denigrated Jesus. Rather, by being obedient, he was most fully who he really is. He was perfect in his response to God's will. Likewise, when we sin we are rejecting who God made us to be, while when we live in obedience to God's will, we are actually most fully ourselves.

A reading from the Letter to the Hebrews

Brothers and sisters:
Since we have a great high priest who has passed through the heavens,
Jesus, the Son of God,
let us hold fast to our confession.
For we do not have a high priest
who is unable to sympathize with our weaknesses,
but one who has similarly been tested in every way,
yet without sin.
So let us confidently approach the throne of grace
to receive mercy and to find grace for timely help.

In the days when Christ was in the flesh,
he offered prayers and supplications with loud cries and tears
to the one who was able to save him from death,
and he was heard because of his reverence.
Son though he was, he learned obedience from what he suffered;
and when he was made perfect,
he became the source of eternal salvation for all who obey him.

The word of the Lord.

Lect. No. 40

VERSE BEFORE THE GOSPEL: Philippians 2:8-9

This verse, taken from the Philippians' hymn, speaks of Jesus' profound obedience to the will of the Father and his exaltation as LORD.

Christ became obedient to the point of death,
even death on a cross.
Because of this, God greatly exalted him
and bestowed on him the name which is above every other name.

Lect.
No. 40

GOSPEL: John 18:1—19:42

The Passion of our Lord Jesus Christ.

The passion narrative in the Gospel of John agrees with the other gospels in most details except those that are specifically Johannine. One example of this is that wherever possible the divinity of Jesus is emphasized. Jesus knows all things and controls all things from the beginning to the end of the account.

Although the place where Jesus led the disciples is not mentioned by name, it is obviously the garden of Gethsemane. We can see the violent intent of the soldiers of the high priests by the weapons they are carrying. This contrasts with the way that Jesus meets the troops, totally without arms. He is able to defeat them simply with the truth.

Jesus asks them whom they seek. They respond Jesus of Nazareth, and he tells them, "I AM." This phrase is the same as the meaning of the name of God in the Old Testament: Yahweh. Thus, Jesus is identifying himself as God. Those who had come to arrest Jesus fall down in fear and awe, for they are in the presence of the living God.

Peter tries to defend Jesus with a sword, cutting off Malchus' ear. Only in this gospel is the violent disciple identified as Peter. It is compatible with his personality, which is a bit impetuous throughout this gospel. Jesus tells him to put away his sword because he is

The Passion of our Lord Jesus Christ according to John

Jesus went out with his disciples across the Kidron valley
to where there was a garden,
into which he and his disciples entered.
Judas his betrayer also knew the place,
because Jesus had often met there with his disciples.
So Judas got a band of soldiers and guards
from the chief priests and the Pharisees
and went there with lanterns, torches, and weapons.
Jesus, knowing everything that was going to happen to him,
went out and said to them, "Whom are you looking for?"
They answered him, "Jesus the Nazorean."
He said to them, "I AM."
Judas his betrayer was also with them.
When he said to them, "I AM,"
they turned away and fell to the ground.
So he again asked them,
"Whom are you looking for?"
They said, "Jesus the Nazorean."
Jesus answered,
"I told you that I AM.
So if you are looking for me, let these men go."
This was to fulfill what he had said,
"I have not lost any of those you gave me."
Then Simon Peter, who had a sword, drew it,
struck the high priest's slave, and cut off his right ear.
The slave's name was Malchus.

not going to confront violence with violence. Jesus wants to show that only love conquers.

Jesus is brought to the high priest's house. We hear how Caiaphas had predicted that it was better that one person die for the sake of the people. Caiaphas had meant that it was better to kill him before a rebellion began, but the Holy Spirit had given meaning to his words that he did not even understand. Jesus was going to die for the people, for the forgiveness of our sins.

The leaders of the Jews were offended by the fact that Jesus claimed divine prerogatives for himself. He was also considered to be a political danger, for the Jewish leaders feared he might start a rebellion in which they would lose their privileges.

The other disciple, who is probably the beloved disciple, is able to enter the high priest's house. He also arranges to bring Peter into the courtyard.

Jesus answers the questions of the high priest with diffidence. He is the very presence of God, and it is absurd that they should be questioning him. Furthermore, he is truth itself, and had spoken in the light. They were the ones who were working in the dark to hide their evil deeds.

The temple guards are enraged that Jesus would respond to the high priest in this manner and one strikes Jesus. He is trying to protect the dignity of the high priest, but there is an

Jesus said to Peter,
  "Put your sword into its scabbard.
Shall I not drink the cup that the Father gave me?"

So the band of soldiers, the tribune, and the Jewish
    guards seized Jesus,
  bound him, and brought him to Annas first.
He was the father-in-law of Caiaphas,
  who was high priest that year.
It was Caiaphas who had counseled the Jews
  that it was better that one man should die rather
    than the people.

Simon Peter and another disciple followed Jesus.
Now the other disciple was known to the high
    priest,
  and he entered the courtyard of the high priest
    with Jesus.
But Peter stood at the gate outside.
So the other disciple, the acquaintance of the high
    priest,
  went out and spoke to the gatekeeper and brought
    Peter in.
Then the maid who was the gatekeeper said to
    Peter,
  "You are not one of this man's disciples, are you?"
He said, "I am not."
Now the slaves and the guards were standing
    around a charcoal fire
  that they had made, because it was cold,
  and were warming themselves.
Peter was also standing there keeping warm.

The high priest questioned Jesus
  about his disciples and about his doctrine.
Jesus answered him,
  "I have spoken publicly to the world.
I have always taught in a synagogue
  or in the temple area where all the Jews gather,

irony here. How much more important is Jesus, and yet the guard fails to recognize the honor he should be paying him.

We hear of Peter's denial of Jesus (an abbreviated version as compared to the synoptic version). Typical of this gospel is the subtle comparison between Peter who denies Jesus and the beloved disciple who is courageous enough to accompany Jesus to the cross.

Jesus is brought to the palace of Pilate. The leaders of the Jews do not want to enter the palace because that would make them ritually impure and they would not be able to celebrate the Passover meal that night. John's gospel presents the Last Supper as an anticipated Passover meal. In the Gospel of John, Jesus dies on Good Friday, but Passover begins on Friday night and not on Thursday night as in the Synoptic gospels. The best studies on this topic have suggested that John was probably right.

The interrogation of Jesus before Pilate is a brilliant scene. There are seven sections to the drama (divided by leaving or entering the palace). The first and last, second and second last, third and third last sections are related. The central section is the passage where Jesus is hailed as the king of the Jews. This is the core message of this extended section. Jesus, despite appearances, is the true king of the Jews. Yet, he is not a king who rules from the cross, and his crown is not one of gold but one made of thorns.

and in secret I have said nothing. Why ask me?
Ask those who heard me what I said to them.
They know what I said."
When he had said this,
    one of the temple guards standing there struck Jesus and said,
    "Is this the way you answer the high priest?"
Jesus answered him,
    "If I have spoken wrongly, testify to the wrong;
    but if I have spoken rightly, why do you strike me?"
Then Annas sent him bound to Caiaphas the high priest.

Now Simon Peter was standing there keeping warm.
And they said to him,
    "You are not one of his disciples, are you?"
He denied it and said,
    "I am not."
One of the slaves of the high priest,
    a relative of the one whose ear Peter had cut off, said,
    "Didn't I see you in the garden with him?"
Again Peter denied it.
And immediately the cock crowed.

Then they brought Jesus from Caiaphas to the praetorium.
It was morning.
And they themselves did not enter the praetorium,
    in order not to be defiled so that they could eat the Passover.
So Pilate came out to them and said,
    "What charge do you bring against this man?"
They answered and said to him,
    "If he were not a criminal,
    we would not have handed him over to you."
At this, Pilate said to them,

In the first and last sections, Pilate uses Jesus as a pawn to get back at the Jews (whom he hated). He tells the Jews to judge him according to their own law. They respond that they cannot put him to death (which is quoting Roman law and not Jewish law). They have thus implicitly denied their own law.

Likewise, in the last section Pilate asks whether he should put their king to death. They respond that they have no king but Caesar. By saying that, they are denying their king (both Jesus and Yahweh).

In the second and second last portions we see Pilate questioning Jesus. In the second there are questions concerning Jesus' kingdom and truth, and in the second last section there are questions concerning Pilate's authority. Both of these sections question who has the real authority, Pilate or Jesus.

The way that Jesus responds to Pilate throughout this section shows that Jesus possesses true authority while that of Pilate is illusory. All authority comes from God (even that exercised by earthly rulers).

Furthermore, when Pilate asks the question, "What is truth," he is not asking a philosophical question. He is stating a political opinion, "what does truth matter when he could gain political advantage." He knew that Jesus was innocent, but yet he would let Jesus die in order to get back at the Jews.

"Take him yourselves, and judge him according to your law."
The Jews answered him,
"We do not have the right to execute anyone,"
in order that the word of Jesus might be fulfilled
that he said indicating the kind of death he would die.
So Pilate went back into the praetorium
and summoned Jesus and said to him,
"Are you the King of the Jews?"
Jesus answered,
"Do you say this on your own
or have others told you about me?"
Pilate answered,
"I am not a Jew, am I?
Your own nation and the chief priests handed you over to me.
What have you done?"
Jesus answered,
"My kingdom does not belong to this world.
If my kingdom did belong to this world,
my attendants would be fighting
to keep me from being handed over to the Jews.
But as it is, my kingdom is not here."
So Pilate said to him,
"Then you are a king?"
Jesus answered,
"You say I am a king.
For this I was born and for this I came into the world,
to testify to the truth.
Everyone who belongs to the truth listens to my voice."
Pilate said to him, "What is truth?"

When he had said this,
he again went out to the Jews and said to them,
"I find no guilt in him.

In the third and third last sections we see Pilate speaking with the Jewish leaders. He gives them a choice between Jesus and Barabbas in the third, and presents the beaten and humiliated Jesus in the third last. Neither of these presentations quiets their blood-lust. They still seek to crucify him.

As mentioned above, the core to understanding all that is going on in this trial is found in the central section where the soldiers treat Jesus as a king. They intend to humiliate him, but in great irony they are actually proclaiming the hidden truth about Jesus.

All of the characters involved (Pilate, the leaders of the Jews, the soldiers) thought that they were controlling what was going on. Jesus is the true king, and he was in control in spite of what they thought.

The purple cloak they use is a bit problematic. Purple was very rare and it was not clear how they would have obtained it. The Gospel of Matthew speaks of a scarlet robe.

Pilate asks Jesus where he is from. This is a common theme throughout the gospel. People often wonder where Jesus comes from, for they do not recognize that he comes from the Father. He comes from above, and he leads us back there.

After this drama is played out, it is time for all to be completed. Jesus is led out to the place of judgment.

But you have a custom that I release one prisoner to
    you at Passover.
Do you want me to release to you the King of the
    Jews?"
They cried out again,
    "Not this one but Barabbas!"
Now Barabbas was a revolutionary.

Then Pilate took Jesus and had him scourged.
And the soldiers wove a crown out of thorns and
    placed it on his head,
    and clothed him in a purple cloak,
    and they came to him and said,
    "Hail, King of the Jews!"
And they struck him repeatedly.
Once more Pilate went out and said to them,
    "Look, I am bringing him out to you,
    so that you may know that I find no guilt in him."
So Jesus came out,
    wearing the crown of thorns and the purple cloak.
And he said to them, "Behold, the man!"
When the chief priests and the guards saw him they
    cried out,
    "Crucify him, crucify him!"
Pilate said to them,
    "Take him yourselves and crucify him.
I find no guilt in him."
The Jews answered,
    "We have a law, and according to that law he
        ought to die,
    because he made himself the Son of God."
Now when Pilate heard this statement,
    he became even more afraid,
    and went back into the praetorium and said to
        Jesus,
    "Where are you from?"
Jesus did not answer him.
So Pilate said to him,

It is important to remember that all of this is occurring on the preparation day for the Passover celebration. Jesus was being led out to his crucifixion at the very moment that the Passover lambs were being taken to the temple to be killed. In this we see how Jesus is the new Passover Lamb. This symbolism is continued later in the account where we hear about the fact that none of his bones was broken. This was one of the requirements for the Passover lamb, and it was true of Jesus as well.

The leaders of the Jews are strongly blamed for the death of Jesus in this gospel. This gospel and Matthew have often been used as proof texts for anti-Semitism. That is not a correct reading of these texts. It was not "the Jews" who had Jesus put to death. It was their leaders with the collaboration of the Roman authorities. We should remember, however, that we are ultimately responsible for the death of Jesus. He died because of our sins.

Pilate proclaims Jesus as king of the Jews in the inscription that he ordered to be hung over the head of Jesus. The leaders of the Jews objected to the phrase "King of the Jews," but Pilate insisted that it remain.

Jesus is crucified on Golgotha, a small outcropping of rock in a used-out quarry. His cross was anchored in a rock that had a natural flaw and was therefore rejected by the builders (hence, the fulfillment of the verse that speaks of the stone rejected by the builders becoming the cornerstone).

"Do you not speak to me?
Do you not know that I have power to release you
 and I have power to crucify you?"
Jesus answered him,
 "You would have no power over me
 if it had not been given to you from above.
For this reason the one who handed me over to you
 has the greater sin."
Consequently, Pilate tried to release him; but the
 Jews cried out,
 "If you release him, you are not a Friend of Cae-
 sar.
Everyone who makes himself a king opposes Cae-
 sar."

When Pilate heard these words he brought Jesus out
 and seated him on the judge's bench
 in the place called Stone Pavement, in Hebrew,
 Gabbatha.
It was preparation day for Passover, and it was
 about noon.
And he said to the Jews,
 "Behold, your king!"
They cried out,
 "Take him away, take him away! Crucify him!"
Pilate said to them,
 "Shall I crucify your king?"
The chief priests answered,
 "We have no king but Caesar."
Then he handed him over to them to be crucified.

So they took Jesus, and, carrying the cross himself,
 he went out to what is called the Place of the
 Skull,
 in Hebrew, Golgotha.
There they crucified him, and with him two others,
 one on either side, with Jesus in the middle.
Pilate also had an inscription written and put on the
 cross.

The leaders of the Jews object to the inscription placed over the head of Jesus stating that he was the King of the Jews. Ironically, it was a pagan who insisted upon sustaining the truth while Jesus' own people were rejecting their own king.

The soldiers divide Jesus' garments, but they do not cut his cloak, which was a seamless garment.

The mother of Jesus is standing below the cross along with Mary, the wife of Clopas, Mary of Magdala, and the beloved disciple.

Jesus hands his mother over into the care of the beloved disciple. Tradition holds that he cared for her for the rest of her life.

This passage also has a symbolic meaning. Jesus married the Church on the cross (in fulfillment of the matrimonial symbolism found throughout the gospel). According to Jewish tradition, if a man died without having children, his next of kin was to marry the widow to have a child who would bear the deceased man's name.

Jesus had no children from his marriage to the Church, so he adopted the beloved disciple as his brother so that the brother would produce children who would bear his name (Christians).

Jesus is in control until the very minute of his death. He fulfills all that was prophesied

It read,
    "Jesus the Nazorean, the King of the Jews."
Now many of the Jews read this inscription,
    because the place where Jesus was crucified was
        near the city;
    and it was written in Hebrew, Latin, and Greek.
So the chief priests of the Jews said to Pilate,
    "Do not write 'The King of the Jews,'
    but that he said, 'I am the King of the Jews.' "
Pilate answered,
    "What I have written, I have written."

When the soldiers had crucified Jesus,
    they took his clothes and divided them into four
        shares,
    a share for each soldier.
They also took his tunic, but the tunic was seamless,
    woven in one piece from the top down.
So they said to one another,
    "Let's not tear it, but cast lots for it to see whose it
        will be,"
    in order that the passage of Scripture might be
        fulfilled that says:
        They divided my garments among them,
            and for my vesture they cast lots.
This is what the soldiers did.
Standing by the cross of Jesus were his mother
    and his mother's sister, Mary the wife of Clopas,
    and Mary of Magdala.
When Jesus saw his mother and the disciple there
        whom he loved
    he said to his mother, "Woman, behold, your son."
Then he said to the disciple,
    "Behold, your mother."
And from that hour the disciple took her into his
        home.

After this, aware that everything was now finished,
    in order that the Scripture might be fulfilled,

about his death, and he then hands over his spirit. It was he who decided when it was time to die.

The soldiers were sent to break the legs of those who had been crucified. One died on the cross due to suffocation when one no longer had the strength to push one's body up to catch one's breath. By breaking the legs of those who had been crucified, the soldiers hastened their death for they could not push up to breathe.

When they came to Jesus, he was already dead. Therefore, they did not break his legs.

This fulfilled the Paschal lamb symbolism, that none of the lamb's bones were to be broken.

It also fulfilled matrimonial symbolism. God created Adam's wife Eve by placing Adam in a deep sleep and taking a rib from his side. God created the second Adam's (Jesus') wife, the Church, by allowing Jesus to descend into a deep sleep (death) and opening his side (the pierced side), which gave forth blood and water (the symbols for the Eucharist and Baptism).

The burial is problematic. The Synoptics speak of the women going to the tomb on Easter morning to anoint the body because there had been no time to do so on Good Friday. The myrrh and aloes, therefore, must be symbolic to show that they buried the body of Jesus with great care and love.

Jesus said, "I thirst."
There was a vessel filled with common wine.
So they put a sponge soaked in wine on a sprig of hyssop
and put it up to his mouth.
When Jesus had taken the wine, he said,
"It is finished."
And bowing his head, he handed over the spirit.

Here all kneel and pause for a short time.

Now since it was preparation day,
in order that the bodies might not remain on the cross on the sabbath,
for the sabbath day of that week was a solemn one,
the Jews asked Pilate that their legs be broken
and that they be taken down.
So the soldiers came and broke the legs of the first
and then of the other one who was crucified with Jesus.
But when they came to Jesus and saw that he was already dead,
they did not break his legs,
but one soldier thrust his lance into his side,
and immediately blood and water flowed out.
An eyewitness has testified, and his testimony is true;
he knows that he is speaking the truth,
so that you also may come to believe.
For this happened so that the Scripture passage might be fulfilled:
Not a bone of it will be broken.
And again another passage says:
They will look upon him whom they have pierced.

After this, Joseph of Arimathea,
secretly a disciple of Jesus for fear of the Jews,
asked Pilate if he could remove the body of Jesus.
And Pilate permitted it.

This is the only gospel where we see Nicodemus assisting Joseph of Arimathea. Nicodemus appears three times in this gospel. The first time is when he comes to Jesus by night (for he was afraid). The second time is when it is suggested in the Sanhedrin that Jesus be put to death. Nicodemus objects that this is not the proper legal procedure. Notice that he is not defending Jesus as much as the law.

This is the third time we see Nicodemus. Here he courageously assists in the burial of Jesus, a convicted criminal according to Roman law. He risks his life to render this sign of respect toward Jesus. These three appearances show a growth in his faith from fear to lukewarm commitment to the point where he is willing to die for Jesus.

So he came and took his body.

Nicodemus, the one who had first come to him at night,

and also came bringing a mixture of myrrh and aloes weighing about one hundred pounds.

They took the body of Jesus

and bound it with burial cloths along with the spices,

according to the Jewish burial custom.

Now in the place where he had been crucified there was a garden,

and in the garden a new tomb, in which no one had yet been buried.

So they laid Jesus there because of the Jewish preparation day;

for the tomb was close by.

The Gospel of the Lord.

March 30, 2002

THE EASTER VIGIL

Lect. No. 41

FIRST READING:

A Longer Form: Genesis 1:1—2:2

God looked at everything he had made, and he found it very good.

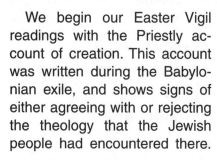

We begin our Easter Vigil readings with the Priestly account of creation. This account was written during the Babylonian exile, and shows signs of either agreeing with or rejecting the theology that the Jewish people had encountered there.

By using the phrases, "In the beginning" and "create," the author is speaking about creation *ex nihilo*, the fact that God created everything that exists from nothing.

The first thing that God creates is light. Ancient people believed that light was the most ethereal of all the things that existed, so it was the first thing created. One should not ask where the light came from (the sun and moon and stars are not created until the fourth day). God is the ultimate source of light.

God creates through the word. He speaks and all is made. This creation story, in fact, has God speaking ten times. The law of God was very important to the authors who wrote this account, and so God is seen as creating with the ten words (Decalogue, another phrase used for the ten commandments). God also names all the things that he creates, thus showing that he has dominion over them all.

A reading from the Book of Genesis

In the beginning, when God created the heavens and the earth,
the earth was a formless wasteland, and darkness covered the abyss,
while a mighty wind swept over the waters.

Then God said,
"Let there be light," and there was light.
God saw how good the light was.
God then separated the light from the darkness.
God called the light "day," and the darkness he called "night."
Thus evening came, and morning followed—the first day.

Then God said,
"Let there be a dome in the middle of the waters,
to separate one body of water from the other."
And so it happened:
God made the dome,
and it separated the water above the dome from the water below it.
God called the dome "the sky."
Evening came, and morning followed—the second day.

Then God said,
"Let the water under the sky be gathered into a single basin,
so that the dry land may appear."

God not only creates, he also separates. He separates the light from darkness, water from dry land, etc. God places order in our universe and gives it certain laws that it must obey. This is the source for the idea of the "laws of nature" (and also "the natural law").

The ancients pictured the sky as a type of bowl that protected the world from the flood of waters over it. Thus, when the great flood occurs in the day of Noah, God opens the floodgates in the heavens. This reminds us of the fragility of creation. If God withholds his care but for a minute, it would cease to exist.

On the third day God commands the earth to bring forth vegetation. This phrasing retains a bit of the idea of Mother Nature, for God uses the earth as his intermediary. Plants were not considered to be living creatures by the Jews. Things had to have breath and blood in order to be considered living creatures.

When God creates the lights in the heavens, he names neither the sun nor the moon. The reason for this is that the names for Moon and Sun in Hebrew were also names of pagan gods. In order to keep all traces of pagan beliefs out of this account, the author does not even mention the names of these heavenly bodies (lest a reader believe that Yahweh had created the moon and the sun as minor deities). They are clearly creatures created by and subject to the LORD alone.

And so it happened:
  the water under the sky was gathered into its
      basin,
  and the dry land appeared.
God called the dry land "the earth,"
  and the basin of the water he called "the sea."
God saw how good it was.
Then God said,
  "Let the earth bring forth vegetation:
  every kind of plant that bears seed
  and every kind of fruit tree on earth
  that bears fruit with its seed in it."
And so it happened:
  the earth brought forth every kind of plant that
      bears seed
  and every kind of fruit tree on earth
  that bears fruit with its seed in it.
God saw how good it was.
Evening came, and morning followed—the third
      day.

Then God said:
  "Let there be lights in the dome of the sky,
  to separate day from night.
Let them mark the fixed times, the days and the
      years,
  and serve as luminaries in the dome of the sky,
  to shed light upon the earth."
And so it happened:
  God made the two great lights,
  the greater one to govern the day,
  and the lesser one to govern the night;
  and he made the stars.
God set them in the dome of the sky,
  to shed light upon the earth,
  to govern the day and the night,
  and to separate the light from the darkness.
God saw how good it was.

Note that evening precedes the morning throughout the account. Jewish people believe the day begins with sunset (specifically, when one can look into the sky and see three stars at the same glance).

On the fifth day God creates fish, sea creatures, and birds. These creatures are at the edge of the world in which we exist. Those creatures closer to us were created the sixth day. Note that the author uses the word "create" on the fifth day. This is the second use of this phrase, for on the first day God created things that were not living, and he was now creating living creatures.

God even created the sea creatures. This is a reference to Leviathan and Rahab, the primordial sea creatures. Pagans believed them to be gods. This author states clearly that they were created by the Lord God. One of the psalms even speaks of how God created them so that he could play with them, as if they were a child's playthings.

The rabbis speculated on when God created the angels. They had two possible answers. Some said that God created the angels on the second day for that is when he created the heavens. Others said that he created the angels on the fifth day, for that is when he created winged creatures.

Throughout the account we continue to hear how good creation was. God created this world to be good. Evil entered through sin, not because it had been created that way.

Evening came, and morning followed—the fourth day.

Then God said,
"Let the water teem with an abundance of living creatures,
and on the earth let birds fly beneath the dome of the sky."
And so it happened:
God created the great sea monsters
and all kinds of swimming creatures with which the water teems,
and all kinds of winged birds.
God saw how good it was, and God blessed them, saying,
"Be fertile, multiply, and fill the water of the seas;
and let the birds multiply on the earth."
Evening came, and morning followed—the fifth day.

Then God said,
"Let the earth bring forth all kinds of living creatures:
cattle, creeping things, and wild animals of all kinds."
And so it happened:
God made all kinds of wild animals, all kinds of cattle,
and all kinds of creeping things of the earth.
God saw how good it was.

Then God said:
"Let us make man in our image, after our likeness.
Let them have dominion over the fish of the sea,
the birds of the air, and the cattle,
and over all the wild animals
and all the creatures that crawl on the ground."

The creation of the human race involves a special intervention on God's part (notice the three uses of the word "create"). Humanity is created as both male and female, implying that we are not complete without each other.

We are created in God's likeness and image. This means that we have been given dominion over all that was created. We have been made God's viceroys and representatives upon the earth. This does not mean that we should be arrogant and misuse creation.

Psalm 8 explains that dominion is treating the world in the same way as a small babe who sings the glory of God's creation. Dominion means to celebrate creation, not abuse it.

All that was created is placed at our disposition. This is how greatly God esteems us.

On the seventh day God rests and consecrates the Sabbath. The weekly day of rest is not another commandment that we must obey, but rather a time when we can imitate God himself. As Jesus said, the Sabbath was created for us, for it gives us a chance to rest, meditate on life and praise God for all his goodness.

God created man in his image;
    in the image of God he created him;
    male and female he created them.
God blessed them, saying:
    "Be fertile and multiply;
    fill the earth and subdue it.
Have dominion over the fish of the sea, the birds of
        the air,
    and all the living things that move on the earth."
God also said:
    "See, I give you every seed–bearing plant all over
        the earth
    and every tree that has seed–bearing fruit on it to
        be your food;
    and to all the animals of the land, all the birds of
        the air,
    and all the living creatures that crawl on the
        ground,
    I give all the green plants for food."
And so it happened.
God looked at everything he had made, and he
        found it very good.
Evening came, and morning followed—the sixth
        day.

Thus the heavens and the earth and all their array
        were completed.
Since on the seventh day God was finished
    with the work he had been doing,
    he rested on the seventh day from all the work he
        had undertaken.

The word of the Lord.

Lect.
No. 41

FIRST READING: **B** Shorter Form: Genesis 1:1, 26-31a

God looked at everything he had made, and he found it very good.

We begin our Easter Vigil readings with the Priestly account of creation. By using the phrases, "In the beginning" and "create," the author is speaking about creation *ex nihilo*, the fact that God created everything that exists from nothing.

The creation of the human race involves a special intervention on God's part (notice the three uses of the word "create"). Humanity is created as both male and female, implying that we are not complete without each other.

We are created in God's likeness and image. This means that we have been given dominion over all that was created.

We have been made God's viceroys and representatives upon the earth. This does not mean that we should be arrogant and misuse creation.

Psalm 8 explains that dominion is treating the world in the same way as a small babe who sings the glory of God's creation. Dominion means to celebrate creation, not abuse it.

All that was created is placed at our disposition. This is how greatly God esteems us.

A reading from the Book of Genesis

In the beginning, when God created the heavens and the earth,
God said: "Let us make man in our image, after our likeness.
Let them have dominion over the fish of the sea,
the birds of the air, and the cattle,
and over all the wild animals
and all the creatures that crawl on the ground."
God created man in his image;
in the image of God he created him;
male and female he created them.
God blessed them, saying:
"Be fertile and multiply;
fill the earth and subdue it.
Have dominion over the fish of the sea, the birds of the air,
and all the living things that move on the earth."
God also said:
"See, I give you every seed–bearing plant all over the earth
and every tree that has seed–bearing fruit on it to be your food;
and to all the animals of the land, all the birds of the air,
and all the living creatures that crawl on the ground,
I give all the green plants for food."
And so it happened.
God looked at everything he had made, and he found it very good.

The word of the Lord.

Lect. No. 41 **RESPONSORIAL PSALM:** 🅰 **Ps 104:1-2, 5-6, 10, 12, 13-14, 24, 35 (℟.: 30)**

Psalm 104 is a hymn of thanksgiving to praise the Lord as the God of creation.

The response requests that God send forth his Spirit and renew the face of the earth. This is a recognition that God created everything that exists through his Spirit.

The word for Spirit in Hebrew is the same word as breath and wind. God spoke, sent forth the breath of his mouth, and all was created.

On Easter, we celebrate the first creation and also the new creation that occurred with the death and resurrection of Jesus and the descent of the Holy Spirit upon the earth.

In this hymn we see both the power of the Lord (for he can command the earth and waters to occupy a place from which they will not move) and also God's loving concern (for he waters the earth, gives vegetation for the needs of its animals, etc.)

Just by looking at the world and all that it contains, the psalmist is led to glorify the God of creation. One cannot look at a bird or flower and not realize that it was created by a loving God. One cannot look into a microscope or a telescope and not realize that God is great. This all fills us with awe.

℟. **Lord, send out your Spirit, and renew the face of the earth.**

Bless the Lord, O my soul!
 O Lord, my God, you are great indeed!
You are clothed with majesty and glory,
 robed in light as with a cloak.

℟. **Lord, send out your Spirit, and renew the face of the earth.**

You fixed the earth upon its foundation,
 not to be moved forever;
with the ocean, as with a garment, you covered it;
 above the mountains the waters stood.

℟. **Lord, send out your Spirit, and renew the face of the earth.**

You send forth springs into the watercourses
 that wind among the mountains.
Beside them the birds of heaven dwell;
 from among the branches they send forth their song.

℟. **Lord, send out your Spirit, and renew the face of the earth.**

You water the mountains from your palace;
 the earth is replete with the fruit of your works.
You raise grass for the cattle,
 and vegetation for man's use,
producing bread from the earth.

℟. **Lord, send out your Spirit, and renew the face of the earth.**

How manifold are your works, O Lord!
 In wisdom you have wrought them all—
the earth is full of your creatures.
 Bless the Lord, O my soul!

℟. **Lord, send out your Spirit, and renew the face of the earth.**

Lect. No. 41

RESPONSORIAL PSALM: **B** Ps 33:4-5, 6-7, 12-13, 20, 22 (℟.: 5b)

Psalm 33 is both a hymn to praise the God of creation and a hymn of trust in the goodness of the Lord.

God's word created the world in goodness. He continuously pronounced all that he created to be good. His word is trustworthy. His law manifests his justice and righteousness, for the law is an expression of his divine will. It is his word revealed to us on Mount Sinai.

Blessed, indeed, is the nation that has such a just and merciful God. This is a God who made all things, and yet God cares about us and protects us.

We might sometimes wonder if God could really be concerned with us. We wonder if God knows what is happening to us or cares. This psalm celebrates the fact that God, who created all things, will still respond to our every need. We truly can place our hope in him.

℟. **The earth is full of the goodness of the Lord.**

Upright is the word of the LORD,
　and all his works are trustworthy.
He loves justice and right;
　of the kindness of the LORD the earth is full.

℟. **The earth is full of the goodness of the Lord.**

By the word of the LORD the heavens were made;
　by the breath of his mouth all their host.
He gathers the waters of the sea as in a flask;
　in cellars he confines the deep.

℟. **The earth is full of the goodness of the Lord.**

Blessed the nation whose God is the LORD,
　the people he has chosen for his own inheritance.
From heaven the LORD looks down;
　he sees all mankind.

℟. **The earth is full of the goodness of the Lord.**

Our soul waits for the LORD,
　who is our help and our shield.
May your kindness, O LORD, be upon us
　who have put our hope in you.

℟. **The earth is full of the goodness of the Lord.**

Lect. No. 41

SECOND READING: **A** Longer Form: Genesis 22:1-18

The sacrifice of Abraham, our father in faith.

The Second Reading this evening is the story of the sacrifice of Isaac (this is also called the binding of Isaac in Jewish tradition). It is an esteemed story in both the Jewish and the Christian tradition.

A reading from the Book of Genesis

God put Abraham to the test.
　He called to him, "Abraham!"
"Here I am," he replied.
Then God said:

God calls Abraham and asks him to sacrifice his only son to the Lord. There is tremendous irony in this request, for Abraham had had another son, Ishmael. Ishmael tried to harm Isaac, and Ishmael was sent away into the desert to die. Furthermore, God asks for the son "whom you love." God knew exactly how great this sacrifice would be for Abraham.

He is also asking for a tremendous act of trust, for the boy Isaac was the only visible sign of God's fulfillment of his promise. Even though God had promised a great land and a descendance as numerous as the sand on the shore of the sea and the stars in the sky, Abraham nevertheless did not yet have any land and only one son (for as far as Abraham knew, his other son Ishmael was dead or at least as good as dead to Abraham).

But Abraham proves his obedience to the will of the Lord by taking his son to Mount Moriah where he fully intends to sacrifice him. The journey is made pathetic by the fact that Abraham carries the knife and fire on the journey up the mountain while his son carries the wood. Abraham is carrying those objects that might harm the boy.

Then it is even worse when the son asks where the sacrifice is, and Abraham responds that the Lord will provide. Abraham is saying this thinking of the son that the Lord had already provided, but the Lord would give these words new meaning.

"Take your son Isaac, your only one, whom you
  love,
  and go to the land of Moriah.
There you shall offer him up as a holocaust
  on a height that I will point out to you."
Early the next morning Abraham saddled his donkey,
  took with him his son Isaac and two of his servants as well,
  and with the wood that he had cut for the holocaust,
  set out for the place of which God had told him.
On the third day Abraham got sight of the place from afar.
Then he said to his servants:
  "Both of you stay here with the donkey,
  while the boy and I go on over yonder.
We will worship and then come back to you."
Thereupon Abraham took the wood for the holocaust
  and laid it on his son Isaac's shoulders,
  while he himself carried the fire and the knife.
As the two walked on together, Isaac spoke to his father Abraham:
  "Father!" Isaac said.
"Yes, son," he replied.
Isaac continued, "Here are the fire and the wood,
  but where is the sheep for the holocaust?"
"Son," Abraham answered,
  "God himself will provide the sheep for the holocaust."
Then the two continued going forward.
When they came to the place of which God had told him,
  Abraham built an altar there and arranged the wood on it.
Next he tied up his son Isaac,
  and put him on top of the wood on the altar.

When the LORD saw that Abraham was totally obedient, he halted the sacrifice. What Abraham had said about the LORD providing was fulfilled when Abraham saw a ram caught in the thicket and sacrificed that animal in place of his son.

Some scholars say that this was originally a story of how the Israelite people rejected human sacrifices. That might even be true, but the form of the story contained in Genesis is clearly a story about the demands of faith. One must be willing to die to oneself and sacrifice everytrhing in order to follow God's will.

This event is a prefiguring of what happened with Jesus on the cross. We had sinned and deserved to be punished. We were to be the holocaust, but God sent a substitute in our place: Jesus, his only beloved Son. Thus, he saved his beloved children through the death of his only Son.

Why did God test Abraham in this manner? Certainly he knew Abraham's faith. Is it possible that this test was for Abraham's benefit, so that he could learn the depths of his trust? This is true in our own faith lives, for we often learn what trust means in times of crisis and suffering.

The account closes with a reaffirmation of God's covenantial promises to Abraham. Until the day he died Abraham would have to continue to trust, for his immediate descendance was not very numerous nor did he possess much land (for he only owned his burial cave).

Then he reached out and took the knife to slaughter his son.
But the LORD's messenger called to him from heaven,
    "Abraham, Abraham!"
"Here I am," he answered.
"Do not lay your hand on the boy," said the messenger.
"Do not do the least thing to him.
I know now how devoted you are to God,
    since you did not withhold from me your own beloved son."
As Abraham looked about,
    he spied a ram caught by its horns in the thicket.
So he went and took the ram
    and offered it up as a holocaust in place of his son.
Abraham named the site Yahweh–yireh;
    hence people now say, "On the mountain the LORD will see."

Again the LORD's messenger called to Abraham from heaven and said:
    "I swear by myself, declares the LORD,
    that because you acted as you did
    in not withholding from me your beloved son,
    I will bless you abundantly
    and make your descendants as countless
    as the stars of the sky and the sands of the seashore;
    your descendants shall take possession
    of the gates of their enemies,
    and in your descendants all the nations of the earth shall find blessing—
    all this because you obeyed my command."

The word of the Lord.

Lect. No. 41 **SECOND READING:** **B** **Shorter Form: Genesis 22:1-2. 9a, 10-13, 15-18**

The sacrifice of Abraham our father in faith.

God calls Abraham and asks him to sacrifice his only son to the Lord. He is asking for the son "whom you love." God knew exactly how great this sacrifice would be for Abraham.

He is also asking for a tremendous act of trust, for the boy Isaac was the only visible sign of God's fulfillment of his promise. Even though God had promised a great land and a descendance as numerous as the sand on the shore of the sea and the stars in the sky, Abraham nevertheless did not yet have any land and only one son (for as far as Abraham knew, his other son Ishmael was dead or at least as good as dead to Abraham).

But Abraham proves his obedience to the will of the Lord by taking his son to Mount Moriah where he fully intends to sacrifice him.

When the Lord saw that Abraham was totally obedient, he halted the sacrifice. What Abraham had said about the Lord providing was fulfilled when Abraham saw a ram caught in the thicket and sacrificed that animal in place of his son.

This story is clearly about the demands of faith. One must be willing to die to self and sacrifice everything in order to follow God's will.

A reading from the Book of Genesis

God put Abraham to the test.
He called to him, "Abraham!"
"Here I am," he replied.
Then God said:
"Take your son Isaac, your only one, whom you love,
and go to the land of Moriah.
There you shall offer him up as a holocaust
on a height that I will point out to you."

When they came to the place of which God had told him,
Abraham built an altar there and arranged the wood on it.
Then he reached out and took the knife to slaughter his son.
But the Lord's messenger called to him from heaven,
"Abraham, Abraham!"
"Here I am," he answered.
"Do not lay your hand on the boy," said the messenger.
"Do not do the least thing to him.
I know now how devoted you are to God,
since you did not withhold from me your own beloved son."
As Abraham looked about,
he spied a ram caught by its horns in the thicket.
So he went and took the ram
and offered it up as a holocaust in place of his son.

Again the Lord's messenger called to Abraham from heaven and said:

This event is a prefiguring of what happened with Jesus on the cross. We had sinned and deserved to be punished. We were to be the holocaust, but God sent a substitute in our place: Jesus, his only beloved Son. Thus, he saved his beloved children through the death of his only Son.

Why did God test Abraham in this manner? Certainly he knew Abraham's faith. Is it possible that this test was for Abraham's benefit, so that he could learn the depths of his trust? This is true in our own lives, for we often learn what trust means in times of crisis and suffering.

"I swear by myself, declares the Lord,
that because you acted as you did
in not withholding from me your beloved son,
I will bless you abundantly
and make your descendants as countless
as the stars of the sky and the sands of the
   seashore;
your descendants shall take possession
of the gates of their enemies,
and in your descendants all the nations of the
   earth shall find blessing—
all this because you obeyed my command."

The word of the Lord.

Lect.
No. 41

RESPONSORIAL PSALM: Ps 16:5, 8, 9-10, 11 (℞.: 1).

Psalm 16 is a powerful expression of trust in the Lord. Not only will God deliver us; God is our entire inheritance. He is our allotted portion and our cup.

This is an appropriate response to the story that we have just read. Abraham risked everything on the Lord. He believed in the Lord's promise even when there was no sign that the Lord was going to be faithful.

God was just as faithful to his own Son when he died on the cross. He did not allow his Son to undergo corruption, nor to be abandoned to the netherworld. This is also true of us, for we have become adopted children of the Lord. We are heirs to his promise and coheirs with Jesus.

℞. **You are my inheritance, O Lord.**

O Lord, my allotted portion and my cup,
   you it is who hold fast my lot.
I set the Lord ever before me;
   with him at my right hand I shall not be disturbed.

℞. **You are my inheritance, O Lord.**

Therefore my heart is glad and my soul rejoices,
   my body, too, abides in confidence;
because you will not abandon my soul to the netherworld,
   nor will you suffer your faithful one to undergo corruption.

℞. **You are my inheritance, O Lord.**

You will show me the path to life,
   fullness of joys in your presence,
   the delights at your right hand forever.

℞. **You are my inheritance, O Lord.**

Lect.
No. 41

THIRD READING: Exodus 14:15—15:1

The Israelites marched on dry land through the midst of the sea.

Our Third Reading tells us of the exodus of the Israelites from slavery in Egypt to freedom in the promised land.

Although the Pharaoh had promised to let the Israelites go free, he repented his decision and followed them with all of his troops. He intended to cut them off and kill them.

The LORD ordered Moses to hold his staff over the waters of the Reed Sea The waters split, and the Israelites were able to pass through the sea without harm.

Various explanations have been given in recent years to interpret what happened. Some have spoken of earthquakes, volcanic explosions, El Niño, etc. God often works through natural means to further his plan. Whatever, the Israelites and we have one explanation for what happened: God delivered his chosen people from certain destruction at the hands of Pharaoh and his soldiers.

We could also speak about the soldiers. God did not want the Israelites to go by way of the Philistines lest they become afraid and return to Egypt. God knew that the people of Israel were not yet courageous. Maybe they even needed the soldiers at their backs to force them across the sea lest they

A reading from the Book of Exodus

The LORD said to Moses, "Why are you crying out to me?
Tell the Israelites to go forward.
And you, lift up your staff and, with hand outstretched over the sea,
  split the sea in two,
  that the Israelites may pass through it on dry land.
But I will make the Egyptians so obstinate
  that they will go in after them.
Then I will receive glory through Pharaoh and all his army,
  his chariots and charioteers.
The Egyptians shall know that I am the LORD,
  when I receive glory through Pharaoh
  and his chariots and charioteers."

The angel of God, who had been leading Israel's camp,
  now moved and went around behind them.
The column of cloud also, leaving the front,
  took up its place behind them,
  so that it came between the camp of the Egyptians
  and that of Israel.
But the cloud now became dark, and thus the night passed
  without the rival camps coming any closer together all night long.
Then Moses stretched out his hand over the sea,
  and the LORD swept the sea
  with a strong east wind throughout the night
  and so turned it into dry land.

turn back out of fear. This has often been used as a symbol of the fact that God often allows us to feel the consequences of our sins in order to push us across the sea from slavery to sin into the freedom of God's children.

We become bogged down in our sinful habits, and it often looks more comfortable to stay in our sins than to convert from them. The sins have become familiar (even if they are a form of slavery), while conversion is the unknown (like marching off into the desert).

God brings us to the point where staying in our sins grows so uncomfortable that we finally have the courage to leave them and wander into the unknown. We have to recognize for ourselves how much our sins are hurting us before we can reject them and choose the freedom of the children of God.

The Egyptians followed the Israelites but their heavy chariots became clogged down in the mud of the recently dried sea bottom. Thus, when Moses stretched his hands out over the sea again and the waters flowed back, they could not extricate themselves and they drowned. The defeat was total, for one cannot fight against the LORD.

The Israelites, who had by now reached dry land, were filled with a sense of awe and wonder. They realized that they owed their entire victory to the LORD. The only thing they could do was to thank and praise the LORD.

When the water was thus divided,
the Israelites marched into the midst of the sea on dry land,
with the water like a wall to their right and to their left.

The Egyptians followed in pursuit;
all Pharaoh's horses and chariots and charioteers went after them
right into the midst of the sea.
In the night watch just before dawn
the LORD cast through the column of the fiery cloud
upon the Egyptian force a glance that threw it into a panic;
and he so clogged their chariot wheels
that they could hardly drive.
With that the Egyptians sounded the retreat before Israel,
because the LORD was fighting for them against the Egyptians.

Then the LORD told Moses, "Stretch out your hand over the sea,
that the water may flow back upon the Egyptians,
upon their chariots and their charioteers."
So Moses stretched out his hand over the sea,
and at dawn the sea flowed back to its normal depth.
The Egyptians were fleeing head on toward the sea,
when the LORD hurled them into its midst.
As the water flowed back,
it covered the chariots and the charioteers of Pharaoh's whole army
which had followed the Israelites into the sea.
Not a single one of them escaped.
But the Israelites had marched on dry land
through the midst of the sea,
with the water like a wall to their right and to their left.

The Israelites sang a great victory song to celebrate their wondrous deliverance. Their song, which is called the Song of Miriam, is one of the oldest parts of the Old Testament to have been written. It is probably one of the earliest parts of the Bible.

By studying the language of the hymn, scholars have determined that it dates back to at least the 11th century B.C. In other words, the hymn now found in the Book of Exodus might be the actual hymn that the Israelites sang on that glorious day.

Thus the LORD saved Israel on that day
    from the power of the Egyptians.
When Israel saw the Egyptians lying dead on the seashore
    and beheld the great power that the LORD
    had shown against the Egyptians,
    they feared the LORD and believed in him and in his servant Moses.

Then Moses and the Israelites sang this song to the LORD:
    I will sing to the LORD, for he is gloriously triumphant;
    horse and chariot he has cast into the sea.

The word of the Lord.

Lect. No. 41 **RESPONSORIAL PSALM: Exodus 15:1-2, 3-4, 5-6, 17-18 (℟.: 1b)**

As we have just seen, this might be one of the oldest hymns of the Bible. It was sung in celebration of the victory that God had given to the Israelite people at the Reed Sea.

One of the important aspects of the hymn is the pattern of parallelism that occurs throughout the hymn. The author repeats the same idea over and over again using slightly different words each time.

In this hymn the LORD is lauded as being a great warrior. He defeated both the forces of Pharaoh and also the forces of the sea.

In the Old Testament, the sea was often thought of as being opposed to the will of God. It was where the great sea monster Leviathan lives. If God can

℟. **Let us sing to the Lord; he has covered himself in glory.**

I will sing to the LORD, for he is gloriously triumphant;
    horse and chariot he has cast into the sea.
My strength and my courage is the LORD,
    and he has been my savior.
He is my God, I praise him;
    the God of my father, I extol him.

℟. **Let us sing to the Lord; he has covered himself in glory.**

The LORD is a warrior,
    LORD is his name!
Pharaoh's chariots and army he hurled into the sea;
    the elite of his officers were submerged in the Red Sea.

℟. **Let us sing to the Lord; he has covered himself in glory.**

use it to further his plans, then he is truly LORD of earth and sea.

God not only redeemed the Israelites, he also brought them into the promised land and planted them on the mountain of his inheritance.

This part of the hymn might have been written after the rest if it refers to Mount Zion. (This was the place where Solomon built his temple in Jerusalem.) It could, however, be an ancient Hebrew expression (for the people of this area conceived of God as living on a great mountain).

Lect. No. 41

The flood waters covered them,
    they sank into the depths like a stone.
Your right hand, O LORD, magnificent in power,
    your right hand, O LORD, has shattered the enemy.

℟. **Let us sing to the Lord; he has covered himself in glory.**

You brought in the people you redeemed
    and planted them on the mountain of your inheritance—
the place where you made your seat, O LORD,
    the sanctuary, LORD, which your hands established.
The LORD shall reign forever and ever.

℟. **Let us sing to the Lord; he has covered himself in glory.**

FOURTH READING: Isaiah 54:5-14

With enduring love, the Lord your redeemer takes pity on you.

This reading comes from the Book of the Prophet Isaiah, from the section of the Book written by Second Isaiah. It was composed during the exile in Babylon, and it is a promise of consolation for a people who had been sorely tried by their suffering.

When Israel had been defeated by the Babylonians, they wondered why the LORD had allowed them to lose to their enemies. They wondered whether Yahweh might be less powerful than Marduk, the national god of the Babylonians. Or else, might Yahweh be angry with them and have rejected them? Was he still angry at them? Would he ever forgive them?

A reading from the Book of the Prophet Isaiah

The One who has become your husband is your Maker;
    his name is the LORD of hosts;
your redeemer is the Holy One of Israel,
    called God of all the earth.
The LORD calls you back,
    like a wife forsaken and grieved in spirit,
    a wife married in youth and then cast off,
    says your God.
For a brief moment I abandoned you,
    but with great tenderness I will take you back.
In an outburst of wrath, for a moment
    I hid my face from you;
but with enduring love I take pity on you,
    says the LORD, your redeemer.

This reading speaks of the commitment that God had made toward them. He was their maker, their spouse. He might have been angry at them for a while, but they were now forgiven. The LORD speaks of his anger as being something that was momentary, forever to be forgotten.

Even though nature itself would be shaken, even though mountains and hills were brought low, God's love for Israel would never be in question. God would rebuild their cities with great splendor. He himself would redeem them and deliver them from the hands of their enemies.

The LORD would also instruct his people so that they would know his will and never again fall from his favor. They would live in justice and peace forever.

This is for me like the days of Noah,
  when I swore that the waters of Noah
  should never again deluge the earth;
so I have sworn not to be angry with you,
  or to rebuke you.
Though the mountains leave their place
  and the hills be shaken,
my love shall never leave you
  nor my covenant of peace be shaken,
  says the LORD, who has mercy on you.
O afflicted one, storm–battered and unconsoled,
  I lay your pavements in carnelians,
  and your foundations in sapphires;
I will make your battlements of rubies,
  your gates of carbuncles,
  and all your walls of precious stones.
All your children shall be taught by the LORD,
  and great shall be the peace of your children.
In justice shall you be established,
  far from the fear of oppression,
  where destruction cannot come near you.

The word of the Lord.

Lect. No. 41 **RESPONSORIAL PSALM: Ps 30:2, 4, 5-6, 11-12, 13 (℞.: 2a)**

Psalm 30 is a thanksgiving for a deliverance. The psalmist was at the point of death and was sure that he had fallen into the hands of his enemies.

The LORD intervened in a miraculous manner and saved him from all of his enemies' plots. The LORD is truly merciful and generous. Even when he becomes angry at people for their sins, his anger lasts but a moment.

℞. **I will praise you, Lord, for you have rescued me.**

I will extol you, O LORD, for you drew me clear
  and did not let my enemies rejoice over me.
O LORD, you brought me up from the netherworld;
  you preserved me from among those going down
    into the pit.

℞. **I will praise you, Lord, for you have rescued me.**

Sing praise to the LORD, you his faithful ones,
  and give thanks to his holy name.

We can ask how to apply this psalm to our Christian lives. It is obvious that we are reading this psalm at the Easter Vigil because we are celebrating Jesus' defeat over our worst enemies: sin, alienation, death, etc.

Our other enemies, people who hurt us, are no longer to be hated because we are a gospel people. We do not hate them in order to destroy them; we love them so that we might heal their brokenness.

For his anger lasts but a moment;
　　a lifetime, his good will.
At nightfall, weeping enters in,
　　but with the dawn, rejoicing.

℟. **I will praise you, Lord, for you have rescued me.**

Hear, O LORD, and have pity on me;
　　O LORD, be my helper.
You changed my mourning into dancing;
　　O LORD, my God, forever will I give you thanks.

℟. **I will praise you, Lord, for you have rescued me.**

Lect.
No. 41

FIFTH READING: Isaiah 55:1-11

Come to me that you may have life.
I will renew with you an everlasting covenant.

The Fifth Reading is another passage from the Book of the Prophet Isaiah, from the writings of Second Isaiah.

The central theme of this prophet is consolation. It is in fact found in the first words of his prophecy (Isaiah 40:1).

This consolation is not something to be earned. God has already paid the price. We should not seek after other sources of comfort for the pain in our hearts. God alone can provide that love and that healing which will bring us true peace.

This healing is so powerful that peoples will seek it from afar. If we give witness to the peace we have found in God, people will seek to find the same peace in their own lives. Even if we never mention the name of the LORD, they will

A reading from the Book of the Prophet Isaiah

Thus says the LORD:
　　All you who are thirsty,
　　come to the water!
You who have no money,
　　come, receive grain and eat;
come, without paying and without cost,
　　drink wine and milk!
Why spend your money for what is not bread,
　　your wages for what fails to satisfy?
Heed me, and you shall eat well,
　　you shall delight in rich fare.
Come to me heedfully,
　　listen, that you may have life.
I will renew with you the everlasting covenant,
　　the benefits assured to David.
As I made him a witness to the peoples,
　　a leader and commander of nations,
so shall you summon a nation you knew not,
　　and nations that knew you not shall run to you,

see that there is something different about us and they will ask to share in the gift that we have received.

Now is the time to seek God. It is time to abandon all foolishness and sinfulness. We must admit our fundamental need of the mercy of God and seek him with all our strength. This is not a time for compromise or hesitation. We must make a leap of faith and place our trust in God.

This leap of faith means adopting a different way of viewing reality. We must look at things through the eyes of God. This means learning the wisdom of God and living by its precepts.

The word of God has been showered down upon the earth and into our hearts. We must allow it to take root and become fertile. God's word is effective (remember how the world was created through God's word), but God also gives us freedom. God will not force himself upon us: we must choose to make our hearts a home for his word.

because of the LORD, your God,
the Holy One of Israel, who has glorified you.

Seek the LORD while he may be found,
call him while he is near.
Let the scoundrel forsake his way,
and the wicked man his thoughts;
let him turn to the LORD for mercy;
to our God, who is generous in forgiving.
For my thoughts are not your thoughts,
nor are your ways my ways, says the LORD.
As high as the heavens are above the earth,
so high are my ways above your ways
and my thoughts above your thoughts.

For just as from the heavens
the rain and snow come down
and do not return there
till they have watered the earth,
making it fertile and fruitful,
giving seed to the one who sows
and bread to the one who eats,
so shall my word be
that goes forth from my mouth;
my word shall not return to me void,
but shall do my will,
achieving the end for which I sent it.

The word of the Lord.

Lect.
No. 41

RESPONSORIAL PSALM: Isaiah 12:2-3, 4, 5-6 (℟.: 3)

This Responsorial Psalm is not even a psalm; it is a hymn found in the first part of the Book of the Prophet Isaiah.

It celebrates the actions of the LORD who is Israel's savior. When this hymn was written, it especially meant that God would save Israel from their earthly enemies. But, as we

℟. **You will draw water joyfully from the springs of salvation.**

God indeed is my savior;
I am confident and unafraid.
My strength and my courage is the LORD,
and he has been my savior.
With joy you will draw water
at the fountain of salvation.

have seen in the previous read-ings, we must spiritualize this hymn and speak of how God saves us from the worst of our enemies: sin, fear, alienation, death, etc.

We must proclaim God as our deliverer. We must praise God with great gratitude. We must recognize how God has showered his blessing upon us and give thanks.

This itself is a great witness, for when people hear us speak-ing about how God has blessed us in so many ways, they will begin to see God working in their own lives.

℟. **You will draw water joyfully from the springs of salvation.**

Give thanks to the LORD, acclaim his name;
    among the nations make known his deeds,
    proclaim how exalted is his name.

℟. **You will draw water joyfully from the springs of salvation.**

Sing praise to the LORD for his glorious achieve-ment;
    let this be known throughout all the earth.
Shout with exultation, O city of Zion,
    for great in your midst
    is the Holy One of Israel!

℟. **You will draw water joyfully from the springs of salvation.**

Lect. No. 41

SIXTH READING: Baruch 3:9-15, 32—4:4

Walk toward the splendor of the Lord.

This Sixth Reading has been attributed to Baruch, the secre-tary of Jeremiah the Prophet. The book is actually a collection of various fragments that have been assembled together. It is not clear if it was actually writ-ten by Baruch.

This particular section speaks about wisdom and the law. Wisdom was considered to be the revelation of the will of God. We could not possibly know what God wanted if he had not revealed it to us.

The fullest expression of this revelation, according to this reading, is the law. God has not left us in the darkness like

A reading from the Book of the Prophet Baruch

Hear, O Israel, the commandments of life:
    listen, and know prudence!
How is it, Israel,
    that you are in the land of your foes,
    grown old in a foreign land,
defiled with the dead,
    accounted with those destined for the nether-world?
You have forsaken the fountain of wisdom!
    Had you walked in the way of God,
    you would have dwelt in enduring peace.
Learn where prudence is,
    where strength, where understanding;
that you may know also
    where are length of days, and life,
    where light of the eyes, and peace.

other peoples. They did not know how to please the LORD. God has revealed exactly what is pleasing in his sight through the law.

That is why we should reexamine our ways and observe the law with all our heart. If we live the law, then we will find true joy. Our lives will be filled with meaning. If we do not follow it, then we will find that we have abandoned the will of God and we will not find peace.

This wisdom, the law of the LORD, is already ingrained in creation. We saw this in the First Reading that we heard this evening, when we saw how God created with ten words (the Decalogue).

These ten words, the ten commandments, are the foundation and blueprint of creation. If we observe nature, we should be able to see the order that exists in it and we should be able to learn what God wants of us.

As Christians, our law is the law of love seen in the gospels. We do not observe precepts for the sake of consistency, but rather as a response to God's revelation of love for us. Only by living God's law can our heart be receptive to the love of God.

Who has found the place of wisdom,
  who has entered into her treasuries?

The One who knows all things knows her;
  he has probed her by his knowledge—
the One who established the earth for all time,
  and filled it with four–footed beasts;
he who dismisses the light, and it departs,
  calls it, and it obeys him trembling;
before whom the stars at their posts
  shine and rejoice;
when he calls them, they answer, "Here we are!"
  shining with joy for their Maker.
Such is our God;
  no other is to be compared to him:
he has traced out the whole way of understanding,
  and has given her to Jacob, his servant,
  to Israel, his beloved son.

Since then she has appeared on earth,
  and moved among people.
She is the book of the precepts of God,
  the law that endures forever;
all who cling to her will live,
  but those will die who forsake her.
Turn, O Jacob, and receive her:
  walk by her light toward splendor.
Give not your glory to another,
  your privileges to an alien race.
Blessed are we, O Israel;
  for what pleases God is known to us!

The word of the Lord.

Lect.
No. 41
RESPONSORIAL PSALM: Ps 19:8, 9, 10, 11 (℟.: John 6:68c)

Psalm 19 is a perfect response to the reading we have just heard from Baruch. The first part is a hymn to celebrate the God of creation. The second part celebrates the law, God's gift to Israel. The two parts, which superficially have little to do with each other, are actually a celebration of the fact that God created the world in and through wisdom as expressed in the law.

The part of the psalm that we are using gives a series of synonyms for the law and its goodness. It is interesting that there are only six references to the LORD in this section. That is unusual for the perfect number in the Bible is seven, and one would expect the psalmist to speak of the LORD seven times. The seventh reference to the LORD occurs at the end of the psalm where the law is "the words of my mouth and the meditation of my heart." The law is only perfect when it is interiorized.

℟. **Lord, you have the words of everlasting life.**

The law of the LORD is perfect,
  refreshing the soul;
the decree of the LORD is trustworthy,
  giving wisdom to the simple.

℟. **Lord, you have the words of everlasting life.**

The precepts of the LORD are right,
  rejoicing the heart;
the command of the LORD is clear,
  enlightening the eye.

℟. **Lord, you have the words of everlasting life.**

The fear of the LORD is pure,
  enduring forever;
the ordinances of the LORD are true,
  all of them just.

℟. **Lord, you have the words of everlasting life.**

They are more precious than gold,
  than a heap of purest gold;
sweeter also than syrup
  or honey from the comb.

℟. **Lord, you have the words of everlasting life.**

Lect.
No. 41
SEVENTH READING: Ezekiel 36:16-17a, 18-28

I shall sprinkle clean water upon you and I shall give you a new heart.

God had intended the covenant with Israel to be an eternal covenant, but the people of Israel had violated God's commandments so insolently that God allowed them to be punished for their iniquities. They deserved everything they received by being led into exile in Babylon.

A reading from the Book of the Prophet Ezekiel

The word of the LORD came to me, saying:
  Son of man, when the house of Israel lived in
    their land,
  they defiled it by their conduct and deeds.
Therefore I poured out my fury upon them
  because of the blood that they poured out on the
    ground,
  and because they defiled it with idols.

In this reading from the Book of the Prophet Ezekiel we hear that God was relenting from the punishment that he had allowed his people to suffer. Yet, this reading makes it clear that he is not relenting because they deserve his mercy.

If anything, their conduct had been worse since they were exiled. The very fact that they were led into exile had been a source of embarrassment to God for his name had been profaned among the pagans (for the pagans said that it was God's fault that his people had ended up this way).

Therefore, God would forgive his people and give them a new beginning. It could not simply be a continuation of what had been going on. It had to be a whole new start. The covenant that God had made with Israel had been degraded by Israel's sins. A new covenant was their only hope.

God would put a new heart and a new spirit within them. Henceforth they would no longer follow the law superficially; they would live it with great fervor because it had been internalized.

We must remember that the rebirth that we are celebrating this evening is not due to anything that we have done. God is showing us an astounding mercy in allowing us to be reborn in his Spirit. Tonight we should be filled with a profound sense of gratitude and awe that God has been so gracious to us.

I scattered them among the nations,
    dispersing them over foreign lands;
    according to their conduct and deeds I judged them.
But when they came among the nations wherever
        they came,
    they served to profane my holy name,
    because it was said of them: "These are the people
        of the LORD,
    yet they had to leave their land."
So I have relented because of my holy name
    which the house of Israel profaned
    among the nations where they came.
Therefore say to the house of Israel: Thus says the
        Lord GOD:
    Not for your sakes do I act, house of Israel,
    but for the sake of my holy name,
    which you profaned among the nations to which
        you came.
I will prove the holiness of my great name, profaned
        among the nations,
    in whose midst you have profaned it.
Thus the nations shall know that I am the LORD,
        says the Lord GOD,
    when in their sight I prove my holiness through
        you.
For I will take you away from among the nations,
    gather you from all the foreign lands,
    and bring you back to your own land.
I will sprinkle clean water upon you
    to cleanse you from all your impurities,
    and from all your idols I will cleanse you.
I will give you a new heart and place a new spirit
        within you,
    taking from your bodies your stony hearts
    and giving you natural hearts.
I will put my spirit within you and make you live by
        my statutes,
    careful to observe my decrees.

We celebrate the new covenant that Jesus inaugurated with his death and resurrection.

Lect.
No. 41

A

Psalms 42 and 43 were probably originally written as one lamentation psalm. Here we use selected verses from the two psalms to add to the spirit of joy and desire for the things of the LORD.

This psalm was probably written by a priest or levite. It speaks of the incredible joy that he felt when he celebrated the liturgy of the LORD. This was, for him, the greatest reward for all that he did. Its memory was all that gave him hope in times of suffering.

He even speaks of his desire for the LORD as being a thirsting, like the deer that longs for running water. We have to remember that this was written in a highly arid climate, and water was the difference between life and death.

This evening we could say that our relationship with God is the difference for us between life that is meaningful and an existence that has no ultimate meaning.

Thus, as we either make or renew our baptismal promises, we vow ourselves to life in God.

You shall live in the land I gave your fathers;
    you shall be my people, and I will be your God.

The word of the Lord.

RESPONSORIAL PSALM:

When baptism is celebrated, responsorial psalm A is used; when baptism is not celebrated, responsorial psalm B or C is used.

Ps 42:3, 5; 43:3, 4 (℟.: 42:2)

When baptism is celebrated

℟. **Like a deer that longs for running streams, my soul longs for you, my God.**

Athirst is my soul for God, the living God.
    When shall I go and behold the face of God?

℟. **Like a deer that longs for running streams, my soul longs for you, my God.**

I went with the throng
    and led them in procession to the house of God,
amid loud cries of joy and thanksgiving,
    with the multitude keeping festival.

℟. **Like a deer that longs for running streams, my soul longs for you, my God.**

Send forth your light and your fidelity;
    they shall lead me on
and bring me to your holy mountain,
    to your dwelling–place.

℟. **Like a deer that longs for running streams, my soul longs for you, my God.**

Then will I go in to the altar of God,
    the God of my gladness and joy;
then will I give you thanks upon the harp,
    O God, my God!

℟. **Like a deer that longs for running streams, my soul longs for you, my God.**

B
Isaiah 12:2-3, 4bcd, 5-6 (℟.: 3)
When baptism is not celebrated

In our readings this evening we have celebrated our creation, our call, and our rebirth in the new covenant written upon our hearts and our spirits.

These are all ways that God has shown himself to be our savior. And God continues to be our savior for he continues to protect us from our enemies.

Therefore, we proclaim his name and glory before all the nations. This is especially important considering what we have just read: that our conduct often gives scandal and betrays our commitment to the covenant.

People know that we call ourselves Christian, but all too often we fail to live as such. We have to make our words and actions powerful witnesses to God's love and mercy. We have to live with integrity and become more of what we say we are.

℟. **You will draw water joyfully from the springs of salvation.**

God indeed is my savior;
  I am confident and unafraid.
My strength and my courage is the LORD,
  and he has been my savior.
With joy you will draw water
  at the fountain of salvation.

℟. **You will draw water joyfully from the springs of salvation.**

Give thanks to the LORD, acclaim his name;
  among the nations make known his deeds,
  proclaim how exalted is his name.

℟. **You will draw water joyfully from the springs of salvation.**

Sing praise to the LORD for his glorious achievement;
  let this be known throughout all the earth.
Shout with exultation, O city of Zion,
  for great in your midst
  is the Holy One of Israel!

℟. **You will draw water joyfully from the springs of salvation.**

C
Ps 51:12-13, 14-15, 18-19 (℟.: 12a)
When baptism is not celebrated

Our last reading has spoken about the rebirth that God offers us, for he places a new heart and a new spirit within us.

This psalm is a penitential psalm that speaks of the need for this rebirth. We cannot hope to turn from sin if we do

℟. **Create a clean heart in me, O God.**

A clean heart create for me, O God,
  and a steadfast spirit renew within me.
Cast me not out from your presence,
  and your Holy Spirit take not from me.

℟. **Create a clean heart in me, O God.**

not receive the grace to do so from God.

We, for our part, must admit our brokenness and need. We cannot be arrogant, pretending that we can do it all by ourselves. We have to have humble and contrite hearts.

In this psalm we also promise to be instruments of God's mercy, for we will share our insights into his mercy with those who do not yet know how much he loves them.

Give me back the joy of your salvation,
  and a willing spirit sustain in me.
I will teach transgressors your ways,
  and sinners shall return to you.

℟. **Create a clean heart in me, O God.**

For you are not pleased with sacrifices;
  should I offer a holocaust, you would not accept it.
My sacrifice, O God, is a contrite spirit;
  a heart contrite and humbled, O God, you will not spurn.

℟. **Create a clean heart in me, O God.**

Lect. No. 41

EPISTLE: Romans 6:3-11

Christ, raised from the dead, dies no more.

When Jesus rose from the dead, he was not reanimated like Lazarus and the widow of Naim's son. They were brought back to life, but one day they would die anew. They were still subject to all of the limitations of this mortal existence.

That was not the case with Jesus. When he rose from the dead, he received a glorified body that no longer suffers from the limitations of this world. He will no longer die. He is so filled with the life of God that death no longer has any power over him.

When we were baptized, we died to this world in order to live with Christ. Saint Paul speaks of being crucified to this world. We have rejected our previous life-style in which we were slaves to sin. We have chosen to live Christ's life and love. But now we have to live in a manner that is consistent with this choice.

A reading from the Letter of Saint Paul
to the Romans

Brothers and sisters:
Are you unaware that we who were baptized into Christ Jesus
were baptized into his death?
We were indeed buried with him through baptism into death,
so that, just as Christ was raised from the dead
by the glory of the Father,
we too might live in newness of life.

For if we have grown into union with him through a death like his,
we shall also be united with him in the resurrection.
We know that our old self was crucified with him,
so that our sinful body might be done away with,
that we might no longer be in slavery to sin.
For a dead person has been absolved from sin.
If, then, we have died with Christ,
we believe that we shall also live with him.

This means that we have to continue to live as if we are dead to sin. Saying yes to God also means saying no to those things that keep us from union with him. When we are weak and feel ourselves slipping back into our old ways, we must reach out to the one who has died so that we might live in him, Jesus our Lord.

We know that Christ, raised from the dead, dies no more;
  death no longer has power over him.
As to his death, he died to sin once and for all;
  as to his life, he lives for God.
Consequently, you too must think of yourselves as being dead to sin
  and living for God in Christ Jesus.

The word of the Lord.

<table>
<tr><td>Lect.
No. 41</td></tr>
</table>

RESPONSORIAL PSALM: Ps 118:1-2, 16-17, 22-23

How could we possibly express our gratitude to someone who was willing to die for us? Words fail. And yet we cannot but try to thank God for his incredible mercy.

Therefore, we live to praise God. Every moment of our lives must be lived as a response to God's gift of life. Furthermore, God does not just give us life: God gives us life filled with meaning and love.

The third section of our Responsorial Psalm speaks of a stone rejected by the builders becoming the cornerstone. This reminds us of the stone that held the cross (for it was a stone left by the builders in a quarry) and also that we ourselves were once rejected but have now become part of God's building, the Church.

℟. **Alleluia, alleluia, alleluia.**

Give thanks to the LORD, for he is good,
  for his mercy endures forever.
Let the house of Israel say,
  "His mercy endures forever."

℟. **Alleluia, alleluia, alleluia.**

The right hand of the LORD has struck with power;
  the right hand of the LORD is exalted.
I shall not die, but live,
  and declare the works of the LORD.

℟. **Alleluia, alleluia, alleluia.**

The stone which the builders rejected
  has become the cornerstone.
By the LORD has this been done;
  it is wonderful in our eyes.

℟. **Alleluia, alleluia, alleluia.**

GOSPEL: Matthew 28:1-10

He has been raised from the dead and is going before you to Galilee.

Each of the four gospels has an account of the resurrection. They all agree in the major details, but many of the minor details are slightly different for symbolic reasons.

Matthew's account emphasizes the Jewish leaders' attempt to deny the resurrection. This is why we hear that the guards saw Jesus come out of the tomb. No one could possibly argue that the disciples had stolen the body of Jesus (a lie that the Jewish leaders would later spread).

All of the resurrection narratives agree that the women went to the tomb very early in the morning, just before the dawn (when one can see light on the horizon). In this account, two women went to the tomb (two was the number needed to give witness in the Old Testament).

Jesus appears in his glorified body, shining like the sun. Everyone who sees him is filled with fear and awe and joy. This is exactly what one would expect when one comes into contact with the holy. One is filled both with attraction and with fear.

He tells the women that he will meet his disciples in Galilee. There he will give them their commission to preach the gospel to all of the nations upon the world.

A reading from the holy Gospel according to Matthew

After the sabbath, as the first day of the week was dawning,
    Mary Magdalene and the other Mary came to see
        the tomb.
And behold, there was a great earthquake;
    for an angel of the Lord descended from heaven,
    approached, rolled back the stone, and sat upon it.
His appearance was like lightning
    and his clothing was white as snow.
The guards were shaken with fear of him
    and became like dead men.
Then the angel said to the women in reply,
    "Do not be afraid!
I know that you are seeking Jesus the crucified.
He is not here, for he has been raised just as he said.
Come and see the place where he lay.
Then go quickly and tell his disciples,
    'He has been raised from the dead,
    and he is going before you to Galilee;
    there you will see him.'
    Behold, I have told you."
Then they went away quickly from the tomb,
    fearful yet overjoyed,
    and ran to announce this to his disciples.
And behold, Jesus met them on their way and
    greeted them.
They approached, embraced his feet, and did him
    homage.
Then Jesus said to them, "Do not be afraid.
Go tell my brothers to go to Galilee,
    and there they will see me."

The Gospel of the Lord.

March 31, 2002

EASTER SUNDAY

THE RESURRECTION OF THE LORD

Lect. No. 42 **FIRST READING: Acts 10:34a, 37-43**

We ate and drank with him after he rose from the dead.

A reading from the Acts of the Apostles

Peter proceeded to speak and said:
"You know what has happened all over Judea,
  beginning in Galilee after the baptism
  that John preached,
  how God anointed Jesus of Nazareth
  with the Holy Spirit and power.
He went about doing good
  and healing all those oppressed by the devil,
  for God was with him.
We are witnesses of all that he did
  both in the country of the Jews and in Jerusalem.
They put him to death by hanging him on a tree.
This man God raised on the third day and granted
    that he be visible,
  not to all the people, but to us,
  the witnesses chosen by God in advance,
  who ate and drank with him after he rose from
    the dead.
He commissioned us to preach to the people
  and testify that he is the one appointed by God
  as judge of the living and the dead.
To him all the prophets bear witness,
  that everyone who believes in him
  will receive forgiveness of sins through his name."

The word of the Lord.

Our First Reading is taken from the speech that Saint Peter gave when he was called to the house of Cornelius, a Roman centurion whom God had led to conversion.

The speech is a form of the "kerygma," the first preaching that the apostles would proclaim concerning the life and mission of Jesus. Unlike Saint Paul's version, which often centered exclusively on the death and resurrection of Jesus, this one includes many of the elements of Jesus' earthly mission.

This is what one would expect, given the fact that Paul only knew the resurrected Jesus while Peter followed Jesus during his public ministry.

In proclaiming this kerygma, Peter is fulfilling his mission, which we hear outlined in this reading: Jesus commissioned him to be a witness and to preach to the nations. He and the other disciples were to continue the work of the prophets to proclaim the word of the Lord.

Lect.
No. 42 **RESPONSORIAL PSALM: Ps 118:1-2, 16-17, 22-23 (℟.: 24)**

Psalm 118 speaks about power and mercy. These are not two ideas that we would naturally associate, but it gives us an important insight into what mercy really is.

We often think of mercy as something that is gentle and even weak. But true mercy is a strong and courageous virtue.

Mercy does not avoid the truth. It fully recognizes that there are difficulties and yet forgives. It loves the other into healing. Mercy always ends up upon the cross.

This is gospel truth. The world tells us that we can force others to do what we want them to do. Therefore, we sometimes try to use force to bring them to conversion.

God, on the other hand, realizes that you cannot force love. The only way to bring people to true love is by loving them over and over again. They do not deserve that love, but they need it. This is true mercy.

The Lord Jesus, through his cross and resurrection, has destroyed the power of sin and death and brought us into his life. He has taken what the world would consider a defeat and turned it into a powerful victory. This is truly the day the Lord has made, and we cannot but rejoice.

℟. **This is the day the Lord has made; let us rejoice and be glad.**

or:

℟. **Alleluia.**

Give thanks to the Lord, for he is good,
    for his mercy endures forever.
Let the house of Israel say,
    "His mercy endures forever."

℟. **This is the day the Lord has made; let us rejoice and be glad.**

or:

℟. **Alleluia.**

The right hand of the Lord has struck with power;
    the right hand of the Lord is exalted.
I shall not die, but live,
    and declare the works of the Lord.

℟. **This is the day the Lord has made; let us rejoice and be glad.**

or:

℟. **Alleluia.**

The stone which the builders rejected
    has become the cornerstone.
By the Lord has this been done;
    it is wonderful in our eyes.

℟. **This is the day the Lord has made; let us rejoice and be glad.**

or:

℟. **Alleluia.**

SECOND READING

Lect. No. 42

A Colossians 3:1-4

Seek what is above, where Christ is.

In this passage from the Letter to the Colossians, we are reminded of the consequences of our baptismal commitment that we renew today. If we have died with Christ in order to rise with him, then we must live in a manner that is consistent with that choice.

The reward we will receive is that when Jesus returns at the end of time, we will share in his glory. We will live with him for all eternity.

A reading from the Letter of Saint Paul to the Colossians

Brothers and sisters:
  If then you were raised with Christ, seek what is above,
where Christ is seated at the right hand of God.
Think of what is above, not of what is on earth.
For you have died, and your life is hidden with Christ in God.
When Christ your life appears,
  then you too will appear with him in glory.

The word of the Lord.

OR: B 1 Corinthians 5:6b-8

Clear out the old yeast, so that you may become a fresh batch of dough.

Saint Paul uses Passover symbolism to talk about the choices that we must make as Christians. Part of the Passover ceremony is to throw out all traces of leavened products at the beginning of the festival of unleavened bread.

We have experienced a new Passover: the death and resurrection of Jesus. We have passed over from death to life. We must reject all the traces of death that can still be found in our conduct. We must live for and in Jesus, our Lord and our all.

A reading from the first Letter of Saint Paul to the Corinthians

Brothers and sisters:
  Do you not know that a little yeast leavens all the dough?
Clear out the old yeast,
  so that you may become a fresh batch of dough,
  inasmuch as you are unleavened.
For our paschal lamb, Christ, has been sacrificed.
Therefore, let us celebrate the feast,
  not with the old yeast, the yeast of malice and wickedness,
  but with the unleavened bread of sincerity and truth.

The word of the Lord.

Lect.
No. 42

SEQUENCE: *Victimae paschali laudes*

Sequences are ancient poems written to celebrate some of the major feasts of the liturgical year. This particular Sequence is filled with Easter symbolism. Jesus the Paschal Lamb is also the shepherd (many ancient churches in Europe have mosaics that depict a lamb in the center of a flock).

Jesus the sinless one redeems us from our sin. Life and death collide on the cross. Death thinks itself victorious, but it has been defeated by love that gives life eternal.

The second part of the Sequence creates a dialog between the Sequence's narrator and Mary of Magdala. She is encouraged to give witness to what she had seen at the tomb.

We call upon the risen Christ, our victorious King, to have mercy on us.

Christians, to the Paschal Victim
　　Offer your thankful praises!
A Lamb the sheep redeems;
　　Christ, who only is sinless,
　　Reconciles sinners to the Father.
Death and life have contended in that combat stupendous:
　　The Prince of life, who died, reigns immortal.
Speak, Mary, declaring
　　What you saw, wayfaring.
"The tomb of Christ, who is living,
　　The glory of Jesus' resurrection;
Bright angels attesting,
　　The shroud and napkin resting.
Yes, Christ my hope is arisen;
　　To Galilee he goes before you."
Christ indeed from death is risen, our new life obtaining.
　　Have mercy, victor King, ever reigning!
　　Amen. Alleluia.

Lect.
No. 42

ALLELUIA: cf. 1 Corinthians 5:7b-8a

For the first time in many weeks we proclaim the Alleluia Verse. We celebrate Jesus who is our Paschal Lamb and who died out of love for us.

℟. **Alleluia, alleluia.**

Christ, our paschal lamb, has been sacrificed;
let us then feast with joy in the Lord.

℟. **Alleluia, alleluia.**

At an afternoon or evening Mass, another Gospel may be read: Luke 24:13-35, p. 196.

The Gospel from the Easter Vigil, p. 182, may also be read in place of the following Gospel at any time of the day.

Lect.
No. 42

GOSPEL: John 20:1-9

He had to rise from the dead.

In the Gospel of John only one woman goes to the tomb on the morning of the resurrection: Mary of Magdala. She represents the Church who is seeking her savior. She is the first to give witness to the resurrection and is often called the proto-apostle.

She runs to Peter and the beloved disciple and announces that Jesus is no longer in the tomb (she has not yet encountered the risen Jesus and therefore does not yet understand what has happened).

Peter and the beloved disciple run to the tomb. The latter arrives first, but waits at the entrance until Peter can arrive. The beloved disciple arrived first because he was running with his heart (he deeply loved the savior). He waited to enter because love bows to authority (represented by Peter).

Peter enters and sees, while the beloved disciple enters, sees, and believes (his heart leads him to faith). The beloved disciple is not named for, at one level, he represents all of us. Today we all run to the tomb to see and believe and to give witness to the resurrection.

A reading from the holy Gospel according to John

On the first day of the week,
    Mary of Magdala came to the tomb early in the morning,
    while it was still dark,
    and saw the stone removed from the tomb.
So she ran and went to Simon Peter
    and to the other disciple whom Jesus loved, and told them,
    "They have taken the Lord from the tomb,
    and we don't know where they put him."
So Peter and the other disciple went out and came to the tomb.
They both ran, but the other disciple ran faster than Peter
    and arrived at the tomb first;
    he bent down and saw the burial cloths there, but did not go in.
When Simon Peter arrived after him,
    he went into the tomb and saw the burial cloths there,
    and the cloth that had covered his head,
    not with the burial cloths but rolled up in a separate place.
Then the other disciple also went in,
    the one who had arrived at the tomb first,
    and he saw and believed.
For they did not yet understand the Scripture
    that he had to rise from the dead.

The Gospel of the Lord.

April 7, 2002

SECOND SUNDAY OF EASTER

FIRST READING: Acts 2:42-47

All who believed were together and had all things in common.

Our First Reading gives us a description of the early Christian community.

This description (and that found at the end of chapter 4 of Acts) is typical of Luke. He tends to be very optimistic in his view of community life. He was trying to bring pagans to conversion, so he wanted them to see how wonderful Christian life was. In this sense, we could call him the community's first vocation director.

The members of that early Christian community are described as being dedicated to the breaking of bread (celebrations of the Eucharist), prayer, and mutual support. Often we get so caught up with the difficulties of the community that we fail to see how God is working in our midst. This reading reminds us to look beyond the surface difficulties to see God working in our midst.

A reading from the Acts of the Apostles

They devoted themselves
to the teaching of the apostles and to the communal life,
to the breaking of bread and to the prayers.
Awe came upon everyone,
and many wonders and signs were done through the apostles.
All who believed were together and had all things in common;
they would sell their property and possessions
and divide them among all according to each one's need.
Every day they devoted themselves
to meeting together in the temple area
and to breaking bread in their homes.
They ate their meals with exultation and sincerity of heart,
praising God and enjoying favor with all the people.
And every day the Lord added to their number those who were being saved.

The word of the Lord.

Lect. No. 43

RESPONSORIAL PSALM: Ps 118:2-4, 13-15, 22-24 (℟.: 1)

The Easter Season is filled with a sense of wonder and gratitude. We sing along with the psalmist that the mercy of God endures forever. We have experienced that mercy in our celebrations over this past week. We have commemorated the death and resurrection of the Lord Jesus. We have renewed our commitment to our baptismal promises.

One of our responses to these wondrous events is fear—not the fear in which we do not trust God's mercy (for we sing that the mercy of God endures forever). Rather, it is the sense of awe that we feel when we recognize how good and merciful God is.

When we think of how difficult it is to forgive others, we have a small glimpse into the mercy of God. Yet we cannot even begin to understand how profound that mercy is. God loves us all, and destroys the power of sin by responding to us with ever greater mercy.

As we continue to sing our Easter songs and alleluias, we join in the joyful shouts of victory in the tents of the just. As we arrive at the end of our Easter octave celebration, we continue to rejoice.

This Easter joy does not mean that we have to ignore problems that we face in life. When we confront them, we know that nothing can separate us from God's love. If God died for us, then how much more will he lead us through our present difficulties into his peace.

℟. **Give thanks to the Lord for he is good, his love is everlasting.**

or:

℟. **Alleluia.**

Let the house of Israel say,
  "His mercy endures forever."
Let the house of Aaron say,
  "His mercy endures forever."
Let those who fear the LORD say,
  "His mercy endures forever."

℟. **Give thanks to the Lord for he is good, his love is everlasting.**

or:

℟. **Alleluia.**

I was hard pressed and was falling,
  but the LORD helped me.
My strength and my courage is the LORD,
  and he has been my savior.
The joyful shout of victory
  in the tents of the just:

℟. **Give thanks to the Lord for he is good, his love is everlasting.**

or:

℟. **Alleluia.**

The stone which the builders rejected
  has become the cornerstone.
By the LORD has this been done;
  it is wonderful in our eyes.
This is the day the LORD has made;
  let us be glad and rejoice in it.

℟. **Give thanks to the Lord for he is good, his love is everlasting.**

or:

℟. **Alleluia.**

Lect.
No. 43

SECOND READING: 1 Peter 1:3-9

God has given us new birth to a living hope
through the resurrection of Jesus Christ from the dead.

The First Letter of Peter is a celebration of the dignity we received in our baptism. We have been adopted as God's children.

We have an inheritance that means we will live forever with God. It is described as being an inheritance that is imperishable, undefiled, and unfading.

We should view suffering from this perspective. Saint Peter argues that suffering will lead to our purification for it will help us to learn what is really important and worth living and dying for. It will purify our intentions, for it will teach us to trust without limit in the providence of God.

Our dignity in the Lord also changes our view of sin. Sin is no longer the breaking of rules: it is living in a manner that falls short of the dignity to which we have been called.

Jesus, in his death and resurrection, taught us that we are too good and precious to sell ourselves for such a cheap price. He thought so highly of us that he died for us. Should we not value ourselves as highly?

A reading from the first Letter of Saint Peter

Blessed be the God and Father of our Lord Jesus Christ,
who in his great mercy gave us a new birth to a living hope
through the resurrection of Jesus Christ from the dead,
to an inheritance that is imperishable, undefiled, and unfading,
kept in heaven for you
who by the power of God are safeguarded through faith,
to a salvation that is ready to be revealed in the final time.
In this you rejoice, although now for a little while
you may have to suffer through various trials,
so that the genuineness of your faith,
more precious than gold that is perishable even though tested by fire,
may prove to be for praise, glory, and honor
at the revelation of Jesus Christ.
Although you have not seen him you love him;
even though you do not see him now yet believe in him,
you rejoice with an indescribable and glorious joy,
as you attain the goal of your faith, the salvation of your souls.

The word of the Lord.

Lect. No. 43

The Alleluia Verse recalls Jesus' words to Thomas the apostle. We are those who are blessed because they have believed owing to the things we have heard and not because we have seen.

ALLELUIA: John 20:29

℞. **Alleluia, alleluia.**

You believe in me, Thomas, because you have seen me, says the Lord;

blessed are they who have not seen me, but still believe!

℞. **Alleluia, alleluia.**

Lect. No. 43

GOSPEL: John 20:19-31

Eight days later Jesus came and stood in their midst.

The first part of today's Gospel speaks of Jesus' first apparition to the disciples. They were filled with fear, but Jesus greets them with the words "peace be with you." There are no recriminations or accusations. Rather, there is total acceptance.

Jesus then breathes upon his disciples. Through this gesture, Jesus is breathing his Holy Spirit into the disciples. It recalls the Genesis creation story in which Adam was made into a living being through the breath of God's Spirit. Now, we are made into a new creation by the same means.

In the Gospel of Luke and Acts, the giving of the Spirit occurs on Pentecost Sunday. Here it occurs the evening of Easter. This is typical of John's gospel, which tends to present the death and resurrection of Jesus as events that ended history as we know it. Time has no more

A reading from the holy Gospel according to John

On the evening of that first day of the week,
  when the doors were locked, where the disciples were,
  for fear of the Jews,
  Jesus came and stood in their midst
  and said to them, "Peace be with you."
When he had said this, he showed them his hands
  and his side.
The disciples rejoiced when they saw the Lord.
Jesus said to them again, "Peace be with you.
As the Father has sent me, so I send you."
And when he had said this, he breathed on them
  and said to them,
  "Receive the Holy Spirit.
Whose sins you forgive are forgiven them,
  and whose sins you retain are retained."

Thomas, called Didymus, one of the Twelve,
  was not with them when Jesus came.
So the other disciples said to him, "We have seen the Lord."

meaning for us now that we are living in Jesus.

The handing on of the Holy Spirit is associated with the forgiveness of sins. The Spirit is the Father's love for Jesus and his love for the Father and their love for us. It is only through a powerful outpouring of love that our sins can be forgiven.

The second half of this story concerns Thomas. He did not want to believe in the resurrection until he had concrete evidence. We cannot always have absolute proof for our faith. We often must trust and take a risk (a leap of faith).

We also see that Jesus is truly risen in the flesh (for Thomas could touch his wounds). This was a rejection of an early heresy called Docetism, which denied the reality of the incarnation and sufferings of Jesus.

Finally, those who believe without seeing (those of us in the generations after that of the eyewitnesses) are commended for believing.

But he said to them,
    "Unless I see the mark of the nails in his hands
    and put my finger into the nailmarks
    and put my hand into his side, I will not believe."
Now a week later his disciples were again inside
    and Thomas was with them.
Jesus came, although the doors were locked,
    and stood in their midst and said, "Peace be with
        you."
Then he said to Thomas, "Put your finger here and
        see my hands,
    and bring your hand and put it into my side,
    and do not be unbelieving, but believe."
Thomas answered and said to him, "My Lord and
        my God!"
Jesus said to him, "Have you come to believe because you have seen me?
Blessed are those who have not seen and have believed."

Now, Jesus did many other signs in the presence of
        his disciples
    that are not written in this book.
But these are written that you may come to believe
    that Jesus is the Christ, the Son of God,
    and that through this belief you may have life in
        his name.

The Gospel of the Lord.

THIRD SUNDAY OF EASTER

Lect. No. 46

FIRST READING: Acts 2:14, 22-33

It was impossible for Jesus to be held by death.

A reading from the Acts of the Apostles

Then Peter stood up with the Eleven,
raised his voice, and proclaimed:
"You who are Jews, indeed all of you staying in Jerusalem.
Let this be known to you, and listen to my words.
You who are Israelites, hear these words.
Jesus the Nazarene was a man commended to you by God
with mighty deeds, wonders, and signs,
which God worked through him in your midst, as you yourselves know.
This man, delivered up by the set plan and foreknowledge of God,
you killed, using lawless men to crucify him.
But God raised him up, releasing him from the throes of death,
because it was impossible for him to be held by it.
For David says of him:

I saw the Lord ever before me,
with him at my right hand I shall not be disturbed.
Therefore my heart has been glad and my tongue has exulted;
my flesh, too, will dwell in hope,
because you will not abandon my soul to the netherworld,
nor will you suffer your holy one to see corruption.
You have made known to me the paths of life;
you will fill me with joy in your presence.

The First Reading is a presentation of the "kerygma," this time being the first preaching that Saint Peter gave on the day of Pentecost to the pilgrims who were in town for the Jewish feast of Pentecost.

Many of the important themes of the writings of Saint Luke are contained in this reading. The first and most important is that God had a plan that was fulfilled in the ministry of Jesus. It had been foretold by the prophets of the Old Testament (such as the passage taken from Psalm 16, which is quoted at length).

A second theme is that those who crucified Jesus had rejected the plan of God. They are described as being lawless men.

The third theme, found in all of scripture, is that God would not let the evil deeds of the Jewish leaders destroy his plan. God destroyed their evil designs by raising Jesus from the dead.

All of these deeds are described in terms that Peter's listeners could understand. Peter speaks to them as being eye-witnesses to many of the events. Therefore, they had a special responsibility to respond to the wondrous deeds that God had worked in their midst.

Peter speaks of the promise that David would never see the corruption of death. Yet he did die. Peter states that this had been said not for David, but for Jesus. He was the one whose flesh did not see corruption. God raised him from the dead.

Peter reminds them that they are all witnesses to this. They were also witnesses to the promise of the Holy Spirit whose descent upon the disciples they had just witnessed.

It is interesting that most of the New Testament texts that speak of the resurrection of Jesus speak of the Father having raised him and not of him rising under his own power. The Father exalted him by raising him and by calling him to sit at his right in glory

"My brothers, one can confidently say to you
   about the patriarch David that he died and was
      buried,
   and his tomb is in our midst to this day.
But since he was a prophet and knew that God had
      sworn an oath to him
   that he would set one of his descendants upon his
      throne,
   he foresaw and spoke of the resurrection of the
      Christ,
   that neither was he abandoned to the netherworld
   nor did his flesh see corruption.
God raised this Jesus;
   of this we are all witnesses.
Exalted at the right hand of God,
   he received the promise of the Holy Spirit from
      the Father
   and poured him forth, as you see and hear."

The word of the Lord.

Lect. No. 46

RESPONSORIAL PSALM: Ps 16:1-2, 5, 7-8, 9-10, 11 (℞.: 11a)

The Responsorial Psalm is a longer version of the psalm quoted in the First Reading.

In the First Reading we heard that this psalm had been written by David. We must be a bit cautious in this attribution, for many of the psalms were dedicated to David and not actually written by him. The reason for the confusion is that in Hebrew the phrase for "written by" and "written for" is the same.

Regardless of who its author is, this psalm is one of trust in the deliverance of the LORD.

℞. **Lord, you will show us the path of life.**

or:

℞. **Alleluia.**

Keep me, O God, for in you I take refuge;
   I say to the LORD, "My LORD are you."
O LORD, my allotted portion and my cup,
   you it is who hold fast my lot.

℞. **Lord, you will show us the path of life.**

or:

℞. **Alleluia.**

I bless the LORD who counsels me;
   even in the night my heart exhorts me.

The LORD is described as the psalmist's refuge, portion, and cup. The author considers the LORD to be his hope and life. If the psalmist were cut off from the LORD, there would be no meaning in life, no hope for the future.

Even in the night the author could feel secure. Night was considered to be the time ruled by the enemy. Many verses in scripture speak about the fears of the night and how the evil one rules it. But the LORD's presence would distance every danger.

The LORD would protect the psalmist even from the eternal night: death. He was sure that he would not undergo corruption.

This psalm was fulfilled when God raised Jesus from the dead. His resurrection is a promise for all of us, for we will share in his glory when we rise with him.

I set the LORD ever before me;
   with him at my right hand I shall not be disturbed.

℟. **Lord, you will show us the path of life.**

or:

℟. **Alleluia.**

Therefore my heart is glad and my soul rejoices,
   my body, too, abides in confidence;
because you will not abandon my soul to the netherworld,
   nor will you suffer your faithful one to undergo corruption.

℟. **Lord, you will show us the path of life.**

or:

℟. **Alleluia.**

You will show me the path to life,
   abounding joy in your presence,
   the delights at your right hand forever.

℟. **Lord, you will show us the path of life.**

or:

℟. **Alleluia.**

Lect.
No. 46

SECOND READING: 1 Peter 1:17-21

*You were saved with the precious Blood of Christ,
as with that of a spotless, unblemished lamb.*

The Second Reading speaks of God's gracious gift of our redemption and how we should respond to the new life God has given us.

Our redemption did not come about with formulas or payments of earthly goods. It was brought about with the precious blood of the lamb (Jesus, the new Paschal Lamb of our redemption).

A reading from the first Letter of Saint Peter

Beloved:
If you invoke as Father him who judges impartially
according to each one's works,
conduct yourselves with reverence during the time of your sojourning,
realizing that you were ransomed from your futile conduct,

God so loved us that even before the creation of the world, he had chosen Jesus as our savior. Even before we were created, God had predestined us to be called into his glory.

Our present life is only a sojourn, for our true home is God's glory. We must keep our eyes on that home in order to maintain our perspective lest we get caught up in our daily problems and anxieties.

| Lect. |
| No. 46 |

The Alleluia Verse is taken from the road to Emmaus scene. It is Jesus who sends his Spirit into our hearts to understand the meaning of the sacred scriptures.

| Lect. |
| No. 46 |

The Gospel of Luke is one of the most artistic gospels in presenting the life and mission of Jesus. It often has symbolic scenes that are both incredibly beautiful and powerfully meaningful. This is especially true of the account of the resurrection.

Luke presents three resurrection narratives to speak of what happened when Jesus rose and what it means to us.

In the first scene, the women go to the tomb and see the empty grave and speak with the two angels ("men dressed in shining clothes"), but they do not see the risen Jesus.

handed on by your ancestors,
not with perishable things like silver or gold
but with the precious blood of Christ
as of a spotless unblemished lamb.

He was known before the foundation of the world
but revealed in the final time for you,
who through him believe in God
who raised him from the dead and gave him glory,
so that your faith and hope are in God.

The word of the Lord.

ALLELUIA: cf. Luke 24:32

℟. **Alleluia, alleluia.**

Lord Jesus, open the Scriptures to us;
make our hearts burn while you speak to us.

℟. **Alleluia, alleluia.**

GOSPEL: Luke 24:13-35

They recognized Jesus in the breaking of bread.

A reading from the holy Gospel according to Luke

That very day, the first day of the week,
two of Jesus' disciples were going
to a village seven miles from Jerusalem called Emmaus,
and they were conversing about all the things that had occurred.
And it happened that while they were conversing and debating,
Jesus himself drew near and walked with them,
but their eyes were prevented from recognizing him.
He asked them,
"What are you discussing as you walk along?"
They stopped, looking downcast.
One of them, named Cleopas, said to him in reply,

Today we hear the second scene, the road to Emmaus. Here the two disciples encounter Jesus in the breaking of the bread (a symbol for the celebration of the Eucharist) and the explanation of the word (for the disciples' hearts burned inside of them when he explained the scriptures).

The third scene presents Jesus who appears to his disciples in the flesh.

These three scenes are a paradigm for the Christian life. At first we hear about Jesus from others. Then we come to meet him in word and sacrament. Finally, as our faith grows, we meet him face to face.

Typical of Luke, all three accounts include an explanation of how all that happened to Jesus was in fulfillment of God's plan and had been foretold in the law and prophets.

The phrase, "the breaking of the bread," was a liturgical phrase in use at the end of the first century A.D. Thus, when early Christian readers would read this phrase in this story, they would immediately associate it with the celebration of the Eucharist.

We should notice in this account that Jesus seems to appear in two different places at the same time (for while he was speaking with the disciples on the road to Emmaus, he was also appearing to Simon Peter in Jerusalem). Our glorified body will not be subject to the limitations of this earthly body.

"Are you the only visitor to Jerusalem
who does not know of the things
that have taken place there in these days?"
And he replied to them, "What sort of things?"
They said to him,
"The things that happened to Jesus the Nazarene,
who was a prophet mighty in deed and word
before God and all the people,
how our chief priests and rulers both handed him over
to a sentence of death and crucified him.
But we were hoping that he would be the one to redeem Israel;
and besides all this,
it is now the third day since this took place.
Some women from our group, however, have astounded us:
they were at the tomb early in the morning
and did not find his body;
they came back and reported
that they had indeed seen a vision of angels
who announced that he was alive.
Then some of those with us went to the tomb
and found things just as the women had described,
but him they did not see."
And he said to them, "Oh, how foolish you are!
How slow of heart to believe all that the prophets spoke!
Was it not necessary that the Christ should suffer these things
and enter into his glory?"
Then beginning with Moses and all the prophets,
he interpreted to them what referred to him
in all the Scriptures.
As they approached the village to which they were going,

We will not be limited by time and space. We will not suffer from illness or death. Even our emotions will be purified. Our love will never be tinged by jealousy or confusion. We will be able to love as God himself loves.

We should also notice that the disciples do not recognize Jesus until late in the story. In some resurrection narratives, the disciples immediately recognize Jesus. In others, he is not recognized (Emmaus, Mary of Magdala in the garden, and by the sea in John 21). Jesus' risen body (and ours) is a continuity of this earthly body, but it is also changed and glorified.

The disciples speak of how their hearts burned within them while Jesus explained scripture along the way. Even before Jesus broke bread with them, he was present to them in the word of God.

As we celebrate the Eucharist today, we meet Jesus in both of these moments: the breaking of the word and the breaking of the bread.

he gave the impression that he was going on farther.
But they urged him, "Stay with us,
    for it is nearly evening and the day is almost over."
So he went in to stay with them.
And it happened that, while he was with them at table,
    he took bread, said the blessing,
    broke it, and gave it to them.
With that their eyes were opened and they recognized him,
    but he vanished from their sight.
Then they said to each other,
    "Were not our hearts burning within us
    while he spoke to us on the way and opened the Scriptures to us?"
So they set out at once and returned to Jerusalem
    where they found gathered together
    the eleven and those with them who were saying,
    "The Lord has truly been raised and has appeared to Simon!"
Then the two recounted
    what had taken place on the way
    and how he was made known to them in the breaking of bread.

The Gospel of the Lord.

April 21, 2002

FOURTH SUNDAY OF EASTER

Lect. No. 49

FIRST READING: Acts 2:14a, 36-41

God has made Jesus both Lord and Christ.

A reading from the Acts of the Apostles

Then Peter stood up with the Eleven,
raised his voice, and proclaimed:
"Let the whole house of Israel know for certain
    that God has made both Lord and Christ,
    this Jesus whom you crucified."

Now when they heard this, they were cut to the
    heart,
    and they asked Peter and the other apostles,
    "What are we to do, my brothers?"
Peter said to them,
    "Repent and be baptized, every one of you,
    in the name of Jesus Christ for the forgiveness of
      your sins;
    and you will receive the gift of the Holy Spirit.
For the promise is made to you and to your children
    and to all those far off,
    whomever the Lord our God will call."
He testified with many other arguments, and was
    exhorting them,
    "Save yourselves from this corrupt generation."
Those who accepted his message were baptized,
    and about three thousand persons were added
    that day.

The word of the Lord.

This is a continuation of Saint Peter's discourse on the day of Pentecost. This week we hear the response to his call.

Those listening were convinced by his words and wanted to know what to do. Peter had spoken with conviction, for his words were filled with Spirit and truth.

He invited them to be baptized. There is a sense of urgency throughout this account. Jesus had risen from the dead, and the resurrection of the dead was a sign of the dawning of the end times. There was no time to waste; today was the day for them to convert.

This is why Luke has such a large number being baptized. Although the number 3,000 might be a bit exaggerated, it nevertheless helps us to understand that the message was tremendously successful right from its very first moments. Peter's listeners had to turn from their sins and embrace God with all their hearts.

RESPONSORIAL PSALM: 23:1-3a, 3b-4, 5, 6 (℟.: 1)

Our Responsorial Psalm is the beautiful Psalm 23, which was written during the exile in Babylon. The main image used by the psalmist is that of the shepherd, one who watches and protects the flock over which he has care.

The time of the exile was horrific for the Jewish people. They wondered whether God knew of their plight or cared. The image of the shepherd was a response to that question. God cared for them with great love.

God will lead us through the dark valley (popularly known as "the valley of death"), i.e., a valley as dark as death. He comforts us with his rod and his staff. Every time that we are in the darkest part of our lives and we feel abandoned, God lets us know of his presence much as a shepherd would let his sheep know that he was near by touching their flanks with his rod and staff.

He leads us to restful waters. As always with the psalms, we have to remember where they were written, in a land that was intolerably arid.

He spreads the table before us in the sight of our foes. Normally, the presence of our enemies would cause us to lose our appetite. With God near, we do not suffer from anxiety.

Our head is anointed with oil, again something that would be done in an arid climate.

℟. **The Lord is my shepherd; there is nothing I shall want.**

or:

℟. **Alleluia.**

The LORD is my shepherd; I shall not want.
　In verdant pastures he gives me repose;
beside restful waters he leads me;
　he refreshes my soul.

℟. **The Lord is my shepherd; there is nothing I shall want.**

or:

℟. **Alleluia.**

He guides me in right paths
　for his name's sake.
Even though I walk in the dark valley
　I fear no evil; for you are at my side
with your rod and your staff
　that give me courage.

℟. **The Lord is my shepherd; there is nothing I shall want.**

or:

℟. **Alleluia.**

You spread the table before me
　in the sight of my foes;
you anoint my head with oil;
　my cup overflows.

℟. **The Lord is my shepherd; there is nothing I shall want.**

or:

℟. **Alleluia.**

Only goodness and kindness follow me
　all the days of my life;

Finally, we have the hope of dwelling in the house of God, a place where we will always be at home with the one we love. (Ultimately, whever we find ourselves, we are at home if we are one with God.)

and I shall dwell in the house of the LORD
    for years to come.

℟. **The Lord is my shepherd; there is nothing I shall want.**

or:

℟. **Alleluia.**

Lect.
No. 49

SECOND READING: 1 Peter 2:20b-25

You have returned to the shepherd and guardian of your souls.

Saint Peter begins this passage by encouraging those who suffer to adopt the attitude of Jesus. Through his suffering he was able to bring about the forgiveness of our sins. He suffered meekly, and he bore the weight of our sins upon himself.

Jesus did not deserve the suffering that he received. We were the ones who truly deserved it because of our sinfulness. Yet he bore it all for our sake. As Peter says, "By his wounds you have been healed."

If we, in turn, suffer with patience, especially when we do not deserve it, we cause a great thing to happen. We give witness to a redeeming love.

If, on the other hand, we respond to suffering with anger or bitterness, if we try to get even for wrongs done to us, then there will be no healing. We will have descended into hate, and neither we nor the person we dislike will benefit from it.

A reading from the first Letter of Saint Peter

Beloved:
If you are patient when you suffer for doing what is good,
this is a grace before God.
For to this you have been called,
    because Christ also suffered for you,
    leaving you an example that you should follow in his footsteps.
He committed no sin, and no deceit was found in his mouth.

When he was insulted, he returned no insult;
    when he suffered, he did not threaten;
    instead, he handed himself over to the one who judges justly.
He himself bore our sins in his body upon the cross,
    so that, free from sin, we might live for righteousness.
By his wounds you have been healed.
For you had gone astray like sheep,
    but you have now returned to the shepherd and guardian of your souls.

The word of the Lord.

Lect.
No. 49

Jesus is the good shepherd who calls each one of us by name. He protects us from those things that would harm or destroy us.

Lect.
No. 49

During the time of the Babylonian exile, the image of God as our shepherd was very popular.

The passage we are using as our Gospel is a reflection upon the readings from the Old Testament that used the good shepherd image. Jesus was probably in the temple when these readings were used in the Jewish liturgy (it was read during the feast of the dedication of the temple).

Jesus changes the image, though, by applying it to himself. He is God come to earth to rule and guide his people. He will call them by name for he knows each one of us intimately. We see this fulfilled when Jesus calls Mary of Magdala by name in the garden. We are not an impersonal mass of people. We are his beloved. He will protect us from our enemies.

Jesus also uses the shepherd image as a starting point and alters it slightly by calling himself the sheep gate. It means that if anyone wants to

ALLELUIA: John 10:14

℟. **Alleluia, alleluia.**

I am the good shepherd, says the Lord;
I know my sheep, and mine know me.

℟. **Alleluia, alleluia.**

GOSPEL: John 10:1-10

I am the gate for the sheep.

A reading from the holy Gospel according to John

Jesus said:
"Amen, amen, I say to you,
   whoever does not enter a sheepfold through the gate
but climbs over elsewhere is a thief and a robber.
But whoever enters through the gate is the shepherd of the sheep.
The gatekeeper opens it for him, and the sheep hear his voice,
   as the shepherd calls his own sheep by name and leads them out.
When he has driven out all his own,
   he walks ahead of them, and the sheep follow him,
   because they recognize his voice.
But they will not follow a stranger;
   they will run away from him,
   because they do not recognize the voice of strangers."
Although Jesus used this figure of speech,
   the Pharisees did not realize what he was trying to tell them.

So Jesus said again, "Amen, amen, I say to you,
   I am the gate for the sheep.
All who came before me are thieves and robbers,

203 FOURTH SUNDAY OF EASTER

come to God and find safety, they must come through him. He alone is the source of our peace.

The thieves and brigands of whom Jesus speaks are those false gods and values that would lead us from the truth. They seem to offer life and comfort, but they only delude us and bring us emptiness and frustration.

but the sheep did not listen to them.

I am the gate.

Whoever enters through me will be saved,
   and will come in and go out and find pasture.

A thief comes only to steal and slaughter and destroy;
   I came so that they might have life and have it more abundantly."

The Gospel of the Lord.

April 28, 2002
FIFTH SUNDAY OF EASTER

Lect. No. 52

FIRST READING: Acts 6:1-7

They chose seven men filled with the Spirit.

Saint Luke loves to portray the early Christian community as peaceable. That is why it is so unusual that he would admit that there were some disagreements in that Church.

The Hebrews were those who spoke Aramaic as their mother tongue. This included most if not all of the original apostles.

The Hellenists, on the other hand, were Jews who spoke Greek. Actually, the vast majority of Jews in the world at the time of Jesus spoke Greek they were not appreciated by the Aramaic speaking Jews for they were often accused of being too liberal in their interpretation of the obligations of the faith.

The money that had been collected by the community to help widows and orphans was being distributed to the Hebrews but not the Hellenists. There were complaints, and the apostles turned to God for discernment.

They chose seven Hellenists for charity within the community. This service is called "diaconia" in Greek, hence we call these seven the first deacons. The texts that follow make it clear that their responsibilities soon grew to include preaching.

A reading from the Acts of the Apostles

As the number of disciples continued to grow, the Hellenists complained against the Hebrews because their widows
were being neglected in the daily distribution.
So the Twelve called together the community of the disciples and said,
"It is not right for us to neglect the word of God to serve at table.
Brothers, select from among you seven reputable men,
filled with the Spirit and wisdom,
whom we shall appoint to this task,
whereas we shall devote ourselves to prayer
and to the ministry of the word."
The proposal was acceptable to the whole community,
so they chose Stephen, a man filled with faith and the Holy Spirit,
also Philip, Prochorus, Nicanor, Timon, Parmenas,
and Nicholas of Antioch, a convert to Judaism.
They presented these men to the apostles
who prayed and laid hands on them.
The word of God continued to spread,
and the number of the disciples in Jerusalem increased greatly;
even a large group of priests were becoming obedient to the faith.

The word of the Lord.

Lect.
No. 52

RESPONSORIAL PSALM: Ps 33:1-2, 4-5, 18-19 (℟.: 22)

Psalm 33 praises the Lord for his goodness, especially in saving us from our enemies. Our only hope, our only salvation, is found in God.

We hear that the word of the Lord is trustworthy. All throughout the Old Testament God sent messengers to communicate his word to us. Yet those messengers were mostly rejected and often murdered, for God's people did not really want to hear the truth.

But God did not abandon his promises. He would not allow our infidelity to destroy the word that he had spoken to us. Instead, he sent his Word, Jesus, into the world to save us. Jesus is the incarnate proof that God is always true to his word, for he is the Word of Truth.

There are virtues that we can expect of God and that we should be able to expect of those who say that they are his disciples: justice, rectitude, and kindness.

The "eyes of the Lord" are upon us to watch over us and protect us. God is not watching us to catch us in some fault that we might commit. He is watching to protect his beloved children from harming themselves, even as we might watch over our children to protect them from every danger.

℟. **Lord, let your mercy be on us, as we place our trust in you.**

or:

℟. **Alleluia.**

Exult, you just, in the Lord;
  praise from the upright is fitting.
Give thanks to the Lord on the harp;
  with the ten–stringed lyre chant his praises.

℟. **Lord, let your mercy be on us, as we place our trust in you.**

or:

℟. **Alleluia.**

Upright is the word of the Lord,
  and all his works are trustworthy.
He loves justice and right;
  of the kindness of the Lord the earth is full.

℟. **Lord, let your mercy be on us, as we place our trust in you.**

or:

℟. **Alleluia.**

See, the eyes of the Lord are upon those who fear
    him,
  upon those who hope for his kindness,
to deliver them from death
  and preserve them in spite of famine.

℟. **Lord, let your mercy be on us, as we place our trust in you.**

or:

℟. **Alleluia.**

Lect.
No. 52

SECOND READING: 1 Peter 2:4-9

You are a chosen race, a royal priesthood.

Jesus is the living stone upon which the Church has been built. He is a sure foundation, and we will never be shaken. This reading speaks of him being a cornerstone that is chosen and precious.

We, in turn, are also stones that will be built into a holy temple of the Lord. Jesus is thus the image and the promise of what we are to become.

If we, on the other hand, do not follow in Jesus' footsteps, then the rock that is Jesus causes us to stumble. We will be convicted by his example. He has taught us the truth of God, and we will have chosen that which is false if we do not follow him.

Thus, it is not so much Jesus who condemns us as we who will have chosen our own condemnation. He offered life, and we have chosen to reject it.

But God has not called us for failure. He has called us for an incredible dignity. He has made us a chosen race. We have become a royal priesthood. We share in the priesthood and kingship of Jesus through the grace of our Baptism. We are a holy nation for we have been set aside and consecrated to belong to the Lord alone.

A reading from the first Letter of Saint Peter

Beloved:
Come to him, a living stone, rejected by human beings
but chosen and precious in the sight of God,
and, like living stones,
let yourselves be built into a spiritual house
to be a holy priesthood to offer spiritual sacrifices
acceptable to God through Jesus Christ.
For it says in Scripture:
Behold, I am laying a stone in Zion,
a cornerstone, chosen and precious,
and whoever believes in it shall not be put to shame.
Therefore, its value is for you who have faith, but for those without faith:
The stone that the builders rejected
has become the cornerstone,
a stone that will make people stumble,
and a rock that will make them fall.
They stumble by disobeying the word, as is their destiny.

You are "a chosen race, a royal priesthood,
a holy nation, a people of his own,
so that you may announce the praises" of him
who called you out of darkness into his wonderful light.

The word of the Lord.

Lect. No. 52

Jesus is the way, for we cannot come to the Father except through him. He is the truth, for he is wisdom incarnate. He is the life, for he is the source and goal of our lives.

Lect. No. 52

The Gospel is taken from the Last Supper discourse in the Gospel of John. It is believed that the author of this gospel gathered many of the thoughts of Jesus from all throughout his ministry into this rather extended presentation (it goes from the middle of chapter 13 to the end of chapter 17).

This portion of the discourse shows Jesus preparing his disciples for his departure. He speaks to them of the fact that he must go away so that he might prepare a dwelling place for them with the Father. It was difficult for early Christians to understand why Jesus did not remain upon the earth to guide and protect them. They could not understand why this was not an abandonment. This passage shows that Jesus did not abandon them; he did what was best for them by preparing the way to the Father for them.

The second portion of the dialogue has Jesus explaining that he is the way to the Father. We cannot know God except through him. That is why he was

ALLELUIA: John 14:6

℟. **Alleluia, alleluia.**

I am the way, the truth and the life, says the Lord;
no one comes to the Father, except through me.

℟. **Alleluia, alleluia.**

GOSPEL: John 14:1-12

I am the way and the truth and the life.

A reading from the holy Gospel according to John

Jesus said to his disciples:
"Do not let your hearts be troubled.
You have faith in God; have faith also in me.
In my Father's house there are many dwelling
    places.
If there were not,
    would I have told you that I am going to prepare a
        place for you?
And if I go and prepare a place for you,
    I will come back again and take you to myself,
    so that where I am you also may be.
Where I am going you know the way."
Thomas said to him,
    "Master, we do not know where you are going;
    how can we know the way?"
Jesus said to him, "I am the way and the truth and
    the life.
No one comes to the Father except through me.
If you know me, then you will also know my Father.
From now on you do know him and have seen him."
Philip said to him,
    "Master, show us the Father, and that will be
        enough for us."

born in this world, to reveal to us who the Father is and how much he loves us.

If we have known Jesus, then we have also known the Father. Likewise, if we have not known Jesus, we cannot really say that we have known the Father, for Jesus is the way to the Father. He is the visible revelation of who God is.

Jesus insisted all throughout his ministry that he could do nothing except through the Father. Jesus has revealed the Father to us, and we can do the works that Jesus has done.

We are his disciples both because we have followed him and because we now represent him upon the earth.

Jesus said to him, "Have I been with you for so long a time
and you still do not know me, Philip?
Whoever has seen me has seen the Father.
How can you say, 'Show us the Father'?
Do you not believe that I am in the Father and the Father is in me?
The words that I speak to you I do not speak on my own.
The Father who dwells in me is doing his works.
Believe me that I am in the Father and the Father is in me,
or else, believe because of the works themselves.
Amen, amen, I say to you,
whoever believes in me will do the works that I do,
and will do greater ones than these,
because I am going to the Father."

The Gospel of the Lord.

When the Ascension of the Lord is celebrated the following Sunday, the Second Reading and Gospel from the Seventh Sunday of Easter, pp. 218-219 may be read on the Sixth Sunday of Easter.

May 5, 2002

SIXTH SUNDAY OF EASTER

Lect. No. 55 FIRST READING: Acts 8:5-8, 14-17

Peter and John laid hands on them, and they received the Holy Spirit.

A reading from the Acts of the Apostles

Philip went down to the city of Samaria
and proclaimed the Christ to them.
With one accord, the crowds paid attention to what was said by Philip
    when they heard it and saw the signs he was doing.
For unclean spirits, crying out in a loud voice,
    came out of many possessed people,
    and many paralyzed or crippled people were cured.
There was great joy in that city.

Now when the apostles in Jerusalem
    heard that Samaria had accepted the word of God,
    they sent them Peter and John,
    who went down and prayed for them,
    that they might receive the Holy Spirit,
    for it had not yet fallen upon any of them;
    they had only been baptized in the name of the Lord Jesus.
Then they laid hands on them
    and they received the Holy Spirit.

The word of the Lord.

The First Reading is taken from the Acts of the Apostles. In chapter 1 of Acts we hear that the gospel would spread from Jerusalem to Judea to the very ends of the earth. Today we see the beginning of the fulfillment of this promise.

The present episode shows us an important step in this spread of the gospel. Philip, one of the seven called to the diaconate, shares the gospel with the Samaritans.

The Samaritans were considered to be a type of heretical Jew, for they had mixed elements of the Jewish faith with paganism.

By having the gospel reach the Samaritans, it was now reaching beyond the Jewish people. The next step would be for the gospel to reach the pagans, first in Israel and Asia Minor and then slowly to the ends of the earth (Rome).

The Samaritans accept the gospel with great joy. Peter and John pray over them, and the Holy Spirit descends upon them.

Lect.
No. 55

RESPONSORIAL PSALM: Ps 66:1-3, 4-5, 6-7, 16, 20 (℞.: 1)

This hymn of praise was originally written to celebrate the fact that God had delivered the people of Israel. He had intervened in their history in a powerful way.

Here the psalm has a different sense. All of the nations of the earth are to hear how glorious God is. We are no longer only speaking about how God saved Israel, but how he saved all of us. If our God is the only God who exists, then he must be the God of all people.

The death and resurrection of Jesus is a new Passover. We have passed through the sea on dry land. Our Baptism was that passing through the sea of death, but God created a dry passage for us through his death and resurrection.

All nations and all individuals have been invited to make this passage to life with Jesus. We are no longer divided by race or class or other differences (remember Saint Paul's words that there is no Greek or Jew, male or female, slave or free). We are all one in Christ.

We have to keep up our hope and trust in the providence of God. Often we can become discouraged for evil can seem so strong and all-pervasive. If God has done all of this for us, surely he will protect us.

℞. **Let all the earth cry out to God with joy.**

or:

℞. **Alleluia.**

Shout joyfully to God, all the earth,
   sing praise to the glory of his name;
   proclaim his glorious praise.
Say to God, "How tremendous are your deeds!

℞. **Let all the earth cry out to God with joy.**

or:

℞. **Alleluia.**

Let all on earth worship and sing praise to you,
   sing praise to your name!"
Come and see the works of God,
   his tremendous deeds among the children of
   Adam.

℞. **Let all the earth cry out to God with joy.**

or:

℞. **Alleluia.**

He has changed the sea into dry land;
   through the river they passed on foot.
Therefore let us rejoice in him.
   He rules by his might forever.

℞. **Let all the earth cry out to God with joy.**

or:

℞. **Alleluia.**

Hear now, all you who fear God, while I declare
   what he has done for me.
Blessed be God who refused me not
   my prayer or his kindness!

℞. **Let all the earth cry out to God with joy.**

or:

℞. **Alleluia.**

SECOND READING: 1 Peter 3:15-18

Put to death in the flesh, Christ was raised to life in the Spirit.

Saint Peter encourages us to share the source of our joy with others: our faith in the Lord Jesus. Notice how pastoral he is in his instructions. One does not have to be aggressive.

Peter invites us to be gentle and to act with reverence. Thus, we will not be trying to force others' compliance; we will be inviting them to share a gift we have received from the Lord.

If, after sharing our faith, we receive taunts and other forms of subtle persecution, we should view it as an honor. Jesus suffered for us. If we suffer with hope, we will give an important message to those who persecute us. We, like Jesus, will be putting the flesh to death so that we might live in the Spirit.

A reading from the first Letter of Saint Peter

Beloved:
Sanctify Christ as Lord in your hearts.
Always be ready to give an explanation
    to anyone who asks you for a reason for your
        hope,
    but do it with gentleness and reverence,
    keeping your conscience clear,
    so that, when you are maligned,
    those who defame your good conduct in Christ
    may themselves be put to shame.
For it is better to suffer for doing good,
    if that be the will of God, than for doing evil.
For Christ also suffered for sins once,
    the righteous for the sake of the unrighteous,
    that he might lead you to God.
Put to death in the flesh,
    he was brought to life in the Spirit.

The word of the Lord.

ALLELUIA: John 14:23

In order to be one with the Father, we must live as Jesus lived. This means keeping his word in speech and action. In this way, we will abide with the Father just as Jesus abides with him.

℟. **Alleluia, alleluia.**

Whoever loves me will keep my word, says the Lord,
and my Father will love him and we will come to him.

℟. **Alleluia, alleluia.**

Lect.
No. 55

GOSPEL: John 14:15-21

I will ask the Father and he will give you another Advocate.

As we prepare for the Ascension, we hear Jesus promise that he will send another Advocate. Note that the Advocate being sent is "another Advocate." Jesus is the first Advocate, for he interceded for us with the Father.

The Greek word used for "Paraclete" in this Gospel is a very ambiguous word. It could mean advocate or advisor or counselor or one who gives consolation. All of these meanings are true and all of them are used in the passages that speak about the "Paraclete."

The Spirit of truth will help us to remember what Jesus taught and to understand it. That Spirit will give us courage to bear witness to our faith and will also provide us with the words we need to defend ourselves when we suffer for our faith.

The sign that we are in the Spirit is that we obey the commandments.

A reading from the holy Gospel according to John

Jesus said to his disciples:
"If you love me, you will keep my commandments.
And I will ask the Father,
    and he will give you another Advocate to be with you always,
    the Spirit of truth, whom the world cannot accept,
    because it neither sees nor knows him.
But you know him, because he remains with you,
    and will be in you.
I will not leave you orphans; I will come to you.
In a little while the world will no longer see me,
    but you will see me, because I live and you will live.
On that day you will realize that I am in my Father
    and you are in me and I in you.
Whoever has my commandments and observes them
    is the one who loves me.
And whoever loves me will be loved by my Father,
    and I will love him and reveal myself to him."

The Gospel of the Lord.

Our First Reading for the feast of the Ascension is the only full account of the ascension of Jesus that is found in the New Testament (the account found in the Gospel of Luke is a very perfunctory account).

The account begins with a dedication to Theophilus. We do not know who Theophilus is. Various theories suggest he might be a Roman official whom Luke is trying to bring to conversion, or a rich gentleman who is paying for the work of making copies of this gospel, or else it might be a symbolic name. This third possibility is the most likely. "Theos" means God and "phileo" means to love, so this book (and the Gospel of Luke) might be dedicated to lovers of God, that is, all Christians.

We hear an outline of the ministry, which began in Jerusalem, and then spread to Judea and Samaria, and then to the ends of the earth. This is the exact pattern that one finds throughout the pages of the Acts of the Apostles.

Jesus promises the disciples that they will receive the gift of the Holy Spirit. In the Gospel of John, the disciples received that gift on Easter. Here the apostles and disciples will receive the gift on the day of Pentecost.

In the states of Alaska, California, Hawaii, Idaho, Montana, Nevada, Oregon, Utah, and Washington (as well as other states that may choose this option), the following Mass of the Ascension is celebrated on May 12, in place of the Mass of the Seventh Sunday of Easter that appears on p. 217.

May 9, 2002

THE ASCENSION OF THE LORD

Lect. No. 58

FIRST READING: Acts 1:1-11

As the Apostles were looking on, Jesus was lifted up.

A reading from the beginning of the
Acts of the Apostles

In the first book, Theophilus,
I dealt with all that Jesus did and taught
until the day he was taken up,
after giving instructions through the Holy Spirit
to the apostles whom he had chosen.
He presented himself alive to them
by many proofs after he had suffered,
appearing to them during forty days
and speaking about the kingdom of God.
While meeting with them,
he enjoined them not to depart from Jerusalem,
but to wait for "the promise of the Father
about which you have heard me speak;
for John baptized with water,
but in a few days you will be baptized with the
Holy Spirit."

When they had gathered together they asked him,
"Lord, are you at this time going to restore the
kingdom to Israel?"
He answered them, "It is not for you to know the
times or seasons
that the Father has established by his own authority.
But you will receive power when the Holy Spirit
comes upon you,
and you will be my witnesses in Jerusalem,
throughout Judea and Samaria,
and to the ends of the earth."

213

Jesus ascends into the heavens upon a cloud. The Book of Daniel predicted that the Son of Man would descend upon the clouds. Thus, it was appropriate that he ascend to heaven the same way.

Heaven is not really up above us; it is a different dimension beyond our understanding. But Jesus might have ascended in this manner so that the apostles would better understand what was happening. Thus, when we die, we will be with Jesus in heaven (but not necessarily floating on the clouds).

When he had said this, as they were looking on,
he was lifted up, and a cloud took him from their sight.
While they were looking intently at the sky as he was going,
suddenly two men dressed in white garments stood beside them.
They said, "Men of Galilee,
why are you standing there looking at the sky?
This Jesus who has been taken up from you into heaven
will return in the same way as you have seen him going into heaven."

The word of the Lord.

Lect. No. 58

RESPONSORIAL PSALM: Ps 47:2-3, 6-7, 8-9 (R̃.: 6)

In Psalm 47 we praise God who is the king of heaven and earth. He sits upon his holy throne and judges the nations.

On this feast of the Ascension we remember the day that Jesus ascended into the heavens to be enthroned next to the Father. He has been exalted and proclaimed as Lord of the heavens and the earth. Every knee shall bend and every head bow at the mention of his name.

The Jewish hasidic tradition has a saying that if God is our king, then we are at fault, but if God is not our king, then we are at fault.

The meaning of the saying is that if God is our king, we are at fault because we often do not treat him like our king.

But if God is not our king, we are at fault for we have not made him our king.

R̃. **God mounts his throne to shouts of joy: a blare of trumpets for the Lord.**

or:

R̃. **Alleluia.**

All you peoples, clap your hands,
shout to God with cries of gladness.
For the LORD, the Most High, the awesome,
is the great king over all the earth.

R̃. **God mounts his throne to shouts of joy: a blare of trumpets for the Lord.**

or:

R̃. **Alleluia.**

God mounts his throne amid shouts of joy;
the LORD, amid trumpet blasts.
Sing praise to God, sing praise;
sing praise to our king, sing praise.

R̃. **God mounts his throne to shouts of joy: a blare of trumpets for the Lord.**

or:

R̃. **Alleluia.**

By celebrating God as our Lord and king, we are committing ourselves to the project of living as if he were the Lord of our lives. We praise him, we celebrate his goodness, we observe his commandments, and we live for and in him. Saint Francis of Assisi often used the expression, "My God and my all." This is exactly what it means to make Jesus the king of our lives.

For king of all the earth is God;
    sing hymns of praise.
God reigns over the nations,
    God sits upon his holy throne.

℟. **God mounts his throne to shouts of joy: a blare of trumpets for the Lord.**

or:

℟. **Alleluia.**

Lect. No. 58

SECOND READING: Ephesians 1:17-23

God seated Jesus at his right hand in the heavens.

The Second Reading is a prayer that we might understand the profound nature of the mystery into which God has called us. If we only could comprehend the glory that God has in store for us, then we would never want to abandon our call.

The key to understanding that mystery is to reflect upon the mystery of our redemption in Christ. Jesus died for us, but the Father exalted him. He raised him from the dead and welcomed him into his glory in heaven (through the ascension that we celebrate today).

The Father also proclaimed Jesus as Lord of everything that exists in the heavens and on the earth and under the earth.

We might consider Jesus to have been humiliated when he died on the cross, but the Father considered him most loving when he was obedient even unto death. This was his hour of glory, and it was because of this that the Father exalted Jesus in supreme glory.

A reading from the Letter of Saint Paul
to the Ephesians

Brothers and sisters:
May the God of our Lord Jesus Christ, the Father of glory,
give you a Spirit of wisdom and revelation
resulting in knowledge of him.
May the eyes of your hearts be enlightened,
    that you may know what is the hope that belongs
        to his call,
    what are the riches of glory
    in his inheritance among the holy ones,
    and what is the surpassing greatness of his power
    for us who believe,
    in accord with the exercise of his great might,
    which he worked in Christ,
    raising him from the dead
    and seating him at his right hand in the heavens,
    far above every principality, authority, power, and
        dominion,
    and every name that is named
    not only in this age but also in the one to come.
And he put all things beneath his feet
    and gave him as head over all things to the
        church,

If we reflect upon this, we will realize that when we are obedient to the Father's will in our lives, we are not losing our dignity. We are living at the deepest level of love possible.

which is his body,
the fullness of the one who fills all things in every
    way.

The word of the Lord.

Lect. No. 58

ALLELUIA: Matthew 28:19a, 20b

The Alleluia Verse reminds us of the commission that Jesus gave the apostles (and us) to proclaim the gospel message to all peoples.

℟. **Alleluia, alleluia.**

Go and teach all nations, says the Lord;
I am with you always, until the end of the world.

℟. **Alleluia, alleluia.**

Lect. No. 58

GOSPEL: Matthew 28:16-20

All power in heaven and on earth has been given to me.

The final commission that Jesus gives the apostles in the Gospel of Matthew is filled with a series of themes found all throughout the gospel. Every time that there is a series of teachings (there are five major sections in the gospel), these themes are repeated.

We hear that Jesus has all power in the heavens and on the earth. Jesus gives that authority to his disciples. They are sent to all the nations of the earth, making them disciples and baptizing them in the name of the Holy Trinity.

Yet he will not abandon them or us. He promises to be with us until the end of time. He will guide and protect us until he returns in glory at the end of time.

A reading from the conclusion of the holy Gospel
according to Matthew

The eleven disciples went to Galilee,
    to the mountain to which Jesus had ordered
    them.
When they saw him, they worshiped, but they
    doubted.
Then Jesus approached and said to them,
    "All power in heaven and on earth has been given
    to me.
Go, therefore, and make disciples of all nations,
    baptizing them in the name of the Father,
    and of the Son, and of the Holy Spirit,
    teaching them to observe all that I have commanded you.
And behold, I am with you always, until the end of
    the age."

The Gospel of the Lord.

In the states of Alaska, California, Hawaii, Idaho, Montana, Nevada, Oregon, Utah, and Washington (as well as other states that may choose this option), the Mass of the Ascension that appears on p. 213 is celebrated today in place of the following Mass of the Seventh Sunday of Easter.

May 12, 2002

SEVENTH SUNDAY OF EASTER

We celebrated the feast of the Ascension this past Thursday. Today we remember what the apostles and Mary and some of the other disciples did in the days between that event and Pentecost Sunday. They dedicated themselves to prayer and waiting. They gathered together in the upper room where they had celebrated the Last Supper.

This could be a model for discernment. Before we go off charging into the world, we should dedicate ourselves to prayer to make sure that we are preaching the Lord and not ourselves. We often have to learn to wait in expectation for the Lord's times are not always our times.

Lect. No. 59

FIRST READING: Acts 1:12-14

All these devoted themselves with one accord to prayer.

A reading from the Acts of the Apostles

After Jesus had been taken up to heaven the apostles returned to Jerusalem
from the mount called Olivet, which is near Jerusalem,
a sabbath day's journey away.

When they entered the city
they went to the upper room where they were staying,
Peter and John and James and Andrew,
Philip and Thomas, Bartholomew and Matthew,
James son of Alphaeus, Simon the Zealot,
and Judas son of James.
All these devoted themselves with one accord to prayer,
together with some women,
and Mary the mother of Jesus, and his brothers.

The word of the Lord.

Lect. No. 59

RESPONSORIAL PSALM: Ps 27:1, 4, 7-8 (℟.: 13)

There is a sense of expectation in today's liturgy. We have celebrated the Ascension, but we have not yet received the gift of the Holy Spirit.

The Responsorial Psalm well depicts this sense of both hope and desire. Fear is banished be-

℟. **I believe that I shall see the good things of the Lord in the land of the living.**

or:

℟. **Alleluia.**

The LORD is my light and my salvation;
whom should I fear?

cause God will always be there for us to guide and protect us.

We are filled with hope for we know that God is our light and salvation. We know that he has responded to our prayers so often in the past. There is no need for anxiety, for God will always respond to our need.

Yet there is always a sense of things not yet being fulfilled. Being human, we long for that moment when all will be made perfect in God. We long to dwell in his house.

This sense of the "already" and "not yet" is also the spirit of our life as Christians. The kingdom of God has already dawned with the life, death, and resurrection of Jesus. The gospel has been preached to the ends of the earth.

And yet there is so much to do. The signs of the kingdom are often faint and difficult to discern. When will the kingdom be fully realized? When will we be able to dwell in the house of God for all our days?

The LORD is my life's refuge;
    of whom should I be afraid?
  R⁄. **I believe that I shall see the good things of the Lord in the land of the living.**
  or:
  R⁄. **Alleluia.**

One thing I ask of the LORD; this I seek:
To dwell in the house of the LORD
    all the days of my life,
that I may gaze on the loveliness of the LORD
    and contemplate his temple.
  R⁄. **I believe that I shall see the good things of the Lord in the land of the living.**
  or:
  R⁄. **Alleluia.**

Hear, O LORD, the sound of my call;
    have pity on me, and answer me.
Of you my heart speaks; you my glance seeks.
  R⁄. **I believe that I shall see the good things of the Lord in the land of the living.**
  or:
  R⁄. **Alleluia.**

Lect.
No. 59

SECOND READING: 1 Peter 4:13-16

If you are insulted for the name of Christ, blessed are you.

The First Letter of Peter speaks of our response to suffering. It is not a curse or punishment but a sharing in Christ's sufferings.

If we suffer for doing evil things, there is no credit to that. We should never he caught in those circumstances, because this is contrary to our Christian way of life.

A reading from the first Letter of Saint Peter

Beloved:
Rejoice to the extent that you share in the sufferings of Christ,
    so that when his glory is revealed
    you may also rejoice exultantly.
If you are insulted for the name of Christ, blessed are you,
    for the Spirit of glory and of God rests upon you.

On the other hand, if we suffer because we have tried to live good Christian lives and give witness to the gospel, then there is great honor in this. We have been chosen to share in the sufferings of Christ. Far from being ashamed, we should accept our sufferings and glorify God.

But let no one among you be made to suffer

as a murderer, a thief, an evildoer, or as an intriguer.

But whoever is made to suffer as a Christian should not be ashamed

but glorify God because of the name.

The word of the Lord.

Lect.
No. 59

We can at times feel as if we have been abandoned by God, but Jesus promises that we will never be left alone. He will always be with us.

ALLELUIA: cf. John 14:18

℟. **Alleluia, alleluia.**

I will not leave you orphans, says the Lord.
I will come back to you, and your hearts will rejoice.

℟. **Alleluia, alleluia.**

Lect.
No. 59

GOSPEL: John 17:1-11a

Father, glorify your Son.

This passage from the Gospel of John is taken from the Last Supper discourse. It is a prayer to the Father and for the disciples.

Jesus' entire mission in this gospel is to reveal the Father's love for us. He did this through his ministry of concern. He revealed himself as the only begotten Son of God to show how much God cares for us, that he would send his only Son into the world to die for us.

At the end of his life, Jesus now places his life into the hands of the Father. He asks the Father to glorify him. The word glory has a special meaning in this gospel. Jesus' hour of glory is the cross. Glory is expressing God's love, a love so profound that it would die for us.

A reading from the holy Gospel according to John

Jesus raised his eyes to heaven and said, "Father, the hour has come.
Give glory to your son, so that your son may glorify you,
    just as you gave him authority over all people,
    so that your son may give eternal life to all you gave him.
Now this is eternal life,
    that they should know you, the only true God,
    and the one whom you sent, Jesus Christ.
I glorified you on earth
    by accomplishing the work that you gave me to do.
Now glorify me, Father, with you,
    with the glory that I had with you before the world began.

Jesus prays for his disciples because they have been given to him by the Father, and he is entrusting them back into his hands. It is always important to remember that faith is ultimately a gift from God to which we must respond.

We should always have a sense of profound gratitude for this tremendous gift. At the same time we must recognize the great responsibility that we have to nurture that which God has given us.

Jesus speaks of the world and those who are in the world. They are the ones who have rejected Jesus and his mission. "The world" is not to be confused with creation. That which God created is good, but that which brings us down and makes us worldly is evil, for it separates us from God's love.

"I revealed your name to those whom you gave me
    out of the world.
They belonged to you, and you gave them to me,
    and they have kept your word.
Now they know that everything you gave me is from
    you,
    because the words you gave to me I have given to
      them,
    and they accepted them and truly understood that
      I came from you,
    and they have believed that you sent me.
I pray for them.
I do not pray for the world but for the ones you have
    given me,
    because they are yours, and everything of mine is
      yours
    and everything of yours is mine,
    and I have been glorified in them.
And now I will no longer be in the world,
    but they are in the world, while I am coming to
      you."

The Gospel of the Lord.

PENTECOST SUNDAY
AT THE VIGIL MASS

FIRST READING:

A Genesis 11:1-9

Lect. No. 62

It was called Babel because there the Lord confused the speech of all the world.

A reading from the Book of Genesis

The whole world spoke the same language, using the same words.
While the people were migrating in the east,
    they came upon a valley in the land of Shinar and
        settled there.
They said to one another,
    "Come, let us mold bricks and harden them with
        fire."
They used bricks for stone, and bitumen for mortar.
Then they said, "Come, let us build ourselves a city
    and a tower with its top in the sky,
    and so make a name for ourselves;
    otherwise we shall be scattered all over the earth."

The LORD came down to see the city and the tower
    that the people had built.
Then the LORD said: "If now, while they are one
        people,
    all speaking the same language,
    they have started to do this,
    nothing will later stop them from doing whatever
        they presume to do.
Let us then go down there and confuse their lan-
        guage,
    so that one will not understand what another
        says."
Thus the LORD scattered them from there all over
    the earth,

Saint Luke describes the day of Pentecost as being a new creation. On the first day of creation, the Spirit of the LORD was breathed into a clump of mud and made it into a living being: Adam. Now the Spirit of the Lord was being breathed into the disciples, and they were becoming a new creation in Christ.

This new act of creation involves a healing of all the damage that had been done to the human race through the effects of sin.

The First Reading today offers an example of some of that damage which it did. It presents a story about the early days of humanity that explains the origin of all of the different languages in the world.

The creation of many different languages upon the earth was seen as a punishment for sin for it prevented people from communicating with each other. People had tried to build a tower to the heavens in an attempt to bring God down to earth. God confounds their attempts and prevents them from ever attempting this again.

As with all of the stories in the early chapters in the Book of Genesis, this story is more of a parable than a historical account of the birth of the various languages. It was probably based upon a very ancient story that is now lost.

and they stopped building the city.
That is why it was called Babel,
  because there the Lord confused the speech of all
    the world.
It was from that place that he scattered them all
  over the earth.

The word of the Lord.

Lect. No. 62

OR: B Exodus 19:3-8a, 16-20b

The Lord came down upon Mount Sinai before all the people.

In this reading we hear of a great theophany in which God encounters his people on Mount Sinai. The mountain was wrapped in smoke and fire. There was thunder and the mountain shook violently. (It is interesting to contrast this description with the story of how God appeared to Elijah the prophet in 1 Kings 19.)

This epiphany of the power of God occurred shortly after the people of Israel left Egypt. The LORD had delivered them from the hands of their enemies. The people knew that God had intervened in their history to make them his own people.

Therefore the LORD invited his people into this covenant. He would be their God and they would be his people for all time. He asked them only that they keep the commandments he was giving them so that they might be holy and set apart in his name.

The feast of Pentecost is also a time for setting apart a people for God. In this case, the

A reading from the Book of Exodus

Moses went up the mountain to God.
  Then the LORD called to him and said,
  "Thus shall you say to the house of Jacob;
  tell the Israelites:
  You have seen for yourselves how I treated the
    Egyptians
  and how I bore you up on eagle wings
  and brought you here to myself.
Therefore, if you hearken to my voice and keep my
    covenant,
  you shall be my special possession,
  dearer to me than all other people,
  though all the earth is mine.
You shall be to me a kingdom of priests, a holy
    nation.
That is what you must tell the Israelites."
So Moses went and summoned the elders of the
    people.
When he set before them
  all that the LORD had ordered him to tell them,
  the people all answered together,
  "Everything the LORD has said, we will do."

On the morning of the third day
  there were peals of thunder and lightning,

people being set apart is the Church, the Mystical Body of Christ. The commandment he hands on to them is that they are to love each other as Jesus has loved them.

Like the people of Israel, God now calls the people of the Church to be a kingdom of priests, a holy nation unto the Lord.

God does not always encounter his people on mountains that tremble or with great winds and tongues of fire. This does not mean that God is not there. It simply means that God acts in many different ways, and yet he is always setting apart a holy people to be his own.

and a heavy cloud over the mountain,
and a very loud trumpet blast,
so that all the people in the camp trembled.
But Moses led the people out of the camp to meet God,
and they stationed themselves at the foot of the mountain.
Mount Sinai was all wrapped in smoke,
for the LORD came down upon it in fire.
The smoke rose from it as though from a furnace,
and the whole mountain trembled violently.
The trumpet blast grew louder and louder, while Moses was speaking,
and God answering him with thunder.

When the LORD came down to the top of Mount Sinai,
he summoned Moses to the top of the mountain.

The word of the Lord.

Lect.
No. 62

OR: C Ezekiel 37:1-14

Dry bones of Israel, I will bring spirit into you, that you may come to life.

This passage was written by the Prophet Ezekiel while he was in exile in Babylon. This is one of the first passages that speaks of the resurrection of the dead.

It is probable that when the prophet spoke of these bones coming to life, he intended this as a prophecy of the resurrection of the people of Israel. They were a nation in exile and they were as good as dead. God would breathe his spirit back into them and would bring them back to life. He would heal the wounds caused by their sins.

A reading from the Book of the Prophet Ezekiel

The hand of the LORD came upon me,
and he led me out in the spirit of the LORD
and set me in the center of the plain,
which was now filled with bones.
He made me walk among the bones in every direction
so that I saw how many they were on the surface of the plain.
How dry they were!
He asked me:
Son of man, can these bones come to life?
I answered, "Lord GOD, you alone know that."
Then he said to me:

Nevertheless, this passage makes sense only if the prophet also believed that God could bring individuals back to life. The experience of living in exile in Babylon had taught Ezekiel that there must be a reward after this life.

It is probable that this passage is based upon the beliefs of the Persian people. They were the nation to the east of Babylon. Many of the Persians practiced the cult of Zoroaster. In this religion, the dead were laid out in the fields until the birds of the air picked their bones dry. The people of this religion believed that these bones would be raised from the dead by a good god on the last day.

Thus, when Ezekiel spoke to these bones, he probably had this idea in mind. Of course, like many of the prophets of the Old Testament, he added his own particular Jewish ideas to the passage.

In the same way in which the LORD allowed his Spirit to enter into these bones to make them living creatures, so also God sent his Spirit into us to allow us to become a living people. Before he sent his Spirit, we were as good as dead.

We were separated from each other by false divisions brought about by our sinfulness. We were not joined together like the bones of a living body, we were scattered like dried out bones.

Prophesy over these bones, and say to them:
Dry bones, hear the word of the LORD!
Thus says the Lord GOD to these bones:
See! I will bring spirit into you, that you may come to life.
I will put sinews upon you, make flesh grow over you,
cover you with skin, and put spirit in you
so that you may come to life and know that I am the LORD.
I, Ezekiel, prophesied as I had been told,
and even as I was prophesying I heard a noise;
it was a rattling as the bones came together, bone joining bone.
I saw the sinews and the flesh come upon them,
and the skin cover them, but there was no spirit in them.
Then the LORD said to me:
Prophesy to the spirit, prophesy, son of man,
and say to the spirit: Thus says the Lord GOD:
From the four winds come, O spirit,
and breathe into these slain that they may come to life.
I prophesied as he told me, and the spirit came into them;
they came alive and stood upright, a vast army.
Then he said to me:
Son of man, these bones are the whole house of Israel.
They have been saying,
"Our bones are dried up,
our hope is lost, and we are cut off."
Therefore, prophesy and say to them: Thus says the Lord GOD:
O my people, I will open your graves
and have you rise from them,
and bring you back to the land of Israel.

Now God has made us a living body again. We are one in him. We are God's own people, and we make him present upon the earth.

But we must choose to live in God's love. That means making decisions to reject selfishness, which only brings death, and choosing to live in the freedom of God's own children.

Then you shall know that I am the LORD,
  when I open your graves and have you rise from
    them,
  O my people!
I will put my spirit in you that you may live,
  and I will settle you upon your land;
  thus you shall know that I am the LORD.
I have promised, and I will do it, says the LORD.

The word of the Lord.

Lect.
No. 62

OR: D Joel 3:1-5

I will pour out my spirit upon the servants and handmaids.

This reading from the Book of the Prophet Joel is probably one of the last parts of the Old Testament written. It belongs to the apocalyptic tradition of the Bible. In this tradition, authors speak of how bad things have become, and how only an intervention of the LORD can make it better. Most apocalyptic books also use imaginative imagery to convey the idea of the coming judgment.

The LORD'S intervention would occur through an outpouring of the Holy Spirit of the LORD upon all peoples. The Spirit of God would give us a revelation of the hidden secrets of God.

The prophet speaks of the great marvels that would accompany this outpouring of the Spirit. The image of the Spirit appearing in tongues of fire is taken from this passage. Saint Peter, in fact, quoted this very passage in his discourse to the crowd on Pentecost Sunday.

A reading from the Book of the Prophet Joel

Thus says the LORD:
  I will pour out my spirit upon all flesh.
Your sons and daughters shall prophesy,
  your old men shall dream dreams,
  your young men shall see visions;
even upon the servants and the handmaids,
  in those days, I will pour out my spirit.
And I will work wonders in the heavens and on the
    earth,
  blood, fire, and columns of smoke;
the sun will be turned to darkness,
  and the moon to blood,
at the coming of the day of the LORD,
  the great and terrible day.
Then everyone shall be rescued
  who calls on the name of the LORD;
for on Mount Zion there shall be a remnant,
  as the LORD has said,
and in Jerusalem survivors
  whom the LORD shall call.

The word of the Lord.

| Lect.
No. 62 | **RESPONSORIAL PSALM: Ps 104:1-2, 24, 35, 27-28, 29, 30 (℟.: cf. 30)** |

This Responsorial Psalm is a hymn of praise to the God of all creation. The greatest reason we have to praise God is that when he created, he sent out his Spirit into the world. Then, after we sinned and damaged creation, God sent forth his Spirit again on the day of Pentecost to renew the face of the earth. We are now a new creation.

We are not subject to many of the destructive effects of sin for we have been rescued from them by grace. God has clothed us with majesty and glory and robed us in light.

This is not to say that the renewal is totally completed, for we live in the "already" but also in the "not yet." We have received the Holy Spirit, which is God's down payment of the glory that awaits us, but we are also still waiting for the total fulfillment of all the promises Jesus made. Still, the kingdom has dawned and if we look at things through the eyes of God, we will see his power at work in our midst.

We are totally dependent upon the generosity of God. As with all living creatures, if God withholds his breath, we cannot hope to survive. Likewise, if God withholds his Spirit, our spiritual life will perish. We will suffocate spiritually.

℟. **Lord, send out your Spirit, and renew the face of the earth.**

or:

℟. **Alleluia.**

Bless the LORD, O my soul!
   O LORD, my God, you are great indeed!
You are clothed with majesty and glory,
   robed in light as with a cloak.

℟. **Lord, send out your Spirit, and renew the face of the earth.**

or:

℟. **Alleluia.**

How manifold are your works, O LORD!
   In wisdom you have wrought them all—
the earth is full of your creatures;
   bless the LORD, O my soul! Alleluia.

℟. **Lord, send out your Spirit, and renew the face of the earth.**

or:

℟. **Alleluia.**

Creatures all look to you
   to give them food in due time.
When you give it to them, they gather it;
   when you open your hand, they are filled with good things.

℟. **Lord, send out your Spirit, and renew the face of the earth.**

or:

℟. **Alleluia.**

If you take away their breath, they perish
   and return to their dust.

But if we trust in God and find our refuge in him, then we will not have to fear. God will provide his Spirit to renew our hearts. He never refuses his gift of the Spirit to those who ask him for it in his name.

When you send forth your spirit, they are created,
and you renew the face of the earth.

R̰. **Lord, send out your Spirit, and renew the face of the earth.**

or:

R̰. **Alleluia.**

Lect.
No. 62

SECOND READING: Romans 8:22-27

The Spirit intercedes with inexpressible groanings.

When God created the world, he breathed his Spirit into Adam and made him a living creature, a human being. We are not simply animals; we have something of God within us.

But when we sinned, we denied that presence. We chose to follow that which could not give life. Furthermore, our sinfulness alienated not only us, but also all of creation. All that exists was made to be good, but our sins have made creation ambiguous. That which should lead us to God all too often leads us to sin.

As one example, just think of how often we misuse food. God created it to be good and of service to us, but we frequently eat too little or too much or the wrong thing.

We recognize the emptiness within us, and unfortunately we try to fill the void with sin and bad habits, etc, but none of it works. We are left feeling lonelier. The Spirit that Jesus breathed into his disciples fills the void. It reminds us of who we are, beloved children of God.

A reading from the Letter of Saint Paul
to the Romans

Brothers and sisters:
We know that all creation is groaning in labor
pains even until now;
and not only that, but we ourselves,
who have the firstfruits of the Spirit,
we also groan within ourselves
as we wait for adoption, the redemption of our
bodies.
For in hope we were saved.
Now hope that sees is not hope.
For who hopes for what one sees?
But if we hope for what we do not see, we wait with
endurance.

In the same way, the Spirit too comes to the aid of
our weakness;
for we do not know how to pray as we ought,
but the Spirit himself intercedes with inexpressible groanings.
And the one who searches hearts
knows what is the intention of the Spirit,
because he intercedes for the holy ones
according to God's will.

The word of the Lord.

Lect.
No. 62

The Holy Spirit descended upon the apostles and Mary in the form of tongues of fire. We ask that same Spirit to inflame our hearts.

Lect.
No. 62

In this Gospel passage Jesus identifies himself as the source of living water. This is an image that was found in Ezekiel. The prophet was commanded to pass through a great river that flowed from the temple. The water became so deep that he could not pass through it. The river was a symbol for the acts of worship in the temple that were a source of grace for the people of Israel.

Now Jesus identifies himself as the true source of all grace. This was the water he offered to the Samaritan woman, and this is the water he gives to us.

ALLELUIA

℟. **Alleluia, alleluia.**

Come, Holy Spirit, fill the hearts of the faithful and kindle in them the fire of your love.

℟. **Alleluia, alleluia.**

GOSPEL: John 7:37-39

Rivers of living water will flow.

A reading from the holy Gospel according to John

On the last and greatest day of the feast,
    Jesus stood up and exclaimed,
    "Let anyone who thirsts come to me and drink.
As Scripture says:
    Rivers of living water will flow from within him
    who believes in me."

He said this in reference to the Spirit
    that those who came to believe in him were to receive.
There was, of course, no Spirit yet,
    because Jesus had not yet been glorified.

The Gospel of the Lord.

May 19, 2002

PENTECOST SUNDAY

MASS DURING THE DAY

Lect. No. 63

FIRST READING: Acts 2:1-11

*They were all filled with the Holy Spirit
and began to speak.*

A reading from the Acts of the Apostles

When the time for Pentecost was fulfilled,
they were all in one place together.
And suddenly there came from the sky
a noise like a strong driving wind,
and it filled the entire house in which they were.
Then there appeared to them tongues as of fire,
which parted and came to rest on each one of
them.
And they were all filled with the Holy Spirit
and began to speak in different tongues,
as the Spirit enabled them to proclaim.

Now there were devout Jews from every nation
under heaven staying in Jerusalem.
At this sound, they gathered in a large crowd,
but they were confused
because each one heard them speaking in his own
language.
They were astounded, and in amazement they
asked,
"Are not all these people who are speaking
Galileans?
Then how does each of us hear them in his native
language?
We are Parthians, Medes, and Elamites,
inhabitants of Mesopotamia, Judea and Cappadocia,

The account of the day of Pentecost in Acts is filled with symbolism.

Pentecost was already a pilgrimage festival for the Jewish people. That would explain the large crowd of Jews from all over the world who were there when the Holy Spirit descended upon the apostles and Mary. The fact that they are from all the countries mentioned in the account is a foreshadowing of the fact that the gospel would eventually spread to all those nations. This might, in fact, be a list of all the nations that had already received the gospel when this book was written.

The strong wind is reminiscent of the Spirit of the Lord that hovered over the waters on the first day of creation. This was a new creation in which the people of God were being made into the Church, the Mystical Body of Christ.

The tongues of fire was a fulfillment of the prophecy of Joel that the Spirit would come upon God's people. We are no longer filled with loneliness and alienation and fear.

There was a healing of the confusion of languages in the fact that the apostles could speak in their own language and everyone could understand them. Although this is called the gift of tongues, it is different from the phenomenon described in 1 Corinthians 12—14.

Pontus and Asia, Phrygia and Pamphylia,
Egypt and the districts of Libya near Cyrene,
as well as travelers from Rome,
both Jews and converts to Judaism, Cretans and Arabs,
yet we hear them speaking in our own tongues
of the mighty acts of God."

The word of the Lord.

| Lect.
No. 63 | **RESPONSORIAL PSALM: Ps 104:1, 24, 29-30, 31, 34 (℟.: cf. 30)** |

This is a hymn of praise to the God of creation. We praise God for he sent out his Spirit to create the world. After we sinned and damaged creation, God sent forth his Spirit again to renew the face of the earth. We are a new creation, not subject to the destructive effects of sin.

This is not to say that the renewal is totally complete, for we live in the "already" but "not yet." We have already received the Holy Spirit, which is God's down payment of the glory that awaits us, but we are also still awaiting the total fulfillment of the promises Jesus made. Yet the kingdom has dawned and if we look at things through the eyes of Jesus, we will see God's power at work in our midst.

We are totally dependent upon the generosity of God. As with all living creatures, we cannot survive if he withholds his breath. Likewise, if God withholds his Spirit, our spiritual life will perish. We will suffocate spiritually.

℟. **Lord, send out your Spirit, and renew the face of the earth.**

or:

℟. **Alleluia.**

Bless the LORD, O my soul!
　O LORD, my God, you are great indeed!
How manifold are your works, O LORD!
　the earth is full of your creatures.

℟. **Lord, send out your Spirit, and renew the face of the earth.**

or:

℟. **Alleluia.**

May the glory of the LORD endure forever;
　may the LORD be glad in his works!
Pleasing to him be my theme;
　I will be glad in the LORD.

℟. **Lord, send out your Spirit, and renew the face of the earth.**

or:

℟. **Alleluia.**

If you take away their breath, they perish
　and return to their dust.

But if we trust in Jesus and find all of our strength in God, then we will not have to fear. God will provide his Spirit to those who ask him for it in his name. God will give us life that is so profound that even death will not conquer it.

When you send forth your spirit, they are created,
    and you renew the face of the earth.

℟. **Lord, send out your Spirit, and renew the face of the earth.**

or:

℟. **Alleluia.**

Lect. No. 63

SECOND READING: 1 Corinthians 12:3b-7, 12-13

In one Spirit we were all baptized into one body.

The community of Corinth suffered from some misunderstandings concerning the role of the Holy Spirit. They considered the gifts they had received to be signs of power that made them better than others.

Saint Paul attempts to correct their arrogance by teaching them that gifts are given for the common service. They are not for our own profit. Each person in the community has been given special gifts that complement the gifts given to others. We need each other to be complete.

Furthermore, the gifts of the Spirit should bring us closer together, not create divisions. Before our baptism, we were divided from each other and forced to live as competitors and even enemies. Now we are one body in Christ and we seek to build up that body in love.

A reading from the first Letter of Saint Paul
    to the Corinthians

Brothers and sisters:
    No one can say, "Jesus is Lord," except by the Holy Spirit.
There are different kinds of spiritual gifts but the same Spirit;
    there are different forms of service but the same Lord;
    there are different workings but the same God
    who produces all of them in everyone.
To each individual the manifestation of the Spirit
    is given for some benefit.

As a body is one though it has many parts,
    and all the parts of the body, though many, are one body,
    so also Christ.
For in one Spirit we were all baptized into one body,
    whether Jews or Greeks, slaves or free persons,
    and we were all given to drink of one Spirit.

The word of the Lord.

Lect. No. 63

SEQUENCE: *Veni, Sancte Spiritus*

This beautiful Sequence is a hymn that celebrates the Holy Spirit. It speaks of many of the attributes that we associate with the Spirit.

First of all, the Spirit is called a light divine. We do not know our way to God, but the Spirit illumines our thoughts and prayers.

The Spirit is a comforter. This is one of the meanings of the title "Paraclete."

We often need to experience the love that is communicated through the Spirit. The Spirit is the love between the Father and the Son and between them and us.

The Spirit fills up the void in our heart. We long for fulfillment, yet so often we seek it in things that do not bring true joy and peace. The Spirit responds to our deepest aspirations.

We receive healing, both spiritual and physical, through the action of the Holy Spirit.

We also speak of the seven gifts that the Spirit has given us. The gifts are symbolic of the incredible multiplicity of gifts that the Spirit pours out upon us. They allow us to continue the work of God in the world.

Come, Holy Spirit, come!
And from your celestial home
  Shed a ray of light divine!
Come, Father of the poor!
Come, source of all our store!
  Come, within our bosoms shine.
You, of comforters the best;
You, the soul's most welcome guest;
  Sweet refreshment here below;
In our labor, rest most sweet;
Grateful coolness in the heat;
  Solace in the midst of woe.
O most blessed Light divine,
Shine within these hearts of yours,
  And our inmost being fill!
Where you are not, we have naught,
Nothing good in deed or thought,
  Nothing free from taint of ill.
Heal our wounds, our strength renew;
On our dryness pour your dew;
  Wash the stains of guilt away:
Bend the stubborn heart and will;
Melt the frozen, warm the chill;
  Guide the steps that go astray.
On the faithful, who adore
And confess you, evermore
  In your sevenfold gift descend;
Give them virtue's sure reward;
Give them your salvation, Lord;
  Give them joys that never end. Amen.
  Alleluia.

Lect. No. 63

We invite the Holy Spirit into our lives and our hearts. Without the love that the Spirit imparts, we cannot hope to live in God's love.

ALLELUIA

℟. **Alleluia, alleluia.**

Come, Holy Spirit, fill the hearts of your faithful and kindle in them the fire of your love.

℟. **Alleluia, alleluia.**

Lect. No. 63

GOSPEL: John 20:19-23

As the Father sent me, so I send you: Receive the Holy Spirit.

Having heard the Acts version of the descent of the Holy Spirit, we now hear the version contained in the Gospel of John.

Jesus breathes upon the disciples to give them the gift of the Holy Spirit. This is in imitation of how God created Adam. God breathed his Spirit into Adam and he came to life. In this account, Jesus breathes his Holy Spirit into the disciples and they are given new life in him.

The gift of the Holy Spirit is also associated with the forgiveness of our sins. The Spirit is God's love and is so filled with mercy that it brings us pardon. The sin against the Spirit is to believe that our sins are unforgivable or to presume upon God's mercy and so to sin all the more.

A reading from the holy Gospel according to John

On the evening of that first day of the week,
 when the doors were locked, where the disciples were,
for fear of the Jews,
Jesus came and stood in their midst
 and said to them, "Peace be with you."
When he had said this, he showed them his hands
 and his side.
The disciples rejoiced when they saw the Lord.
Jesus said to them again, "Peace be with you.
As the Father has sent me, so I send you."
And when he had said this, he breathed on them
 and said to them,
 "Receive the Holy Spirit.
Whose sins you forgive are forgiven them,
 and whose sins you retain are retained."

The Gospel of the Lord.

MAY 26, 2002

THE SOLEMNITY OF THE MOST HOLY TRINITY

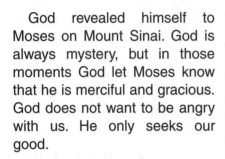

Lect. No. 164

FIRST READING: Exodus 34:4b-6, 8-9

The Lord, the Lord, a merciful and gracious God.

God revealed himself to Moses on Mount Sinai. God is always mystery, but in those moments God let Moses know that he is merciful and gracious. God does not want to be angry with us. He only seeks our good.

Thus, the commandments that God revealed to Moses and the people of Israel are to be seen as a great act of compassion. God so loved us that he taught us how to live in his ways. If we observe the commandments, we will find life; but if we break the commandments, we will have chosen our own spiritual death.

Moses admitted that the people of Israel (and we) are sinners and we will always be in need of God's mercy, but God promises to grant that mercy when we seek it.

A reading from the Book of Exodus

Early in the morning Moses went up Mount Sinai
    as the LORD had commanded him,
    taking along the two stone tablets.

Having come down in a cloud, the LORD stood with Moses there
    and proclaimed his name, "LORD."
Thus the LORD passed before him and cried out,
    "The LORD, the LORD, a merciful and gracious God,
    slow to anger and rich in kindness and fidelity."
Moses at once bowed down to the ground in worship.
Then he said, "If I find favor with you, O LORD,
    do come along in our company.
This is indeed a stiff–necked people; yet pardon our wickedness and sins,
    and receive us as your own."

The word of the Lord.

Lect. No. 164

RESPONSORIAL PSALM: Daniel 3:52, 53, 54, 55 (℟.: 52b)

These verses are taken from the hymn of the three young men in the furnace from the Book of Daniel.

We praise the God of history, the God of our fathers. God reveals himself through his actions in our history.

℟. **Glory and praise for ever!**

Blessed are you, O Lord, the God of our fathers,
    praiseworthy and exalted above all forever;
and blessed is your holy and glorious name,
    praiseworthy and exalted above all for all ages.

℟. **Glory and praise for ever!**

We praise the holy name of God. God revealed his name as Yahweh, which means "I am." Rabbis suggested that this means, "I am who I am for you, who I have always been for you, who I will always be for you."

We praise God in his temple, for God reveals himself in great love and allows us to encounter him.

Finally, we praise the God of mystery who can look into the depths.

Lect.
No. 164

Blessed are you in the temple of your holy glory,
   praiseworthy and glorious above all forever.

℟. **Glory and praise for ever!**

Blessed are you on the throne of your kingdom,
   praiseworthy and exalted above all forever.

℟. **Glory and praise for ever!**

Blessed are you who look into the depths
   from your throne upon the cherubim,
   praiseworthy and exalted above all forever.

℟. **Glory and praise for ever!**

SECOND READING: 2 Corinthians 13:11-13

*The grace of Jesus Christ and the love of God
and the fellowship of the Holy Spirit.*

Saint Paul's two Letters to the Corinthians are the first Letters written in the New Testament that have clear references to the Holy Trinity. Remember that these letters were written long before the gospels were written.

In the last verses of this reading, we hear a blessing given in the name of the Lord Jesus Christ (the word "Lord" means that Jesus is God and the word "Christ" is the Greek equivalent of the word "Messiah"), God (the Father), and the Holy Spirit.

Lect.
No. 164

A reading from the second Letter of Saint Paul
to the Corinthians

Brothers and sisters, rejoice. Mend your ways, encourage one another,
   agree with one another, live in peace,
   and the God of love and peace will be with you.
Greet one another with a holy kiss.
All the holy ones greet you.

The grace of the Lord Jesus Christ
   and the love of God
   and the fellowship of the Holy Spirit be with all of
      you.

The word of the Lord.

ALLELUIA: cf. Revelation 1:8

The Alleluia Verse is taken from the Book of Revelation and is a doxology giving praise to God who is Trinity: Father, Son, and Holy Spirit.

℟. **Alleluia, alleluia.**

Glory to the Father, the Son, and the Holy Spirit;
   to God who is, who was, and who is to come.

℟. **Alleluia, alleluia.**

Lect.
No. 164

GOSPEL: John 3:16-18

God sent his Son that the world might be saved through him.

The Gospel of John presents the final judgment as something that will occur before the end of time. It already occurs today, for when we make Jesus a part of our lives, God will be real and alive to us. When, however, we reject Jesus, we choose to live a life without him.

There could he no greater punishment than that. However this is certainly not what God wants. God did not send Jesus into the world so that we would be condemned. God wants us to be saved; he even called his Son to the cross out of love for us.

A reading from the holy Gospel according to John

God so loved the world that he gave his only Son,
so that everyone who believes in him might not perish
but might have eternal life.
For God did not send his Son into the world to condemn the world,
but that the world might be saved through him.
Whoever believes in him will not be condemned,
but whoever does not believe has already been condemned,
because he has not believed in the name of the only Son of God.

The Gospel of the Lord.

Lect. No. 167

The time that Israel spent in the desert has been viewed in different ways throughout their history.

On the one hand, their time in the desert was a period of difficulties and testing. There were all but unbearable circumstances in which the Israelites often lacked water, food, safety, etc.

On the other hand, it was a time of God's intervention, for God protected them from every danger that oppressed them. God gave them water from a rock. God gave them manna and quail from the skies.

Because the people of Israel had no way to provide for their own needs, they learned to trust in the providence of God.

Ironically, the greatest danger to Israel was not in the desert, it was when they left the desert. They could provide for themselves and they began to forget to trust.

Once a year Jewish people live in tents (the Feast of Booths) to commemorate the period when God nourished them in the desert.

FIRST READING:

Deuteronomy 8:2-3, 14b-16a

He gave you a food unknown to you and your fathers.

A reading from the Book of Deuteronomy

Moses said to the people:
"Remember how for forty years now the LORD, your God,
has directed all your journeying in the desert,
so as to test you by affliction
and find out whether or not it was your intention
to keep his commandments.
He therefore let you be afflicted with hunger,
and then fed you with manna,
a food unknown to you and your fathers,
in order to show you that not by bread alone does one live,
but by every word that comes forth from the mouth of the LORD.

"Do not forget the LORD, your God,
who brought you out of the land of Egypt,
that place of slavery;
who guided you through the vast and terrible desert
with its saraph serpents and scorpions,
its parched and waterless ground;
who brought forth water for you from the flinty rock
and fed you in the desert with manna,
a food unknown to your fathers."

The word of the Lord.

Lect.
No. 167 **RESPONSORIAL PSALM: Ps 147:12-13, 14-15, 19-20 (℟.: 12)**

This psalm is a hymn of praise for the many ways that God has shown his power and providence.

We praise God who has protected us against our enemies, whether they be external brokenness or the demons that haunt our peace.

God has also blessed our homes with children. Every child is a gift from God the creator.

God has also granted peace in our borders. This is both the peace that is the absence of strife and the peace of a heart that is at home in God. Every time we try to establish peace on our own, we end up frustrated.

We are able to see God's word transforming the world. We see creation being transformed before our very eyes. If we see things with the eyes of God, we will see the kingdom of God dawning.

God has also given us his commandments (both those written and those found in our hearts). The commandments are not the dictates of an authoritarian God. They are one of his most precious gifts, for they help us to become the best people that we could possibly be.

℟. **Praise the Lord, Jerusalem.**

or:

℟. **Alleluia.**

Glorify the LORD, O Jerusalem;
   praise your God, O Zion.
For he has strengthened the bars of your gates;
   he has blessed your children within you.

℟. **Praise the Lord, Jerusalem.**

or:

℟. **Alleluia.**

He has granted peace in your borders;
   with the best of wheat he fills you.
He sends forth his command to the earth;
   swiftly runs his word!

℟. **Praise the Lord, Jerusalem.**

or:

℟. **Alleluia.**

He has proclaimed his word to Jacob,
   his statutes and his ordinances to Israel.
He has not done thus for any other nation;
   his ordinances he has not made known to them.
    Alleluia.

℟. **Praise the Lord, Jerusalem.**

or:

℟. **Alleluia.**

Lect.
No. 167

SECOND READING: 1 Corinthians 10:16-17

The bread is one, and we, though many, are one body.

In these short verses, Saint Paul is able to communicate several important truths about the sacrament of the Eucharist. We hear that the Eucharist is the body and blood of Jesus. Participating in this sacrament is union with our Lord.

Furthermore, when we eat the body and blood of the Lord, we are also becoming one with each other. We have to live this reality in the way we treat our neighbor.

Lect.
No. 167

This rather long Sequence is a beautiful hymn that speaks of the miracle of God's love for us expressed in the sacrament of the Eucharist.

We begin by praising Jesus the Lord and shepherd of our lives. He is our Lord and our all. We have no other choice but to praise him because this is our greatest joy in life.

When we really love someone, the words of love we express to that person are not seen as taking anything away from us. They fulfill us, for we are most truly ourselves when we are giving of ourselves to the other.

We especially praise Jesus when we recall the sacrament

A reading from the first Letter of Saint Paul to the Corinthians

Brothers and sisters:
The cup of blessing that we bless,
is it not a participation in the blood of Christ?
The bread that we break,
is it not a participation in the body of Christ?
Because the loaf of bread is one,
we, though many, are one body,
for we all partake of the one loaf.

The word of the Lord.

SEQUENCE: *Lauda Sion*

The sequence Laud, O Zion (Lauda Sion), or the shorter form beginning with the verse Lo! the angel's food is given, may be sung optionally before the Alleluia.

Laud, O Zion, your salvation,
Laud with hymns of exultation,
Christ, your king and shepherd true:

Bring him all the praise you know,
He is more than you bestow.
Never can you reach his due.

Special theme for glad thanksgiving
Is the quick'ning and the living
Bread today before you set:

From his hands of old partaken,
As we know, by faith unshaken,
Where the Twelve at supper met.

Full and clear ring out your chanting,
Joy nor sweetest grace be wanting,
From your heart let praises burst:

of the Eucharist. Just thinking of this sacrament reminds us of the first time that this sacrament was celebrated

We think of the twelve apostles gathered together to celebrate the Passover meal. We also think of how Jesus transformed the meaning of that feast. Our meal is no longer the commemoration of something that happened in Egypt. We now celebrate the new Passover, that in which Jesus passed over from death into life.

This meal was intended to be repeated again and again within the community.

Jesus told us to take bread and wine and to say the words that he had said over these substances.

These words are not simply a commemoration, they also make real the event they celebrate. The bread is made into flesh, the wine into blood. We cannot understand this only at the level of our senses, for they fail to perceive the great change that has occurred. Yet we believe!

This celebration makes present again (in an unbloody manner) the sacrifice of Jesus on the cross. We experience his sacrificial love when we partake of this meal.

In a miraculous manner, there are no limitations in our Eucharistic Lord. He is risen, so he no longer suffers from the limitations of this present condition. He can be in many places

For today the feast is holden,
When the institution olden
　　Of that supper was rehearsed.

Here the new law's new oblation,
By the new king's revelation,
　　Ends the form of ancient rite:

Now the new the old effaces,
Truth away the shadow chases,
　　Light dispels the gloom of night.

What he did at supper seated,
Christ ordained to be repeated,
　　His memorial ne'er to cease:

And his rule for guidance taking,
Bread and wine we hallow, making
　　Thus our sacrifice of peace.

This the truth each Christian learns,
Bread into his flesh he turns,
　　To his precious blood the wine:

Sight has fail'd, nor thought conceives,
But a dauntless faith believes,
　　Resting on a pow'r divine.

Here beneath these signs are hidden
Priceless things to sense forbidden;
　　Signs, not things are all we see:

Blood is poured and flesh is broken,
Yet in either wondrous token
　　Christ entire we know to be.

Whoso of this food partakes,
Does not rend the Lord nor breaks;
　　Christ is whole to all that taste:

Thousands are, as one, receivers,
One, as thousands of believers,
　　Eats of him who cannot waste.

Bad and good the feast are sharing,
Of what divers dooms preparing,
　　Endless death, or endless life.

and even times at once. He is fully present even in the smallest fragment of the host.

The good and the evil both participate in this sacrament. But while this meal brings the good into union with the Lord, the evil are actually harmed. They have committed an act of deceit that leaves them lonelier than before.

Our breaking of the bread does not destroy the presence of Jesus. He is risen, and our actions only serve to celebrate the mystery of his glorified body.

This shorter form of the eucharistic hymn is permeated with symbolism. The first part speaks of the sacredness of this sacrament. Only those who have purified their hearts should dare to participate in it.

This sacrament had been prefigured in the Old Testament by Isaac who was offered up as a sacrifice in obedience to the Father. It was also prefigured by the paschal lamb whose blood brought safety and salvation to the people of Israel.

The third stanza calls upon Jesus to protect and nourish us.

Finally, the fourth stanza asks that the promise of the sacrament of the Eucharist be fulfilled. It is the bread of heaven, and we ask that we be able to participate in the heavenly banquet forever.

Life to these, to those damnation,
See how like participation
   Is with unlike issues rife.

When the sacrament is broken,
Doubt not, but believe 'tis spoken,
   That each sever'd outward token
    Doth the very whole contain.

Nought the precious gift divides,
Breaking but the sign betides
   Jesus still the same abides,
    Still unbroken does remain.

The shorter form of the sequence begins here.

Lo! the angel's food is given
  To the pilgrim who has striven;
   See the children's bread from heaven,
    Which on dogs may not be spent.

Truth the ancient types fulfilling,
Isaac bound, a victim willing,
   Paschal lamb, its lifeblood spilling,
    Manna to the fathers sent.

Very bread, good shepherd, tend us,
Jesu, of your love befriend us,
   You refresh us, you defend us,
   Your eternal goodness send us
In the land of life to see.

You who all things can and know,
Who on earth such food bestow,
   Grant us with your saints, though lowest,
   Where the heav'nly feast you show,
Fellow heirs and guests to be. Amen. Alleluia.

Lect.
No. 167

This Alleluia Verse is taken from the discourse on the bread of life found in the Gospel of John. It identifies Jesus as the only bread that can truly nourish us.

Lect.
No. 167

This is the latter part of the discourse on the bread of life. The first part portrayed Jesus primarily as the Wisdom of God and secondarily as the Eucharistic bread of life. In this second part, the entire emphasis is upon the Real Presence of Jesus in the bread and wine that have become his body and blood.

We hear that the bread is the flesh of Jesus. The word for flesh in Greek is "sarx," and it means physical body. When the prologue of this gospel spoke about the incarnation, it said that the word became flesh. By using the same word for the Eucharist, this gospel is saying that whatever Jesus was in the incarnation, that is what the Eucharist is.

Those listening to him are horrified, for it sounds as if he is proposing cannibalism (this was, in fact, one of the calumnies used against early Christians). Jesus even proposes drinking his blood (blood was sacred to the Hebrews and belonged only to God, which is why in Kosher butchering the animal is bled completely).

In this holy sacrament, Jesus offers to come into a profound and intimate union with each one of us.

ALLELUIA: John 6:51

℟. **Alleluia, alleluia.**

I am the living bread that came down from heaven,
  says the Lord;
whoever eats this bread will live forever.

℟. **Alleluia, alleluia.**

GOSPEL: John 6:51-58

My flesh is true food, and my blood is true drink.

A reading from the holy Gospel according to John

Jesus said to the Jewish crowds:
"I am the living bread that came down from heaven;
  whoever eats this bread will live forever;
  and the bread that I will give
  is my flesh for the life of the world."

The Jews quarreled among themselves, saying,
  "How can this man give us his flesh to eat?"
Jesus said to them,
  "Amen, amen, I say to you,
  unless you eat the flesh of the Son of Man and
    drink his blood,
  you do not have life within you.
Whoever eats my flesh and drinks my blood
  has eternal life,
  and I will raise him on the last day.
For my flesh is true food,
  and my blood is true drink.
Whoever eats my flesh and drinks my blood
  remains in me and I in him.
Just as the living Father sent me
  and I have life because of the Father,
  so also the one who feeds on me
  will have life because of me.
This is the bread that came down from heaven.
Unlike your ancestors who ate and still died,
  whoever eats this bread will live forever."

The Gospel of the Lord.

TENTH SUNDAY IN ORDINARY TIME

Lect.
No. 88

FIRST READING:

Hosea 6:3-6

It is love that I desire, not sacrifice.

This First Reading presents a dialog between God and the people of Israel. The people are sure that that LORD would intervene upon their behalf. They believe that this was as certain as the fact that rain falls upon the earth.

God uses a water image in his response, but one that is the opposite of that used by the people. He speaks of their fidelity as being as unsure as the dew that disappears in the morning.

The people had presumed upon God's fidelity, but God desired a change in their interior disposition and not their external actions.

A reading from the Book of the Prophet Hosea

In their affliction, people will say:
"Let us know, let us strive to know the LORD;
   as certain as the dawn is his coming,
   and his judgment shines forth like the light of
      day!
He will come to us like the rain,
   like spring rain that waters the earth."

What can I do with you, Ephraim?
   What can I do with you, Judah?
Your piety is like a morning cloud,
   like the dew that early passes away.
For this reason I smote them through the prophets,
   I slew them by the words of my mouth;
for it is love that I desire, not sacrifice,
   and knowledge of God rather than holocausts.

The word of the Lord.

Lect.
No. 88

RESPONSORIAL PSALM: Ps 50:1, 8, 12-13, 14-15 (℟.: 23b)

The Responsorial Psalm continues the theme that God desires a conversion of the heart and not a conformity measured by external actions.

This psalm is a type of trial. God accuses the people of their sins against the covenant. He tells them that they might have performed numerous animal sacrifices, but that is not really what God wanted. God did not need their sacrifices.

Our worship is supposed to be an expression of our interior disposition. If it is nothing more than a ritual action that is performed because we feel that we are supposed to do it, or worse, an action that we perform because we feel that it will buy God's favor, then our actions are meaningless.

℟. **To the upright I will show the saving power of God.**

God the LORD has spoken and summoned the earth,
  from the rising of the sun to its setting.
"Not for your sacrifices do I rebuke you,
  for your holocausts are before me always."

℟. **To the upright I will show the saving power of God.**

"If I were hungry, I would not tell you,
  for mine are the world and its fullness.
Do I eat the flesh of strong bulls,
  or is the blood of goats my drink?"

℟. **To the upright I will show the saving power of God.**

"Offer to God praise as your sacrifice
  and fulfill your vows to the Most High;
then call upon me in time of distress;
  I will rescue you, and you shall glorify me."

℟. **To the upright I will show the saving power of God.**

Lect.
No. 88

SECOND READING: Romans 4:18-25

Abraham was strengthened by faith and gave glory to God.

This Reading is taken from a part of the Letter to the Romans that is written in a distinctive form of argumentation. Saint Paul had been accused of being anti-Jewish, so he adopts a rabbinic form of argumentation to show that this is not true.

This form is called Midrash. In it one uses verses of Scripture (often disconnected verses) to interpret the meaning of the text.

The point of Paul's argument is that faith and not works produces righteousness. He therefore speaks of Abraham as the father of faith. Abraham trusted in God's promise even though the external circumstances would have made its fulfillment seem impossible. Because he trusted, he was considered to be righteous.

Abraham is therefore the exemplar and father of those who trust in Jesus who died and rose for us. It is through that faith that they are justified (at peace with God).

A reading from the Letter of Saint Paul
to the Romans

Brothers and sisters:
Abraham believed, hoping against hope,
that he would become "the father of many nations,"
according to what was said, "Thus shall your descendants be."
He did not weaken in faith when he considered his own body
as already dead—for he was almost a hundred years old—
and the dead womb of Sarah.
He did not doubt God's promise in unbelief;
rather, he was strengthened by faith and gave glory to God
and was fully convinced that what he had promised
he was also able to do.
That is why *it was credited to him as righteousness.*
But it was not for him alone that it was written
that *it was credited to him;*
it was also for us, to whom it will be credited,
who believe in the one who raised Jesus our Lord from the dead,
who was handed over for our transgressions
and was raised for our justification.

The word of the Lord.

Lect. No. 88

God reaches out to those whom the world would consider to be unworthy of his attention, the poor and those who are imprisoned, for they are the ones who most need him.

Lect. No. 88

The Gospel continues the theme found in the First Reading that God does not desire external observance, but rather calls for conversion of the heart.

This account tells of the call of Matthew (Levi), the tax collector. This was considered to be an unclean profession, and tax collectors were shunned.

Jesus, on the other hand, reached out to them and to sinners and offered them his love and forgiveness. The righteous (most often self-righteous) felt that they were self-sufficient. Sinners and tax collectors knew that they were broken and needed Jesus' intervention, and they were therefore ready to respond to his call with all their heart.

ALLELUIA: cf. Lk 4:18

℟. **Alleluia, alleluia.**

The Lord sent me to bring glad tidings to the poor, and to proclaim liberty to captives.

℟. **Alleluia, alleluia.**

GOSPEL: Matthew 9:9-13

I did not come to call the righteous but sinners.

A reading from the holy Gospel according to Matthew

As Jesus passed on from there,
he saw a man named Matthew sitting at the customs post.
He said to him, "Follow me."
And he got up and followed him.
While he was at table in his house,
  many tax collectors and sinners came
  and sat with Jesus and his disciples.
  The Pharisees saw this and said to his disciples,
  "Why does your teacher eat with tax collectors
    and sinners?"
He heard this and said,
  "Those who are well do not need a physician, but
    the sick do.
Go and learn the meaning of the words,
  'I desire mercy, not sacrifice.'
I did not come to call the righteous but sinners."

The Gospel of the Lord.

ELEVENTH SUNDAY IN ORDINARY TIME

Lect. No. 91

FIRST READING: Exodus 19:2-6a

You shall be to me a kingdom of priests, a holy nation.

In the First Reading we hear of an episode that occurred during Israel's sojourn in the desert.

God spoke to Israel to remind them of how he protected them. He spoke of having borne them up on eagle wings. He had proved to them how much he loved them. They were precious to him.

He was now inviting them into the covenant. If they would only keep his commandments, they would live in his love for all time. They would be a holy nation, one that had been consecrated and set aside by the LORD as his own.

He was making them into a kingdom of priests. All the people of the nation would be holy and precious to the LORD. Their prayer and actions would be sacred.

A reading from the Book of Exodus

In those days, the Israelites came to the desert of Sinai and pitched camp.
While Israel was encamped here in front of the mountain,
    Moses went up the mountain to God.
Then the LORD called to him and said,
    "Thus shall you say to the house of Jacob;
    tell the Israelites:
    You have seen for yourselves how I treated the Egyptians
    and how I bore you up on eagle wings
    and brought you here to myself.
Therefore, if you hearken to my voice and keep my covenant,
    you shall be my special possession,
    dearer to me than all other people,
    though all the earth is mine.
You shall be to me a kingdom of priests, a holy nation."

The word of the Lord.

Lect. No. 91

RESPONSORIAL PSALM: Ps 100:1-2, 3, 5 (℟.: 3c)

We have heard how God chose us as his holy people and how he protected us from all that would have harmed us.

℟. **We are his people: the sheep of his flock.**

Sing joyfully to the LORD, all you lands;
    serve the LORD with gladness;
    come before him with joyful song.

We celebrate that election in our Responsorial Psalm. God made us his holy people, his own flock. He protects us forever and promises never to abandon us.

What is interesting about this psalm is that it is not only Israel that will celebrate this election. All nations are called to sing God's praises, for they have all been called into his covenant. They are all his chosen people.

℟. **We are his people: the sheep of his flock.**

Know that the LORD is God;
　he made us, his we are;
　his people, the flock he tends.

℟. **We are his people: the sheep of his flock.**

The LORD is good:
　his kindness endures forever,
　and his faithfulness to all generations.

℟. **We are his people: the sheep of his flock.**

Lect. No. 91

SECOND READING: Romans 5:6-11

If we were reconciled to God through the death of his Son,
how much more will we be saved by his life.

The idea of election that we saw in the First Reading is also found in this Second Reading, a passage from the Letter to the Romans.

Saint Paul marvels at the fact that Jesus would have died for us. It was not that we deserved this in any way. In fact, the opposite is true; we really deserve to be punished. Paul spent the first four chapters of this letter saying this: that all had sinned and all deserved God's wrath.

Yet Jesus proved his love for us in such a powerful way by showing us that he loved us more than life itself.

This miracle of God's grace fills us with a sense of joy. Yet this miracle has only begun. Paul asks what marvels the Lord must have in store for us now that we have been justified. If Jesus would die for us when we were still sinners and undeserving of his love, then what will he do for us now that we

A reading from the Letter of Saint Paul
to the Romans

Brothers and sisters:
　Christ, while we were still helpless,
　yet died at the appointed time for the ungodly.
Indeed, only with difficulty does one die for a just
　person,
　though perhaps for a good person
　one might even find courage to die.
But God proves his love for us
　in that while we were still sinners Christ died for
　us.
How much more then, since we are now justified by
　his blood,
　will we be saved through him from the wrath.
Indeed, if, while we were enemies,
　we were reconciled to God through the death of
　his Son,
　how much more, once reconciled,
　will we be saved by his life.
Not only that,
　but we also boast of God through our Lord Jesus
　Christ,

live in God's peace! It is beyond understanding; it fills us with awe.

Lect.
No. 91

Our Alleluia Verse repeats the words that the disciples preached in every nation: we must repent, for God's kingdom is at hand. It is already dawning in our midst.

Lect.
No. 91

Today's Gospel is divided into three segments, each of which is related to the others.

The first speaks of Jesus' attitude toward the crowds of people who were following him. He saw their profound need. He recognized that they were reaching out, but they seemed so frustrated in their attempts to find the Lord.

They were like sheep without a shepherd. There is both a negative and a positive sense to this saying. The negative dimension is that those who had been appointed as shepherds over them had obviously not fulfilled their duty (the Sadducees and Pharisees). The positive dimension is that Jesus himself would be their shepherd. They did not even know where to turn to find the peace that their hearts so desired.

through whom we have now received reconciliation.

The word of the Lord.

ALLELUIA: Mark 1:15

℟. **Alleluia, alleluia.**

The kingdom of God is at hand.
Repent and believe in the Gospel.

℟. **Alleluia, alleluia.**

GOSPEL: Matthew 9:36—10:8

Jesus summoned his twelve disciples and sent them out.

A reading from the holy Gospel according
to Matthew

At the sight of the crowds, Jesus' heart was moved with pity for them
because they were troubled and abandoned,
like sheep without a shepherd.
Then he said to his disciples,
    "The harvest is abundant but the laborers are few;
    so ask the master of the harvest
    to send out laborers for his harvest."

Then he summoned his twelve disciples
    and gave them authority over unclean spirits
    to drive them out and to cure every disease and
        every illness.
The names of the twelve apostles are these:
    first, Simon called Peter, and his brother Andrew;
    James, the son of Zebedee, and his brother John;
    Philip and Bartholomew, Thomas and Matthew
        the tax collector;
    James, the son of Alphaeus, and Thaddeus;

The second section gives the names of the twelve apostles. This is the customary list of the apostles found in the Synoptic Gospels. The only difference is that Thaddeus is named. We believe that this is Jude.

The third section gives their commission. They are to go forth to the tribes of Israel and proclaim the kingdom of God. Note that they were not to go to the pagans until after the resurrection. This is emphasized in this very Jewish gospel, for Jesus came to save the lost sheep of Israel.

Simon from Cana, and Judas Iscariot who betrayed him.

Jesus sent out these twelve after instructing them thus,

"Do not go into pagan territory or enter a Samaritan town.

Go rather to the lost sheep of the house of Israel.

As you go, make this proclamation: 'The kingdom of heaven is at hand.'

Cure the sick, raise the dead, cleanse lepers, drive out demons.

Without cost you have received; without cost you are to give."

The Gospel of the Lord.

June 23, 2002

TWELFTH SUNDAY IN ORDINARY TIME

Lect. No. 94

FIRST READING: Jeremiah 20:10-13

*He has rescued the life of the poor
from the power of the wicked.*

A reading from the Book of the Prophet Jeremiah

J eremiah said:
"I hear the whisperings of many:
    'Terror on every side!
    Denounce! let us denounce him!'
All those who were my friends
    are on the watch for any misstep of mine.
'Perhaps he will be trapped; then we can prevail,
    and take our vengeance on him.'
But the LORD is with me, like a mighty champion:
    my persecutors will stumble, they will not tri-
    umph.
In their failure they will be put to utter shame,
    to lasting, unforgettable confusion.
O LORD of hosts, you who test the just,
    who probe mind and heart,
let me witness the vengeance you take on them,
    for to you I have entrusted my cause.
Sing to the LORD,
    praise the LORD,
for he has rescued the life of the poor
    from the power of the wicked!"

The word of the Lord.

This reading is one of the passages known as the Confessions of Jeremiah (e.g., Jeremiah 15:10-21; 17:14-18, etc.) The Confessions express a profound feeling of despair. The prophet had been betrayed by his friends. He had done everything that the LORD had asked of him, but when difficulties came, God seemed to be nowhere in sight.

Yet Jeremiah could not even stop proclaiming God's word. Elsewhere he speaks of how he tried to keep silent, but God's word burned in his bones like fire.

The thing that hurt most is that everything Jeremiah said was intended to help his friends, but they took his words as a threat and used them as an excuse to attack him. He had loved them, and they threw it in his face.

Ultimately, there is nowhere the prophet could turn except to the LORD. He had done everything that he could, and now he would have to place his trust in God.

Lect. No. 94

RESPONSORIAL PSALM: Ps 69:8-10, 14, 17, 33-35 (℟.: 14c)

This Responsorial Psalm is constructed of the three main elements of all lamentation psalms.

The first element is the catalog of difficulties. It describes the disasters that have befallen the psalmist. This particular psalm continues the idea of suffering due to one's fidelity to the LORD that was found in the First Reading.

The second element is an appeal for help. God is reminded that he has always helped him in the past, and he is beseeched to continue his beneficence. The LORD is the source of all kindness and mercy.

The third element is the part of the psalm that is called the *todah.* This is found at the end of all lamentation psalms. It is a thanksgiving for what the psalmist is sure will be a quick delivery from all of his difficulties.

℟. **Lord, in your great love, answer me.**

For your sake I bear insult,
    and shame covers my face.
I have become an outcast to my brothers,
    a stranger to my mother's children,
because zeal for your house consumes me,
    and the insults of those who blaspheme you fall
      upon me.

℟. **Lord, in your great love, answer me.**

I pray to you, O LORD,
    for the time of your favor, O God!
In your great kindness answer me
    with your constant help.
Answer me, O LORD, for bounteous is your kindness;
    in your great mercy turn toward me.

℟. **Lord, in your great love, answer me.**

"See, you lowly ones, and be glad;
    you who seek God, may your hearts revive!
For the LORD hears the poor,
    and his own who are in bonds he spurns not.
Let the heavens and the earth praise him,
    the seas and whatever moves in them!'

℟. **Lord, in your great love, answer me.**

Lect. No. 94

SECOND READING: Romans 5:12-15

The gift is not like the transgression.

Adam brought sin into the world and with it death (most probably Saint Paul means spiritual death). We all participated in sin by committing our own sins. We all invited death into our souls. But Jesus brought life into the world. His death on the cross destroyed death. Love conquered hate.

A reading from the Letter of Saint Paul
to the Romans

Brothers and sisters:
Through one man sin entered the world,
and through sin, death,
and thus death came to all men, inasmuch as all
    sinned—

The effect of the sin that Adam brought into the world was horrific. Death reigned. Even before we received the commandments we were trapped in sin.

The effect of Jesus' sacrifice on the cross is life. The second Adam is so much greater than the first. Anyone can kill oneself or another. That happens all the time. But how many can bring a dead person back to life? That is what Jesus did by dying on the cross for us.

for up to the time of the law, sin was in the world,
though sin is not accounted when there is no law.
But death reigned from Adam to Moses,
even over those who did not sin
after the pattern of the trespass of Adam,
who is the type of the one who was to come.

But the gift is not like the transgression.
For if by the transgression of the one the many died,
how much more did the grace of God
and the gracious gift of the one man Jesus Christ
overflow for the many.

The word of the Lord.

Lect. No. 94

The Alleluia Verse reminds us that when we proclaim the gospel message, we are not speaking on our own authority. The Spirit of God is speaking through us.

ALLELUIA: John 15:26b, 27a

R̝. **Alleluia, alleluia.**

The Spirit of truth will testify to me, says the Lord;
and you also will testify.

R̝. **Alleluia, alleluia.**

Lect. No. 94

Last week we heard Jesus invite us to preach the dawning of the kingdom of God. This week we hear that God will protect us in our mission.

This does not mean that we will not face opposition. We certainly will face problems if we speak the truth. Often we will be ridiculed for trying to live according to Christian values.

GOSPEL: Matthew 10:26-33

Do not be afraid of those who kill the body.

A reading from the holy Gospel according to Matthew

Jesus said to the Twelve:
"Fear no one.
Nothing is concealed that will not be revealed,
nor secret that will not be known.
What I say to you in the darkness, speak in the light;
what you hear whispered, proclaim on the house-tops.

But God has revealed his deepest secrets to us. He has invited us to share in his mission. How could we wonder whether he will protect us?

Jesus speaks of how our heavenly Father even protects the smallest bird. How could we doubt his providence?

The Gospel passage closes with a promise that if we give witness to Jesus before all, he will give witness to our devotion before the Father at the final judgment. But if we deny him, he will deny us for he can only tell the truth.

And do not be afraid of those who kill the body but
    cannot kill the soul;
  rather, be afraid of the one who can destroy
  both soul and body in Gehenna.
Are not two sparrows sold for a small coin?
Yet not one of them falls to the ground without your
    Father's knowledge.
Even all the hairs of your head are counted.
So do not be afraid; you are worth more than many
    sparrows.
Everyone who acknowledges me before others
  I will acknowledge before my heavenly Father.
But whoever denies me before others,
  I will deny before my heavenly Father."

The Gospel of the Lord.

THIRTEENTH SUNDAY IN ORDINARY TIME

Lect. No. 97

FIRST READING: 2 Kings 4:8-11, 14-16a

Elisha is a holy man of God, let him remain.

A reading from the second Book of Kings

One day Elisha came to Shunem,
    where there was a woman of influence, who
    urged him to dine with her.
Afterward, whenever he passed by, he used to stop
    there to dine.
So she said to her husband, "I know that Elisha is a
    holy man of God.
Since he visits us often, let us arrange a little room
    on the roof
    and furnish it for him with a bed, table, chair, and
    lamp,
    so that when he comes to us he can stay there."
Sometime later Elisha arrived and stayed in the
    room overnight.

Later Elisha asked, "Can something be done for
    her?"
His servant Gehazi answered, "Yes!
    She has no son, and her husband is getting on in
    years."
Elisha said, "Call her."
When the woman had been called and stood at the
    door,
    Elisha promised, "This time next year
    you will be fondling a baby son."

The word of the Lord.

This story is about a woman who recognized that Elisha was a man of God and acted accordingly. She arranged for a place where he could stay every time that he passed through her village. She did not ask any favors of the LORD or the prophet of God. Rather, she only served.

It is interesting that her service was not something extraordinary. She offered simple hospitality, and in this she served the LORD.

The prophet inquired about her needs, however, and discovered through a servant that she did not have any children. He called her over and promised that by that time the next year she would have a child.

This reading speaks about how God will reward us for the good deeds we do for others in his name. Sometimes that reward comes in things we receive now on earth; other times it is received in our eternal reward. Ultimately, the greatest reward is that we received the chance to express our love and generosity.

Lect.
No. 97

RESPONSORIAL PSALM: Ps 89:2-3, 16-17, 18-19 (℟.: 2a)

This psalm is an act of trust in the providence of God. We recognize that in him we find our fulfillment, and apart from him we will never find peace.

And so we trust in God completely. We become a people dedicated to the service of God and neighbor. We find our total meaning for existence in this commitment.

This certainly involves a leap of faith. First of all, we must trust in the promises of the gospel. Then, and even more difficult, we must trust in our brothers and sisters who together with us form the Church.

We must see beyond the superficial to the deepest level of truth. Together in the Lord Jesus we form the Mystical Body of Christ.

℟. **Forever I will sing the goodness of the Lord.**

The promises of the LORD I will sing forever,
   through all generations my mouth shall proclaim
      your faithfulness.
For you have said, "My kindness is established forever";
   in heaven you have confirmed your faithfulness.

℟. **Forever I will sing the goodness of the Lord.**

Blessed the people who know the joyful shout;
   in the light of your countenance, O LORD, they
      walk.
At your name they rejoice all the day,
   and through your justice they are exalted.

℟. **Forever I will sing the goodness of the Lord.**

You are the splendor of their strength,
   and by your favor our horn is exalted.
For to the LORD belongs our shield,
   and to the Holy One of Israel, our king.

℟. **Forever I will sing the goodness of the Lord.**

Lect.
No. 97

SECOND READING: Romans 6:3-4, 8-11

Buried with Christ in baptism, we shall walk in the newness of life.

Choosing Jesus to be the center of our lives means making a positive and negative decision. The positive decision is to place our hope and trust in our Lord. The negative decision is to stop trusting in the things of the world. We must die to them. They cannot bring us the peace and joy that we seek.

A reading from the Letter of Saint Paul
to the Romans

Brothers and sisters:
   Are you unaware that we who were baptized
      into Christ Jesus
were baptized into his death?
We were indeed buried with him through baptism
      into death,
   so that, just as Christ was raised from the dead

Saint Paul elsewhere speaks of dying to our slavery to sin and passions. We have to be able to say no to those things that distance us from what is truly important.

We do this once and for all at our Baptism, but we must also do it every day in each decision that we make.

This leaves us free to choose God. We are no longer trying to serve God and mammon. We place our hearts totally in our God.

Lect.
No. 97

God has presented two choices: life and death; light and darkness. The life that God offers us is so profound and purposeful that it is a share in God's own life. God calls us from death to life in him.

Lect.
No. 97

The Gospel combines two of the themes contained in today's readings.

The first theme is that there is a price to pay in order to follow our Lord. We will have to suffer for the sake of the gospel. We must be willing to sacrifice our comforts and even our way of looking at reality, for the ways of God are not our ways.

by the glory of the Father,
we too might live in newness of life.

If, then, we have died with Christ,
we believe that we shall also live with him.
We know that Christ, raised from the dead, dies no
more;
death no longer has power over him.
As to his death, he died to sin once and for all;
as to his life, he lives for God.
Consequently, you too must think of yourselves as
dead to sin
and living for God in Christ Jesus.

The word of the Lord.

ALLELUIA: 1 Peter 2:9

R̸. **Alleluia, alleluia.**

You are a chosen race, a royal priesthood, a holy nation;
announce the praises of him who called you out of
darkness into his wonderful light.

R̸. **Alleluia, alleluia.**

GOSPEL: Matthew 10:37-42

Whoever does not take up his cross is not worthy of me.
Whoever receives you, receives me.

A reading from the holy Gospel according
to Matthew

Jesus said to his apostles:
"Whoever loves father or mother more than me is
not worthy of me,
and whoever loves son or daughter more than me
is not worthy of me;
and whoever does not take up his cross
and follow after me is not worthy of me.

The second theme is that those who care for one of the messengers of the gospel will be rewarded. Whoever offers a cup of water for the sake of the Lord Jesus is serving the Lord himself

This offers an interesting possibility as to how we can serve the gospel. Not all of us will go off into foreign mission lands. Not all of us will serve the gospel in heroic ways. Yet, we can all be part of the support staff for those who are more actively involved in the ministry.

Furthermore, we have to reevaluate the importance of the small things that we do out of faith. Sometimes we under-value them because they do not seem to be earthshaking. A better way to view our actions is that we are planting the seeds of the kingdom.

Whoever finds his life will lose it,
   and whoever loses his life for my sake will find it.
Whoever receives you receives me,
   and whoever receives me receives the one who
      sent me.
Whoever receives a prophet because he is a prophet
   will receive a prophet's reward,
   and whoever receives a righteous man
   because he is a righteous man
   will receive a righteous man's reward.
And whoever gives only a cup of cold water
   to one of these little ones to drink
   because the little one is a disciple—
   amen, I say to you, he will surely not lose his re-
      ward."

The Gospel of the Lord.

FOURTEENTH SUNDAY IN ORDINARY TIME

Lect. No. 100

FIRST READING: Zechariah 9:9-10

See, your king comes to you humbly.

This prophecy from the Book of the Prophet Zechariah presents an alternative view of what the Messiah will be like. The Jews expected the Messiah to be a conquering hero. This reading speaks of a Messiah who is meek and gentle. He will ride a donkey through the streets of Jerusalem and not a great charger as a conqueror might. He will even banish the tools of violence from the land for they will not be needed any more.

Yet he will be victorious. He will establish the same borders for the promised land as had the great King David. Love truly conquers.

A reading from the Book of the Prophet Zechariah

Thus says the LORD:
   Rejoice heartily, O daughter Zion,
   shout for joy, O daughter Jerusalem!
See, your king shall come to you;
   a just savior is he,
meek, and riding on an ass,
   on a colt, the foal of an ass.
He shall banish the chariot from Ephraim,
   and the horse from Jerusalem;
the warrior's bow shall be banished,
   and he shall proclaim peace to the nations.
His dominion shall be from sea to sea,
   and from the River to the ends of the earth.

The word of the Lord.

Lect. No. 100

RESPONSORIAL PSALM: Ps 145:1-2, 8-9, 10-11, 13-14 (℞.: cf. 1)

This is a hymn of praise for our God and King, who is great and powerful, yet also gracious and merciful.

We praise God especially because he has not left us to suffer alone. He has not abandoned us to our own folly. He has reached out into our lives with profound compassion. He understands our pain, and is

℞. **I will praise your name forever, my king and my God.**

or:

℞. **Alleluia.**

I will extol you, O my God and King,
   and I will bless your name forever and ever.
Every day will I bless you,
   and I will praise your name forever and ever.

willing to heal us by bearing our pain upon himself. He has healed us by his wounds.

The LORD is also slow to anger. We often view the God of the Old Testament as an angry God, one who would be ready to destroy us and all of creation if we were to commit the smallest infraction against his law.

This is not at all a fair portrayal of the LORD. God is, of course, angry when we sin, but he is not angry at us. We are God's beloved children, and any parent is angry at those things that hurt his or her children. God is angry, but at our sin and not at us.

This shows the deepest level of compassion. God understands and feels our pain. God hurts for us when we sin. Jesus bore this pain when he died upon the cross for us.

God especially reaches out into our lives when we are falling and bowed down. The reason for this is twofold. From God's side, he will never abandon us in our pain. From our side, it is when we are humbled that we are capable of understanding that we need God's help. It is only when we have failed that we realize that we cannot succeed by our own efforts.

℟. **I will praise your name forever, my king and my God.**

or:

℟. **Alleluia.**

The LORD is gracious and merciful,
    slow to anger and of great kindness.
The LORD is good to all
    and compassionate toward all his works.

℟. **I will praise your name forever, my king and my God.**

or:

℟. **Alleluia.**

Let all your works give you thanks, O LORD,
    and let your faithful ones bless you.
Let them discourse of the glory of your kingdom
    and speak of your might.

℟. **I will praise your name forever, my king and my God.**

or:

℟. **Alleluia.**

The LORD is faithful in all his words
    and holy in all his works.
The LORD lifts up all who are falling
    and raises up all who are bowed down.

℟. **I will praise your name forever, my king and my God.**

or:

℟. **Alleluia.**

Lect. No. 100

SECOND READING: Romans 8:9, 11-13

If by the Spirit you put to death the deeds of the body, you will live.

In this continuation of our readings from the Letter to the Romans, we see a contrast between the flesh and the spirit.

The flesh does not mean the material world. God created the world and it is good. When we sinned, we not only hurt ourselves. We also corrupted the things of the world. The things of the world, even though they were created to be good, can lead us to sin if they are misused. Furthermore, there is a voice that cries in our hearts to misuse these good things. This is the voice of sin and death, the voice of the evil one.

The Spirit, on the other hand, calls us to freedom and truth. It calls us to live in the freedom of the children of God. One cannot live by both the flesh and the Spirit. One must choose to live for one and die to the other.

A reading from the Letter of Saint Paul to the Romans

Brothers and sisters:
You are not in the flesh;
on the contrary, you are in the spirit,
if only the Spirit of God dwells in you.
Whoever does not have the Spirit of Christ does not belong to him.
If the Spirit of the one who raised Jesus from the dead dwells in you,
the one who raised Christ from the dead
will give life to your mortal bodies also,
through his Spirit that dwells in you.
Consequently, brothers and sisters,
we are not debtors to the flesh,
to live according to the flesh.
For if you live according to the flesh, you will die,
but if by the Spirit you put to death the deeds of the body,
you will live.

The word of the Lord.

Lect. No. 100

ALLELUIA: cf. Matthew 11:25

The wisdom of God is not like the wisdom of the world. In the wisdom of God it is the small and humble who know the mysteries of the kingdom of God.

℟. **Alleluia, alleluia.**

Blessed are you, Father, Lord of heaven and earth;
you have revealed to little ones the mysteries of the kingdom.

℟. **Alleluia, alleluia.**

Lect.
No. 100

GOSPEL: Matthew 11:25-30

I am meek and humble of heart.

Jesus speaks of those who are invited into the wisdom of the Lord of heaven and earth. It is not the rich and powerful; it is the little ones (the "anawim").

It is the simple who are humble enough to listen to God. They know that they are not self-sufficient and that they need the help of the Lord.

The proud, on the other hand, think themselves to be in charge. They are not ready to listen; they tell God what they want him to say and do.

That is why Jesus invites the meek and humble of heart to come to him. He offers comfort and healing.

Once we place our troubles in the hands of the Lord and acknowledge that he alone can save us, then we find an incredible peace. This is not resignation, it is surrender to the will of God.

A reading from the holy Gospel according to Matthew

At that time Jesus exclaimed:
"I give praise to you, Father, Lord of heaven and earth,
for although you have hidden these things from the wise and the learned
you have revealed them to little ones.
Yes, Father, such has been your gracious will.
All things have been handed over to me by my Father.
No one knows the Son except the Father,
and no one knows the Father except the Son
and anyone to whom the Son wishes to reveal him.
"Come to me, all you who labor and are burdened,
and I will give you rest.
Take my yoke upon you and learn from me,
for I am meek and humble of heart;
and you will find rest for yourselves.
For my yoke is easy, and my burden light."

The Gospel of the Lord.

July 14, 2002

FIFTEENTH SUNDAY IN ORDINARY TIME

Lect. No. 103

FIRST READING: Isaiah 55:10-11

The rain makes the earth fruitful.

A reading from the Book of the Prophet Isaiah

Thus says the LORD:
Just as from the heavens
the rain and snow come down
and do not return there
till they have watered the earth,
making it fertile and fruitful,
giving seed to the one who sows
and bread to the one who eats,
so shall my word be
that goes forth from my mouth;
my word shall not return to me void,
but shall do my will,
achieving the end for which I sent it.

The word of the Lord.

In Hebrew theology "the word" is an expression of the will of God. Furthermore, words are not simply symbolic representations. In some way, they make the object represented by the word present. Words produce reality. In the creation story in Genesis we hear God speak words and all things are made.

Thus, when God's word is poured out upon the earth, it makes God's reality present. God's word, which created the world, was now recreating it. It is not fruitless, it is a seed that will produce an abundant harvest.

Lect. No. 103

RESPONSORIAL PSALM: Ps 65:10, 11, 12-13, 14 (℟.: Luke 8:8)

Our Responsorial Psalm today is taken from Psalm 65, a hymn of praise.

We are using those verses that speak about the bounty that God showers upon the earth.

This psalm was written when people still wondered who produced fertility upon the earth. The people of Canaan had worshiped fertility gods, especially

℟. **The seed that falls on good ground will yield a fruitful harvest.**

You have visited the land and watered it;
greatly have you enriched it.
God's watercourses are filled;
you have prepared the grain.

℟. **The seed that falls on good ground will yield a fruitful harvest.**

the god Baal whom they worshiped as the god of the storms.

The Israelites, by proclaiming Yahweh as the God of the harvest, were making a profession of faith. They were saying that Yahweh is the only God who exists, and he is the one who causes all good things to happen upon the earth. This was a courageous profession, for they had previously thought of Yahweh as a God of the desert.

This psalm is being used in association with the First Reading, which speaks about the word of God producing fertility upon the earth, and the Gospel, which also speaks about the word of God being like the seed that is sown in the fields.

Thus have you prepared the land: drenching its furrows,
breaking up its clods,
softening it with showers,
blessing its yield.

℟. **The seed that falls on good ground will yield a fruitful harvest.**

You have crowned the year with your bounty,
and your paths overflow with a rich harvest;
the untilled meadows overflow with it,
and rejoicing clothes the hills.

℟. **The seed that falls on good ground will yield a fruitful harvest.**

The fields are garmented with flocks
and the valleys blanketed with grain.
They shout and sing for joy.

℟. **The seed that falls on good ground will yield a fruitful harvest.**

Lect. No. 103

SECOND READING: Romans 8:18-23

Creation awaits the revelation of the children of God.

When God created the world, he pronounced it to be good. But when Adam and Eve sinned, they brought death and alienation into the world.

Adam and Eve were alienated from God (they hid from him), from each other (they blamed each other for causing this difficulty), and from creation (we hear of this in the enmity between Adam and Eve and the snake). Sin destroyed the unity and corrupted the goodness of creation.

A reading from the Letter of Saint Paul to the Romans

Brothers and sisters:
I consider that the sufferings of this present time are as nothing
compared with the glory to be revealed for us.
For creation awaits with eager expectation
the revelation of the children of God;
for creation was made subject to futility,
not of its own accord but because of the one who subjected it,
in hope that creation itself
would be set free from slavery to corruption

But the Spirit of God has been breathed into us. We and creation have been renewed. The Spirit cries out in our hearts that we are children of God.

The Spirit also works in creation for it is already proclaiming the glory of God and leading us to praise the God who created it in love.

and share in the glorious freedom of the children of God.
We know that all creation is groaning in labor pains
    even until now;
    and not only that, but we ourselves,
    who have the firstfruits of the Spirit,
    we also groan within ourselves
    as we wait for adoption, the redemption of our
        bodies.

The word of the Lord.

Lect. No. 103

ALLELUIA

℟. **Alleluia, alleluia.**

The seed is the word of God, Christ is the sower.
All who come to him will have life forever.

℟. **Alleluia, alleluia.**

Jesus sows the word of God into our hearts. If we prepare the ground with care and love through acts of penance and conversion, it will bear a rich harvest for life everlasting.

Lect. No. 103

GOSPEL: A Longer Form: Matthew 13:1-23

A sower went out to sow.

The parable of the seed that is sown is an example of how Jesus explained the mysteries of faith in language that the people listening to him could understand.

The great commandment is that we should love the Lord with all our heart and soul and strength. The rabbis asked what this meant. The response they developed was that we should love the Lord with our intellectual ability, with our lives by giving witness to his truth even to the point of death, and with all of our financial resources.

A reading from the holy Gospel according to Matthew

On that day, Jesus went out of the house and sat down by the sea.
Such large crowds gathered around him
    that he got into a boat and sat down,
    and the whole crowd stood along the shore.
And he spoke to them at length in parables, saying:
    "A sower went out to sow.
And as he sowed, some seed fell on the path,
    and birds came and ate it up.
Some fell on rocky ground, where it had little soil.
It sprang up at once because the soil was not deep,

JULY 14, 2002

FIFTEENTH SUNDAY IN ORDINARY TIME   266

To love the Lord with all our heart means to love the Lord with our intellectual ability. The heart in the Bible is not where we feel, it is where we think. According to Jewish thought, the place we feel is our gut or stomach or even kidneys. So when we love the Lord with our heart, we are loving him with our mind.

To love the Lord with all our soul means to love the Lord with our lives. The rabbis said that it meant to love the Lord even if they should try to tear the soul out of our bodies (this means even if they should threaten to put us to death).

To love the Lord with all our strength means to love the Lord with all that we possess. The rabbis said that strength meant our material possessions.

When Jesus says that some of the seed fell on the path and it represents those who heard the word without understanding it, it means that they did not love the Lord with all their heart. They did not apply their intellectual ability to know the word.

When Jesus says that some of the seed fell on rocky ground and that it represents those who hear the word but deny it during times of tribulation or persecution, it means that they did not love the Lord with their souls. They were not willing to give up their lives for the faith. They chose to remain in their ignorance because they did not want to know the truth.

and when the sun rose it was scorched,
and it withered for lack of roots.
Some seed fell among thorns, and the thorns grew up and choked it.
But some seed fell on rich soil, and produced fruit,
a hundred or sixty or thirtyfold.
Whoever has ears ought to hear."

The disciples approached him and said,
"Why do you speak to them in parables?"
He said to them in reply,
"Because knowledge of the mysteries of the kingdom of heaven
has been granted to you, but to them it has not been granted.
To anyone who has, more will be given and he will grow rich;
from anyone who has not, even what he has will be taken away.
This is why I speak to them in parables, because
they look but do not see and hear but do not listen or understand.
Isaiah's prophecy is fulfilled in them, which says:
You shall indeed hear but not understand,
you shall indeed look but never see.
Gross is the heart of this people,
they will hardly hear with their ears,
they have closed their eyes,
lest they see with their eyes
and hear with their ears
and understand with their hearts and be converted,
and I heal them.

"But blessed are your eyes, because they see,
and your ears, because they hear.
Amen, I say to you, many prophets and righteous people
longed to see what you see but did not see it,
and to hear what you hear but did not hear it.

When Jesus says that some of the seed fell among the thorns and that represents those who were lured from the word by worldly anxieties, it means that they did not love the Lord with all their strength.

Finally, when Jesus speaks of those who do not understand, it is not because Jesus is hiding the truth from them. They refuse to listen and understand, fulfilling the prophecy in Isaiah about their hardened heart.

Jesus told this parable so that we would realize that we have a solemn responsibility to cooperate with the grace of God in our lives. It is not enough to think nice thoughts about God to call ourselves Christian. We must dedicate our minds, our lives, and all that we own to the service of the kingdom. Anything less will not produce true peace in the kingdom.

"Hear then the parable of the sower.
The seed sown on the path is the one
  who hears the word of the kingdom without understanding it,
  and the evil one comes and steals away
  what was sown in his heart.
The seed sown on rocky ground
  is the one who hears the word and receives it at once with joy.
But he has no root and lasts only for a time.
When some tribulation or persecution comes because of the word,
  he immediately falls away.
The seed sown among thorns is the one who hears the word,
  but then worldly anxiety and the lure of riches choke the word
  and it bears no fruit.
But the seed sown on rich soil
  is the one who hears the word and understands it,
  who indeed bears fruit and yields a hundred or sixty or thirtyfold."

The Gospel of the Lord.

Lect.
No. 103

GOSPEL: B Shorter Form: Matthew 13:1-9

A sower went out to sow.

The parable of the seed that is sown is an example of how Jesus explained the mysteries of faith in language that the people listening to him could understand.

The great commandment is that we should love the Lord with all our heart and soul and strength. The rabbis asked what this meant. The response they developed was that we should

A reading from the holy Gospel according
to Matthew

On that day, Jesus went out of the house and sat down by the sea.
Such large crowds gathered around him
  that he got into a boat and sat down,
  and the whole crowd stood along the shore.
And he spoke to them at length in parables, saying:
  "A sower went out to sow.

love the Lord with our intellectual ability, with our lives, and with all of our financial resources.

Jesus told this parable so that we would realize that we have a solemn responsibility to cooperate with the grace of God in our lives. It is not enough to think nice thoughts about God to call ourselves Christian. We must dedicate our minds, our lives, and all that we own to the service of the kingdom. Anything less will not produce true peace in the kingdom.

And as he sowed, some seed fell on the path,
and birds came and ate it up.
Some fell on rocky ground, where it had little soil.
It sprang up at once because the soil was not deep,
and when the sun rose it was scorched,
and it withered for lack of roots.
Some seed fell among thorns, and the thorns grew
up and choked it.
But some seed fell on rich soil and produced fruit,
a hundred or sixty or thirtyfold.
Whoever has ears ought to hear."

The Gospel of the Lord.

July 21, 2002

SIXTEENTH SUNDAY IN ORDINARY TIME

Lect. No. 106

FIRST READING: Wisdom 12:13, 16-19

You give repentance for sins.

A reading from the Book of Wisdom

This reading from the Book of Wisdom speaks about God who is both the God of power and the God of mercy.

This is an odd mixture. Usually we do not associate these two ideas with each other. We think of mercy as a weak attribute, while we think of power as the ability to impose one's will on others.

God possesses power and justice. God knows what is good and what is not. God could condemn us all. Yet, God treats us with great leniency. God shows us a powerful mercy.

God also teaches us that we should be willing to treat each other in the same way, not seeking absolute justice as much as great mercy.

There is no god besides you who have the care of all,
  that you need show you have not unjustly condemned.
For your might is the source of justice;
  your mastery over all things makes you lenient to all.
For you show your might when the perfection of your power is disbelieved;
  and in those who know you, you rebuke temerity.
But though you are master of might, you judge with clemency,
  and with much lenience you govern us;
  for power, whenever you will, attends you.
And you taught your people, by these deeds,
  that those who are just must be kind;
and you gave your children good ground for hope
  that you would permit repentance for their sins.

The word of the Lord.

Lect. No. 106

RESPONSORIAL PSALM: Ps 86:5-6, 9-10, 15-16 (℟.: 5a)

In the Responsorial Psalm we hear of God's wondrous deeds and his remarkable mercy. We celebrate our God as good and forgiving. This was the great proclamation of Jesus' ministry: how good and loving and merciful God is.

℟. **Lord, you are good and forgiving.**

You, O LORD, are good and forgiving,
  abounding in kindness to all who call upon you.
Hearken, O LORD, to my prayer
  and attend to the sound of my pleading.

℟. **Lord, you are good and forgiving.**

This mercy is no longer just for the people of the first covenant. It is now for all of the nations upon the earth. No one is excluded from that mercy. Yet, we must admit that we need it before we can receive it.

That is why we turn to God and beg for his mercy. We admit that we cannot make it without him. We beg for mercy, not because God does not readily offer it, but because we need to recognize our need.

Lect.
No. 106

So often we do not even know how to pray. Our hearts become confused and sluggish due to the sinful habits that we have acquired and the weakness of our own spirits. The Holy Spirit whispers the things of God in the deepest part of our hearts so that we might know what we really need.

The Spirit gives breath to our prayers and grants us the courage to ask for the things that are our deepest aspiration: that there be someone who loves us without limit.

Lect.
No. 106

The Alleluia Verse celebrates the fact that God speaks his wisdom to the little ones, those who are humble and meek. Unless we become like children, we cannot hope to see the kingdom of God.

All the nations you have made shall come
　and worship you, O Lord,
　and glorify your name.
For you are great, and you do wondrous deeds;
　you alone are God.

℟. **Lord, you are good and forgiving.**

You, O Lord, are a God merciful and gracious,
　slow to anger, abounding in kindness and fidelity.
Turn toward me, and have pity on me;
　give your strength to your servant.

℟. **Lord, you are good and forgiving.**

SECOND READING: Romans 8:26-27

The Spirit intercedes with inexpressible groanings.

A reading from the Letter of Saint Paul
to the Romans

Brothers and sisters:
　The Spirit comes to the aid of our weakness;
　for we do not know how to pray as we ought,
　but the Spirit himself intercedes with inexpressible groanings.
And the one who searches hearts
　knows what is the intention of the Spirit,
　because he intercedes for the holy ones
　according to God's will.

The word of the Lord.

ALLELUIA: cf. Matthew 11:25

℟. **Alleluia, alleluia.**

Blessed are you, Father, Lord of heaven and earth;
you have revealed to little ones the mysteries of the
　kingdom.

℟. **Alleluia, alleluia.**

Lect.
No. 106

GOSPEL: **A** Longer Form: Matthew 13:24-43

Let them grow together until harvest.

Jesus proclaimed the dawning of the kingdom of God. When people heard this, they were sure that God the Father would soon send his angels upon the earth to put all things right. They were anxious for this to occur, for evil seemed to have reigned for far too long.

That is why some of his listeners were disappointed both during his ministry and during the early days of the Church. They wondered where the promised miraculous intervention was. They wondered why God was waiting to reward the just and punish the evil.

The parables in today's Gospel give a partial answer to these difficulties. The first message is that the kingdom has begun to grow, but it will take a long time for it to come to fruition.

The word of God was like the wheat seed that had been planted in the fields. It was growing, but there was evil growing right alongside of it. That evil would continue to co-exist with those who had chosen the kingdom until the end of time.

God was not going to make it all better until then. In the meantime, people must make a choice for or against the kingdom.

A reading from the holy Gospel according to Matthew

Jesus proposed another parable to the crowds, saying:
"The kingdom of heaven may be likened
to a man who sowed good seed in his field.
While everyone was asleep his enemy came
and sowed weeds all through the wheat, and then went off.
When the crop grew and bore fruit, the weeds appeared as well.
The slaves of the householder came to him and said,
'Master, did you not sow good seed in your field?
Where have the weeds come from?'
He answered, 'An enemy has done this.'
His slaves said to him,
'Do you want us to go and pull them up?'
He replied, 'No, if you pull up the weeds
you might uproot the wheat along with them.
Let them grow together until harvest;
then at harvest time I will say to the harvesters,
"First collect the weeds and tie them in bundles for burning;
but gather the wheat into my barn."'"

He proposed another parable to them.
"The kingdom of heaven is like a mustard seed
that a person took and sowed in a field.
It is the smallest of all the seeds,
yet when full-grown it is the largest of plants.
It becomes a large bush,
and the 'birds of the sky come and dwell in its branches.'"

He spoke to them another parable.

A second parable concerning the kingdom has to do with the mustard seed. Again, people wondered why they were not seeing powerful signs of the dawning of the kingdom. They expected Jesus to call his angels down from the skies to defeat the forces of evil. Why, then, was this not happening?

The answer is that the kingdom dawns like the mustard seed. It begins in very small, all but invisible ways. Yet it will slowly grow in magnitude. Jesus speaks of the mustard seed being the smallest of the seeds of the earth. That is not quite true for there are smaller seeds. (Remember, the gospels have the truth of faith, not botanical truth.)

The parable of the yeast is similar. The yeast is all but invisible, but yet it has tremendous effects upon the dough. So it is with the kingdom. In its earliest moments it can seem totally insignificant, but Christians can have a tremendous effect upon society.

These parables should be an encouragement to us. We often wonder why it is that the forces of good seem to be so powerless against so many evils. These parables give us the answer. We are most effective when we realize that the changes come in small ways. We also have to remember that there will be evil in the world until the last day. We will never totally defeat it, but we must not give up the fight.

"The kingdom of heaven is like yeast
   that a woman took and mixed with three measures of wheat flour
until the whole batch was leavened."

All these things Jesus spoke to the crowds in parables.
He spoke to them only in parables,
   to fulfill what had been said through the prophet:
     I will open my mouth in parables,
      I will announce what has lain hidden from the foundation of the world.

Then, dismissing the crowds, he went into the house.
His disciples approached him and said,
   "Explain to us the parable of the weeds in the field."
He said in reply, "He who sows good seed is the Son of Man,
   the field is the world, the good seed the children of the kingdom.
The weeds are the children of the evil one,
   and the enemy who sows them is the devil.
The harvest is the end of the age, and the harvesters are angels.
Just as weeds are collected and burned up with fire,
   so will it be at the end of the age.
The Son of Man will send his angels,
   and they will collect out of his kingdom
   all who cause others to sin and all evildoers.
They will throw them into the fiery furnace,
   where there will be wailing and grinding of teeth.
Then the righteous will shine like the sun
   in the kingdom of their Father.
Whoever has ears ought to hear."

The Gospel of the Lord.

Lect.
No. 106

GOSPEL: **B** Shorter Form: Matthew 13:24-30

Let them grow together until the harvest.

Jesus proclaimed the dawning of the kingdom of God. When people heard this, they were sure that God the Father would soon send his angels upon the earth to put all things right. They were anxious for this to occur, for evil seemed to have reigned for far too long.

That is why some of his listeners were disappointed both during his ministry and during the early days of the Church. They wondered where the promised miraculous intervention was. They wondered why God was waiting to reward the just and punish the evil.

The parables in today's Gospel give a partial answer to these difficulties. The first message is that the kingdom has begun to grow, but it will take a long time for it to come to fruition.

The word of God was like the wheat seed that had been planted in the fields. It was growing, but there was evil growing right alongside of it. That evil would continue to co-exist with those who had chosen the kingdom until the end of time. God was not going to make it all better until then. In the meantime, people must make a choice for or against the kingdom.

A reading from the holy Gospel according to Matthew

Jesus proposed another parable to the crowds, saying:

"The kingdom of heaven may be likened to a man who sowed good seed in his field.

While everyone was asleep his enemy came
  and sowed weeds all through the wheat, and then went off.

When the crop grew and bore fruit, the weeds appeared as well.

The slaves of the householder came to him and said,
  'Master, did you not sow good seed in your field?

Where have the weeds come from?'

He answered, 'An enemy has done this.'

His slaves said to him, 'Do you want us to go and
  pull them up?'

He replied, 'No, if you pull up the weeds
  you might uproot the wheat along with them.

Let them grow together until harvest;
  then at harvest time I will say to the harvesters,
  "First collect the weeds and tie them in bundles
    for burning;
  but gather the wheat into my barn."'"

The Gospel of the Lord.

July 28, 2002

SEVENTEENTH SUNDAY IN ORDINARY TIME

Lect. No. 109 **FIRST READING: 1 Kings 3:5, 7-12**

You have asked for wisdom.

This episode takes place at the beginning of Solomon's reign as king of Israel and Judah. Solomon went to the shrine in Gibeon (at this time there were many shrines of the LORD throughout the land of Israel). There he performed a great sacrifice, and then went to sleep. While he was asleep, he had a dream in which the LORD asked him to request whatever he wanted.

Solomon responded that he wanted wisdom so that he could rule God's people justly. Because he asked for wisdom and not for riches or victories, the LORD granted his request. Solomon came to be known as the wisest king on the earth.

Wisdom, at this time, was understood as knowing how to live the good life. Much of the accumulated wisdom of Israel was collected and today forms the latter part of the Book of Proverbs. These folk sayings were the way that the community wisdom would be passed on from one generation to the next. Solomon was known as the wisest of kings in the history of Israel. It is known, in fact, that he even collected books of wisdom from neighboring countries (e.g., Egypt).

A reading from the first Book of Kings

The LORD appeared to Solomon in a dream at night.

God said, "Ask something of me and I will give it to you."

Solomon answered:

"O LORD, my God, you have made me, your servant, king

to succeed my father David;

but I am a mere youth, not knowing at all how to act.

I serve you in the midst of the people whom you have chosen,

a people so vast that it cannot be numbered or counted.

Give your servant, therefore, an understanding heart

to judge your people and to distinguish right from wrong.

For who is able to govern this vast people of yours?"

The LORD was pleased that Solomon made this request.

So God said to him:

"Because you have asked for this—

not for a long life for yourself,

nor for riches,

nor for the life of your enemies,

but for understanding so that you may know what is right—

274

While the First Reading speaks of the gift of wisdom that the LORD gave to King Solomon, the Responsorial Psalm celebrates one form of wisdom: the law. We will only find true peace if we keep God's commandments, for they call us to a life filled with meaning and generosity.

I do as you requested.
I give you a heart so wise and understanding
 that there has never been anyone like you up to now,
 and after you there will come no one to equal you."

The word of the Lord.

Lect. No. 109

RESPONSORIAL PSALM:

Ps 119:57, 72, 76-77, 127-128, 129-130 (℟.: 97a)

We sometimes think of the law as being a thing that robs us of our freedom and dignity.

This was not the concept of the law in the Old Testament. For the people of Israel, the law was an incredible gift of mercy. God revealed to Israel how its people might live the good life.

That is why the psalmist uses words like compassion, kindness, and comfort when he speaks of the law. That is why he considers the law of God's mouth to be more precious than thousands of gold and silver pieces.

This psalm challenges us to consider how we look at the commandments and the laws of the Church. Are they esteemed as gifts from God? Are they seen as revelations of how to live the good life? Or are they considered to be imposed upon us from powers beyond our control?

℟. **Lord, I love your commands.**

I have said, O LORD, that my part
 is to keep your words.
The law of your mouth is to me more precious
 than thousands of gold and silver pieces.

℟. **Lord, I love your commands.**

Let your kindness comfort me
 according to your promise to your servants.
Let your compassion come to me that I may live,
 for your law is my delight.

℟. **Lord, I love your commands.**

For I love your commands
 more than gold, however fine.
For in all your precepts I go forward;
 every false way I hate.

℟. **Lord, I love your commands.**

Wonderful are your decrees;
 therefore I observe them.
The revelation of your words sheds light,
 giving understanding to the simple.

℟. **Lord, I love your commands.**

JULY 28, 2002 SEVENTEENTH SUNDAY IN ORDINARY TIME 276

No. 109

SECOND READING: Romans 8:28-30

God predestined us to be conformed to the image of his Son.

This passage from the Letter to the Romans speaks of God's plan to bring us to salvation. God foreknew us even before we existed. He called us into existence with love and predestined us to share in his life. (Predestination does not mean that we have to do something, only that we are invited to do it.) He has called us, justified us, and glorified us.

In other words, God's mystery (plan) of salvation is too wonderful to understand. How could anyone love us this much? How could God invite us into his own glory? This fills us with a sense of awe and tremendous gratitude.

A reading from the Letter of Saint Paul to the Romans

Brothers and sisters:
We know that all things work for good for those who love God,
who are called according to his purpose.
For those he foreknew he also predestined
to be conformed to the image of his Son,
so that he might be the firstborn
among many brothers and sisters.
And those he predestined he also called;
and those he called he also justified;
and those he justified he also glorified.

The word of the Lord.

No. 109

ALLELUIA: cf. Matthew 11:25

Our Alleluia Verse praises God who has revealed his mystery of salvation to the little ones, those who were humble and meek enough to understand this love and respond with gratitude.

R. **Alleluia, alleluia.**

Blessed are you Father, Lord of heaven and earth;
for you have revealed to little ones the mysteries of the kingdom.

R. **Alleluia, alleluia.**

No. 109

GOSPEL: A Longer Form: Matthew 13:44-52

He sells all that he has and buys the field.

In today's Gospel, there are three different allegories that speak about our response to an encounter with the kingdom of God. In the first two, there is a sense of being willing to abandon what had previously been considered to be of prime importance in order to acquire that which is far more precious.

A reading from the holy Gospel according to Matthew

Jesus said to his disciples:
"The kingdom of heaven is like a treasure buried in a field,
which a person finds and hides again,

This is more than only rejecting sin and all of its allure. It often means giving up things that are good, but not of the same value as the kingdom. When we love someone, we often have to say no to things that otherwise might have been part of our experience.

The last of the allegories is slightly different. It is similar to last week's Gospel in which the final separation between good and bad would not occur until the end of time. In the meantime, we must make our choice between the kingdom of light and that of darkness.

Finally, there is a saying that speaks of the good scribe as being the one who can use both the old and the new. This is an important reminder that we should not reject something simply because it does not measure up to our point of view. We should be willing to go beyond our usual preferences to find that which is good and true wherever it might lie. Otherwise, we might be ignoring one of the ways God is speaking to us.

and out of joy goes and sells all that he has and
  buys that field.
Again, the kingdom of heaven is like a merchant
  searching for fine pearls.
When he finds a pearl of great price,
  he goes and sells all that he has and buys it.
Again, the kingdom of heaven is like a net thrown
    into the sea,
  which collects fish of every kind.
When it is full they haul it ashore
  and sit down to put what is good into buckets.
What is bad they throw away.
Thus it will be at the end of the age.
The angels will go out and separate the wicked from
    the righteous
  and throw them into the fiery furnace,
  where there will be wailing and grinding of teeth.

"Do you understand all these things?"
They answered, "Yes."
And he replied,
  "Then every scribe who has been instructed in the
    kingdom of heaven
  is like the head of a household
  who brings from his storeroom both the new and
    the old."

The Gospel of the Lord.

Lect.
No. 109

GOSPEL: B Shorter Form: Matthew 13:44-46

He sells all that he has and buys the field.

In today's Gospel, there are two different allegories that speak about our response to an encounter with the kingdom of God. There is a sense of being willing to abandon what had previously been considered to be of prime importance in order

A reading from the holy Gospel according
        to Matthew

Jesus said to his disciples:
"The kingdom of heaven is like a treasure buried
    in a field,
  which a person finds and hides again,

to acquire that which is far more precious.

This is more than only rejecting sin and all of its allure. It often means giving up things that are good, but not of the same value as the kingdom. When we love someone, we often have to say no to things that otherwise might have been part of our experience.

and out of joy goes and sells all that he has and buys that field.
Again, the kingdom of heaven is like a merchant searching for fine pearls.
When he finds a pearl of great price, he goes and sells all that he has and buys it."

The Gospel of the Lord.

August 4, 2002

EIGHTEENTH SUNDAY IN ORDINARY TIME

Lect. No. 112

FIRST READING: Isaiah 55:1-3

Hasten and eat.

A reading from the Book of the Prophet Isaiah

Thus says the LORD:
  All you who are thirsty,
come to the water!
You who have no money,
  come, receive grain and eat;
come, without paying and without cost,
  drink wine and milk!
Why spend your money for what is not bread;
  your wages for what fails to satisfy?
Heed me, and you shall eat well,
  you shall delight in rich fare.
Come to me heedfully,
  listen, that you may have life.
I will renew with you the everlasting covenant,
  the benefits assured to David.

The word of the Lord.

This reading comes from the second part of the Book of the Prophet Isaiah. It speaks of the incredible graciousness of God. God offers to nourish us and satisfy our thirst. There is no price to pay, for he has already paid it on our behalf.

God offers us life and that in abundance. Why would we seek after things that do not satisfy? We often think that this thing or that will offer us the joy and peace that we seek, but these things just leave us disillusioned for they cannot answer our deepest need. It is only God who can fill the void in our hearts.

The covenant into which God invites us will be an everlasting covenant. It is a promise of love without end.

Lect. No. 112

RESPONSORIAL PSALM: Ps 145:8-9, 15-16, 17-18 (℟.: cf. 16)

The Responsorial Psalm speaks of the fidelity and good-ness of the LORD. This litany of praise expresses the psalmist's trust in God. The LORD is gracious, merciful, kind, and compassionate. The response to the psalm speaks about how God nourishes us and answers all of our needs. The psalm portrays a God whose every wish is to express his love for us.

℟. **The hand of the Lord feeds us; he answers all our needs.**

The LORD is gracious and merciful,
  slow to anger and of great kindness.
The LORD is good to all
  and compassionate toward all his works.

℟. **The hand of the Lord feeds us; he answers all our needs.**

This is why we can hope in God. He will not necessarily give us everything we want, but he will always give us everything we need. That is why we can speak of God being holy and just, for he protects us from what will harm us, even if we ask for it. Like any good parent, God sometimes says, "No."

Sometimes God gives us the miracle we request, sometimes he invites us to the cross. Either way, though, he will always uphold us with his love.

The eyes of all look hopefully to you,
  and you give them their food in due season;
you open your hand
  and satisfy the desire of every living thing.

℟. **The hand of the Lord feeds us; he answers all our needs.**

The LORD is just in all his ways
  and holy in all his works.
The LORD is near to all who call upon him,
  to all who call upon him in truth.

℟. **The hand of the Lord feeds us; he answers all our needs.**

Lect.
No. 112

SECOND READING: Romans 8:35, 37-39

*No creature will be able to separate us from
the love of God in Christ Jesus.*

The Second Reading speaks of the providence of God. His love is more powerful than any other force in the world. Love alone conquers.

Once we have experienced that love and allowed it to heal the brokenness at the bottom of our heart, nothing can rob the peace we will have found.

Even when disastrous things happen, we are able to find serenity. This does not mean that we ignore what is happening or deny the pain. It simply means that we recognize that no matter what happens, God still loves us and will never abandon us.

A reading from the Letter of Saint Paul
to the Romans

Brothers and sisters:
  What will separate us from the love of Christ?
Will anguish, or distress, or persecution, or famine,
  or nakedness, or peril, or the sword?
No, in all these things we conquer overwhelmingly
  through him who loved us.
For I am convinced that neither death, nor life,
  nor angels, nor principalities,
  nor present things, nor future things,
  nor powers, nor height, nor depth,
  nor any other creature will be able to separate us
  from the love of God in Christ Jesus our Lord.

The word of the Lord.

Lect.
No. 112

The Alleluia Verse reminds us that the true consolation we receive from God is not the material things we get, it is the word of God that tells us of his love for us.

Lect.
No. 112

The Gospel presents the account of the miraculous multiplication of loaves and fish. It is an example of a nature miracle: one in which Jesus changes the laws of nature.

This particular miracle portrays Jesus as the Good Shepherd. This is why the account mentions that there was grass upon which the crowd could sit (for the good shepherd leads the sheep to verdant pastures).

Jesus takes the loaves and fish and blesses them and multiplies them. Some would say that this is a social miracle: that Jesus shared all the food he had, and everyone in the crowd followed his example.

This is a beautiful story, but simply not what is written here. It is a miraculous multiplication. To give further proof that Jesus has power over the laws of nature, we see him walking upon the water in the passage that immediately follows this account.

ALLELUIA: Matthew 4:4b

℟. **Alleluia, alleluia.**

One does not live on bread alone,
but on every word that comes forth from the mouth
    of God.

℟. **Alleluia, alleluia.**

GOSPEL: Matthew 14:13-21

They all ate and were satisfied.

A reading from the holy Gospel according
to Matthew

When Jesus heard of the death of John the Baptist,
    he withdrew in a boat to a deserted place by himself.
The crowds heard of this and followed him on foot
    from their towns.
When he disembarked and saw the vast crowd,
    his heart was moved with pity for them, and he
    cured their sick.
When it was evening, the disciples approached him
    and said,
    "This is a deserted place and it is already late;
    dismiss the crowds so that they can go to the villages
    and buy food for themselves."
Jesus said to them, "There is no need for them to go
    away;
    give them some food yourselves."
But they said to him,
    "Five loaves and two fish are all we have here."
Then he said, "Bring them here to me,"
    and he ordered the crowds to sit down on the
    grass.

The blessing of the bread, its being broken, and its fragments being collected are all allusions to the Eucharist (for the words used in this account are the same as would be used in the celebration of the sacrament).

There were twelve baskets of fragments left over. That is enough to nourish the twelve tribes of Israel. In the multiplication of loaves and fish that fed four thousand there were seven baskets of fragments, enough for the whole world.

Taking the five loaves and the two fish, and looking
    up to heaven,
  he said the blessing, broke the loaves,
  and gave them to the disciples,
  who in turn gave them to the crowds.
They all ate and were satisfied,
  and they picked up the fragments left over—
  twelve wicker baskets full.
Those who ate were about five thousand men,
  not counting women and children.

The Gospel of the Lord.

August 11, 2002

NINETEENTH SUNDAY IN ORDINARY TIME

The First Reading recounts the episode when Elijah encountered the LORD on the holy mountain.

Since it was the mountain where God appeared to his people with fire and wind and earthquakes, one would expect that he would use the same means to express his presence to Elijah. Instead, God appears to the prophet in the whispering sound of the breeze.

The LORD was revealing to Elijah that he does not always work in miraculous ways. Sometimes God works in humble, simple, everyday ways.

People always flock to events that seem to have a miraculous tenor to them. We should be ready to recognize his presence in our everyday lives as much as we do in those tremendous events.

Lect. No. 115 **FIRST READING: 1 Kings 19:9a, 11-13a**

Go outside and stand on the mountain before the Lord.

A reading from the first Book of Kings

At the mountain of God, Horeb,
  Elijah came to a cave where he took shelter.
Then the LORD said to him,
  "Go outside and stand on the mountain before the
    LORD;
  the LORD will be passing by."
A strong and heavy wind was rending the mountains
  and crushing rocks before the LORD—
  but the LORD was not in the wind.
After the wind there was an earthquake—
  but the LORD was not in the earthquake.
After the earthquake there was fire—
  but the LORD was not in the fire.
After the fire there was a tiny whispering sound.
When he heard this,
  Elijah hid his face in his cloak
  and went and stood at the entrance of the cave.

The word of the Lord.

Lect. No. 115 **RESPONSORIAL PSALM: Ps 85:9, 10, 11-12, 13-14 (℟.: 8)**

The Responsorial Psalm for today is the last part of a lamentation. All lamentation psalms end the same way: with a hymn of thanksgiving for the deliverance that the psalmist was sure the LORD would grant. That is why these verses are so exuberantly positive.

℟. **Lord, let us see your kindness, and grant us your salvation.**

I will hear what God proclaims;
  the LORD—for he proclaims peace.
Near indeed is his salvation to those who fear him,
  glory dwelling in our land.

The psalmist speaks of peace, salvation, kindness, truth, and justice. All of these benefits would be showered upon those who hope in the LORD.

Justice is a prerequisite for peace, as Pope Paul VI proclaimed. We learn of justice from God, and we are called to practice that justice in the way we treat those around us. What is especially important to remember, though, is that justice must be combined with mercy. While strict justice is giving each person what they deserve, God's justice goes far beyond this. He forgives us and heals us even though we do not deserve it. This is the way we have to treat others.

R̸. **Lord, let us see your kindness, and grant us your salvation.**

Kindness and truth shall meet;
   justice and peace shall kiss.
Truth shall spring out of the earth,
   and justice shall look down from heaven.

R̸. **Lord, let us see your kindness, and grant us your salvation.**

The LORD himself will give his benefits;
   our land shall yield its increase.
Justice shall walk before him,
   and prepare the way of his steps.

R̸. **Lord, let us see your kindness, and grant us your salvation.**

Lect.
No. 115

SECOND READING: Romans 9:1-5

I could wish that I were accursed for the sake of my own people.

There were times when Saint Paul was accused of hating his fellow Israelites and working for their ruin. Here we see how far from the truth that accusation is.

Paul speaks of how he would accept being sent to hell if only it would mean that his fellow Jews would be welcomed into heaven. This certainly gives us a difficult measure of our Christian love. If our worst enemy in the world and we were at the gates of heaven, and only one could get in, would we be willing to let our enemy go in instead of us?

Paul closes this section by speaking of the fact that the Jewish people are still the people of the promise. Even if some

A reading from the Letter of Saint Paul
to the Romans

Brothers and sisters:
   I speak the truth in Christ, I do not lie;
   my conscience joins with the Holy Spirit in bearing me witness
   that I have great sorrow and constant anguish in my heart.
For I could wish that I myself were accursed and cut off from Christ
   for the sake of my own people,
   my kindred according to the flesh.
They are Israelites;
   theirs the adoption, the glory, the covenants,
   the giving of the law, the worship, and the promises;
   theirs the patriarchs, and from them,

of them were unfaithful, God is never unfaithful to his promises. They are still the chosen people.

Lect.
No. 115

The Alleluia Verse speaks of the trust that we are called to place in God. We depend upon him for everything that we have and are.

Lect.
No. 115

As we saw last week, Jesus transforms the laws of nature. Last week we saw how he took five loaves of bread and two fish and made enough food to nourish over five thousand people. This week he performs another nature miracle when he walks upon the waters.

The disciples were terrified when they saw him coming toward them. They thought that it was a ghost or some other evil force. He assured them that it was he.

The assumption that it was an evil force approaching their boat is not all that extraordinary. It was the middle of the night and in the middle of the sea. These were considered to be the time and the place where the forces of evil held sway. The fact that Jesus has control over both the night and the sea shows that Jesus was in charge of nature, but also that Jesus is superior to the forces of evil. They are impotent before him.

according to the flesh, is the Christ,
who is over all, God blessed forever. Amen.

The word of the Lord.

ALLELUIA: cf. Psalm 130:5

℟. **Alleluia, alleluia.**

I wait for the Lord;
my soul waits for his word.

℟. **Alleluia, alleluia.**

GOSPEL: Matthew 14:22-33

Command me to come to you on the water.

A reading from the holy Gospel according
to Matthew

After he had fed the people, Jesus made the disciples get into a boat
and precede him to the other side,
while he dismissed the crowds.
After doing so, he went up on the mountain by himself to pray.
When it was evening he was there alone.
Meanwhile the boat, already a few miles offshore,
was being tossed about by the waves, for the wind was against it.
During the fourth watch of the night,
he came toward them walking on the sea.
When the disciples saw him walking on the sea they were terrified.
"It is a ghost," they said, and they cried out in fear.
At once Jesus spoke to them, "Take courage, it is I; do not be afraid."
Peter said to him in reply,
"Lord, if it is you, command me to come to you on the water."

The Gospel of Matthew is the only one in which this episode includes the story of Saint Peter walking on the water. Peter demonstrates his typical impetuosity by stepping out onto the water to meet Jesus, but then he lets his fear take over. He begins to sink. Jesus chides him for his lack of faith.

While our natural talents can get us so far (just as Peter's natural impetuosity got him to leave the boat), ultimately we have to abandon ourselves in trust to the Lord Jesus. God does not call us to reject who we are, but he does call us to allow his grace to transform our hearts in his love.

He said, "Come."

Peter got out of the boat and began to walk on the water toward Jesus.

But when he saw how strong the wind was he became frightened;

and, beginning to sink, he cried out, "Lord, save me!"

Immediately Jesus stretched out his hand and caught Peter,

and said to him, "O you of little faith, why did you doubt?"

After they got into the boat, the wind died down.

Those who were in the boat did him homage, saying,

"Truly, you are the Son of God."

The Gospel of the Lord.

THE ASSUMPTION OF THE BLESSED VIRGIN MARY

AT THE VIGIL MASS

The First Reading speaks of the day that King David brought the Ark of the Covenant into Jerusalem. He had recently conquered the city, and now he wanted to make it a focal point of the faith.

The first attempt to bring the Ark into the city ended in failure. One of the soldiers accompanying the Ark touched it. He was immediately struck dead, for he had touched a sacred object. The Ark was left where it was until David saw that the Ark brought blessing to the owner of the property where it was placed.

Notice that David performs sacrifices and gives blessings. In ancient Israel, the king was also considered to be a priest.

The reason that this reading was chosen for this feast is that Mary is the Ark of the New Covenant. She held the presence of the living God within her womb, even as the Ark was the place where God manifested his presence.

This psalm seems to have been written for a liturgical feast. It celebrates the kingship of David and the day that he brought the Ark of the Covenant into Jerusalem.

Lect. No. 621

FIRST READING:

1 Chronicles 15:3-4, 15-16; 16:1-2

They brought in the ark of God and set it within the tent which David had pitched for it.

A reading from the first Book of Chronicles

David assembled all Israel in Jerusalem to bring the ark of the LORD
   to the place that he had prepared for it.
David also called together the sons of Aaron and the Levites.

The Levites bore the ark of God on their shoulders with poles,
   as Moses had ordained according to the word of the LORD.

David commanded the chiefs of the Levites
   to appoint their kinsmen as chanters,
   to play on musical instruments, harps, lyres, and cymbals,
   to make a loud sound of rejoicing.

They brought in the ark of God and set it within the tent
   which David had pitched for it.
Then they offered up burnt offerings and peace offerings to God.
When David had finished offering up the burnt offerings and peace offerings,
   he blessed the people in the name of the LORD.

The word of the Lord.

Lect.
No. 621

RESPONSORIAL PSALM: Ps 132:6-7, 9-10, 13-14 (℟.: 8)

The conquest of Jerusalem was a question of power politics. David saw that the city lay between the northern and the southern tribes. He conquered the city and made it his capital because he wanted to unite the tribes. He moved the Ark into the city so that pilgrims would be forced to enter the city periodically and see the grandeur of the palace that he had built. His political machinations were brilliant.

And yet the LORD used David's base political motives to reveal his mercy. He chose Zion (the mountain associated with the city Jerusalem) to be his dwelling place upon the earth.

God often uses our actions to fulfill his will, even when we do not necessarily intend for that to happen. God could even make a cross into an instrument of salvation.

℟. **Lord, go up to the place of your rest, you and the ark of your holiness.**

Behold, we heard of it in Ephrathah;
　we found it in the fields of Jaar.
Let us enter into his dwelling,
　let us worship at his footstool.

℟. **Lord, go up to the place of your rest, you and the ark of your holiness.**

May your priests be clothed with justice;
　let your faithful ones shout merrily for joy.
For the sake of David your servant,
　reject not the plea of your anointed.

℟. **Lord, go up to the place of your rest, you and the ark of your holiness.**

For the Lord has chosen Zion;
　he prefers her for his dwelling.
"Zion is my resting place forever;
　in her will I dwell, for I prefer her."

℟. **Lord, go up to the place of your rest, you and the ark of your holiness.**

Lect.
No. 621

SECOND READING: 1 Corinthians 15:54b-57

God gave us the victory through Jesus Christ.

This passage is taken from the end of a consideration on the resurrection of the dead. Saint Paul wants the Corinthians to understand that we will all rise on the last day. Death is no longer victorious, for Christ has conquered death and sin.

Paul speaks of the power of sin being the law. Sin had entered the world and it was terrible. But the law made sin even more horrific. We thought that

A reading from the first Letter of Saint Paul to the Corinthians

Brothers and sisters:
　When that which is mortal clothes itself with immortality,
then the word that is written shall come about:
　Death is swallowed up in victory.
　Where, O death, is your victory?
　Where, O death, is your sting?

the law would liberate us from sin, but the best that it could do was point out how much we are sinners. It left us more frustrated than before. Our only true liberation is Christ.

Lect. No. 621

This Beatitude speaks of those who listen to the word of God and make it part of their hearts and lives. Of all who ever lived, Mary did this most fully, for in her the word truly became incarnate.

Lect. No. 621

When a woman cried out that Mary was blessed for she was the mother of Jesus, Jesus responded that a person is blessed who hears the word of God and observes it.

This is not an insult for Mary, for of all people who ever lived, she most successfully heard the word of God (e.g., in the invitation from the Archangel Gabriel to be the mother of the Son of God) and observed it. In her the word of God, Jesus, became incarnate.

The sting of death is sin,
    and the power of sin is the law.
But thanks be to God who gives us the victory
    through our Lord Jesus Christ.

The word of the Lord.

ALLELUIA: Luke 11:28

℟. **Alleluia, alleluia.**

Blessed are they who hear the word of God and observe it.

℟. **Alleluia, alleluia.**

GOSPEL: Luke 11:27-28

Blessed is the womb that carried you!

A reading from the holy Gospel according to Luke

While Jesus was speaking,
    a woman from the crowd called out and said to him,
    "Blessed is the womb that carried you
    and the breasts at which you nursed."
He replied,
    "Rather, blessed are those
    who hear the word of God and observe it."

The Gospel of the Lord.

August 15, 2002

THE ASSUMPTION OF THE BLESSED VIRGIN MARY

MASS DURING THE DAY

Lect. No. 622

FIRST READING:
Revelation 11:19a; 12:1-6a, 10ab

A woman clothed with the sun, with the moon beneath her feet.

The First Reading is taken from the Book of Revelation. On one level, it speaks of the birth of Jesus upon the earth. On another level, it presents an image of the Church making Christ present again each day.

Like the woman in this passage, Mary gave birth to a child who was immediately endangered by the evil one who wanted to devour him (this is probably a reference to the plot of King Herod to put the child to death). God protected the child and destroyed the power of the serpent. The image of this woman clothed with the sun, with the moon under her feet and wearing a crown of twelve stars, has become an image for the Immaculate Conception.

But in this account, the woman also represents the Church. She is constantly being attacked by the forces of evil. Yet she makes Christ present in the world. This is especially true when she suffers for the sake of the gospel.

It is appropriate that the image would stand both for Mary and for the Church. Mary is the model of the Church. She is the example of what the Church should be, for she made the word of God incarnate.

A reading from the Book of Revelation

God's temple in heaven was opened,
and the ark of his covenant could be seen in the temple.

A great sign appeared in the sky, a woman clothed with the sun,
with the moon beneath her feet,
and on her head a crown of twelve stars.
She was with child and wailed aloud in pain as she labored to give birth.
Then another sign appeared in the sky;
it was a huge red dragon, with seven heads and ten horns,
and on its heads were seven diadems.
Its tail swept away a third of the stars in the sky
and hurled them down to the earth.
Then the dragon stood before the woman about to give birth,
to devour her child when she gave birth.
She gave birth to a son, a male child,
destined to rule all the nations with an iron rod.
Her child was caught up to God and his throne.
The woman herself fled into the desert
where she had a place prepared by God.

Then I heard a loud voice in heaven say:
"Now have salvation and power come,
and the kingdom of our God
and the authority of his Anointed One."

The word of the Lord.

290

Lect.
No. 622

RESPONSORIAL PSALM: Ps 45:10, 11, 12, 16 (℟.: 10bc)

The Responsorial Psalm is taken from Psalm 45, a psalm written to celebrate the wedding feast of a king of Israel to his bride.

The queen stands at the right hand of the king in gold of Ophir. Gold of Ophir is a very precious form of gold. The queen at the right of the king is not his bride. His bride is the princess borne in before them. The queen is actually the queen mother.

Kings of Israel had many wives and none of them was the queen. The queen was the queen mother. One of her most important responsibilities was to prepare the wedding feast of her son. This is what she is doing at the right hand of the king.

The presence of Mary at the wedding feast of Cana is based upon this image. She is the queen mother who invites her son to his wedding, the cross.

℟. **The queen stands at your right hand, arrayed in gold.**

The queen takes her place at your right hand in gold of Ophir.

℟. **The queen stands at your right hand, arrayed in gold.**

Hear, O daughter, and see; turn your ear,
forget your people and your father's house.

℟. **The queen stands at your right hand, arrayed in gold.**

So shall the king desire your beauty;
for he is your lord.

℟. **The queen stands at your right hand, arrayed in gold.**

They are borne in with gladness and joy;
they enter the palace of the king.

℟. **The queen stands at your right hand, arrayed in gold.**

Lect.
No. 622

SECOND READING: 1 Corinthians 15:20-27

Christ, the firstfruits; then those who belong to him.

Jesus is described as being the firstfruits of those who have fallen asleep. The firstfruits are generally known for two things. First of all, they are known as being the best. Second, they are the promise of more that will shortly arrive. Jesus is the best of those who have been risen from the dead, and he is also a promise to us that we will one day rise from the dead to live with him in heaven.

A reading from the first Letter of Saint Paul to the Corinthians

Brothers and sisters:
   Christ has been raised from the dead,
the firstfruits of those who have fallen asleep.
For since death came through man,
   the resurrection of the dead came also through man.
For just as in Adam all die,
   so too in Christ shall all be brought to life,
   but each one in proper order:

Adam's sin brought death into the world. We are not sure if Paul means physical death or spiritual death. Whichever, we were left hopeless due to the power of sin.

Now that Jesus has risen from the dead, sin and death no longer have any power over us. Jesus has already risen, and on the last day we will all rise with him to share in his glory. That is when Jesus' defeat of his last enemy, death, will be made manifest, for we will live forever with him to share in his glory.

Lect.
No. 622

Christ the firstfruits;
then, at his coming, those who belong to Christ;
then comes the end,
when he hands over the kingdom to his God and
    Father,
when he has destroyed every sovereignty
and every authority and power.
For he must reign until he has put all his enemies
    under his feet.
The last enemy to be destroyed is death,
    for "he subjected everything under his feet."

The word of the Lord.

ALLELUIA

℞. **Alleluia, alleluia.**

Mary is taken up to heaven;
a chorus of angels exults.

℞. **Alleluia, alleluia.**

Our Alleluia Verse celebrates the reason for this feast: that our Blessed Mother was taken up into heaven body and soul to share in God's glory forever.

Lect.
No. 622

GOSPEL: Luke 1:39-56

The Almighty has done great things for me: he has raised up the lowly.

The Gospel presents the story of the visitation of Mary to her cousin Elizabeth.

The traditional site of Elizabeth's and Zechariah's house is Ein Karim, a small village not far outside of Jerusalem.

The child that Elizabeth is carrying gives witness to the presence of Jesus in their midst. The first person who ever recognized the presence of Jesus in the world was an unborn child. Typically, it is those whom society would evaluate as insignificant who are able to respond to God's call.

A reading from the holy Gospel according to Luke

Mary set out
    and traveled to the hill country in haste
to a town of Judah,
where she entered the house of Zechariah
and greeted Elizabeth.
When Elizabeth heard Mary's greeting,
    the infant leaped in her womb,
    and Elizabeth, filled with the Holy Spirit,
    cried out in a loud voice and said,
"Blessed are you among women,
    and blessed is the fruit of your womb.

Elizabeth is filled with the Holy Spirit and thus is able to greet Mary with the phrase that we still use in the "Hail Mary." The Holy Spirit is important throughout the writings of Saint Luke.

Mary is especially blessed for her trust in the words of the Lord. She was generous and willing to place herself at the disposition of God.

Mary responds to this remarkable greeting with the hymn that we call the "Magnificat." This hymn is largely based upon the hymn of Hannah in 1 Samuel 2 (with the verses of various psalms added).

This beautiful hymn expresses the feelings of the "anawim," the poor ones of Yahweh. In the time of Jesus, the poor were despised by the powers that be. Jesus portrayed the exact opposite attitude toward the poor. He considered them to be the chosen of the Father.

Mary, in this hymn and throughout the Gospel of Luke, is portrayed as a representative of the "anawim." She was humble enough to respond lovingly to God's call to become the mother of his Son. When God called her, she replied that she was the servant of the Lord and that it should be done unto her according to his will.

And how does this happen to me,
that the mother of my Lord should come to me?
For at the moment the sound of your greeting reached my ears,
the infant in my womb leaped for joy.
Blessed are you who believed
that what was spoken to you by the Lord
would be fulfilled."

And Mary said:
"My soul proclaims the greatness of the Lord;
my spirit rejoices in God my Savior
for he has looked upon his lowly servant.
From this day all generations will call me blessed:
the Almighty has done great things for me,
and holy is his Name.
He has mercy on those who fear him
in every generation.
He has shown the strength of his arm,
and has scattered the proud in their conceit.
He has cast down the mighty from their thrones,
and has lifted up the lowly.
He has filled the hungry with good things,
and the rich he has sent away empty.
He has come to the help of his servant Israel
for he has remembered his promise of mercy,
the promise he made to our fathers,
to Abraham and his children forever."

Mary remained with her about three months
and then returned to her home.

The Gospel of the Lord.

August 18, 2002

TWENTIETH SUNDAY IN ORDINARY TIME

Lect. No. 118

FIRST READING: Isaiah 56:1, 6-7

I will bring foreigners to my holy mountain.

This reading comes from the third part of the Book of the Prophet Isaiah. It was written after the Israelites' return from exile in Babylon (c. 539 B.C.).

After the exile, there were two opinions in Israel. One wanted to purify Israel by expelling all foreigners from their midst. This reading represents the other opinion, that Yahweh was the God of all peoples and pagans should therefore be welcomed into Israel. There they could worship the only true God in the temple upon God's holy mountain.

This outreach is a theme repeated in the Gospel passage about the Syro-Phoenician woman.

A reading from the Book of the Prophet Isaiah

Thus says the LORD:
  Observe what is right, do what is just;
for my salvation is about to come,
  my justice, about to be revealed.

The foreigners who join themselves to the LORD,
  ministering to him,
loving the name of the LORD,
  and becoming his servants—
all who keep the sabbath free from profanation
  and hold to my covenant,
them I will bring to my holy mountain
  and make joyful in my house of prayer;
their burnt offerings and sacrifices
  will be acceptable on my altar,
for my house shall be called
  a house of prayer for all peoples.

The word of the Lord.

Lect.
No. 118

RESPONSORIAL PSALM: Ps 67:2-3, 5, 6, 8 (℞.: 4)

The Responsorial Psalm continues the theme that Yahweh is the God of all nations. The peoples of every nation upon the earth are called upon to praise the LORD.

For much of Israel's history, the people thought of the LORD as their own national God. The pagan nations had their own gods, but these gods were considered to be inferior to the LORD.

When the Jewish people realized that there was only one God upon the earth, they also came to understand that their God had to be the God of all peoples upon the earth.

℞. **O God, let all the nations praise you!**

May God have pity on us and bless us;
    may he let his face shine upon us.
So may your way be known upon earth;
    among all nations, your salvation.

℞. **O God, let all the nations praise you!**

May the nations be glad and exult
    because you rule the peoples in equity;
    the nations on the earth you guide.

℞. **O God, let all the nations praise you!**

May the peoples praise you, O God;
    may all the peoples praise you!
May God bless us,
    and may all the ends of the earth fear him!

℞. **O God, let all the nations praise you!**

Lect.
No. 118

SECOND READING: Romans 11:13-15, 29-32

The gifts and the call of God for Israel are irrevocable.

The Second Reading speaks of the mystery of God's plan for the Jewish people and the pagans. The majority of the Christians to whom Saint Paul was writing in Rome were originally pagan. Paul tells them that God allowed the Jews to be disobedient so that they might be rejected. This left room for the pagans who could then convert and become part of the people of God.

But this was not the end of the story. God had a plan to make the Jewish people jealous of the pagans who were now part of the new Israel. This would make them want to convert their ways and return to obedience to God.

God would certainly accept them back, for God was always faithful to his promises (even if we are, at times, not faithful). God's mercy is much greater than our guilt, it is beyond our comprehension.

A reading from the Letter of Saint Paul
to the Romans

Brothers and sisters:
I am speaking to you Gentiles.
Inasmuch as I am the apostle to the Gentiles,
　I glory in my ministry in order to make my race
　　jealous
and thus save some of them.
For if their rejection is the reconciliation of the
　world,
　what will their acceptance be but life from the
　　dead?

For the gifts and the call of God are irrevocable.
Just as you once disobeyed God
　but have now received mercy because of their dis-
　　obedience,
　so they have now disobeyed in order that,
　by virtue of the mercy shown to you,
　they too may now receive mercy.
For God delivered all to disobedience,
　that he might have mercy upon all.

The word of the Lord.

Lect.
No. 118

ALLELUIA: cf. Matthew 4:23

The Alleluia Verse speaks of how Jesus proclaimed the dawning of the Kingdom of God upon the earth. All who listen to his call to conversion are part of that kingdom.

℞. **Alleluia, alleluia.**

Jesus proclaimed the Gospel of the kingdom
and cured every disease among the people.

℞. **Alleluia, alleluia.**

Lect. No. 118

GOSPEL: Matthew 15:21-28

O woman, great is your faith!

The Gospel of Matthew speaks of how Jesus came to save the lost sheep of Israel. This was a Jewish Gospel written for a Jewish-Christian community.

Yet, there are a few passages that hint that the mission would extend beyond the boundaries of Israel. One is the fact that the Magi (pagans) come to pay homage to the child Jesus.

Another passage is the one found in today's Gospel. A woman from the Phoenician region who was a pagan came to ask a favor from Jesus. Her daughter was tormented by a demon, and she knew that Jesus possessed the healing power of God.

At first Jesus seems to put her off. It is possible that he was simply repeating a saying of his day (that the pagans were nothing but dogs). The woman would not let this diminish her desire.

Jesus praises her for her faith. He grants her request, for his message was now reaching beyond the people of Israel.

A reading from the holy Gospel according to Matthew

At that time, Jesus withdrew to the region of Tyre and Sidon.

And behold, a Canaanite woman of that district came and called out,

"Have pity on me, Lord, Son of David!

My daughter is tormented by a demon."

But Jesus did not say a word in answer to her.

Jesus' disciples came and asked him,

"Send her away, for she keeps calling out after us."

He said in reply,

"I was sent only to the lost sheep of the house of Israel."

But the woman came and did Jesus homage, saying,

"Lord, help me."

He said in reply,

"It is not right to take the food of the children and throw it to the dogs."

She said, "Please, Lord, for even the dogs eat the scraps that fall from the table of their masters."

Then Jesus said to her in reply,

"O woman, great is your faith!

Let it be done for you as you wish."

And the woman's daughter was healed from that hour.

The Gospel of the Lord.

August 25, 2002

TWENTY-FIRST SUNDAY IN ORDINARY TIME

Lect. No. 121

FIRST READING: Isaiah 22:19-23

I will place the key of the House of David upon his shoulder.

This reading has been chosen because it speaks of keys (the Gospel will present the story of Peter receiving the keys of the kingdom).

In this particular story, Shebna, the majordomo of the palace, was told that he would lose his office and that it would be given to Eliakim. Eliakim would receive all of the signs of office, including the robe, sash, and the keys of office.

Eliakim would be given authority to make decisions that were binding. He could open and shut as he saw fit. He would also be a peg in a sure spot, which means that his responsibilities would not be transitory. He would have great security in his office (unlike Shebna).

A reading from the Book of the Prophet Isaiah

Thus says the LORD to Shebna, master of the palace:
"I will thrust you from your office
    and pull you down from your station.
On that day I will summon my servant
    Eliakim, son of Hilkiah;
I will clothe him with your robe,
    and gird him with your sash,
    and give over to him your authority.
He shall be a father to the inhabitants of Jerusalem,
    and to the house of Judah.
I will place the key of the House of David on
        Eliakim's shoulder;
    when he opens, no one shall shut;
    when he shuts, no one shall open.
I will fix him like a peg in a sure spot,
    to be a place of honor for his family."

The word of the Lord.

Lect. No. 121

RESPONSORIAL PSALM: Ps 138:1-2, 2-3, 6, 8 (℟.: 8bc)

The Responsorial Psalm is a hymn of thanksgiving for the many ways in which the LORD has blessed the psalmist.

He promises to praise the LORD in the holy places, for God had been gracious and loving to him. He speaks of the LORD as being kind and truthful. The

℟. **Lord, your love is eternal; do not forsake the work of your hands.**

I will give thanks to you, O LORD, with all my heart,
    for you have heard the words of my mouth;
in the presence of the angels I will sing your praise;
    I will worship at your holy temple.

298

word "truthful" does not mean that God did not lie to him, but rather that God was always faithful to his promises.

The LORD answered the psalmist's prayers and built up his strength. We are to be child-like, always depending upon God, but not in the sense of being overly passive. It has been said that we must do everything as if it depended upon us, knowing that it all depends upon God.

God listens to the prayers of the lowly. They are the ones who recognize that God is their only strength and bulwark against all of their difficulties.

℟. **Lord, your love is eternal; do not forsake the work of your hands.**

I will give thanks to your name,
    because of your kindness and your truth:
when I called, you answered me;
    you built up strength within me.

℟. **Lord, your love is eternal; do not forsake the work of your hands.**

The LORD is exalted, yet the lowly he sees,
    and the proud he knows from afar.
Your kindness, O LORD, endures forever;
    forsake not the work of your hands.

℟. **Lord, your love is eternal; do not forsake the work of your hands.**

| Lect. |
| No. 121 |

SECOND READING: Romans 11:33-36

From God and through him and for him are all things.

The Second Reading is a type of hymn to celebrate the profundity of the mystery of God's plan. The mystery is not something that God is hiding from us. Rather God's plan is so great and wise that we cannot even begin to understand it fully.

This does not mean that we should not try to understand it—only that we should have the humility to recognize that after we have studied and prayed all our life we will not even have begun to plumb that mystery. And so we like Saint Paul give praise to the Lord.

A reading from the Letter of Saint Paul
to the Romans

Oh, the depth of the riches and wisdom and knowledge of God!
How inscrutable are his judgments and how unsearchable his ways!
For who has known the mind of the Lord
    or who has been his counselor?
Or who has given the Lord anything
    that he may be repaid?
For from him and through him and for him are all things.
To him be glory forever. Amen.

The word of the Lord.

The Alleluia Verse cites the words that Jesus spoke to Peter when he gave him the keys of the kingdom and invited him to become the Vicar of Christ.

ALLELUIA: Matthew 16:18

℟. **Alleluia, alleluia.**

You are Peter and upon this rock I will build my Church

and the gates of the netherworld shall not prevail against it.

℟. **Alleluia, alleluia.**

GOSPEL: Matthew 16:13-20

You are Peter, and to you I will give the keys of the kingdom of heaven.

When Peter says Jesus is "the Christ," he is saying that Jesus is the Messiah. Peter goes on to say that Jesus is the only-begotten Son of the Father. Peter means rock in Greek. Peter is the rock or foundation of the Church.

The "gates of the netherworld" probably refers to a cave that overlooked the site where all of this occurred. For centuries there had been pagan worship there and it was called the "gates to hell." Jesus tells Peter that the forces of evil will not prevail over him and his Church.

The keys to the kingdom refer to the authority given him. In the Old Testament only God had keys: to life, death, and rain. Jesus has God's authority and he passes it on to Peter.

The power to loose and bind was the power that rabbis possessed to make decisions over what was binding in the law. In a sense Jesus is making Peter the chief rabbi of the Church.

Though the other gospels do not speak of keys, they show Peter receiving authority over the Church (e.g., Luke 22; John 21).

A reading from the holy Gospel according to Matthew

Jesus went into the region of Caesarea Philippi and he asked his disciples,
"Who do people say that the Son of Man is?"
They replied, "Some say John the Baptist, others Elijah,
still others Jeremiah or one of the prophets."
He said to them, "But who do you say that I am?"
Simon Peter said in reply,
"You are the Christ, the Son of the living God."
Jesus said to him in reply,
"Blessed are you, Simon son of Jonah.
For flesh and blood has not revealed this to you, but my heavenly Father.
And so I say to you, you are Peter,
and upon this rock I will build my church,
and the gates of the netherworld shall not prevail against it.
I will give you the keys to the kingdom of heaven.
Whatever you bind on earth shall be bound in heaven;
and whatever you loose on earth shall be loosed in heaven."
Then he strictly ordered his disciples
to tell no one that he was the Christ.

The Gospel of the Lord.

TWENTY-SECOND SUNDAY IN ORDINARY TIME

Lect. No. 124

FIRST READING: Jeremiah 20:7-9

The word of the Lord has brought me derision.

This is one of the passages from the Book of the Prophet Jeremiah called the Confessions of Jeremiah. They express the strong feelings that the prophet felt concerning his vocation. He tried to serve the LORD with his entire heart, but he suffered terribly for all of his effort.

Jeremiah felt duped. He felt that he had done his part but he was beginning to feel that the LORD was using him and not living up to his part of the bargain.

He even speaks of trying not to prophesy. He tried to keep quiet and stop preaching, but it did no good. The message became like a fire in his bones and he could not hold it in.

A reading from the Book of the Prophet Jeremiah

You duped me, O LORD, and I let myself be duped;
  you were too strong for me, and you triumphed.
All the day I am an object of laughter;
  everyone mocks me.

Whenever I speak, I must cry out,
  violence and outrage is my message;
the word of the LORD has brought me
  derision and reproach all the day.

I say to myself, I will not mention him,
  I will speak in his name no more.
But then it becomes like fire burning in my heart,
  imprisoned in my bones;
I grow weary holding it in, I cannot endure it.

The word of the Lord.

Lect. No. 124

RESPONSORIAL Psalm: Ps 63:2, 3-4, 5-6, 8-9 (℟.: 2b)

This psalm is a lamentation usually proclaimed by an individual (as opposed to communal laments).

The psalmist speaks of how much he needs an intervention of the LORD. He speaks of the land being dry and parched. It is almost desperate. It is a question of life and death. With the LORD there is life and hope, but if the LORD is not present

℟. **My soul is thirsting for you, O Lord my God.**

O God, you are my God whom I seek;
  for you my flesh pines and my soul thirsts
  like the earth, parched, lifeless and without water.

℟. **My soul is thirsting for you, O Lord my God.**

Thus have I gazed toward you in the sanctuary
  to see your power and your glory,
for your kindness is a greater good than life;
  my lips shall glorify you.

then there is only death and despair. The philosopher Soren Kierkegaard said that the choice was not between belief and non-belief but between belief and despair.

The psalmist searches for ways to express his gratitude for all the goodness that the LORD had shown him. He speaks of raising his hands in praise and exaltation. He also speaks of the sense of peace and satisfaction in his heart that could only be compared to what one would feel at a great banquet.

Lect. No. 124

℞. **My soul is thirsting for you, O Lord my God.**

Thus will I bless you while I live;
　lifting up my hands, I will call upon your name.
As with the riches of a banquet shall my soul be satisfied,
　and with exultant lips my mouth shall praise you.

℞. **My soul is thirsting for you, O Lord my God.**

You are my help,
　and in the shadow of your wings I shout for joy.
My soul clings fast to you;
　your right hand upholds me.

℞. **My soul is thirsting for you, O Lord my God.**

SECOND READING: Romans 12:1-2

Offer your bodies as a living sacrifice.

Saint Paul was writing to a community that had a large percentage of Gentile-Christians. Gentiles were famous for their sexual immorality. This is why Paul begs them to live lives of sexual purity. They were to offer up their bodies as spiritual sacrifices i.e., to live chaste lifestyles.

He begs them not to conform to the values of their age. This advice is timeless, for Christians have always been called to be countercultural.

Lect. No. 124

A reading from the Letter of Saint Paul
to the Romans

I urge you, brothers and sisters, by the mercies of God,
　to offer your bodies as a living sacrifice,
　holy and pleasing to God, your spiritual worship.
Do not conform yourselves to this age
　but be transformed by the renewal of your mind,
　that you may discern what is the will of God,
　what is good and pleasing and perfect.

The word of the Lord.

ALLELUIA: cf. Ephesians 1:17-18

The Alleluia Verse is a paraphrase of a short prayer found in the Letter to the Ephesians. It calls for the spiritual enlightenment of the believers so that they might be filled with hope.

℞. **Alleluia, alleluia.**

May the Father of our Lord Jesus Christ
enlighten the eyes of our hearts,
that we may know what is the hope
that belongs to our call.

℞. **Alleluia, alleluia.**

Lect.
No. 124

GOSPEL: Matthew 16:21-27

Whoever wishes to come after me must deny himself.

In the passage that immediately precedes today's Gospel, Saint Peter is given the keys of the kingdom and is proclaimed as the rock upon which the Church would be built.

Today's Gospel has almost the exactly opposite sentiment. Jesus speaks about the necessity for him to suffer and die. This is one of the many predictions about the passion that Jesus made during his ministry.

Peter's response to this proclamation is abhorrence. Peter wanted Jesus to be a Messiah who was a conquering hero. He wanted Jesus to be a king so that he could share in Jesus' glory. He told Jesus "God forbid." Jesus responded to this protest with the rebuke "Get behind me, Satan!" While Peter's profession that Jesus was the Christ, the Son of the living God, was from God, this sentiment was not. It was from Satan.

Peter did not understand that Jesus would be king upon the cross and that would be his hour of glory. Although he did not yet know it, Peter would share in this glory by the manner of his own death.

A reading from the holy Gospel according to Matthew

Jesus began to show his disciples
that he must go to Jerusalem and suffer greatly
    from the elders, the chief priests, and the scribes,
    and be killed and on the third day be raised.
Then Peter took Jesus aside and began to rebuke him,
    "God forbid, Lord! No such thing shall ever happen to you."
He turned and said to Peter,
    "Get behind me, Satan! You are an obstacle to me.
You are thinking not as God does, but as human beings do."

Then Jesus said to his disciples,
    "Whoever wishes to come after me must deny himself,
    take up his cross, and follow me.
For whoever wishes to save his life will lose it,
    but whoever loses his life for my sake will find it.
What profit would there be for one to gain the whole world
    and forfeit his life?
Or what can one give in exchange for his life?
For the Son of Man will come with his angels in his Father's glory,
    and then he will repay all according to his conduct."

The Gospel of the Lord.

September 8, 2002

TWENTY-THIRD SUNDAY IN ORDINARY TIME

Lect. No. 127

FIRST READING: Ezekiel 33:7-9

*If you do not speak out to dissuade the wicked from his way,
I will hold you responsible for his death.*

This reading from Ezekiel speaks of the obligation of the prophet to give witness to the truth, especially when it involves the conduct of those around us. We are our brothers' keeper.

When we observe people who have gotten themselves in trouble by sinning against God's law, we have the obligation to intervene. If we do not, then we are responsible. If, on the other hand, we have been honest with them and we have shared our insights with them and they still refuse to change their ways, it is then their responsibility. Finally, when we are correcting others, we must be careful not to be self-righteous, for the ability to see the truth and give witness to it is a gift from God and not something we have earned.

A reading from the Book of the Prophet Ezekiel

Thus says the LORD:
You, son of man, I have appointed watchman for the house of Israel;
when you hear me say anything, you shall warn them for me.
If I tell the wicked, "O wicked one, you shall surely die,"
and you do not speak out to dissuade the wicked from his way,
the wicked shall die for his guilt,
but I will hold you responsible for his death.
But if you warn the wicked,
trying to turn him from his way,
and he refuses to turn from his way,
he shall die for his guilt,
but you shall save yourself.

The word of the Lord.

Lect. No. 127

RESPONSORIAL PSALM: Ps 95:1-2, 6-7, 8-9 (R℣.: 8)

There are two dimensions to our Responsorial Psalm today. On the one hand, it is a song of praise to the LORD. God is described as being the rock of our salvation and the shepherd who guides us.

On the other hand, this psalm is also a call to conversion. It re-

R℣. **If today you hear his voice, harden not your hearts.**

Come, let us sing joyfully to the LORD;
let us acclaim the rock of our salvation.
Let us come into his presence with thanksgiving;
let us joyfully sing psalms to him.

minds us that God is, in fact, our shepherd. This means that we are his flock, and we must be willing to obey him.

Furthermore, in the third section it speaks of the necessity of not being rebellious as the Hebrews were at Meribah and Massah in the desert. This refers to the fact that when they asked God for water, they doubted that he would respond to their prayers.

What is the effect of our sins? By our sins we reject God's guidance. God does not stop loving us, but we have turned our backs on his love. Sin hardens our hearts and brings us death.

R. **If today you hear his voice, harden not your hearts.**

Come, let us bow down in worship;
　let us kneel before the LORD who made us.
For he is our God,
　and we are the people he shepherds, the flock he guides.

R. **If today you hear his voice, harden not your hearts.**

Oh, that today you would hear his voice:
　"Harden not your hearts as at Meribah,
　as in the day of Massah in the desert,
where your fathers tempted me;
　they tested me though they had seen my works."

R. **If today you hear his voice, harden not your hearts.**

Lect. No. 127

SECOND READING: Romans 13:8-10

Love is the fulfillment of the law.

When Jesus was asked what the greatest commandment was, he responded that it was to love the Lord with all one's heart, soul, and strength and to love one's neighbor as oneself.

Saint Paul speaks of our Christian obligation toward one another. All of the precepts of the law are summed up in the commandment that we love one another. This commandment, in fact, goes far beyond the others, for it is not enough not to do evil toward others. One must actually seek what is good for them. We must avoid sins of omission as well as those of commission.

A reading from the Letter of Saint Paul to the Romans

Brothers and sisters:
　Owe nothing to anyone, except to love one another;
　for the one who loves another has fulfilled the law.
The commandments, "You shall not commit adultery;
　you shall not kill; you shall not steal; you shall not covet,"
　and whatever other commandment there may be,
　are summed up in this saying, namely,
　"You shall love your neighbor as yourself."
Love does no evil to the neighbor;
　hence, love is the fulfillment of the law.

The word of the Lord.

Lect. No. 127

Jesus is the sign of God's love for us. As such he is the source of peace between us and God. Jesus is the sacrament of God's fidelity and mercy.

Lect. No. 127

This Gospel contains some guidelines for community conduct.

The first saying concerns what to do with someone with whom one is in conflict. The recommendation is that one first try to solve it directly with the person involved (and not try to deal with it behind that person's back). If this does not work, then one should seek the help of a couple of witnesses from the community.

It is important to remember that the reason to confront the person is for that person's good and not for revenge or to establish control over that person's life. Finally one should seek the help of the Church community. If all of that fails, then one should cast that person out of the community (a type of excommunication).

The other two sayings concern loosing and binding (the disciples are given authority over the community) and the power of prayer (that the Lord Jesus would be present to them when they called upon him).

ALLELUIA: 2 Corinthians 5:19

℟. **Alleluia, alleluia.**

God was reconciling the world to himself in Christ and entrusting to us the message of reconciliation.

℟. **Alleluia, alleluia.**

GOSPEL: Matthew 18:15-20

If your brother or sister listens to you, you have won them over.

A reading from the holy Gospel according to Matthew

Jesus said to his disciples:
"If your brother sins against you,
   go and tell him his fault between you and him
      alone.
If he listens to you, you have won over your brother.
If he does not listen,
   take one or two others along with you,
   so that 'every fact may be established
   on the testimony of two or three witnesses.'
If he refuses to listen to them, tell the church.
If he refuses to listen even to the church,
   then treat him as you would a Gentile or a tax collector.
Amen, I say to you,
   whatever you bind on earth shall be bound in
      heaven,
   and whatever you loose on earth shall be loosed
      in heaven.
Again, amen, I say to you,
   if two of you agree on earth
   about anything for which they are to pray,
   it shall be granted to them by my heavenly Father.
For where two or three are gathered together in my
      name,
   there am I in the midst of them."

The Gospel of the Lord.

TWENTY-FOURTH SUNDAY IN ORDINARY TIME

Lect. No. 130

FIRST READING: Sirach 27:30—28:9

Forgive your neighbor's injustice; then when you pray, your own sins will be forgiven.

A reading from the Book of Sirach

Wrath and anger are hateful things,
  yet the sinner hugs them tight.
The vengeful will suffer the LORD's vengeance,
  for he remembers their sins in detail.
Forgive your neighbor's injustice;
  then when you pray, your own sins will be forgiven.
Could anyone nourish anger against another
  and expect healing from the LORD?
Could anyone refuse mercy to another like himself,
  can he seek pardon for his own sins?
If one who is but flesh cherishes wrath,
  who will forgive his sins?
Remember your last days, set enmity aside;
  remember death and decay, and cease from sin!
Think of the commandments, hate not your neighbor;
  remember the Most High's covenant, and overlook faults.

The word of the Lord.

This reading speaks of how wrath and anger are not the ways of God. If one refuses to forgive, then one cannot expect to be forgiven. If one does not show mercy, then mercy will not be shown that person.

How can you forgive another who has done something terrible? The most important thing is to remember that what the person has done is a symptom of the person's brokenness. That person is hurting, and the hateful things that he or she has done is only a sign of that difficulty.

One does not bring that person to healing by adding more hate to the situation. One can only heal that person through love and forgiveness.

This does not mean that one should be oblivious to what the person is doing or to the person's problem. It simply means that we must hate the sin but love the sinner.

Lect. No. 130

RESPONSORIAL PSALM: Ps 103:1-2, 3-4, 9-10, 11-12 (℞.: 8)

The Responsorial Psalm praises God who forgives our sins. The theme of today's liturgy is forgiveness, and one of the greatest sources of the strength to forgive is the recognition of how much God has forgiven us.

We hear in our psalm that God redeems our lives from destruction. We have brought ruin into our own lives through our sinfulness. Sin is an illusion, for it seems as if it is an act of freedom and something that brings us joy. Yet sin is not a free act. Saint Paul speaks about how sin is really just a sign that we are slaves to our passions and not free at all. Likewise, sin does not bring us joy. It brings us a few minutes of diversion, but the ultimate effect of sin is to leave us alienated and frustrated.

God realizes all of this and heals us of our self-destructive activities (for sin is the ultimate act of self-destructiveness). God does this with kindness and compassion. He realizes that our sinfulness is a disease, and the only way to heal this disease is through love and mercy.

And so God uses our sinfulness as an opportunity to love us all the more. God treats our acts of rebellion as a chance to love and heal us. As we have heard in the First Reading, we must learn from the example of God who transforms the world with love.

℞. **The Lord is kind and merciful, slow to anger, and rich in compassion.**

Bless the LORD, O my soul;
  and all my being, bless his holy name.
Bless the LORD, O my soul,
  and forget not all his benefits.

℞. **The Lord is kind and merciful, slow to anger, and rich in compassion.**

He pardons all your iniquities,
  heals all your ills,
he redeems your life from destruction,
  he crowns you with kindness and compassion.

℞. **The Lord is kind and merciful, slow to anger, and rich in compassion.**

He will not always chide,
  nor does he keep his wrath forever.
Not according to our sins does he deal with us,
  nor does he requite us according to our crimes.

℞. **The Lord is kind and merciful, slow to anger, and rich in compassion.**

For as the heavens are high above the earth,
  so surpassing is his kindness toward those who fear him.
As far as the east is from the west,
  so far has he put our transgressions from us.

℞. **The Lord is kind and merciful, slow to anger, and rich in compassion.**

Lect. No. 130

SECOND READING: Romans 14:7-9

Whether we live or die, we are the Lord's.

This short reading teaches us the profound truth that we are not our own. God created us out of love, and called us into his love. We are not complete if we try to live in a totally autonomous manner. We are only complete in the Lord.

Thus, our question must be how we can live each day as a response to God's call. But even death, a passing from this world to the next, must be viewed as a response to God's call.

A reading from the Letter of Saint Paul to the Romans

Brothers and sisters:
  None of us lives for oneself, and no one dies for oneself.
For if we live, we live for the Lord,
  and if we die, we die for the Lord;
  so then, whether we live or die, we are the Lord's.
For this is why Christ died and came to life,
  that he might be Lord of both the dead and the living.

The word of the Lord.

Lect. No. 130

ALLELUIA: John 13:34

God has taught us the true meaning of love by being willing to die for us. This is the measure of the love that we must have for each other.

℟. **Alleluia, alleluia.**

I give you a new commandment, says the Lord;
love one another as I have loved you.

℟. **Alleluia, alleluia.**

Lect. No. 130

GOSPEL: Matthew 18:21-35

I say to you, forgive not seven times, but seventy–seven times.

The theme of forgiveness continues in the Gospel.

Saint Peter asks Jesus how often he must forgive a brother who sins against him. Must he forgive him seven times? The number seven is symbolic in the Bible. It is the perfect number for it represents universality or perfection (for the ancients be-

A reading from the holy Gospel according to Matthew

Peter approached Jesus and asked him,
  "Lord, if my brother sins against me,
  how often must I forgive?
As many as seven times?"
Jesus answered, "I say to you, not seven times but
  seventy-seven times.

lieved that this was the number of planets in the universe and therefore seven represented the entirety of all that existed). By asking if he should forgive his brother seven times, Peter is already being very generous.

Jesus responds that we have to forgive "seventy-seven" times. This means that there is no limit to the times that we must forgive those who have sinned against us.

There are two ways of interpreting this forgiveness. It means that we should forgive people even if they hurt us time after time, or it could mean that we should forgive the same thing every time it resurfaces (for a deep hurt often has to be forgiven over and over again).

Jesus then presents a parable that speaks of forgiveness.

A king was owed a great debt by a man who had no way of paying the debt. The man threw himself upon the king's mercy, and the king was moved with compassion and let him go, forgiving the debt.

Considering the mercy that had been shown to him, one would expect the man to be understanding with others. A man owed him a debt that was only a fraction of what he had owed the king. Yet he was unwilling to show that man the mercy that had been shown him. He imprisoned his debtor until the entire debt was repaid. The king found out about this and punished the man who was unwilling to forgive.

That is why the kingdom of heaven may be likened
  to a king
who decided to settle accounts with his servants.
When he began the accounting,
  a debtor was brought before him who owed him a
    huge amount.
Since he had no way of paying it back,
  his master ordered him to be sold,
  along with his wife, his children, and all his property,
  in payment of the debt.
At that, the servant fell down, did him homage, and
    said,
  'Be patient with me, and I will pay you back in
    full.'
Moved with compassion the master of that servant
  let him go and forgave him the loan.
When that servant had left, he found one of his fellow servants
  who owed him a much smaller amount.
He seized him and started to choke him, demanding,
  'Pay back what you owe.'
Falling to his knees, his fellow servant begged him,
  'Be patient with me, and I will pay you back.'
But he refused.
Instead, he had the fellow servant put in prison
  until he paid back the debt.
Now when his fellow servants saw what had happened,
  they were deeply disturbed, and went to their
    master
  and reported the whole affair.
His master summoned him and said to him, 'You
    wicked servant!
I forgave you your entire debt because you begged
    me to.

The lesson from this parable is obvious. When our heavenly Father forgives us our sins, we should be willing to forgive others. The forgiveness of our own sins is the foundation of our ability to show others compassion and mercy (for it has already been shown to us). We realize that we have received a gift we do not deserve, and therefore we should be generous with others as well (even if they do not deserve it).

Should you not have had pity on your fellow servant,
    as I had pity on you?'
Then in anger his master handed him over to the torturers
    until he should pay back the whole debt.
So will my heavenly Father do to you,
    unless each of you forgives your brother from your heart."

The Gospel of the Lord.

September 22, 2002

TWENTY-FIFTH SUNDAY IN ORDINARY TIME

Lect. No. 133

FIRST READING: Isaiah 55:6-9

My thoughts are not your thoughts.

The First Reading is a call to conversion. We are told to seek God while he might be found. The message is that there is no time to waste. Now is the moment to seek mercy, for God is offering his forgiveness and we should not lose this opportunity. All God wants is that we turn away from sin and turn toward him to obtain his mercy.

The last part of the reading speaks of the ways of God and how they are not like our ways. God's thoughts and reasoning are filled with love and mercy and not vengeance. God's wisdom is beyond our ability to fathom.

A reading from the Book of the Prophet Isaiah

Seek the LORD while he may be found,
   call him while he is near.
Let the scoundrel forsake his way,
   and the wicked his thoughts;
let him turn to the LORD for mercy;
   to our God, who is generous in forgiving.
For my thoughts are not your thoughts,
   nor are your ways my ways, says the LORD.
As high as the heavens are above the earth,
   so high are my ways above your ways
   and my thoughts above your thoughts.

The word of the Lord.

Lect. No. 133

RESPONSORIAL PSALM: Ps 145:2-3, 8-9, 17-18 (℟.: 18a)

This psalm is a hymn of praise to God who is gracious and merciful and compassionate.

God is near to all who call upon him. One of the things that the psalmist realized was that the LORD always reaches out to us. All that God wants is that we realize how much we need for him to be a part of our lives.

When God created us, he called us into his life and his love, but we chose sin instead. But God did not reject us forever. He protects us and calls us into his mercy and even into his glory.

℟. **The Lord is near to all who call upon him.**

Every day will I bless you,
   and I will praise your name forever and ever.
Great is the LORD and highly to be praised;
   his greatness is unsearchable.

℟. **The Lord is near to all who call upon him.**

The LORD is gracious and merciful,
   slow to anger and of great kindness.
The LORD is good to all
   and compassionate toward all his works.

These are things that we cannot fully understand, for we often try to apply our human standards to God's actions. We want God to think the way that we do. But God's ways are not like our ways, and God's mercy is beyond our understanding.

℟. **The Lord is near to all who call upon him.**

The LORD is just in all his ways
    and holy in all his works.
The LORD is near to all who call upon him,
    to all who call upon him in truth.

℟. **The Lord is near to all who call upon him.**

Lect.
No. 133

SECOND READING: Philippians 1:20c-24, 27a

For me to live is Christ.

Saint Paul shows an incredible availability to the will of God in this reading. It is written toward the end of his ministry. He was in prison, and he seems to have felt that he might have died at any moment.

Paul speaks of being ready to die. He is ready to meet our Lord. After all he had suffered, that prospect actually looked appealing. Yet if he were to continue to live, that would also be fine. He could serve the Lord and the community. For him, it did not matter all that much whether he lived or died as long as God's will was done.

This level of surrender to God's will is our goal. It is not easy to attain, but over a lifetime we slowly learn to submit to God's call, wherever it might lead us.

A reading from the Letter of Saint Paul
    to the Philippians

Brothers and sisters:
    Christ will be magnified in my body, whether by
        life or by death.
For to me life is Christ, and death is gain.
If I go on living in the flesh,
    that means fruitful labor for me.
And I do not know which I shall choose.
I am caught between the two.
I long to depart this life and be with Christ,
    for that is far better.
Yet that I remain in the flesh
    is more necessary for your benefit.

Only, conduct yourselves in a way worthy of the
    gospel of Christ.

The word of the Lord.

Lect.
No. 133

ALLELUIA: cf. Acts 16:14b

The Alleluia Verse calls us to open our hearts so that we might hear God's word at the most profound level of our being and respond to it with generosity.

℟. **Alleluia, alleluia.**

Open our hearts, O Lord,
    to listen to the words of your Son.

℟. **Alleluia, alleluia.**

Lect.
No. 133

GOSPEL: Matthew 20:1-16a

Are you envious because I am generous?

This Gospel is one in which human justice is confronted with God's justice. This is certainly one area in which God's ways are not like our ways.

Jesus speaks of the owner of a vineyard who went out and sought people to work in his vineyard. Some went out early in the morning, others at nine in the morning, some at noon, others at three in the afternoon, and finally some went out at five.

When the workday was over, the owner of the vineyard had all of the workers called in so that they might be paid. He had the foreman of the workers give each one of them the salary that he had earned. He paid those who had worked only a couple of hours an entire day's wage.

Those who worked all day long were pleased, for they reasoned that if those who had worked only a couple of hours got all that money, then they should get more. Yet, when they came forward, they were given the same amount of money as those who had worked only a couple of hours.

At this point they became very upset. It just did not seem fair. But the owner of the vineyard answered them by saying that it was none of their business if he wanted to show generosity. They were paid what they deserved, and that should have been enough for them.

A reading from the holy Gospel according to Matthew

Jesus told his disciples this parable:
"The kingdom of heaven is like a landowner
who went out at dawn to hire laborers for his vineyard.
After agreeing with them for the usual daily wage,
he sent them into his vineyard.
Going out about nine o'clock,
the landowner saw others standing idle in the marketplace,
and he said to them, 'You too go into my vineyard,
and I will give you what is just.'
So they went off.
And he went out again around noon,
and around three o'clock, and did likewise.
Going out about five o'clock,
the landowner found others standing around, and said to them,
'Why do you stand here idle all day?'
They answered, 'Because no one has hired us.'
He said to them, 'You too go into my vineyard.'
When it was evening the owner of the vineyard said to his foreman,
'Summon the laborers and give them their pay,
beginning with the last and ending with the first.'
When those who had started about five o'clock came,
each received the usual daily wage.
So when the first came, they thought that they would receive more,
but each of them also got the usual wage.

Would we be pleased if the person we least liked in the world ended up in heaven alongside of us? Do we pray for the good of those who harm us? Are we concerned when someone hurts us not so much that they hurt us, but because we realize that in hurting us, they are hurting themselves even more?

These are all examples of the incredible mercy of God, a mercy that we have already received and that we should be willing to offer to those around us.

And on receiving it they grumbled against the
    landowner, saying,
  'These last ones worked only one hour,
  and you have made them equal to us,
  who bore the day's burden and the heat.'
He said to one of them in reply,
  'My friend, I am not cheating you.
Did you not agree with me for the usual daily wage?
Take what is yours and go.
What if I wish to give this last one the same as you?
Or am I not free to do as I wish with my own
    money?
Are you envious because I am generous?'
Thus, the last will be first, and the first will be last."

The Gospel of the Lord.

September 29, 2002

TWENTY-SIXTH SUNDAY IN ORDINARY TIME

Lect. No. 136

FIRST READING: Ezekiel 18:25-28

By turning from wickedness, a wicked person shall preserve his life.

Once again we hear how the ways of God are not like our ways. Again, as we have over the past few weeks, we speak of justice and mercy. This time, however, the readings present a different perspective.

Our actions have consequences. We cannot presume upon the mercy of God, doing whatever we feel like doing and believing that God will then forgive us. If we choose sin, then we must live with the effects of sin.

Thus, we have to make a choice between life and death. God wants us to choose that which is good and live. But if we choose that which is evil, then we will have to live with the implications.

A reading from the Book of the Prophet Ezekiel

Thus says the LORD:
  You say, "The LORD's way is not fair!"
Hear now, house of Israel:
  Is it my way that is unfair, or rather, are not your ways unfair?
When someone virtuous turns away from virtue to commit iniquity, and dies,
  it is because of the iniquity he committed that he must die.
But if he turns from the wickedness he has committed,
  and does what is right and just,
  he shall preserve his life;
  since he has turned away from all the sins that he has committed,
  he shall surely live, he shall not die.

The word of the Lord.

Lect. No. 136

RESPONSORIAL PSALM: Ps 25:4-5, 6-7, 8-9 (℟.: 6a)

The psalm requests the mercy of God, as many of the psalms have done over the past several weeks. This time, however, there is a slightly different nuance.

The psalmist asks that his sins be forgiven, especially the sins of his youth. But he also asks for something more important. He asks that the LORD

℟. **Remember your mercies, O Lord.**

Your ways, O LORD, make known to me;
  teach me your paths,
guide me in your truth and teach me,
  for you are God my savior.

℟. **Remember your mercies, O Lord.**

316

teach the sinner his ways. He no longer wants to be submerged in his sinfulness. He wants to escape his sins' effects. He knows that the only way that this is possible is for the LORD to change his heart.

Therefore, he is willing to be humble, for God guides the humble to justice and teaches them his way. If one is humble and admits that he or she needs instruction and guidance, God will help that person find the way. But whoever is arrogant and does not seek God's help is condemned to frustration.

Remember that your compassion, O LORD,
　　and your love are from of old.
The sins of my youth and my frailties remember not;
　　in your kindness remember me,
　　because of your goodness, O LORD.

℟. **Remember your mercies, O Lord.**

Good and upright is the LORD;
　　thus he shows sinners the way.
He guides the humble to justice,
　　and teaches the humble his way.

℟. **Remember your mercies, O Lord.**

Lect. No. 136

SECOND READING: 🅰 Longer Form: Philippians 2:1-11

Have in you the same attitude that is also in Christ Jesus.

The Second Reading comes from the Letter to the Philippians and presents the beautiful Christological hymn about who Jesus is from all eternity (for even before Jesus was born in Bethlehem he was already God).

Saint Paul borrowed this hymn from an early Christian source. We do not know who wrote it (although it most probably was not Paul for it uses a different vocabulary than he normally uses). Nevertheless, Paul must have agreed with its theology or else he would not have borrowed it and used it as an example of Jesus' incredible humility.

Paul speaks of Jesus being in the form of God, and later of Jesus taking on the form of a slave. Normally, the word "form" means that he masqueraded his appearance. Here, it does not mean that. Paul believes that Jesus was both truly God and truly man.

A reading from the Letter of Saint Paul to the Philippians

Brothers and sisters:
　　If there is any encouragement in Christ,
any solace in love,
any participation in the Spirit,
any compassion and mercy,
complete my joy by being of the same mind, with
　　the same love,
united in heart, thinking one thing.
Do nothing out of selfishness or out of vainglory;
　　rather, humbly regard others as more important
　　than yourselves,
　　each looking out not for his own interests,
　　but also for those of others.

Have in you the same attitude
　　that is also in Christ Jesus,
　　　　Who, though he was in the form of God,
　　　　　　did not regard equality with God
　　　　　　something to be grasped.

Yet Jesus did not cling to his godliness. He surrendered the prerogatives of his godliness to assume our humanity. The Greek word for his not clinging to his godliness is "kenosis," and it means a surrender or emptying out.

The kenosis was not only the fact that he was born as a human, but also that he was willing to die on the cross in obedience to the will of the Father.

Because of this, God exalted Jesus above everyone and everything in the heavens and on the earth and under the earth. Jesus is proclaimed as Lord. This was the title that was used for Yahweh in the Old Testament. By saying that Jesus is Lord, the author of this hymn is proclaiming Jesus to be God.

Rather, he emptied himself,
    taking the form of a slave,
    coming in human likeness;
    and found human in appearance,
    he humbled himself,
    becoming obedient to the point of death,
    even death on a cross.
Because of this, God greatly exalted him
    and bestowed on him the name
    which is above every name,
    that at the name of Jesus
    every knee should bend,
    of those in heaven and on earth and under
        the earth,
    and every tongue confess that
    Jesus Christ is Lord,
    to the glory of God the Father.

The word of the Lord.

Lect. No. 136

SECOND READING: **B** Shorter Form: Philippians 2:1-5

Have in you the same attitude that is also in Christ Jesus.

Paul enumerates five benefits of God's love that have been given us through Christ's Paschal Mystery: encouragement, solace, participation in the Spirit, compassion, and mercy.

But we should not glory in having such great benefits at our disposal. Rather, we should imitate Christ, who despite being God, did not cling to his godliness. He surrendered the prerogatives of his godliness to assume our humanity.

Paul then exhorts us to be "united in heart" and "thinking one thing." We are to avoid sin-

A reading from the Letter of Saint Paul
        to the Philippians

Brothers and sisters:
    If there is any encouragement in Christ,
any solace in love,
any participation in the Spirit,
any compassion and mercy,
complete my joy by being of the same mind, with
    the same love,
united in heart, thinking one thing.
Do nothing out of selfishness or out of vainglory;
    rather, humbly regard others as more important
        than yourselves,
    each looking out not for his own interests,
    but also for those of others.

fulness or vainglory and look out for the interests of others.

In a word, Paul urges all Christians to have the same attitude as Christ's.

Lect.
No. 136

Those who follow the Lord Jesus listen to God's voice and respond to it on a daily basis. They are like sheep that listen to the voice of the shepherd and follow wherever he would lead them.

Lect.
No. 136

Have in you the same attitude
  that is also in Christ Jesus.

The word of the Lord.

ALLELUIA: John 10:27

℟. **Alleluia, alleluia.**

My sheep hear my voice, says the Lord;
I know them, and they follow me.

℟. **Alleluia, alleluia.**

GOSPEL: Matthew 21:28-32

*He changed his mind and went. Tax collectors and prostitutes are entering
the kingdom of heaven before you.*

Today we hear a parable concerning those who do the will of God and those who do not. Jesus speaks of a man with two sons. Their father tells them to go out to the vineyard. One says that he will go, but does not. The other says that he will not go, but does. Jesus asks his listeners which son did the father's will.

His listeners answer: the son who said no but then did it. Jesus then tells them that this is an example of what will happen at the Last Judgment. Religious people say they will do the Father's will, but they do not. Prostitutes and tax collectors say they will not do God's will, but then they end up doing it. They will enter the kingdom of heaven before the so-called religious people.

A reading from the holy Gospel according
to Matthew

Jesus said to the chief priests and elders of the
  people:
 "What is your opinion?
A man had two sons.
He came to the first and said,
  'Son, go out and work in the vineyard today.'
He said in reply, 'I will not,'
  but afterwards changed his mind and went.
The man came to the other son and gave the same
  order.
He said in reply, 'Yes, sir,' but did not go.
Which of the two did his father's will?"
They answered, "The first."
Jesus said to them, "Amen, I say to you,
  tax collectors and prostitutes
  are entering the kingdom of God before you.

Jesus often warned people who are religious that they should be careful, for their judgment would be more severe than that of great sinners. They have received a gift from the Lord in being able to practice their religion. From those to whom much has been given, much will be expected.

When John came to you in the way of righteousness,
  you did not believe him;
  but tax collectors and prostitutes did.
Yet even when you saw that,
  you did not later change your minds and believe him."

The Gospel of the Lord.

TWENTY-SEVENTH SUNDAY IN ORDINARY TIME

Lect. No. 139

FIRST READING: Isaiah 5:1-7

The vineyard of the Lord of hosts is the house of Israel.

A reading from the Book of the Prophet Isaiah

Let me now sing of my friend,
　　my friend's song concerning his vineyard.
My friend had a vineyard
　　on a fertile hillside;
he spaded it, cleared it of stones,
　　and planted the choicest vines;
within it he built a watchtower,
　　and hewed out a wine press.
Then he looked for the crop of grapes,
　　but what it yielded was wild grapes.

Now, inhabitants of Jerusalem and people of Judah,
　　judge between me and my vineyard:
What more was there to do for my vineyard
　　that I had not done?
Why, when I looked for the crop of grapes,
　　did it bring forth wild grapes?
Now, I will let you know
　　what I mean to do with my vineyard:
take away its hedge, give it to grazing,
　　break through its wall, let it be trampled!
Yes, I will make it a ruin:
　　it shall not be pruned or hoed,
　　but overgrown with thorns and briers;
I will command the clouds
　　not to send rain upon it.
The vineyard of the LORD of hosts is the house of Israel,
　　and the people of Judah are his cherished plant;

This song of the vineyard is probably one of the first of Isaiah's prophecies. He uses an agricultural image to speak of Israel's infidelity to the call of the LORD.

This hymn is very similar to a legal process to accuse those who had broken the stipulations of a covenant. The process normally began with an outline of how one party had been faithful to all of the elements of a covenant, but how the other party had been wickedly unfaithful. When the case was proven, there was a list of the consequences that the unfaithful party would experience.

These consequences are actually a part of the original covenant formula. When people made a covenant, they would call upon themselves a series of blessings and curses. The blessings are what one would receive if that person were faithful, but the curses are what would happen if that party were unfaithful.

God had promised Israel great fertility. He promised Israel that he would be their God and they would be his people. Now that they had broken the covenant, they would suffer the punishment they deserved. They would lose the fertility of their land and protection. They would be like a vineyard whose fence was broken down, and which was neither hoed nor pruned and received no rain. They would receive only desolation and ruin.

**Lect.
No. 139**

The Responsorial Psalm continues the vineyard theme that we saw in the First Reading and we will see again in the Gospel.

This psalm is a communal lament. Unlike the covenant lawsuit that we saw in the First Reading, this is a call for mercy based upon the promises of the covenant.

God planted the garden. He cleared a place for it by dispossessing other peoples. The plant flourished and spread. Now, however, they were suffering. The people of Israel had been attacked and defeated by their enemies. They no longer experienced the protection that God had promised.

The third stanza of the psalm is an appeal for help. The psalmist begs God in the name of the people of Israel to intervene and rescue them from the hands of all their enemies.

Finally, in the fourth stanza, there is an implicit promise. If God comes through with the deliverance for which the people hoped, then they will be faithful to him. This sounds almost like blackmail, but what the psalmist is saying is that if God does not intervene quickly, they will certainly cease to exist.

he looked for judgment, but see, bloodshed!
 for justice, but hark, the outcry!

The word of the Lord.

RESPONSORIAL PSALM:

Ps 80:9, 12, 13-14, 15-16, 19-20 (℟.: Isaiah 5:7a)

℟. **The vineyard of the Lord is the house of Israel.**

A vine from Egypt you transplanted;
 you drove away the nations and planted it.
It put forth its foliage to the Sea,
 its shoots as far as the River.

℟. **The vineyard of the Lord is the house of Israel.**

Why have you broken down its walls,
 so that every passer–by plucks its fruit,
the boar from the forest lays it waste,
 and the beasts of the field feed upon it?

℟. **The vineyard of the Lord is the house of Israel.**

Once again, O LORD of hosts,
 look down from heaven, and see;
take care of this vine,
 and protect what your right hand has planted,
 the son of man whom you yourself made strong.

℟. **The vineyard of the Lord is the house of Israel.**

Then we will no more withdraw from you;
 give us new life, and we will call upon your name.
O LORD, God of hosts, restore us;
 if your face shine upon us, then we shall be saved.

℟. **The vineyard of the Lord is the house of Israel.**

Lect.
No. 139

SECOND READING: Philippians 4:6-9

Do these things, and the God of peace will be with you.

These exhortations are found toward the end of the Letter to the Philippians. Most of Saint Paul's letters finish with a series of admonitions to the community.

Paul begins by exhorting the community to pray for what they need from God and also to be filled with a spirit of gratitude.

He continues to beseech them to live a virtuous life. Paul was always concerned that others be able to see the good example that Christians gave by their life-style. But here it is not simply a question of what others might think. He is asking them to live up to the dignity to which God had called them.

Finally, he presents himself as an example of how they should live. This is typical of Paul who often tells them to imitate him and the other apostles in order to live like Christ.

A reading from the Letter of Saint Paul to the Philippians

Brothers and sisters:
  Have no anxiety at all, but in everything,
  by prayer and petition, with thanksgiving,
  make your requests known to God.
Then the peace of God that surpasses all understanding
  will guard your hearts and minds in Christ Jesus.

Finally, brothers and sisters,
  whatever is true, whatever is honorable,
  whatever is just, whatever is pure,
  whatever is lovely, whatever is gracious,
  if there is any excellence
  and if there is anything worthy of praise,
  think about these things.
Keep on doing what you have learned and received
  and heard and seen in me.
Then the God of peace will be with you.

The word of the Lord.

Lect.
No. 139

ALLELUIA: cf. John 15:16

We are God's vineyard. We must bear fruit that is worthy of the call we have received. We must give witness to God's goodness in our thoughts and actions.

℟. **Alleluia, alleluia.**

I have chosen you from the world, says the Lord,
to go and bear fruit that will remain.

℟. **Alleluia, alleluia.**

Lect. No. 139

GOSPEL: Matthew 21:33-43

He will lease his vineyard to other tenants.

Jesus uses the vineyard theme to speak of his coming suffering and death. He speaks of how the landowner lent out the vineyard to tenants. They refused to uphold their part of the bargain for when it was time for them to pay their rent, they first abused the servants sent to receive it, and then killed them. When the landowner sent his son to collect the rent, they decided to kill him too.

This story is an obvious parallel to what the Jewish leaders did to Jesus. God had entrusted the Jewish people with the covenant. They had abused and killed the prophets that God sent. Then, when in the fullness of time God sent his only Son, they killed him. They would be punished for rejecting God's only-begotten Son, and others would be invited to take their place as the chosen people (e.g., the Gentiles).

The version of the story contained in this gospel is slightly different from that contained in the Gospel of Mark. In that version, the son is killed inside the vineyard and then his body is thrown out of the vineyard. It is probably the oldest version of the story. Here, the son is killed outside the vineyard. The difference between these two stories is based on what actually happened to Jesus.

A reading from the holy Gospel according to Matthew

Jesus said to the chief priests and the elders of the people:
"Hear another parable.
There was a landowner who planted a vineyard,
    put a hedge around it, dug a wine press in it, and
        built a tower.
Then he leased it to tenants and went on a journey.
When vintage time drew near,
    he sent his servants to the tenants to obtain his
        produce.
But the tenants seized the servants and one they
        beat,
    another they killed, and a third they stoned.
Again he sent other servants, more numerous than
        the first ones,
    but they treated them in the same way.
Finally, he sent his son to them, thinking,
    'They will respect my son.'
But when the tenants saw the son, they said to one
        another,
    'This is the heir.
Come, let us kill him and acquire his inheritance.'
They seized him, threw him out of the vineyard, and
        killed him.
What will the owner of the vineyard do to those ten-
        ants when he comes?"
They answered him,
    "He will put those wretched men to a wretched
        death
    and lease his vineyard to other tenants
    who will give him the produce at the proper
        times."

Jesus predicted his passion (the version contained in Mark), having only a small detail that differed from what actually happened. When Matthew wrote his version, he corrected that detail to match what happened. Mark's version is important for it shows that Jesus knew that he would die for us long before it actually happened. Yet he embraced his suffering and death for our sake.

Jesus said to them, "Did you never read in the Scriptures:

The stone that the builders rejected
  has become the cornerstone;
by the Lord has this been done,
  and it is wonderful in our eyes?

Therefore, I say to you,
  the kingdom of God will be taken away from you
  and given to a people that will produce its fruit."

The Gospel of the Lord.

October 13, 2002

TWENTY-EIGHTH SUNDAY IN ORDINARY TIME

Lect. No. 142

FIRST READING: Isaiah 25:6-10a

The Lord will prepare a feast and wipe away the tears from every face.

The First Reading comes from a portion of the Book of the Prophet Isaiah that is somewhat different from the rest of Isaiah's prophecies. Most of the rest of the first part of the Book speaks of Israel and Judah. Here we see prophecies that speak of the restoration that will bring bounty to the entire earth. The veil of death would be lifted and the reproach would be removed. (Does he mean that the imminent danger of death would be removed or is he speaking about the total defeat of death in the age to come?)

This period of peace and bounty is compared to a great banquet that the LORD would provide, one of the early examples of the idea of the Messianic Banquet. There would be choice wines and rich food. There would be great joy and security. All would be well on God's holy mountain.

A reading from the Book of the Prophet Isaiah

On this mountain the LORD of hosts
    will provide for all peoples
a feast of rich food and choice wines,
    juicy, rich food and pure, choice wines.
On this mountain he will destroy
    the veil that veils all peoples,
the web that is woven over all nations;
    he will destroy death forever.
The Lord GOD will wipe away
    the tears from every face;
the reproach of his people he will remove
    from the whole earth; for the LORD has spoken.
    On that day it will be said:
"Behold our God, to whom we looked to save us!
    This is the LORD for whom we looked;
    let us rejoice and be glad that he has saved us!"
For the hand of the LORD will rest on this mountain.

The word of the Lord.

Lect. No. 142

RESPONSORIAL PSALM: Ps 23:1-3a, 3b-4, 5, 6 (R̸.: 6cd)

This is a hymn of trust in the goodness of the LORD It was probably written during the exile in Babylon when the people of Israel desperately needed the consolation of the LORD. Before the exile, the prophets had often complained that the kings of Israel were evil shepherds

R̸. **I shall live in the house of the Lord all the days of my life.**

The LORD is my shepherd; I shall not want.
    In verdant pastures he gives me repose;
beside restful waters he leads me;
    he refreshes my soul.

326

who did not guide their flocks in the way of the LORD. Now God himself would guide it.

There are several images in the first part of the psalm to show how God is a good shepherd. He brings the flock to verdant pastures, leads them to restful waters, and guides them through dangerous places. The valley through which we are led is called the "dark valley" (more popularly known as the "valley of death"). The Hebrew meaning is a valley that is as dark as death. God's rod and staff give us comfort, for while we are wandering in the dark we can feel his presence as he gently touches us with them.

The image then changes from shepherding to hospitality. God feeds us with more food than we could possibly eat. We even feel safe eating in the presence of our enemies, for we know that God will protect us. The oil on the head is also a sign of hospitality. Likewise, he gives us an overflowing cup, one that never runs dry.

℟. **I shall live in the house of the Lord all the days of my life.**

He guides me in right paths
    for his name's sake.
Even though I walk in the dark valley
    I fear no evil; for you are at my side
with your rod and your staff
    that give me courage.

℟. **I shall live in the house of the Lord all the days of my life.**

You spread the table before me
    in the sight of my foes;
you anoint my head with oil;
    my cup overflows.

℟. **I shall live in the house of the Lord all the days of my life.**

Only goodness and kindness follow me
    all the days of my life;
and I shall dwell in the house of the LORD
    for years to come.

℟. **I shall live in the house of the Lord all the days of my life.**

Lect.
No. 142

SECOND READING: Philippians 4:12-14, 19-20

I can do all things in him who strengthens me.

We have seen in previous weeks how Saint Paul developed a profound sense of surrender to God. If he lived or died was not as important as the fact that he was willing to serve the gospel.

In today's reading we find a similar attitude toward the physical circumstances in which he found himself. There were times on Paul's journeys when he

A reading from the Letter of Saint Paul
to the Philippians

Brothers and sisters:
    I know how to live in humble circumstances;
    I know also how to live with abundance.
In every circumstance and in all things
    I have learned the secret of being well fed and of
        going hungry,
    of living in abundance and of being in need.

found himself surprisingly well off. He would be hosted in some cities by people who were quite rich (e.g., Lydia, a seller of purple goods in Philippi). At other times, he found himself destitute, not knowing where he would find his next meal. None of it really mattered as long as he served the Lord.

I can do all things in him who strengthens me.
Still, it was kind of you to share in my distress.

My God will fully supply whatever you need,
   in accord with his glorious riches in Christ Jesus.
To our God and Father, glory forever and ever.
      Amen.

The word of the Lord.

Lect. No. 142

ALLELUIA: cf. Ephesians 1:17-18

We speak of the hope to which we are called in our Alleluia Verse. The image of that hope that we heard in the First Reading and will encounter again in the Gospel is that of a banquet at which the Lord Jesus himself nourishes us.

℟. **Alleluia, alleluia.**

May the Father of our Lord Jesus Christ
enlighten the eyes of our hearts,
so that we may know what is the hope
that belongs to our call.

℟. **Alleluia, alleluia.**

Lect. No. 142

GOSPEL: A Longer Form: Matthew 22:1-14

Invite to the wedding feast whomever you find.

Both this Gospel and the Gospel of Luke contain the story of a banquet to which many are invited who ultimately refuse to attend. The message of the original version of this parable is quite clear. Many of those whom God has invited to salvation would refuse that invitation and thus lose their opportunity to share in the heavenly banquet.

Part of the idea of their refusal could be due to human weakness, the tendency to choose sin rather than the good. But another aspect of this refusal is certainly the his-

A reading from the holy Gospel according
to Matthew

Jesus again in reply spoke to the chief priests and
      elders of the people
   in parables, saying,
   "The kingdom of heaven may be likened to a king
   who gave a wedding feast for his son.
He dispatched his servants
   to summon the invited guests to the feast,
   but they refused to come.
A second time he sent other servants, saying,
   'Tell those invited: "Behold, I have prepared my
      banquet,
   my calves and fattened cattle are killed,
   and everything is ready; come to the feast."'

torical reality of the refusal of many of the Jewish people to accept Jesus as their Messiah. The invitation to those who are on the road is a prefiguring of the call to the Gentiles who would then participate in the banquet.

Historical elements might have also been included in one of the elements in Matthew's version (e.g., the king's reaction to those who refused the invitation—he destroyed the murderers and burned their city). That is not how the story is told in Luke. There the people who refused the invitation are simply not allowed into the banquet afterward. The difference might be a reflection of the destruction of Jerusalem in 70 A.D. by the Romans. This might be an attempt by Matthew to say that Jesus had foretold that disaster during his ministry.

The king invited the good and the bad to come to the meal, but it was expected that they make themselves ready (convert their hearts). The guest who was not dressed well represents those who are invited but who refuse to change their ways.

Some ignored the invitation and went away,
> one to his farm, another to his business.
The rest laid hold of his servants,
> mistreated them, and killed them.
The king was enraged and sent his troops,
> destroyed those murderers, and burned their city.
Then he said to his servants, 'The feast is ready,
> but those who were invited were not worthy to come.
Go out, therefore, into the main roads
> and invite to the feast whomever you find.'
The servants went out into the streets
> and gathered all they found, bad and good alike,
> and the hall was filled with guests.
But when the king came in to meet the guests,
> he saw a man there not dressed in a wedding garment.
The king said to him, 'My friend, how is it
> that you came in here without a wedding garment?'
But he was reduced to silence.
Then the king said to his attendants, 'Bind his hands and feet,
> and cast him into the darkness outside,
> where there will be wailing and grinding of teeth.'
Many are invited, but few are chosen."

The Gospel of the Lord.

Lect.
No. 142

GOSPEL: B Shorter Form: Matthew 22:1-10

Invite to the wedding feast whomever you find.

Both this Gospel and the Gospel of Luke contain the story of a banquet to which many are invited who ultimately refuse to attend. The message of the original version of this parable is quite clear. Many of

A reading from the holy Gospel according to Matthew

Jesus again in reply spoke to the chief priests and elders of the people
in parables, saying,

those whom God has invited to salvation would refuse that invitation and thus lose their opportunity to share in the heavenly banquet.

Part of the idea of their refusal could be due to human weakness, the tendency to choose sin rather than the good. But another aspect of this refusal is certainly the historical reality of the refusal of many of the Jewish people to accept Jesus as their Messiah. The invitation to those who are on the road is a prefiguring of the call to the Gentiles who would then participate in the banquet.

Historical elements might have also been included in one of the elements in Matthew's version (e.g., the king's reaction to those who refused the invitation—he destroyed the murderers and burned their city). That is not how the story is told in Luke. There the people who refused the invitation are simply not allowed into the banquet afterward. The difference might be a reflection of the destruction of Jerusalem in 70 A.D. by the Romans. This might be an attempt by Matthew to say that Jesus had foretold that disaster during his ministry.

The king invited the good and the bad to come to the meal, but it was expected that they make themselves ready (convert their hearts).

"The kingdom of heaven may be likened to a king
who gave a wedding feast for his son.
He dispatched his servants
to summon the invited guests to the feast,
but they refused to come.
A second time he sent other servants, saying,
'Tell those invited: "Behold, I have prepared my banquet,
my calves and fattened cattle are killed,
and everything is ready; come to the feast."'
Some ignored the invitation and went away,
one to his farm, another to his business.
The rest laid hold of his servants,
mistreated them, and killed them.
The king was enraged and sent his troops,
destroyed those murderers, and burned their city.
Then he said to his servants, 'The feast is ready,
but those who were invited were not worthy to come.
Go out, therefore, into the main roads
and invite to the feast whomever you find.'
The servants went out into the streets
and gathered all they found, bad and good alike,
and the hall was filled with guests."

The Gospel of the Lord.

TWENTY-NINTH SUNDAY IN ORDINARY TIME

Lect. No. 145

FIRST READING: Isaiah 45:1, 4-6

I have grasped the right hand of Cyrus to subdue the nations before him.

A reading from the Book of the Prophet Isaiah

Thus says the LORD to his anointed, Cyrus,
    whose right hand I grasp,
subduing nations before him,
    and making kings run in his service,
opening doors before him
    and leaving the gates unbarred:
For the sake of Jacob, my servant,
    of Israel, my chosen one,
I have called you by your name,
    giving you a title, though you knew me not.
I am the LORD and there is no other,
    there is no God besides me.
It is I who arm you, though you know me not,
    so that toward the rising and the setting of the sun
    people may know that there is none besides me.
I am the LORD, there is no other.

The word of the Lord.

Cyrus was the emperor of Persia who defeated the forces of Babylon. One of his first actions when he conquered the Babylonians was to allow the captive populations of Babylon to return to their homeland. This included the Jews in exile there. They were given permission to return to Jerusalem and rebuild the temple.

This prophetic message is unusual because it calls Cyrus "God's anointed one". The phrase "anointed one" means Messiah. Cyrus was doing God's will by saving the Jews from their exile. He was God's chosen instrument.

There is only one God, and therefore the God of the Jews is also the God of Cyrus. He is the God of all. Cyrus' authority as the emperor of Persia could only come from God alone, for he is the source of all power upon the earth.

Lect. No. 145

RESPONSORIAL PSALM: Ps 96:1, 3, 4-5, 7-8, 9-10 (℟.: 7b)

Originally, the Jewish people were henotheists, believing that Yahweh was the God of all, but that the other nations all had their own gods. This psalm was written after the period when Israel became monotheist. Yahweh was the only God who existed. He was God of all the nations.

℟. **Give the Lord glory and honor.**

Sing to the LORD a new song;
    sing to the LORD, all you lands.
Tell his glory among the nations;
    among all peoples, his wondrous deeds.

℟. **Give the Lord glory and honor.**

And so the psalmist calls upon all of the nations to give praise to the LORD. They are all his people, and all authority in the heavens and on the earth belongs to him.

Everyone who exercises authority over others has obtained that authority from God. This is why scripture calls upon us to obey and pray for governors and kings and judges, etc. We have to respect them, not because they are necessarily good people or even because they do a good job, but because God has given them authority. (It is important to remember that these sentiments were written when those ruling were often tyrants.)

For great is the LORD and highly to be praised;
  awesome is he, beyond all gods.
For all the gods of the nations are things of nought,
  but the LORD made the heavens.

R. **Give the Lord glory and honor.**

Give to the LORD, you families of nations,
  give to the LORD glory and praise;
  give to the LORD the glory due his name!
Bring gifts, and enter his courts.

R. **Give the Lord glory and honor.**

Worship the LORD, in holy attire;
  tremble before him, all the earth;
say among the nations: The LORD is king,
  he governs the peoples with equity.

R. **Give the Lord glory and honor.**

Lect. No. 145

SECOND READING: 1 Thessalonians 1:1-5b

Calling to mind faith, love and hope.

The First Letter to the Thessalonians offers lessons that are still important today.

The first is the thanksgiving that Saint Paul offers. Usually his thanksgivings are a few verses long. This one continues for three chapters. Things were going very well for this community, and they were beginning to think they were responsible for their own success. Paul reminds them that their every success comes from God. He is warning them against spiritual pride and arrogant self-sufficiency.

The other lesson is that there is a triangle of relationships: the disciples, the community, and God. He is reminding them that there are horizontal and vertical dimensions to our faith and both are important.

A reading from the first Letter of Saint Paul to the Thessalonians

Paul, Silvanus, and Timothy to the church of the Thessalonians
  in God the Father and the Lord Jesus Christ:
  grace to you and peace.
We give thanks to God always for all of you,
  remembering you in our prayers,
  unceasingly calling to mind your work of faith and labor of love
  and endurance in hope of our Lord Jesus Christ,
  before our God and Father,
  knowing, brothers and sisters loved by God,
  how you were chosen.
For our gospel did not come to you in word alone,
  but also in power and in the Holy Spirit and with much conviction.

The word of the Lord.

Lect. No. 145

ALLELUIA: Philippians 2:15d, 16a

The Alleluia Verse comes from an exhortation in the Letter to the Philippians to live a lifestyle that is filled with light and truth.

℟. **Alleluia, alleluia.**

Shine like lights in the world
as you hold on to the word of life.

℟. **Alleluia, alleluia.**

Lect. No. 145

GOSPEL: Matthew 22:15-21

*Repay to Caesar what belongs to Caesar and to God
what belongs to God.*

The Pharisees and the Herodians (scholars are not entirely sure who they were) had already decided that Jesus was dangerous, and they wanted to trap him in a misstatement that would get him into trouble. If Jesus answered that they should pay their taxes to Caesar, then the Jews of Israel who judged the Romans to be an occupying power would be opposed to Jesus. If, on the other hand, Jesus were to answer that they should not pay taxes, then they could accuse him of opposing Roman authority and they could denounce him to the Roman procurator.

Jesus understood the trap that they had set for him. Ironically, they said they were approaching Jesus with this question because they considered him to be a truthful man. They were not concerned with the truth at all. The only thing that concerned them was subterfuge. Hence, Jesus responds with an answer that confounds them—they should give to Caesar what is Caesar's and give to God what is God's.

A reading from the holy Gospel according to Matthew

The Pharisees went off
and plotted how they might entrap Jesus in speech.
They sent their disciples to him, with the Herodians, saying,
"Teacher, we know that you are a truthful man
and that you teach the way of God in accordance with the truth.
And you are not concerned with anyone's opinion,
for you do not regard a person's status.
Tell us, then, what is your opinion:
Is it lawful to pay the census tax to Caesar or not?"
Knowing their malice, Jesus said,
"Why are you testing me, you hypocrites?
Show me the coin that pays the census tax."
Then they handed him the Roman coin.
He said to them, "Whose image is this and whose inscription?"
They replied, "Caesar's."
At that he said to them,
"Then repay to Caesar what belongs to Caesar
and to God what belongs to God."

The Gospel of the Lord.

October 27, 2002

THIRTIETH SUNDAY IN ORDINARY TIME

Lect. No. 148

FIRST READING: Exodus 22:20-26

*If you wrong the widow and the orphan,
my wrath will flare up against you.*

We sometimes think of the law of the Old Testament as a series of meticulous instructions that have little to do with life. This is not really true. It was a precious gift from God for it communicated his will to us.

Furthermore, the law was concerned with a spirit of compassion that should be shown to all, and especially to those who could not defend themselves. The most obvious of the powerless were the widows and orphans. They had no one to defend them if those in power did not take this responsibility upon themselves.

Aliens and the poor were also considered to be in need of our compassion. God asked the Israelites to remember when they were aliens in Egypt. They were to treat others as they wished that they had been treated.

Likewise, when they lent money, they were not to make the stipulations of the loan humiliating. They should treat the debtor with respect .

A reading from the Book of Exodus

Thus says the LORD:
"You shall not molest or oppress an alien,
for you were once aliens yourselves in the land of Egypt.
You shall not wrong any widow or orphan.
If ever you wrong them and they cry out to me,
I will surely hear their cry.
My wrath will flare up, and I will kill you with the sword;
then your own wives will be widows, and your children orphans.

"If you lend money to one of your poor neighbors among my people,
you shall not act like an extortioner toward him
by demanding interest from him.
If you take your neighbor's cloak as a pledge,
you shall return it to him before sunset;
for this cloak of his is the only covering he has for his body.
What else has he to sleep in?
If he cries out to me, I will hear him; for I am compassionate."

The word of the Lord.

Lect.
No. 148

RESPONSORIAL PSALM: Ps 18:2-3, 3-4, 47, 51 (℟.: 2)

There are times in our lives when everything seems to be changing all at once. Things that we thought would always be one way change radically. Where are we going to find a sense of security and stability?

This psalm responds that the only true source of stability in our lives is God. He is our rock and fortress. When we are shaken by the waves of misfortune and confusion, God is there to give us a moral compass. He protects us from everything that could harm us.

This does not mean that things always end up well. Bad things happen, and there is much suffering in life. But if God is the foundation of our life and faith, then we will be able to get through whatever happens.

℟. **I love you, Lord, my strength.**

I love you, O LORD, my strength,
   O LORD, my rock, my fortress, my deliverer.

℟. **I love you, Lord, my strength.**

My God, my rock of refuge,
   my shield, the horn of my salvation, my stronghold!
Praised be the LORD, I exclaim,
   and I am safe from my enemies.

℟. **I love you, Lord, my strength.**

The LORD lives and blessed be my rock!
   Extolled be God my savior.
You who gave great victories to your king
   and showed kindness to your anointed.

℟. **I love you, Lord, my strength.**

Lect.
No. 148

SECOND READING: 1 Thessalonians 1:5c-10

*You turned from idols to serve the living and true God
and to await his Son from heaven.*

The Second Reading is a continuation of the thanksgiving that we began to read last week. Saint Paul thanks God for the conversion of the Thessalonians. This was a clear sign of the power of God, for they had understood that the words that Paul was preaching were the words of God (even though Paul arrived there beaten up from his last missionary journey).

Paul also thanks God for the fact that the disciples were able to serve them. He speaks of

A reading from the first Letter of Saint Paul
to the Thessalonians

Brothers and sisters:
   You know what sort of people we were among you for your sake.
And you became imitators of us and of the Lord,
   receiving the word in great affliction, with joy from the Holy Spirit,
   so that you became a model for all the believers
   in Macedonia and in Achaia.
For from you the word of the Lord has sounded forth

how the disciples became what the people needed to convert. It is not that the disciples pretended to be what they were not, only that they presented the message in a way that the Thessalonians could accept it.

Finally, the Thessalonians were able to respond to their sufferings and persecution with great joy. That is a clear sign that the Spirit was guiding them, for the normal response to suffering is resentment and anger.

not only in Macedonia and in Achaia,
but in every place your faith in God has gone
forth,
so that we have no need to say anything.
For they themselves openly declare about us
what sort of reception we had among you,
and how you turned to God from idols
to serve the living and true God
and to await his Son from heaven,
whom he raised from the dead,
Jesus, who delivers us from the coming wrath.

The word of the Lord.

Lect.
No. 148

How can we tell whether our faith is an expression of love for God? It is that we keep the word of God and make it alive every day of our lives.

ALLELUIA: John 14:23

℟. **Alleluia, alleluia.**

Whoever loves me will keep my word, says the
Lord,
and my Father will love him and we will come to
him.

℟. **Alleluia, alleluia.**

Lect.
No. 148

GOSPEL: Matthew 22:34-40

You shall love the Lord your God and your neighbor as yourself.

Once again we hear the leaders of the Jews trying to confound Jesus. Again, they are not interested in the truth. All they are interested in is to gain the upper hand over him.

They ask Jesus what the greatest commandment is. Jesus responds with the great commandment: that we should

A reading from the holy Gospel according
to Matthew

When the Pharisees heard that Jesus had silenced the Sadducees,
they gathered together, and one of them,
a scholar of the law, tested him by asking,
"Teacher, which commandment in the law is the
greatest?"

love the Lord, our God, with all our heart, soul, and mind, and that we should love our neighbors as ourselves.

As we saw last week, love has two dimensions. Love, for it to be true, must have a vertical dimension (love of God) and a horizontal dimension (love of neighbor). One without the other is unbalanced and not true love.

He said to him,
"You shall love the Lord, your God,
with all your heart,
with all your soul,
and with all your mind.
This is the greatest and the first commandment.
The second is like it:
You shall love your neighbor as yourself.
The whole law and the prophets depend on these
two commandments."

The Gospel of the Lord.

November 1, 2002

ALL SAINTS

Lect. No. 667 **FIRST READING: Revelation 7:2-4, 9-14**

I had a vision of a great multitude, which no one could count, from every nation, race, people and tongue.

We hear about how the chosen ones were to be marked with the seal of the living God upon their foreheads. In the Book of the Prophet Ezekiel this mark was the Hebrew letter "tau," the first letter of the word Torah, which means "the law." All faithful Jews were to be observers of the law to the deepest part of their being.

In the New Testament, the elect are to be sealed with the Greek letter "tau," which looks like the modern "T." It is a symbol for the cross, for all of Christ's children are to be sealed with the sign of the cross.

We hear that there are one hundred and forty-four thousand to be sealed. Some Christian sects argue that this is the number of people who will be going to heaven.

This is a misunderstanding of the symbolism of the Book of Revelation. In this book, that which we see is the superficial meaning, while that which we hear is the spiritual significance.

John saw a crowd without number from every nation and race and people and tongue. These are the people who are going to heaven. They are numberless.

A reading from the Book of Revelation

I, John, saw another angel come up from the East, holding the seal of the living God.
He cried out in a loud voice to the four angels
who were given power to damage the land and the sea,
"Do not damage the land or the sea or the trees
until we put the seal on the foreheads of the servants of our God."
I heard the number of those who had been marked with the seal,
one hundred and forty-four thousand marked
from every tribe of the Israelites.

After this I had a vision of a great multitude,
which no one could count,
from every nation, race, people, and tongue.
They stood before the throne and before the Lamb,
wearing white robes and holding palm branches in their hands.
They cried out in a loud voice:
"Salvation comes from our God,
who is seated on the throne,
and from the Lamb."
All the angels stood around the throne
and around the elders and the four living creatures.
They prostrated themselves before the throne,
worshiped God, and exclaimed:
"Amen. Blessing and glory, wisdom and thanksgiving,

But John also heard that they were one hundred and forty-four thousand. This number is twelve times twelve times one thousand. Twelve stands for the twelve patriarchs of the Old Testament. Twelve also stands for the twelve apostles. One thousand stands for a very large number.

Thus, one hundred and forty-four thousand means the Old and New Israel. The number is their spiritual identify, not the actual number of those going to heaven.

honor, power, and might
be to our God forever and ever. Amen."
Then one of the elders spoke up and said to me,
"Who are these wearing white robes, and where did they come from?"
I said to him, "My lord, you are the one who knows."
He said to me,
"These are the ones who have survived the time of great distress;
they have washed their robes
and made them white in the blood of the Lamb."

The word of the Lord.

| Lect. No. 667 |

RESPONSORIAL PSALM: Ps 24:1-2, 3-4, 5–6 (℞.: 6)

Psalm 24 is a wisdom psalm that was probably used for pilgrimages to the temple. Wisdom literature speaks of how to live the good life, a life pleasing to the LORD.

This psalm asks who can ascend the mountain of the LORD, the mountain leading to Jerusalem and its temple. Only that person whose hands are sinless and whose heart is clean can participate in the worship of the LORD.

This does not mean that we must be perfect to belong to God's holy people. All of us are sinners, but we must all make the effort to convert and change our ways. This is a life-time project and we will not be totally perfect until the last day. But in the meantime, we commit ourselves more and more to service of our God and our brothers and sisters. This is the way that we will be those who seek "the face of the God of Jacob."

℞. **Lord, this is the people that longs to see your face.**

The LORD'S are the earth and its fullness;
the world and those who dwell in it.
For he founded it upon the seas
and established it upon the rivers.

℞. **Lord, this is the people that longs to see your face.**

Who can ascend the mountain of the LORD?
or who may stand in his holy place?
One whose hands are sinless, whose heart is clean,
who desires not what is vain.

℞. **Lord, this is the people that longs to see your face.**

He shall receive a blessing from the LORD,
a reward from God his savior.
Such is the race that seeks for him,
that seeks the face of the God of Jacob.

℞. **Lord, this is the people that longs to see your face.**

Lect.
No. 667

SECOND READING: 1 John 3:1-3

We shall see God as he is.

The First Letter of John is a masterful treatise on the love of God. It is here, in fact, that we hear the phrase that God is love.

God has demonstrated how much he loves us by the fact that we are called children of God. God does not call us slaves; God calls us his friends and even his beloved children.

This does not mean that everyone will love us. The world hated Jesus because it could not stand Jesus and his message. It wanted selfishness, and Jesus preached love and sacrifice.

We are already God's children. What we shall be in the future cannot even be imagined, for it will be a participation in the glory of God.

A reading from the first Letter of Saint John

Beloved:
  See what love the Father has bestowed on us
  that we may be called the children of God.
Yet so we are.
The reason the world does not know us
  is that it did not know him.
Beloved, we are God's children now;
  what we shall be has not yet been revealed.
We do know that when it is revealed we shall be like him,
  for we shall see him as he is.
Everyone who has this hope based on him makes himself pure,
  as he is pure.

The word of the Lord.

Lect.
No. 667

ALLELUIA: Matthew 11:28

The Lord Jesus offers to be our refuge when life becomes a burden to us. He is the source of peace for our hearts, and our only true joy. Only in him will we find true rest.

℟. **Alleluia, alleluia.**

Come to me, all you who labor and are burdened,
and I will give you rest, says the Lord.

℟. **Alleluia, alleluia.**

Lect.
No. 667

GOSPEL: Matthew 5:1-12a

Rejoice and be glad, for your reward will be great in heaven.

Today's Gospel presents the Beatitudes from the Gospel of Matthew. In Matthew's gospel, Jesus is the new Moses. He is the founder of the New Israel, the Church. Like Moses who climbed Mount Sinai to receive the law, Jesus climbed a moun-

A reading from the holy Gospel according to Matthew

When Jesus saw the crowds, he went up the mountain,
  and after he had sat down, his disciples came to him.

tain in order to give the new law to the New Israel (the Sermon on the Mount).

Unlike the ten commandments of the old law, the Beatitudes are not a series of do's and don'ts. They are a call to generosity. One no longer asks what one can do lest one commit a sin. One must ask what one can do to become a better Christian.

The poor in spirit are those who are not proud (unlike the Pharisees). Those who hunger and thirst for righteousness are the Christians. They were unjustly thrown out of the synagogue for their profession of faith in Jesus. Likewise, they are persecuted for the sake of the kingdom.

Those who are clean of heart are those whose every thought is of God. If one's every thought is of God, then one will see signs of God everywhere (for creation is a gift from God). One will judge everything that one sees to be a sign of God's goodness and generosity.

He began to teach them, saying:
"Blessed are the poor in spirit,
  for theirs is the kingdom of heaven.
Blessed are they who mourn,
  for they will be comforted.
Blessed are the meek,
  for they will inherit the land.
Blessed are they who hunger and thirst for righteousness,
  for they will be satisfied.
Blessed are the merciful,
  for they will be shown mercy.
Blessed are the clean of heart,
  for they will see God.
Blessed are the peacemakers,
  for they will be called children of God.
Blessed are they who are persecuted for the sake of righteousness,
  for theirs is the kingdom of heaven.
Blessed are you when they insult you and persecute you
  and utter every kind of evil against you falsely because of me.
Rejoice and be glad,
  for your reward will be great in heaven."

The Gospel of the Lord.

November 3, 2002

THIRTY-FIRST SUNDAY IN ORDINARY TIME

Lect. No. 151

FIRST READING:

Malachi 1:14b—2:2b, 8-10

You have turned aside from the way, and have caused many to falter by your instruction.

In this oracle from Malachi we hear a severe condemnation of the priests of Israel. They had a special obligation to lead the people to the truth. They were mediators between the LORD and his people. But they failed in their obligations. They lived immoral life-styles. They were prejudiced against some of the people and treated them poorly.

For all of this, God was going to condemn them in a profound way. Because so much was given to them, much was expected of them. They, of all people, should have been faithful to the covenant. Instead they had made a mockery of it.

This serves as a warning for all of us who have received the gift of faith. We should not look upon that gift as something that makes us better than others, or look upon them with contempt because they do not yet have the gift. We should be filled with gratitude to God and be willing to share that gift with others.

A reading from the Book of the Prophet Malachi

A great King am I, says the LORD of hosts,
 and my name will be feared among the nations.
And now, O priests, this commandment is for you:
 If you do not listen,
if you do not lay it to heart,
 to give glory to my name, says the LORD of hosts,
I will send a curse upon you
 and of your blessing I will make a curse.
You have turned aside from the way,
 and have caused many to falter by your instruction;
you have made void the covenant of Levi,
 says the LORD of hosts.
I, therefore, have made you contemptible
 and base before all the people,
since you do not keep my ways,
 but show partiality in your decisions.
Have we not all the one father?
 Has not the one God created us?
Why then do we break faith with one another,
 violating the covenant of our fathers?

The word of the Lord.

Lect. No. 151

RESPONSORIAL PSALM: Ps 131:1, 2, 3

In the Responsorial Psalm we see the exact opposite of what we saw in the First Reading. There we saw people who used the gifts and responsibility that had been given them to establish superiority over others. In the psalm, we see the psalmist exercise tremendous humility.

It is only when we become like children, humble and willing to serve God, that we find a sense of peace.

And so we should look with gratitude at all the ways that God has blessed us and all the talents that he has showered upon us. Those things that we have received from God are to be used in the service of others, and not for our own profit.

℟. **In you, Lord, I have found my peace.**

O LORD, my heart is not proud,
  nor are my eyes haughty;
I busy not myself with great things,
  nor with things too sublime for me.

℟. **In you, Lord, I have found my peace.**

Nay rather, I have stilled and quieted
  my soul like a weaned child.
Like a weaned child on its mother's lap,
  so is my soul within me.

℟. **In you, Lord, I have found my peace.**

O Israel, hope in the LORD,
  both now and forever.

℟. **In you, Lord, I have found my peace.**

Lect. No. 151

SECOND READING: 1 Thessalonians 2:7b-9, 13

We were determined to share with you not only the Gospel of God, but our very selves as well.

When Saint Paul shared the gospel message with the Thessalonians, he sought to proclaim it in a manner that did not impede their acceptance of the truth.

Therefore, he worked day and night in order not to be a burden upon the community. In his days there were philosophers who traveled from city to city proclaiming new ideas for profit (financial and sexual). Paul did not want the Thessalonians to think that this is what he was doing.

A reading from the first Letter of Saint Paul to the Thessalonians

Brothers and sisters:
  We were gentle among you, as a nursing mother cares for her children.
With such affection for you, we were determined to share with you
  not only the gospel of God, but our very selves as well,
  so dearly beloved had you become to us.
You recall, brothers and sisters, our toil and drudgery.

So even though he had every right to expect them to help him financially, he worked for his own living as a tent-maker.

Another of the ways Paul was of service to the community was his gentleness with them. He speaks of loving them like a nursing mother. He realized that they needed this unconditional love in order to understand how much the Lord loved them and wanted what was good for them.

Lect. No. 151

The Alleluia Verse reminds us that our heavenly Father is our only true master. All others are servants who have been placed in our life to minister to our needs.

Lect. No. 151

The Pharisees were not evil people. They were dedicated laymen who wanted to live the prescriptions of the law fully. They spent many hours each day studying the law and determining what it meant. They were constantly trying to build a fence around the law, meaning to take the law to its widest possible application so that they would never break even the smallest requirement of the law.

The problem was not their study. It was their tendency to consider the law more important than people.

Working night and day in order not to burden any of you,
  we proclaimed to you the gospel of God.

And for this reason we too give thanks to God unceasingly,
  that, in receiving the word of God from hearing us,
  you received not a human word but, as it truly is, the word of God,
  which is now at work in you who believe.

The word of the Lord.

ALLELUIA: Matthew 23:9b, 10b

℟. **Alleluia, alleluia.**

You have but one Father in heaven
and one master, the Christ.

℟. **Alleluia, alleluia.**

GOSPEL: Matthew 23:1-12

They preach but they do not practice.

A reading from the holy Gospel according to Matthew

Jesus spoke to the crowds and to his disciples, saying,
  "The scribes and the Pharisees
  have taken their seat on the chair of Moses.
Therefore, do and observe all things whatsoever they tell you,
  but do not follow their example.
For they preach but they do not practice.
They tie up heavy burdens hard to carry
  and lay them on people's shoulders,
  but they will not lift a finger to move them.
All their works are performed to be seen.

Furthermore, they had a tendency to use their studies and their offices as sources of power. They loved their importance within the community and sought signs of respect. In all of this, they were using a gift God had given them for their own profit.

This is why Jesus rejects titles of respect for those working in the community. Those who exercised authority in the community were to see their role as one of service and not an opportunity to be served. They were to follow Jesus' own example in serving the most humble in the community.

They widen their phylacteries and lengthen their tassels.
They love places of honor at banquets, seats of honor in synagogues,
greetings in marketplaces, and the salutation 'Rabbi.'
As for you, do not be called 'Rabbi.'
You have but one teacher, and you are all brothers.
Call no one on earth your father;
you have but one Father in heaven.
Do not be called 'Master';
you have but one master, the Christ.
The greatest among you must be your servant.
Whoever exalts himself will be humbled;
but whoever humbles himself will be exalted."

The Gospel of the Lord.

November 10, 2002

THIRTY-SECOND SUNDAY IN ORDINARY TIME

Lect. No. 154 **FIRST READING: Wisdom 6:12-16**

Wisdom is found by those who seek her.

The Book of Wisdom is one of the last books of the Old Testament to have been written and one of those most influenced by Greek culture.

The ancient idea of wisdom was a collection of sayings that teach one how to live the good life. When the Greeks began to influence Judaism, the concept of wisdom changed. No longer was it impersonal: wisdom was now a woman who presented instruction to the foolish.

She is portrayed as pure and loving. One does not even need to hunt for her, for she is always seeking out those who can learn from her instruction. If one does seek wisdom, that person will never be disappointed. She offers life eternal to all who seek it.

A reading from the Book of Wisdom

Resplendent and unfading is wisdom,
and she is readily perceived by those who love her,
and found by those who seek her.
She hastens to make herself known in anticipation of their desire;
whoever watches for her at dawn shall not be disappointed,
for he shall find her sitting by his gate.
For taking thought of wisdom is the perfection of prudence,
and whoever for her sake keeps vigil
shall quickly be free from care;
because she makes her own rounds, seeking those worthy of her,
and graciously appears to them in the ways,
and meets them with all solicitude.

The word of the Lord.

Lect. No. 154

RESPONSORIAL PSALM: Ps 63:2, 3-4, 5-6, 7-8 (℟.: 2b)

This psalm speaks of the thirst that the psalmist feels for the LORD. This psalm was written in a country that was terribly arid. Thirst was something that this person knew well. But the physical suffering of this thirst was nothing compared with

℟. **My soul is thirsting for you, O Lord my God.**

O God, you are my God whom I seek;
for you my flesh pines and my soul thirsts
like the earth, parched, lifeless and without water.

℟. **My soul is thirsting for you, O Lord my God.**

346

the thirst of one's heart. This author knows that he cannot be complete without God being a part of his life. The LORD is a greater good than life itself.

The psalmist speaks of raising up his hands to praise the LORD. This is an ancient form of prayer, to raise one's arms to the heavens. A good number of catacombs have pictures of people in prayer with this stance.

He remembers the LORD upon the couch during the night. In poetry, the night was often a time of fear when one felt abandoned. Here we see that the LORD is near to the psalmist, whether by day or by night. The psalmist feels as if he is under the shadow of his wings, that he is shadowed by his protection. And so he and we shout for joy, for truly our God is our all.

Thus have I gazed toward you in the sanctuary
    to see your power and your glory,
for your kindness is a greater good than life;
    my lips shall glorify you.

℞. **My soul is thirsting for you, O Lord my God.**

Thus will I bless you while I live;
    lifting up my hands, I will call upon your name.
As with the riches of a banquet shall my soul be satisfied,
    and with exultant lips my mouth shall praise you.

℞. **My soul is thirsting for you, O Lord my God.**

I will remember you upon my couch,
    and through the night–watches I will meditate on you:
you are my help,
    and in the shadow of your wings I shout for joy.

℞. **My soul is thirsting for you, O Lord my God.**

Lect. No. 154

SECOND READING: 🅰 **Longer Form: 1 Thessalonians 4:13-18**

God, through Jesus, will bring with him those who have fallen asleep.

Part of the reason that Saint Paul wrote to this community is that they had questions concerning those who had recently died. When Paul had preached to them, he had spoken of the return of the Lord in glory at the end of time. From the way he spoke, they expected that to happen in the near future.

After Paul left Thessalonica, someone died. The community was distraught for they thought that this person had missed out on the opportunity to greet Jesus on the last day. (It is obvious from this that Paul had not

A reading from the first Letter of Saint Paul to the Thessalonians

We do not want you to be unaware, brothers and sisters,
    about those who have fallen asleep,
    so that you may not grieve like the rest, who have no hope.
For if we believe that Jesus died and rose,
    so too will God, through Jesus,
    bring with him those who have fallen asleep.
Indeed, we tell you this, on the word of the Lord,
    that we who are alive,
    who are left until the coming of the Lord,

had much time to teach them the basics of the faith.)

Paul responds that they need not worry. Those who had died would rise from the dead on the last day. Those who were still alive would be caught up into the clouds to meet Jesus. "Caught up into the clouds," means that they would be with Jesus without having to die. They would simply be transformed from this life to the world to come. Some people call this transformation "the rapture."

will surely not precede those who have fallen asleep.
For the Lord himself, with a word of command,
   with the voice of an archangel and with the trumpet of God,
   will come down from heaven,
   and the dead in Christ will rise first.
Then we who are alive, who are left,
   will be caught up together with them in the clouds
   to meet the Lord in the air.
Thus we shall always be with the Lord.
Therefore, console one another with these words.

The word of the Lord.

Lect. No. 154 **SECOND READING: B Shorter Form: 1 Thessalonians 4:13-14**

God, through Jesus, will bring with him those who have fallen asleep.

When Paul had preached to the Thessalonians, he had spoken of the return of the Lord in glory at the end of time. From the way he spoke, they expected that to happen in the near future.

After Paul left Thessalonica, someone died. The community was distraught for they thought that this person had missed out on the opportunity to greet Jesus on the last day.

Paul says they need not worry. Those who had died will rise on the last day.

A reading from the first Letter of Saint Paul to the Thessalonians

We do not want you to be unaware, brothers and sisters,
   about those who have fallen asleep,
   so that you may not grieve like the rest, who have no hope.
For if we believe that Jesus died and rose,
   so too will God, through Jesus,
   bring with him those who have fallen asleep.

The word of the Lord.

Lect. No. 154

ALLELUIA: Matthew 24:42a, 44

The Alleluia Verse reminds us that we should always be ready for the return of Jesus in glory. We know neither the hour nor the day. We must always be prepared to meet our Lord.

℟. **Alleluia, alleluia.**

Stay awake and be ready!
For you do not know on what day your Lord will come.

℟. **Alleluia, alleluia.**

Lect.
No. 154

GOSPEL: Matthew 25:1-13

Behold, the bridegroom! Come out to meet him!

This parable concerns the end of the world and how we should always be ready for it because we do not know when it will occur.

In the early history of the Church, most people believed that Jesus would return in glory within the very near future. This is when all of the parables and sayings were collected that spoke about Jesus' return as if it were about to happen.

But as the return of the Lord did not happen immediately, the Church began to collect those sayings that spoke of the last days as if we did not know when it would occur. This is one of those parables. It speaks of always being prepared to meet Jesus on the Day of the Lord.

The five virgins who took oil with them and prepared their lamps in time for the return of the bridegroom are symbols of those who live in a way that they are prepared for the return of the Lord at the end of time (whenever that might happen). They were always ready. On the other hand, the five who ran out of oil were those who did not live in a way that they were ready to meet the Lord.

We might ask why the five with oil were so selfish. That is going beyond the scope of the parable No parable can tell the whole truth, so we should learn from them what we can.

A reading from the holy Gospel according to Matthew

Jesus told his disciples this parable:
"The kingdom of heaven will be like ten virgins
  who took their lamps and went out to meet the
    bridegroom.
Five of them were foolish and five were wise.
The foolish ones, when taking their lamps,
  brought no oil with them,
  but the wise brought flasks of oil with their lamps.
Since the bridegroom was long delayed,
  they all became drowsy and fell asleep.
At midnight, there was a cry,
  'Behold, the bridegroom! Come out to meet him!'
Then all those virgins got up and trimmed their lamps.
The foolish ones said to the wise,
  'Give us some of your oil,
  for our lamps are going out.'
But the wise ones replied,
  'No, for there may not be enough for us and you.
Go instead to the merchants and buy some for your-
    selves.'
While they went off to buy it,
  the bridegroom came
  and those who were ready went into the wedding
    feast with him.
Then the door was locked.
Afterwards the other virgins came and said,
  'Lord, Lord, open the door for us!'
But he said in reply,
  'Amen, I say to you, I do not know you.'
Therefore, stay awake,
  for you know neither the day nor the hour."

The Gospel of the Lord.

November 17, 2002

THIRTY-THIRD SUNDAY IN ORDINARY TIME

Lect.
No. 157

FIRST READING:

Proverbs 31:10-13, 19-20, 30-31

She works with loving hands.

Throughout the Book of Proverbs there are instructions on how young men can learn the ways of the LORD and live the good life.

These verses are one of the few places where instructions such as these are applied to women. They come from a poem that is built around a pattern in which each verse begins with one of the letters of the Hebrew alphabet (consecutively).

Some of the instruction is based upon the role of woman as wife (this was the ideal state of life for women in the Bible). Other verses deal with woman in her own stead (e.g., she reaches out her hand to the poor, she fears the LORD, etc.). In what we would consider a very modern sentiment, the poem speaks of outer beauty being fleeting, while beauty of the soul is eternal.

A reading from the Book of Proverbs

When one finds a worthy wife,
   her value is far beyond pearls.
Her husband, entrusting his heart to her,
   has an unfailing prize.
She brings him good, and not evil,
   all the days of her life.
She obtains wool and flax
   and works with loving hands.
She puts her hands to the distaff,
   and her fingers ply the spindle.
She reaches out her hands to the poor,
   and extends her arms to the needy.
Charm is deceptive and beauty fleeting;
   the woman who fears the LORD is to be praised.
Give her a reward for her labors,
   and let her works praise her at the city gates.

The word of the Lord.

Lect.
No. 157

RESPONSORIAL PSALM: Ps 128:1-2, 3, 4-5 (℟.: cf. 1a)

The first step of living wisdom is fear of God. This does not mean that we are afraid that God will punish us. It means that we must recognize God's greatness and are willing to obey him wherever he should lead us. He is the only true guide for our lives.

℟. **Blessed are those who fear the Lord.**

Blessed are you who fear the LORD,
   who walk in his ways!
For you shall eat the fruit of your handiwork;
   blessed shall you be, and favored.

℟. **Blessed are those who fear the Lord.**

If we do this, then our lives will be blessed. The psalm gives typical images that express blessedness in the biblical tradition. We would have a wonderful spouse, many children, successful crops, etc.

This blessedness is also not an individual blessing, for in the Old Testament it was all but impossible to think of the person apart from the nation. All Israel would share in the blessings of the LORD.

Your wife shall be like a fruitful vine
   in the recesses of your home;
your children like olive plants
   around your table.

℟. **Blessed are those who fear the Lord.**

Behold, thus is the man blessed
   who fears the LORD.
The Lord bless you from Zion:
   may you see the prosperity of Jerusalem
all the days of your life.

℟. **Blessed are those who fear the Lord.**

| Lect. |
| No. 157 |

SECOND READING: 1 Thessalonians 5:1-6

Let the day of the Lord not overtake you like a thief.

In the early Church, there was a belief that Jesus would return in glory within a very short while. Saint Paul, in fact, recommends to the Corinthians that they not get married because the end of the world was at hand.

But when the end of the world failed to appear, people began to believe that maybe the return of Jesus would not happen immediately. Nevertheless, it was important that people be ready for it whenever it might occur. They began to speak of it occurring unannounced, like a thief in the night. They would not know when, but they should always be ready.

The reading concludes with an admonition to be children of the light. They were to reject everything that hinted of the dark one, and to choose to live in the ways of the Lord.

A reading from the first Letter of Saint Paul
to the Thessalonians

Concerning times and seasons, brothers and sisters,
   you have no need for anything to be written to you.
For you yourselves know very well that the day of the Lord will come
   like a thief at night.
When people are saying, "Peace and security,"
   then sudden disaster comes upon them,
   like labor pains upon a pregnant woman,
   and they will not escape.

But you, brothers and sisters, are not in darkness,
   for that day to overtake you like a thief.
For all of you are children of the light
   and children of the day.
We are not of the night or of darkness.
Therefore, let us not sleep as the rest do,
   but let us stay alert and sober.

The word of the Lord.

| Lect. |
| No. 157 |

The Alleluia Verse presents a wisdom message that those who live in the ways of the Lord will be blessed. Their lives will be fruitful and complete.

ALLELUIA: John 15:4a, 5b

℟. **Alleluia, alleluia.**

Remain in me as I remain in you, says the Lord.
Whoever remains in me bears much fruit.

℟. **Alleluia, alleluia.**

| Lect. |
| No. 70 |

GOSPEL: 🅰 Longer Form: Matthew 25:14-30

Since you were faithful in small matters, come, share your master's joy.

The Gospel continues the wisdom theme that we have seen in the readings and the psalm.

It speaks of the fact that we have all received gifts from God. These gifts are to be developed and used in the service of others. They are not to be buried in the ground, as we hear in this parable.

The word "talent" in the parable is actually a large amount of money, not the ability to do something. Yet it is symbolic of exactly that: whatever ability or skill a person might possess.

We have to remember that all talents come from God. We could not possibly succeed at anything if it were not for God's goodness.

The First Letter to the Corinthians speaks of how the Holy Spirit showers charisms upon us. Charism means the same thing as the word "talent" in this reading. Gifts are given for the service of others. We cannot use them for our own purposes. We must use our charisms to help to build up the community.

A reading from the holy Gospel according to Matthew

Jesus told his disciples this parable:
"A man going on a journey
 called in his servants and entrusted his possessions to them.
To one he gave five talents; to another, two; to a
 third, one—
 to each according to his ability.
Then he went away.
Immediately the one who received five talents went
  and traded with them,
 and made another five.
Likewise, the one who received two made another
 two.
But the man who received one went off and dug a
 hole in the ground
 and buried his master's money.

After a long time
 the master of those servants came back
 and settled accounts with them.
The one who had received five talents came forward
 bringing the additional five.
He said, 'Master, you gave me five talents.
See, I have made five more.'
His master said to him, 'Well done, my good and
 faithful servant.

We usually apply this parable to the idea of receiving good talents from God. We realize that they should not be sources of boasting or pride, for they have been given to us as gifts, and they should be shared as gifts.

Sometimes when we read parables, though, we can take them beyond their original meaning to apply them better to our lives today. That is one reason why Jesus used parables. They are more flexible in their application than simple commandments or narratives.

One possible example of this is that we always thank God for the good things that we have received. What about our weaknesses and brokenness? Should we not also thank God for these?

Admittedly, some of our brokenness is due to our own sinfulness. But some of it is simply life. We have tendencies that sometimes embarrass us, e.g., a quick temper, a tendency toward jealousy, etc. Often we try to deny or suppress these tendencies. Yet, if we embrace these tendencies and make the best we can of them, we often find that they are not the curses that we thought. They often turn out, in fact, to be the way that we find God.

In other words, we do not deny or reject who we are, but we allow the Lord to transform us so that God's light might shine through us.

Since you were faithful in small matters,
    I will give you great responsibilities.
Come, share your master's joy.'
Then the one who had received two talents also
        came forward and said,
    'Master, you gave me two talents.
See, I have made two more.'
His master said to him, 'Well done, my good and
        faithful servant.
Since you were faithful in small matters,
    I will give you great responsibilities.
Come, share your master's joy.'
Then the one who had received the one talent came
        forward and said,
    'Master, I knew you were a demanding person,
    harvesting where you did not plant
    and gathering where you did not scatter;
    so out of fear I went off and buried your talent in
        the ground.
Here it is back.'
His master said to him in reply, 'You wicked, lazy
        servant!
So you knew that I harvest where I did not plant
    and gather where I did not scatter?
Should you not then have put my money in the bank
        so that I could have got it back with interest on
        my return?
Now then! Take the talent from him and give it to
        the one with ten.
For to everyone who has,
    more will be given and he will grow rich;
    but from the one who has not,
    even what he has will be taken away.
And throw this useless servant into the darkness
        outside,
    where there will be wailing and grinding of teeth.'"

The Gospel of the Lord.

Lect.
No. 157

GOSPEL: **B** Shorter Form: Matthew 25:14-15, 19-21

Since you were faithful in small matters, come, share your master's joy.

The Gospel continues the wisdom theme that we have seen in the readings and the psalm.

It speaks of the fact that we have all received gifts from God. These gifts are to be developed and used in the service of others. They are not to be buried in the ground.

The word "talent" in the parable is actually a large amount of money, not the ability to do something. Yet it is symbolic of exactly that: whatever ability or skill a person might possess.

We have to remember that all talents come from God. We could not possibly succeed at anything if it were not for God's goodness.

The First Letter to the Corinthians speaks of how the Holy Spirit showers charisms upon us. Charism means the same thing as the word "talent" in this reading. Gifts are given for the service of others. We cannot use them for our own purposes. We must use our charisms to help to build up the community.

A reading from the holy Gospel according
to Matthew

Jesus told his disciples this parable:
"A man going on a journey
    called in his servants and entrusted his possessions to them.
To one he gave five talents; to another, two; to a
    third, one—
to each according to his ability.
Then he went away.

After a long time
    the master of those servants came back
    and settled accounts with them.
The one who had received five talents came forward
    bringing the additional five.
He said, 'Master, you gave me five talents.
See, I have made five more.'
His master said to him, 'Well done, my good and
    faithful servant.
Since you were faithful in small matters,
    I will give you great responsibilities.
Come, share your master's joy.'"

The Gospel of the Lord.

THE SOLEMNITY OF OUR LORD JESUS CHRIST THE KING

Lect. No. 160

FIRST READING: Ezekiel 34:11-12, 15-17

As for you, my flock, I will judge between one sheep and another.

A reading from the Book of the Prophet Ezekiel

Thus says the Lord GOD:
  I myself will look after and tend my sheep.
As a shepherd tends his flock
    when he finds himself among his scattered sheep,
    so will I tend my sheep.
I will rescue them from every place where they were
      scattered
    when it was cloudy and dark.
I myself will pasture my sheep;
    I myself will give them rest, says the Lord GOD.
The lost I will seek out,
    the strayed I will bring back,
    the injured I will bind up,
    the sick I will heal,
    but the sleek and the strong I will destroy,
    shepherding them rightly.

As for you, my sheep, says the Lord GOD,
    I will judge between one sheep and another,
    between rams and goats.

The word of the Lord.

Just before the exile in Babylon, the prophets of Israel began to speak of the LORD as the shepherd of his people.

The LORD had given Israel and Judah kings and had commanded them to shepherd his people, but the kings had turned into evil shepherds. They exploited their flock for their own profit.

Therefore, the LORD was going to remove those evil shepherds and he himself would shepherd his people. He would not allow them to be exploited by any who would harm them.

During the exile (587-539 B.C.), this image became all the more important. The people of Judah felt that they had been abandoned or condemned for their sinfulness. They wondered if God loved them or cared about them. The shepherd image spoke of how much God loved his people.

Lect.
No. 160

RESPONSORIAL PSALM: Ps 23:1-2, 2-3, 5-6 (℟.: 1)

This is a hymn of trust in the goodness of the LORD. It was probably written during the exile.

There are several images in the first part of the psalm to show how God is a good shepherd. He brings the flock to verdant pastures, leads them to restful waters, and guides them through dangerous places. The valley through which we are led is called the "dark valley" (more popularly known as the "valley of death"). The Hebrew meaning is a valley that is as dark as death. God's rod and staff give us comfort for while we are wandering in the dark, we can feel his presence as he gently touches us with them.

The image then changes from shepherding to hospitality. God feeds us with more food than we could possibly eat. We even feel safe eating in the presence of our enemies, for we know that God will protect us. The oil on the head is also a sign of hospitality. Hosts would pour oil on the heads of their guests as a remedy for the damage of the dry climate. Likewise, he gives us an overflowing cup, one that never runs dry.

℟. **The Lord is my shepherd; there is nothing I shall want.**

The LORD is my shepherd; I shall not want.
    In verdant pastures he gives me repose.

℟. **The Lord is my shepherd; there is nothing I shall want.**

Beside restful waters he leads me;
    he refreshes my soul.
He guides me in right paths
    for his name's sake.

℟. **The Lord is my shepherd; there is nothing I shall want.**

You spread the table before me
    in the sight of my foes;
you anoint my head with oil;
    my cup overflows.

℟. **The Lord is my shepherd; there is nothing I shall want.**

Only goodness and kindness follow me
    all the days of my life;
and I shall dwell in the house of the LORD
    for years to come.

℟. **The Lord is my shepherd; there is nothing I shall want.**

Lect.
No. 160

SECOND READING: 1 Corinthians 15:20-26, 28

*Christ will hand over the kingdom to his God and Father
so that God may be all in all.*

Jesus, through his death and resurrection, defeated death and gave us life. He is the "firstfruits" of those who will rise. The firstfruits are usually the best (at least the first corn or tomatoes taste that way) and the

A reading from the first Letter of Saint Paul
to the Corinthians

Brothers and sisters:
    Christ has been raised from the dead,
the firstfruits of those who have fallen asleep.

promise of a greater harvest to come. Jesus is that for us, the best and the promise that we, too, will rise.

This destroys the effect of the first sin. Adam's sin brought death into the world. We are not sure whether Saint Paul means that we would not have died before the first sin, or that death would have been a painless passing from this state to the next if there had been no sin. Since that first sin, death has been horrific and alienating. Now that sin is defeated, death can no longer control us. We await that day when we will rise with Christ.

On that day, every enemy will be destroyed. Sin, fear, alienation will all be defeated, and we will be one with Christ who will reign forever. We will share in his reign and his glory, for we are beloved children of the Lord.

Lect.
No. 160

Jesus is the son of David and he has inherited his throne upon which he will reign for all time. This is the fulfillment of the promise of Nathan the prophet that David's dynasty would last forever.

For since death came through man,
the resurrection of the dead came also through man.
For just as in Adam all die,
so too in Christ shall all be brought to life,
but each one in proper order:
Christ the firstfruits;
then, at his coming, those who belong to Christ;
then comes the end,
when he hands over the kingdom to his God and Father,
when he has destroyed every sovereignty
and every authority and power.
For he must reign until he has put all his enemies under his feet.
The last enemy to be destroyed is death.
When everything is subjected to him,
then the Son himself will also be subjected
to the one who subjected everything to him,
so that God may be all in all.

The word of the Lord.

ALLELUIA: Mark 11:9, 10

℟. **Alleluia, alleluia.**

Blessed is he who comes in the name of the Lord!
Blessed is the kingdom of our father David that is to come!

℟. **Alleluia, alleluia.**

Lect.
No. 160

GOSPEL: Matthew 25:31-46

*The Son of Man will sit upon his glorious throne and he will
separate them one from another.*

On this feast of Christ the King, we hear a parable about the final judgment. Jesus will sit upon his glorious throne and divide those who were good from those who were sinners.

Jesus uses the image of a shepherd to make his point. He speaks of separating the sheep from the goats. This was something that would have to be done when the sheep and the goats, which often pastured in the same field, were brought in from those fields.

The judgment is not based upon how well one kept a series of prescriptions of the law. This would have been considered to be the measure of the righteousness of people by the Pharisees. Jesus has a different set of criteria. He judges people according to how well they treated their sisters and brothers. If they treated them with charity, then they were to be welcomed into his kingdom. If not, they would be kept out.

This reading is the source of many of the corporal works of mercy. These works are a reminder that we must serve those who need our help.

All throughout the New Testament, there are teachings concerning charity toward our neighbor. We hear in the Letter of James that the person who says that he has faith but does not help his brother or sister is like the person who looks in the mirror and forgets what he looks

A reading from the holy Gospel according
to Matthew

Jesus said to his disciples:
"When the Son of Man comes in his glory,
　and all the angels with him,
　he will sit upon his glorious throne,
　and all the nations will be assembled before him.
And he will separate them one from another,
　as a shepherd separates the sheep from the goats.
He will place the sheep on his right and the goats on
　　his left.
Then the king will say to those on his right,
　'Come, you who are blessed by my Father.
Inherit the kingdom prepared for you from the foun-
　　dation of the world.
For I was hungry and you gave me food,
　I was thirsty and you gave me drink,
　a stranger and you welcomed me,
　naked and you clothed me,
　ill and you cared for me,
　in prison and you visited me.'
Then the righteous will answer him and say,
　'Lord, when did we see you hungry and feed you,
　or thirsty and give you drink?
When did we see you a stranger and welcome you,
　or naked and clothe you?
When did we see you ill or in prison, and visit you?'
And the king will say to them in reply,
　'Amen, I say to you, whatever you did
　for one of the least brothers of mine, you did for
　　me.'
Then he will say to those on his left,
　'Depart from me, you accursed,

like. That person's faith is nothing more than an illusion that has no real substance.

Likewise, the First Letter of John speaks of loving God and loving each other. Its author asks how we can say that we love God if we do not love God's children. He counsels the community to love in word and deed.

The most important thing to remember when we do works of charity is that they are not actions that make us superior to others. Charity is simply an expression of who and what we are. Therefore we should always feel gratitude toward those for whom we do things (for they gave us the opportunity to express our love).

into the eternal fire prepared for the devil and his
  angels.
For I was hungry and you gave me no food,
  I was thirsty and you gave me no drink,
  a stranger and you gave me no welcome,
  naked and you gave me no clothing,
  ill and in prison, and you did not care for me.'
Then they will answer and say,
  'Lord, when did we see you hungry or thirsty
  or a stranger or naked or ill or in prison,
  and not minister to your needs?'
He will answer them, 'Amen, I say to you,
  what you did not do for one of these least ones,
  you did not do for me.'
And these will go off to eternal punishment,
  but the righteous to eternal life."

The Gospel of the Lord.

APPENDIX 1: INTRODUCTION TO THE BOOKS OF THE BIBLE THAT ARE READ IN THE THREE-YEAR CYCLE

GENESIS

The first book of the Bible tells of the history of the world in its earliest stages (the Primordial History) and during the period of the Patriarchs up to the time that the people of Israel went down to Egypt to escape the great drought during the days of Joseph.

The first eleven chapters contain stories that are not strictly historical in the sense of being a day to day account of the early history of the world. These chapters nevertheless contain important truths about the early days of humanity.

God created us out of love and called us to live in obedience to his commands. We, in the person of Adam and Eve, sinned against God and were punished for our disobedience. Sin grew in the world until God sent his punishment in the form of a great flood.

Beginning with chapter 12, we hear of the history of Abraham and Sarah, Isaac and Rebekah, Jacob and his wives and children, especially Joseph. These stories seem to contain more historic information than the earlier chapters. Some of the customs mentioned in the stories, for example, have been dated back to the period in which the Patriarchs were said to have lived.

It is believed that the information contained in this book comes from three major sources.

The first source is the Yahwist source. It was written during the reigns of David and Solomon (c. 950 B.C.) and in the southern part of Israel. It emphasizes the role of the monarchy and the importance of Judah and his tribe in salvation history. This source is called the Yahwist source because it often refers to God by using the name Yahweh.

The second source is the Elohist source. This dates to around 850 B.C. and was written in the north of Israel. It emphasizes the importance of prophets and the Sinai covenant. Because the kings of the north were often unfaithful to the ways of the Lord, kings are not seen as laudable figures.

The third source is the Priestly source. It was written during the exile in Babylon (587-539 B.C.). It emphasizes the importance of law and tradition. This source tends to be very accurate in measurements of time and space.

The book achieved its present form sometime around the Babylonian exile (c. 587-539 B.C.).

EXODUS

This book tells of the miraculous events that surrounded the exodus of the people of Israel from their slavery in Egypt. It begins with the infancy of Moses and ends with a description of the construction of the objects of cult that Israel was to use when it worshiped the Lord.

The same sources that appear in the Book of Genesis are also found in this book. This would explain why certain events are sometimes described twice in slightly different circumstances (for the two versions were derived from different sources).

This book contains one version of the ten commandments (20:17; the other version is found in the Book of Deuteronomy 5:6-21). The law is seen as a gift from God, for it instructs Israel on how it can follow the ways of the Lord and be faithful to their covenant.

The hymn that the community sings to celebrate its escape from the forces of Pharaoh in Exodus 15 is actually a very ancient hymn. Scholars believe the grammar and vocabulary of the hymn show it to date to the actual time of the exodus. Thus, this is one of the earliest parts of the Bible to have been written.

It is also in this book that God reveals his name, YHWH (i.e., Yahweh), to Moses (3:14). It is said that this name means "I am who I am." It has been interpreted by some rabbis as meaning, "I am who I am for you, who I have always been for you, who I will always be for you." (In modern Bibles LORD in capital letters stands for the name of God, because the Jews never pronounced it.)

LEVITICUS

This is the third of the five books of the Pentateuch. Its name is derived from the word "Levite," for most of the material contained in the book is Levitical law. Unlike Genesis, Exodus, and Numbers, which are amalgamations of various sources, this book is almost entirely derived from the Priestly Source written during the Babylonian Exile (587-539 B.C.).

The people of Israel were living in exile, and the priestly authors felt that they needed to define the obligations of the law in a clear manner so that the Israelites would not lose their cultural identity while living in a foreign land. Among the topics presented are laws concerning sacrifice, the priesthood of Aaron and his descendants, cleanliness and uncleanness, the ritual for the day of atonement, votive offerings, and the law of holiness.

NUMBERS

The Book of Numbers continues the story of Israel during the period in which they dwelt in the desert for forty years while they were being purified by the Lord so that they might enter the promised land.

It is composed of the same sources that we saw in Genesis and Exodus.

It obtained its name from the fact that Israel took a census of those who were with them in the desert. The number of men who left Egypt is cited as being over 600,000, most probably an exaggerated number.

It also contains many instructions for worship and other community actions.

Important episodes include the first attempt to enter the promised land (which failed because of the fear of the people and their lack of trust in the providence of the Lord), Balaam's curse upon Israel (which actually turns out to be a blessing), the choice of the seventy-two elders to assist Moses in governing the people of Israel, and instructions for the division of the promised land when Israel would conquer it.

DEUTERONOMY

Deuteronomy means "the second law." A scroll of the law was discovered by King Josiah when he was reforming the temple cult. It is not known whether the book is ancient and had been lost in the temple during a period of decline in the faith of Israel or whether it was placed in the temple to be found at that time.

Its teachings represent a reform of the way that Israel practiced its religion. Previous to its promulgation, there were shrines to the Lord upon most of the heights of the land. Many of these shrines were dedicated both to Yahweh and to Baal, the pagan god of fertility. The main reform of this book was that it established that one could only worship the Lord with sacrifices in the temple in Jerusalem.

There is an extensive series of legislation throughout the book, including another version of the ten commandments (one version is found in Exodus). Many of the laws are aimed at the pagan practices that had entered into the faith of Israel. The *She'ma Israel*, the profession of faith of the Jewish people, is contained in 6:4ff.

The book closes with Moses designating Joshua as his successor and then dying. He was buried by God on Mount Nebo. These chapters might have originally been in another of the books of the Pentateuch, and were then tacked on to the end of this particular book.

The school that produced this book is called the Deuteronomist school. They not only wrote this book of law but also edited many of the other books that had been written previous to this period. Their major tendency was to write history as it should have happened, and not as it necessarily happened. Thus, they describe the conquest of the holy land as a series of spectacular successes against pagan armies (e.g., Joshua) as opposed to a slow infiltration of tribes into a land where they faced bitter opposition (e.g., Judges).

JOSHUA

The Book of Joshua is the sixth Book of the Old Testament, named after the successor of Moses, who led the Israelites into Canaan. The book contains a systematic account of the conquest of the Promised Land. Its purpose is to demonstrate God's fidelity in giving the Israelites the land he had promised them for an inheritance. It includes: (1) the conquest of Canaan; (2) division of the land; and (3) return of the Trans-jordanian tribes and Joshua's farewell. Like the first five Books of the Bible, Joshua was built up by a long and complex process of editing traditional materials. The whole history of the conquest of the Promised Land is a prophecy of the spiritual conquest of the world through the Church under the leadership of Jesus the Messiah.

Although the victories of Joshua are an action of God, they also call for the active collaboration and faith of his People. God's will is always done, for he controls the forces of nature and history. We must pray and ponder in order to make the right choices so as to be in tune with God's will.

FIRST SAMUEL

First Samuel describes the history of Israel from the end of the period of Judges until the time when Saul and his sons die in battle against the Philistines.

The book opens with the story of the birth of Samuel, the last and greatest of the judges. Judges were charismatic leaders who exercised executive, legislative, judicial, and even priestly power. Chapter 2 presents the hymn that Hannah chanted to celebrate the birth of her son Samuel. This hymn was used as the basis of Mary's hymn in the Gospel of Luke.

The early part of the book describes some of the disasters that Israel suffered in this period. The people became frightened and they asked for a king. God and Samuel chose Saul, a Benjaminite, as the king of Israel. There are two judgments concerning Israel's request (each judgment derives from a different source). One judgment is that the request is understandable, but the other is that the people of Israel were subtly rejecting God, their true king, by requesting a human king.

Saul displeased God, and Samuel had to choose another king who was more pleasing to God. He chose David and anointed him. The latter chapters of this book speak of the growing enmity between Saul and David based upon Saul's jealousy.

SECOND SAMUEL

Second Samuel describes the history of Israel from the death of Samuel until the end of the reign of David (his death is described at the beginning of First Kings). The book begins with David's mourning for the death of King Saul and especially for his son David and David's friend Jonathan.

David accedes to the throne of the southern tribes while Ishbaal, one of Saul's sons, becomes king of the ten northern tribes. At the end of a long civil war, David is proclaimed king of the united tribes. He conquers Jerusalem, makes it his capital, and moves the ark of the covenant there.

The rest of the book is a history of David's deeds and even misdeeds. While he is spectacularly successful in political terms, his personal and family life are another matter. He sins against the LORD by committing adultery with Bathsheba, the wife of Uriah the Hittite, and by conducting a census of Israel implying that they were his possession. He witnessed the death of his son Amnon who raped his daughter Tamar, and of another son Absalom, who rose up in rebellion against David.

FIRST KINGS

The First Book of Kings describes the period of history that began with the death of David and the succession of Solomon as king until the days of King Jehoshaphat of Judah and of King Ahaziah of Israel.

The book opens with the twelve tribes forming a united kingdom. After the death of Solomon, however, King Rehoboam acted foolishly and alienated the ten northern tribes, which seceded and formed their own kingdom, Israel. The southern kingdom was henceforth known as Judah.

The early chapters describe the successes of Solomon, e.g., his construction of the temple in Jerusalem and massive cities and fortifications throughout the land. They also speak of his sinfulness, for he built shrines to the pagan gods of his many wives.

The latter chapters speak of the prophetic career of Elijah. He led Israel away from syncretism to greater fidelity in the Lord. He condemned King Ahab and his wife Jezebel for their religious errors and their social conduct (e.g., robbing the field of Naboth the Jezreelite by having him killed).

In chapter 18 we hear about the contest on Mount Carmel between Elijah and the priests of Baal to determine who was the true God in Israel. In chapter 19 we hear of Elijah's encounter with God on Mount Sinai when he met him not in earthquake or fire or wind as Moses had when he received the law, but in the gentle breeze. The meaning of this passage is that God does not always act in a miraculous, spectacular fashion, but rather he often brings about his will in ordinary, everyday events.

SECOND KINGS

The Second Book of Kings tells the history of the kingdoms of Israel and Judah from the days of Elijah and Elisha until the time of the Babylonian exile.

The early chapters of the book speak of the ascent of Elijah into heaven on a fiery chariot and the ministry of Elisha. The account of Elisha resembles the story of a famous miracle worker.

Much of the book is a chronicle of the infidelity of the kings of both kingdoms and how God allowed his judgment to be visited upon them through the hands of pagan kings.

In 722 B.C. the northern kingdom of Israel was annihilated and its nobility carried off into exile in Assyria. In 587 B.C. the same fate befell the citizens of the southern kingdom of Judah (although they, at least, returned from exile in Babylon).

One of the high points of the book is the accession of King Josiah to the throne of Judah and his reform of the religion of his people (during which the Book of Deuteronomy was discovered and promulgated).

The book also reports the period of Kings Ahaz and Hezekiah. These were two kings who reigned during much of the prophetic career of Isaiah.

FIRST CHRONICLES

The First Book of Chronicles outlines the history of Israel from the creation of Adam until the construction of the temple in Jerusalem. Much of the information contained in this book is also contained in the Books of Samuel and the Books of Kings. It is probably produced by the Deuteronomist school, which tended to tell history as it should have happened and not necessarily as it happened. Thus, its story of King David excludes all of the more scandalous material concerning his adultery, the scandals in his family, etc.

SECOND CHRONICLES

Like First Chronicles, this book is a Deuteronomist revision of the information contained in the First and Second Books of Kings. It begins with the accession of Solomon to the throne and closes with the decree of Cyrus permitting the Jewish people to return from exile in Babylon (c. 539 B.C.). Typical of this school of literature, an idealized view of Israel's history is presented. Solomon is portrayed as being one of the greatest kings of Israel, second only to David. His role in constructing the temple of God in Jerusalem is strongly emphasized.

The history of the kings of the north is all but ignored (for this school considered those kings to be faithless and deceitful), while that of the kings of Judah is presented in greater detail.

NEHEMIAH

Nehemiah was a Jewish official of the Persian emperor who was appointed governor of Judah around 445 B.C. The book named after him speaks of the actions of the prophet and Ezra (a priest). Nehemiah arrived in Jerusalem at a time when the Jewish nation was demoralized and drifting. He rebuilt the walls of the city. He reestablished Jewish law as the law of the land. He promoted social justice (e.g., giving loans with no interest). He ordered those who had married foreign wives to send them away (in his days, this was seen as a purification of the religion of Israel).

JOB

The Book of Job presents an extended reflection upon the problem of pain and suffering. Satan (who is presented as being God's district attorney) convinces God to withdraw his beneficence from Job to see whether Job would curse the LORD. No matter how much Job suffers, he refuses to curse God. Yet he acknowledges that what he was suffering was unjust.

The theory that sin is the cause of all suffering is strongly rejected. Job expresses his anger at the injustice that he was experienc-

ing, even challenging God to explain why he would allow these things to happen.

The saying, "the patience of Job," is a bit misleading. He is patient for two chapters, and then rants and raves against God for more than thirty chapters. In the end, God appears and puts Job to the test. Job realizes that he does not understand all things, and that he must respond to all trials with trust in God.

PSALMS

The Book of Psalms is a collection of 150 psalms written during a period of almost 1,000 years, and it has become the Prayer Book of the Church. They are divided into five books of psalms, each ending with a doxology. The numbers assigned to the psalms are different in the original Hebrew version and the Greek translation. Although many of them are attributed to great historic figures such as David, they were actually dedicated to those people and not written by them.

The psalms are poetry and many demonstrate the most common attribute of Hebrew poetry (parallelism). A large number of the words used in the psalms are *hapax legomena* (words used only once in the Bible).

There are several identifiable literary genres in the psalms. A large number of the psalms are individual or communal lamentations. There are also hymns, royal psalms, hymns of trust, wisdom psalms, thanksgivings, historic psalms, penitential psalms, etc.

PROVERBS

The Book of Proverbs is really two different books written at very different periods of Israel's history.

The older portion of the book is that beginning with chapter 10 and running to the end of the book. It is a series of folk sayings on how to live the good life. It was written to instruct the young on how they could live in the ways of the Lord and receive God's blessings.

This portion is very similar to wisdom books of neighboring cultures (especially Egypt). Some of the sayings, in fact, seem to have been borrowed from those cultures.

The first nine chapters of the book are much more Greek in tone. They must have been written after the conquest of Alexander the Great, so they probably date to the third century B.C. or later. They speak of wisdom as a personalized attribute of God, lady wisdom. The reason for this presentation is that Jewish people adopted the Greek idea that God was totally removed from our experience, that he was the uncreated creator who never had anything to do with his creation. They thus spoke of some of God's attributes as mediators to communicate God's will to us. Among those attributes were God's glory, holiness, spirit, and wisdom.

Wisdom calls to the foolish to instruct them in the ways of the Lord. She offers to nourish them, giving them bread and wine (this idea is used symbolically in the Discourse on the Bread of Life in John 6). She tells them that if they embrace her knowledge, they will receive everlasting life.

ECCLESIASTES

In addition to its Greek name ("Ecclesiastes"), this book is also known by its Hebrew name, Qoheleth. It is a wisdom book written late in the Old Testament period (c. 250 B.C.). The name of the author is uncertain, for the word Qoheleth could be symbolic since it means "the preacher." The book speaks of the impossibility of discerning God's will. God has a plan (for there is a season for everything), but we cannot adequately know it. Thus, it is best to live a reasonably virtuous life. Do not work too much or too little, nor eat too much or too little, etc. Everything else is a chasing after wind.

Rabbis argued about whether to accept this book into the canon or not for quite some time because of its cynicism. Yet this book serves as a good corrective for the overly optimistic attitude of other wisdom literature.

WISDOM

The Book of Wisdom is one of the younger books of the Old Testament. It displays many signs of having been written during the period in which Greek culture heavily influenced Judaism. Because it was only written in Greek, it was not accepted into the Hebrew Bible and is not found in Protestant Bibles as well.

Wisdom is personified as a spirit that is totally pure. We hear of how King Solomon prayed for and received the gift of wisdom in order to rule the people of Israel in the ways of the Lord.

We hear how the evil would be punished for their iniquity and the good would receive an eternal reward. This is one of the few books of the Old Testament that speak about our destiny in the afterlife as being one that is filled with joy.

The latter part of the book gives a panorama of the history of Israel and explains how wisdom was present in each of those stages. One interesting teaching contained in this section is that the plagues of Egypt involved many animals because the people of Egypt had worshiped animals. There is a rabbinic teaching that as the sin, so the punishment.

SIRACH

The Book of Sirach is one of the wisdom books of literature of the Old Testament. It is included in Catholic Bibles but is not found in Protestant Bibles because until recently we only possessed the Greek version of this book (and Protestants follow the rabbis' definition of the Old Testament, that only those books written in Hebrew or Aramaic were acceptable).

The premise of the book is that it was written by Jesus Sirach and translated into Greek by his grandson. Some manuscripts of portions of the original Hebrew text have been found in Qumran and Egypt.

Typical of wisdom literature, the book contains a series of instructions on how to live the good life. The reader is advised to follow the path of virtue. There are instructions for almost every dimension of individual, family, and community life.

The hymn to wisdom in chapter 24 shows heavy Greek influence. It speaks of wisdom who was an architect helping God create the world. Wisdom visited the people of Israel and pitched her tent among them (an image used in the prologue of the Gospel of John when it speaks of the incarnation).

The book closes with a series of accounts of the deeds of the great men of Israel and a hymn of thanksgiving to the Lord.

ISAIAH

The Book of Isaiah is actually a combination of the prophecies of three different prophets (or schools of prophecy).

The first part of the book, from chapter 1 to 39, is attributed to Isaiah the prophet who ministered to the southern kingdom of Judah from around 740 B.C. until around 700 B.C.

His major theme was that God was holy, and we were called to live in that holiness. That meant that we had to exhibit a way of life that was consistent with the holiness of God.

The first chapters of the book are similar to those of the Prophet Amos. Isaiah admonishes the people to live social justice and to care for the poor, for this is what the holiness of God demands.

From chapters 7 to 11 we hear various episodes and oracles that shaped Isaiah's understanding of the coming Messiah. At first Isaiah hoped for a new king who would be better than the old king (remember, all of the kings of Judah and Israel were considered to be the anointed of the Lord and thus each one of them was a messiah). Eventu-

ally, he stopped hoping for a better king and he began to speak of a coming era in which God would intervene through one particular Messiah. This era would be filled with peace and justice. Even nature would experience this, for animals that were natural enemies such as the lion and the lamb could lie down together in peace.

Much of the rest of his prophecy is a series of oracles against nations that had attacked Judah or against his own people for their infidelity.

The second part of the book runs from chapter 40 to 55. This was written during the exile in Babylon (587 - 539 B.C.). It is a book of consolation. God promises Israel that it will be wondrously restored.

This section of the book also contains four poems called the songs of the suffering servant of Yahweh. They speak about a mysterious figure who will bring salvation to Israel and also to the Gentiles. He will be meek and gentle. He will suffer for our sins and die for us, but the Lord will raise him from the dead.

The third section of the book runs from chapter 56 to 66. It was written after the exile. The people thought that when they returned to Israel all would be well, but it did not turn out that way. This prophecy encourages them and admonishes them to convert their ways. Chapter 58 speaks of fasting, telling the people that God does not want us to get involved in empty rituals. He wants us to transform the way we live with him and each other.

JEREMIAH

Of all of the prophets of the Old Testament, Jeremiah is the one who is said to have best foreshadowed Jesus. The reason for this is his heroic suffering for the sake of the message that God had given him to share with his people. He called them to conversion and warned them of the consequences of their actions, but they refused to listen to him. Then, when they suffered the consequences of their own choices, they blamed Jeremiah for what was happening to them. He was beaten, saw his writings burned by the king, was thrown in a cistern to die, and eventually died while being dragged down to Egypt.

Jeremiah preached during one of the most turbulent periods of the history of the kingdom of Judah. One king was following another with fearful rapidity. The people of Judah and their kings were at one moment subjects of Egypt, at the next of Babylon.

Early in Jeremiah's career he witnessed the finding of the Book of Deuteronomy in the temple. This book contained a new law that outlawed all shrines of the Lord in the land with the exception of the temple in Jerusalem. His own family lost their livelihood for they were a family of priests at a shrine to the north of Jerusalem. Yet Jeremiah rejoiced and embraced the reform.

But it brought him only trouble. He speaks in a series of poems of his feelings of abandonment by the Lord (these are called his Confessions, e.g., 20:7-18). Yet he felt that he could not run away from his responsibility to proclaim God's word, so he continued to preach.

In chapter 31 Jeremiah speaks of a new covenant that the Lord will make with the people of Israel. This covenant will not be written upon tablets of stone; it will be written upon their hearts.

Jeremiah also spoke of individual responsibility for sin. We will not be punished for the sins of our ancestors, but rather for our own sins.

Jeremiah's ministry ended shortly after the destruction of Jerusalem and the deportation of most of the nobility to Babylon. During the siege he had told the king and the people to surrender to the Babylonians and receive their punishment for God had sent this chastisement. Because he told the people to surrender and not fight, the princes of the land accused him of sedition and punished him. When the city was conquered, he was not mistreated by the Babylonians. Shortly after the conquest someone assassinated the Babylonian governor, and Jeremiah was forced to accompany those who were fleeing to Egypt to avoid the coming punishment. He died along the way.

BARUCH

The Book of Baruch was purported to have been written by Baruch, the secretary to Jeremiah, during the Babylonian exile. Because the only version of the book extant is written in Greek, it was not included in the Hebrew or Protestant Old Testaments.

It begins with an appeal for the people to turn back to wisdom, which would lead them to the Lord. The law of God is seen as wisdom incarnate.

There are also some songs of lamentation and a purported letter of Jeremiah to the exiles in Babylon.

EZEKIEL

Ezekiel was the only major prophet to prophesy outside of Israel (for he prophesied while he lived in exile in Babylon). Because of this, it was quite some time before his book was accepted by the elders of the Jewish community. His book is filled with extraordinary visions, oracles, and prophetic actions.

Ezekiel was a priest carried away into exile during the first partial exile of 597 B.C. For the next ten years he preached to the exiles and to the community that still resided in Jerusalem. After the second exile of 587 B.C., he continued his ministry addressing himself to the old and new exiles with whom he lived.

His book begins with the account of a theophany, the appearance of the Lord in the form of a fiery chariot.

He performed a number of symbolic actions to draw the attention of his audience to the serious nature of their situation. They refused to listen and change their ways.

In the latter part of the book, we hear of the restoration that the Lord will bring upon Israel. The temple will be rebuilt and purified (he describes its dimensions in great detail toward the end of the book). That which was dead in them will be filled with life (the meaning of the story of the valley filled with dry bones in chapter 37). The temple will become the source of a font of grace and divine love that will renew the land (the story of the river flowing from the altar in the temple and running out into the entire land in chapter 47). God will give his people hearts of flesh to replace their hearts of stone (chapter 36).

DANIEL

Although this book was attributed to a Prophet named Daniel during the period of the Babylonian Exile, it was actually written during the period of persecution at the time of the Maccabees (c. 175 B.C.). (We know this because many of the historic details contained in this book are incorrect.)

The first half of the book is a series of stories set during the Babylonian period that are intended to be parables concerning the need to give witness to the faith. The second half of the book is apocalyptic in style and speaks of the eventual triumph of the people of God over every adversity.

Chapters 13 and 14 (the story of Susanna and Bel and the Dragon) were written only in Greek (as well as part of chapter 3, the hymn of the three young men in the furnace). They are thus not accepted by Protestant churches, while they are part of the canon accepted by Catholic and Orthodox churches.

HOSEA

Hosea was a minor prophet from the northern kingdom of Israel (c. 750 B.C.). He was married to a woman named Gomer who was unfaithful. No matter how much she strayed, he continued to love her. He even allowed himself to be made a fool of in order to try to win her back.

Hosea realized that his relationship with Gomer paralleled God's relationship with Israel. God had made a covenant with Israel and had blessed his people with prosperity, but God's people had strayed and worshiped false gods. The Prophet also used the image of God being a loving parent and Israel being a disobedient child who refused to be corrected, or who even refused to be born when the time had come.

The book has suffered from a considerable amount of editorial reordering of material. This has made it difficult to understand the meaning of certain passages.

JOEL

The Book of Joel is one of the most apocalyptic books in the Old Testament. It speaks about the coming judgment of the Day of the Lord. The enemies of the Lord will be punished while those faithful to his covenant will be rewarded.

This book speaks about a coming outpouring of the Spirit of the Lord upon the whole nation. This passage is quoted by Peter on the day of Pentecost to explain what was happening to those who had received the gift of the Holy Spirit that day.

AMOS

Amos was one of the Minor Prophets (c. 750 B.C.). He was from the southern kingdom of Judah, but his mission was to the people of the north. Amos speaks of himself as being a herdsman and a dresser of sycamore trees (which probably indicates a relatively poor person).

He was not a professional Prophet, and most of his message seems to have come from his observations of the world rather than through special revelations. He calls Israel to task for allowing social injustice in which the poor were oppressed while the rich lived in luxury.

JONAH

While the Book of Jonah is said to be a prophetic book, it is most probably a parable written during the post-exilic period (after 539 B.C.). It speaks of a Prophet named Jonah who is called by God to proclaim the destruction of the pagan city of Nineveh for its sins. Jonah at first refuses because he fears that the Ninevites might repent and thus avoid the punishment that they deserve.

He tries to flee on a ship, but it runs into a storm. He is eventually thrown overboard and swallowed by a large fish, which spews him up on shore. He preaches repentance to the Ninevites, and they immediately begin a period of penance. God withholds his punishment, and Jonah is very depressed for what he feared had come true. God speaks to him of how all people are his own, and how he loves and cares for them all.

Many scholars believe that this was a parable written to speak of the fact that Yahweh was the God of all nations. Israel had been swallowed by a large fish (Babylon), and now they were being called to recognize the fact that God was concerned for everyone (for if there is only one God, then God is the God of all peoples).

MICAH

Micah was a minor prophet in the middle of the eighth century B.C. He came from the small town of Moresheth-Gath. He fostered small town values and fought the corruption of army officials and court officials from Jerusalem. He fought social injustice and oppression. He, like Amos, condemned a formal liturgical life that did not result in a transformation of one's conduct. He speaks of the destruction of the dynasty ruling in Jerusalem and the rise of a new dynasty from the descendants of David living in Bethlehem. This prophecy would later be seen to foretell the birthplace of the Messiah.

HABAKKUK

Habakkuk was one of the minor prophets, and his book was written at the end of the seventh century B.C. The prophet questions why God allows his people to suffer. Why does God allow one pagan nation (Assyria) to be punished by another pagan nation (Babylon), for that second pagan nation only becomes arrogant? The prophet eventually concludes that God will right all things in God's own time. Chapter 3 of the book is a hymn of praise for God who will save his people.

ZEPHANIAH

The Book of Zephaniah is one of the books of the minor prophets. It gives a series of oracles against the people of the nations surrounding Israel and against the people of Israel itself. They will all be punished on the Day of the Lord. It describes that day as a day of woe and of distress.

Yet, the book closes with a hymn of praise of the Lord. Both the people of Israel and even the people of the nations would turn to the Lord and pray to him alone. All the dispersed will be gathered together and healed by the Lord.

ZECHARIAH

The Book of Zechariah is actually produced in two stages. The first part dates to the period shortly after the Jewish people had returned from their exile in Babylon. It is a series of warnings that they should walk in the ways of the Lord but it also speaks of encouragement and hope. This continues through the first eight chapters of the book.

The second section of the book is a series of judgments and oracles that were written much later (some probably dating to the Greek period, after 330 B.C.). The most important passage for us is that which speaks of the entrance of the Messiah into the city of Jerusalem. He is described as riding a donkey, the colt of an ass (9:9). The humble manner in which he entered the city was intended to be contrasted with the arrogance of all of the kings and generals who had conquered Jerusalem and had entered it riding on great chargers. The Messiah would be a ruler who would restore peace to the land. This passage was fulfilled when Jesus entered the city of Jerusalem on Palm Sunday riding on a donkey.

MALACHI

Malachi is believed to be the last of the prophets. He was a minor prophet. We are not sure whether this is actually the author's name, for the word Malachi means "my messenger," so it might be more of a title than a proper name.

He complains especially that the Jewish people have not been faithful to their covenant responsibilities. Their priests offer inferior sacrifices, men divorce the wives of their youth, etc. There will be a coming judgment when God will reward the good and punish the evil.

The book closes with a promise of the return of Elijah to prepare for the Day of the Lord. This was fulfilled in the ministry of John the Baptist, who performed Elijah's mission in New Testament times.

GOSPEL OF MATTHEW

Matthew is the longest and the most Jewish of the gospels. It has numerous quotations from the Old Testament to show how Jesus fulfilled the law and the prophets and numerous references to Jewish customs all throughout.

Ancient tradition speaks of it being the first gospel written. This is why it is always listed as the first gospel in the list of the four. This tradition also speaks of it having been written in Aramaic.

Modern scholarship calls this into question. It is obvious that Matthew copied much of his material from Mark and not vice versa (for Mark is short and ungrammatical and Matthew is longer and better organized).

Furthermore, these same scholars have determined that the Greek version of the gospel that we now possess is not a translation from another language. Rather, the gospel was originally written in Greek.

We can still sustain the ancient tradition if we propose that Matthew, the tax collector, wrote part of today's Gospel of Matthew. Then, some decades later, a second author took that book, combined it with material from Mark and other sources, and produced the Gospel of Matthew as we know it today. This second author kept the original name of the Gospel of Matthew, because this name showed that the gospel had apostolic authority.

This second author was probably a converted Pharisee (for there are so many quotes from the Old Testament throughout the gospel). He probably wrote around 80 A.D. as a response to a persecution that his community was suffering. It was about this time that Christians were definitively excluded from the synagogue.

This was a response to the destruction of the temple. Jewish authorities felt that without the binding force of the temple, they could no longer afford the luxury of allowing several different versions of their faith to co-exist. Christians were shunned, and sometimes murdered for their faith. They were told that they had rejected the God of Israel and would burn in hell forever.

This second Matthew told Christians that they were not cut off from Israel. They were, in fact, the true Israel, while the Jews who had not accepted Jesus were a false Israel for they had not accepted the Messiah whom Yahweh had sent.

Second Matthew combined the material of the gospel into sections of narrative (action) and discourse (teaching). He produced five major sections of teaching to mirror the first five books of the Old Testament that Jews called the Torah.

He presented Jesus as the new Moses for the new Israel. Like Moses, Jesus was endangered as a child by an evil king. Like him he fasted in the desert. Like him, he climbed a mountain where he presented a new law (the Sermon on the Mount).

Throughout the gospel there is a polemic against the leaders of the Jews, especially the Pharisees. This is because they were the ones who had excluded Christians from the synagogues. Furthermore, there are refutations of lies spread about Jesus by the leaders of the Jews, e.g., the resurrection scene. Jesus also uses the Pharisees as an example of what the apostles should not be in their exercise of authority.

This gospel contains more parables than Mark. Many of them speak about the coming judgment and how people must choose to live in the path of the Lord.

GOSPEL OF MARK

The Gospel of Mark is probably the first gospel written. It is believed that it was written in Rome around the year 70 A.D. It was written by John Mark, a disciple who accompanied Paul and Barnabas on one missionary journey (but departed from their company before the journey was finished). John Mark eventually traveled to Rome and became a disciple of Peter.

The gospel presents the story of Jesus in a straightforward manner with little embellishment. If one were to compare it to a modern media, one might speak of it as the home movies of Jesus' ministry. The writing style is poor. Stories are often pasted together with little transition or connection.

Mark presents Jesus as the Messiah who is most of all the Son of Man. Every time that someone is prepared to proclaim Jesus as the Messiah, Jesus silences him. Rather, he says that he is the Son of Man. This title is derived from two Old Testament sources: Daniel 7 where the Son of Man would receive power and authority and dominion, and the Songs of the Suffering Servant in Isaiah where the servant of the Lord would suffer in order to expiate our sins.

The disciples of Jesus and his own family do not fully understand his mission until after the resurrection. Three times Jesus predicts his passion (chapters 8, 9, and 10), and three times the disciples respond inappropriately because they understand his role of being Messiah in terms of power and not in terms of service.

Even the resurrection scene presents this message. The shorter ending (ends at 16:8) speaks of the women hearing about the resurrection but not seeing Jesus themselves. This was most probably the original ending to the gospel. Mark's message, especially to the Church of Rome that was undergoing persecution, was that one does not see the risen Jesus until one has died with him.

There are relatively few parables in the gospel (only chapter 4, the parables on the kingdom). There is a further chapter of teaching in chapter 13, which speaks about the coming apocalyptic era when God will judge the earth.

Many of the expressions heard and the scenes portrayed show Jesus in an embarrassingly human stance. The other Synoptic Gospels, Matthew and Luke, tend to modify that material to show Jesus as more dignified and more divine.

GOSPEL OF LUKE

We believe that the Gospel of Luke was written around 80-85 A.D. Tradition holds that it was written by Luke, a Gentile convert and disciple of Paul. He is also traditionally said to have been a physician. All of this is credible considering the content and the style of the gospel.

Like the Gospel of Matthew, Luke begins with the story of the infancy of Jesus. There are actually a pair of annunciation and birth stories: that of John the Baptist, which is miraculous, and that of Jesus, which is even more astounding.

Throughout Luke's gospel Jesus reaches out to the poorest of the poor, the "anawim."

This phrase means the poor ones of Yahweh. Jewish authorities in the time of Jesus looked with disdain upon the poor for they did not study or observe the law. Jesus, on the other hand, considered them the chosen of God. They could not rely upon their own resources, so they had to rely upon the grace of God to survive. This made them ready to accept the message of God whenever it was addressed to them, and especially when it came in the person of Jesus.

The poor in this gospel are those who are physically poor, but also those who are spiritually poor or excluded from society for any reason. Thus, Jesus reaches out to sinners, to foreigners, to women, etc. The first to hear of his birth were the shepherds (this was not an honorable occupation at the time of the birth of Jesus) and the last was the good thief on the cross.

Jesus invited these people to experience salvation. Salvation is a present reality, for the minute we meet Jesus and encounter his love, we are already saved.

Jesus speaks of how God reaches out to the sinner and rejoices when that person turns from sin. Many of the parables that are specific to this gospel are centered on that theme.

For Luke, the city of Jerusalem holds a special importance for it is the holy city where God's will would be manifested in the death and resurrection of Jesus. Thus, the gospel begins in Jerusalem, and Jesus is on journey toward Jerusalem for most of the gospel (from 9:51). Then in the Acts of the Apostles, the gospel message spreads from Jerusalem (the spiritual center of the world) to Rome (the political center of the world).

This is also the gospel of prayer. The other Synoptic Gospels speak of Jesus praying a couple of times, but this gospel tells of eleven episodes in which he prayed. The purpose of Jesus' prayer was to discern the will of the Father so that he might be obedient to it. One of the ways that Jesus saves us is that he teaches how we can be obedient to the will of God so that the disobedience of the first sin might be repaired. Jesus also speaks of praying for those things that are needed with insistence (e.g., the parable of the widow who insists upon her rights from the judge).

GOSPEL OF JOHN

John is the only gospel that is not considered to be a Synoptic Gospel. The word synoptic means that one is seeing the story from one point of view. The Gospel of John sees the Jesus story from a very different point of view than the other gospels.

There are fewer miracles in this gospel and they are never called miracles. They are always signs that point to a greater reality, the depth of the Father's love for us.

This is why Jesus came to earth, to reveal to us how much God loves us. When we recognize this love, we can turn from our sins and experience the life of God, which is so profound that even death cannot affect it.

There is only one sin in this gospel: not to believe Jesus is the Son of God. All other sins and commandments are derived from this.

Throughout the gospel we see the beloved disciple who most perfectly follows the will of the Father by loving Jesus with a profound love. The other disciples of Jesus, and especially the apostles, do not succeed as well. Peter often appears in the same scenes as the beloved disciple, but he always falls short of that disciple's faith response.

The prologue, the beginning of the gospel, is a beautiful poem that the author of this gospel borrowed and adapted to speak of Jesus as one who pre-existed even before he was born in Bethlehem. He is the word through whom the world was created, and the wisdom that instructed the people of Israel.

The Last Supper Discourse is an extended collection of teachings that instruct the community on the relationship between the Father and Jesus, between them and the disciples, and on who the Paraclete is, etc.

The beautiful bread of life discourse lies at the very heart of the gospel. It is not the midway point in terms of material, but it is the fourth of seven signs that appear in the gospel. The Eucharist was the central sacrament for this community and the very meaning of who they were as a community. In this discourse we hear that the bread of life is the very flesh of Jesus. The word flesh is the same word that is used in the prologue to say that the word became human. Thus, the author is stating that whatever Jesus became in the incarnation, that is what the Eucharist is.

At the Last Supper Jesus further instructs the disciples upon the meaning of the Eucharist when he washes their feet. Eucharist is also Jesus serving us and we being called to serve each other.

Many of the scenes throughout the gospel are written in symbolic language and can only be understood fully when one understands the key to the symbolic interpretation. For example, the abundance of wine at the wedding feast of Cana is due to the fact that Jesus was preparing his own messianic banquet where he would marry the Church.

There are a number of characters who only appear in this gospel, e.g., Nathanael and Nicodemus. There are also characters whom we know only by a title and not by their name, e.g., the Samaritan woman at the well, the man born blind, etc.

This is the gospel that most emphasizes the divinity of Jesus. He knows all things. He is in control of everything from beginning to end. He is the pre-existent Word of God. When people ask him who he is, he often responds with a phrase that begins, "I am," in order to mirror the name Yahweh. Even when he is being arrested and he inquires whom his would-be captors are seeking and they respond, "Jesus of Nazareth," Jesus simply answers, "I am." This response causes them to fall on the ground, for they are in the presence of the living God.

ACTS OF THE APOSTLES

The Acts of the Apostles is the second volume of a two-volume work written by Luke. The first volume was the Gospel of Luke and this told of the ministry of Jesus while he resided in this world in the flesh. The second volume tells of the ministry of Jesus that the Spirit of God guided through the actions of the apostles.

The first part of the book emphasizes the actions of Peter and the other apostles who resided in Jerusalem, and the latter part of the book centers on the missionary journeys of Paul.

In the first chapter we hear Jesus tell the apostles that they must give witness to the gospel in Jerusalem, in Judea, and in Samaria, and to the ends of the earth. This list serves as a short table of contents for Acts. We hear how the gospel began in Jerusalem (the religious center of the world) and in the last chapters we hear how the gospel reaches the ends of the earth (Rome, the political center of the world).

It is absolutely clear that all missionary activities are guided by the Holy Spirit. It is the Spirit that gives the apostles the courage to first proclaim the gospel message on the day of Pentecost. It is the Spirit that leads them to accept Cornelius into the community. The Spirit guides Paul wherever he goes, etc.

The book does not close with the martyrdom of Paul in Rome. Many have asked why. The most obvious reason is that this book is not about Paul. It is about the gospel, and when the gospel reached Rome, the book was complete.

Some of the details of the book are questionable historically. We know this because they contradict what Paul says in his own letters. It is possible that Luke did not have a full account of all that happened, and whenever he ran short of material, he still provided a story. Nevertheless, the majority of details in the book are at least credible, and sometimes even affirmed by what is found in Paul's letters.

Luke shows a tremendous prejudice toward order and comradeship within the community. He deemphasizes difficulties and speaks of the harmony of the early Christian community (2:43-47 and 4:32-37). He was trying to win converts from among the Gentiles, and so he tried to show them the community in its best light. Even he, though, cannot ignore the difficulties in chapter 6, which led to the naming of the seven Greek-speaking disciples to do the work of the diaconate, and the confusion over what obligations the Gentile converts had toward the law of Israel (chapter 15).

ROMANS

The Letter to the Romans is one of Paul's last, if not his last letter. He was writing to a community that he had not founded and that he had never visited.

Paul was planning to visit Jerusalem within the near future. He was carrying the proceeds of a collection that he had made in Greece and Asia Minor to help the poor of the mother Church. Yet he was worried, for many rumors had been spread about his teachings and especially about his attitude toward Judaism.

Therefore, he wrote to the community at Rome to explain his teaching concerning faith and salvation. The reasoning was that, since that community had been founded by missionaries from Jerusalem, they could communicate to that Church that Paul was really not teaching things contrary to the faith.

There is an overall Jewish tenor to the letter from its first words. Paul speaks of Jesus being a fulfillment of the promises of the prophets and having descended according to the flesh from King David.

Throughout the first chapters he argues that we are all worthy of God's condemna-

tion, both Jew and Gentile. We have all sinned, and we are all subject to the wrath of God. But God has responded to our plight with incredible mercy. God, through the death and resurrection of his Son, has ransomed us from sin and called us into the liberty of the children of God.

Later in the letter he speaks of the fate of those Jews who had not yet converted. Paul says that they are subject to disobedience for a good reason, for they have been removed from the tree of the people of God for a while so that the Gentiles who believed in Jesus might be grafted on to that tree. The future hope was that the Jews would then become jealous and would themselves accept Jesus.

Paul also speaks of the proper attitude toward civil authorities. They have received their commission from the Lord, so they should be respected and obeyed.

The letter closes with a long list of people who are to be greeted. Scholars have often wondered where this list originated, for Paul did not know the members of this community. It is now believed that this might be part of a covering letter for a copy of the Letter to the Romans that Paul sent to another community (possibly Ephesus, for many of the people mentioned are associated with that region).

FIRST CORINTHIANS

The First Letter to the Corinthians was a letter written to a community that was deeply troubled by divisions and heretical tendencies.

When Paul arrived in Corinth, he was only one of many preachers proclaiming a new religion from the East. Most of the other religions had ecstatic tendencies in which the believer would seek to be possessed by the spirits of the gods. From the tenor of this letter, it would seem that some in the community interpreted Paul's message in this same manner.

They claimed that they had received a special revelation from the Holy Spirit that was superior to any human teaching. This led to factionalism in the community, for one group felt itself superior to the others. It led to problems of sexual immorality, for the adherents of this belief either practiced an attitude that they were spiritual creatures and it did not matter what they did in the flesh (licentiousness) or stated that they were spiritual creatures and they should never have anything to do with the flesh (absolute abstemiousness).

There were difficulties concerning the eating of meat offered to idols. Most meat sold in the markets had previously been offered to pagan idols. Could a Christian eat it? The response that the problem makers gave was that since the pagan god did not really exist, they could do whatever they wanted. Paul responded that while that was true, they might be giving poor example, especially to those whose consciences were weak.

There were problems in the celebration of the Lord's Supper. At this time the entire Passover meal was celebrated at the Eucharist, but some in the community had little to eat while others had too much. Paul spoke to them of the fact that the Eucharist is communion both with Jesus and with each other. By not practicing charity, they were sinning against the Eucharist.

There were problems with speaking in tongues, a practice in which one allows the Holy Spirit to speak through oneself. Unfortunately, some vaunted their ability to speak in tongues, even disrupting services in the community. Paul gave clear instructions on how this gift should be used.

Finally, there were some who denied the bodily resurrection. They wanted to be entirely spiritual, so they rejected the idea that they would regain their body at the resurrection. Paul responded that if Jesus did not rise from the dead, then we are the most pitiable of creatures.

An important teaching is found in chapter 3, verses 10-15. This is one of the few places in the New Testament where there is a teaching on the existence of Purgatory.

SECOND CORINTHIANS

The Second Letter to the Corinthians is a continuation of the discussion begun in First Corinthians. The first nine chapters are an attempt by Paul to reconcile with the community. He felt that the difficulties had gone on long enough, and those who had been responsible for the problems had repented from their evil ways.

The last four chapters are an angry denunciation of the troublemakers.

Scholars now believe that the last four chapters were actually a letter written before the first nine chapters. In those nine chapters, in fact, he refers to an earlier angry letter, which could well be the last chapters of what is now Second Corinthians. Because the letters were copied from papyri to scrolls, it is possible that a scribe simply made a mistake in the order of the chapters and inverted them. This makes even more sense when one considers the fact that toward the end of the first nine chapters Paul asks the Corinthians to be generous in a collection that he is gathering for the community in Jerusalem. It would be very odd to ask for money and then berate the community for four chapters.

There is even a fragment toward the end of chapter six and the beginning of chapter seven (6:14—7:1) that scholars believe might be from a letter that preceded the present First Letter to the Corinthians. In First Corinthians Paul speaks of an earlier correspondence in which he had given them rules concerning how they should interact with nonbelievers. The verses mentioned above do not fit in their present context and speak of the very things that Paul said he spoke of in that first letter.

This would mean that Second Corinthians is actually composed of fragments of at least three letters. It also means that Paul had to write at least four letters to this community to address their difficulties, an indication of how deeply ingrained they were. Saint Clement of Rome, the fourth Pope, wrote them again toward the end of the first century to discuss the exact same difficulties that Paul addressed all throughout his Corinthians correspondence.

The most beautiful image presented in this letter is that in which Paul speaks of the ministers of the gospel being earthen vessels that contain a great treasure, the gospel message they are sharing.

GALATIANS

The Letter to the Galatians was one of the most difficult letters Paul wrote. He was writing to a community that had fallen into error, and throughout the letter there is a sense of anger and fear.

Galatians, unlike Paul's other letters, is not addressed to one community. Galatia was a region, and Paul was writing to all of the small Christian communities dispersed throughout that region.

He had preached the gospel to them, and many had converted to the faith. The vast majority of those who converted were pagans.

Sometime later, a group of Jewish-Christian missionaries arrived from Jerusalem. They undercut Paul's teaching by saying that Paul had preached an "easy" gospel to them. Paul had told them that it was not necessary to be circumcised or to follow Jewish law after they had been baptized. Remember that when one was baptized, one was really becoming a Jew who believed in the Messiah whom Yahweh had sent. They said that Paul had only tried to buy their favor.

Many in the community favored adopting Jewish ways. Paul wrote them to admonish them severely. He told them that they were liberated from their sins not by Jewish customs, but by the death and resurrection of Jesus. Their sins had already been washed away in their Baptism. If they adopted Jewish ways, it meant that they did not suffi-

ciently trust in this message and that they did not have faith.

Paul adopted a very Jewish way of presenting this message. It is called Midrash, a type of rabbinic argumentation. In Midrash, one takes a verse from scripture and combines it with a similar verse from another place to produce a third meaning. This is not often used today, especially in Christian circles, but in Paul's day is was accepted as the proper way to argue Jewish questions.

Paul also gives an account of the "Council of Jerusalem," a meeting between Paul (and his disciples) and the apostles that occurred in Jerusalem sometime during the middle to the late 40's. At that meeting, they all reached the decision that pagans did not have to follow Jewish law if they converted to Christianity.

EPHESIANS

Colossians and Ephesians are two letters that are related (for they have many expressions in common). They are both attributed to Paul, but it is possible that he did not write either. There are expressions and situations described in the letters that cause some scholars to doubt their Pauline origin.

The author begins the letter with a hymn that praises Jesus and that proclaims that all existing things are to be put under Christ's headship in the fullness of time. As in Colossians, even heavenly powers are said to be subject to the authority of Jesus.

Paul's other letters speak of the fact that there is no importance if one is Jew or Gentile; this letter goes further and says that Jews and Gentiles have been made into one people through the death and resurrection of Christ.

Ephesians presents a developed theology of the Church as the body of Christ. In the course of his discussion on the Church, Paul speaks of the union of Christ and the Church in terms of something that is as intimate as the marriage union between a husband and a wife. This is a much more positive portrait of marriage than we find in Paul's other letters where marriage is something that must be done to avoid sin.

Much of the second part of the letter is an exhortation to live according to the values that give witness to the love of God in daily life. Christians are to combat vice and the powers of evil and live a totally blameless life. As in Colossians, there is an instruction on proper conduct within families and between slaves and masters, although this particular version is more elaborate.

PHILIPPIANS

The Letter to the Philippians is one of Paul's last and most intimate letters. He is writing from prison, and the fact that he faced possible death colors many of the thoughts he includes in this communication. He speaks of the necessity to make peace in the community. He tells the community that he does not know whether he will live or die, but that it does not make all that much difference because if he lives, he will preach and work for the Lord, but if he dies he will be with the Lord. He speaks about his conversion and how he changed his way of looking at things. The very things that he had previously considered most important were now considered to be rubbish in light of knowing and loving the Lord.

Chapter 2 contains a beautiful hymn that speaks of Jesus and his humility. Jesus, who was in the form of God (this means that he was God), gave up the prerogatives of his state to serve us by dying on the cross. God responded to this sacrifice by proclaiming him Lord of all of creation.

COLOSSIANS

Colossians and Ephesians are two letters that are related (for many expressions are in common). They are both attributed to Paul, but it is possible that he did not write either. There are expressions and situations described in the letters that cause some scholars to doubt their Pauline origin.

This letter's author speaks of Jesus in whom the fullness of divinity dwells. He is the visible likeness of the invisible God. All creatures, even those that are spiritual, are subject to him. This is important, for Greek philosophy taught that the more spiritual a creature was, the more it resembled God. Angels were totally spiritual creatures, while Jesus was incarnate. Some thought that this meant that the angels were superior to Jesus. This letter insists on Christians not worshiping angels, and on the fact that Jesus is far superior to them. Some types of behavior are condemned that seem to have originated in Jewish practices.

The letter closes with an instruction on how members of families and the community should treat one another and also with some information about Paul's travels and ministry. It is interesting that Mark is spoken of in positive terms, for Acts had spoken of a rift between Mark and Paul after he abandoned Paul on a missionary journey.

FIRST THESSALONIANS

The First Letter to the Thessalonians is most probably the first letter that Paul wrote. He was writing to a community that was very successful in turning from the errors of their previous days to the truth of the gospel. Paul even speaks of the faith of the Thessalonians being famous throughout the entire world.

This is actually one of the problems that Paul had to address. They were so successful that they started to become boastful, thinking that they had arrived at success through their own efforts. He writes an extensive thanksgiving (the entire first three chapters of this letter) to remind them that all of their success is a gift from the Lord.

In these chapters he speaks of the rapport that exists between the missionaries, the community, and God. The relationship between the missionaries and the Thessalonians is critical, for they learned about their faith through them. Yet the missionaries could never have preached if the Lord had not called them and given them the courage to proclaim the gospel, and the Thessalonians could never have accepted their message if the Spirit of the Lord had not prompted their hearts to listen to the missionaries and interpret their message as the word of God. Our faith has both a horizontal and a vertical dimension.

The last chapters speak of the end times. Paul teaches in chapter 4 that on the last day those who have died will rise from the dead to be with the Lord, while those who are still alive will not have to die. They will be "caught up into the clouds." This particular expression should not be interpreted literally. It was simply Paul's way of expressing the fact that they would be with the Lord in heaven.

Finally, the last chapter talks about when the return of the Lord would occur (we do not know, so we should always be ready) and how we must combat against evil with the armor of the virtues.

SECOND THESSALONIANS

Second Thessalonians is one of the letters attributed to St. Paul. Many modern scholars doubt this attribution because of the dissimilarities in language and theology between it and First Thessalonians. Eschatology is one of the major themes of the letter. Paul warns the community not to be fooled by those who claim to foretell the end of the world.

FIRST TIMOTHY

This is one of the Pastoral Epistles. The authorship is in doubt, for though it purports to have been written by St. Paul, its language and theology is different from that found in Paul's authentic letters.

This letter contains a warning concerning the false teachers that were troubling the community. There are a number of pastoral recommendations (e.g., presenting the attributes of bishops and deacons,

outlining proper relationships within families, etc.). Many of the teachings are based upon Stoic ideas concerning the proper ways to do things. The author of this letter was very concerned with giving good witness in whatever one did.

SECOND TIMOTHY

Second Timothy is one of the Pastoral Epistles. It is supposedly sent to Timothy, a convert whose father was pagan but whose mother was Jewish. Paul had him circumcised because he was technically Jewish since one obtained one's Jewishness through the mother.

This letter is purported to be Paul's last instruction to Timothy before he was martyred (it is doubtful that Paul actually wrote this letter). He wants to encourage him and instruct him that his own and Timothy's sufferings are a share in the suffering of Christ.

Paul speaks of the need to give witness, especially in what he calls the end times. He also warns Timothy concerning certain individuals who were spreading heresy.

This is one of the few writings in the Bible that speak of inspiration of these sacred texts (3:14-17).

TITUS

The Letter to Titus is one of the three pastoral letters. It is attributed to Paul, although many scholars believe that it was probably written by one of his disciples. Titus, the recipient, was a pagan who was baptized by Paul. He accompanied Paul to the Council of Jerusalem. At the time he received this letter, he was a bishop and organizer of the Church in Crete.

The letter speaks of the qualifications that leaders of the Church should possess. It gives instructions on the proper way for Christians to act in family and in the community. It warns the reader not to become involved in silly arguments about questions of faith.

PHILEMON

This is the only undisputed letter of St. Paul to be written to an individual. Paul writes to Philemon, asking him to welcome his returning slave Onesimus. That slave had been with Paul in prison and had converted to the faith. Although Paul does not specifically ask for the release of the slave, he seems to imply this course of action.

HEBREWS

Paul's Letter to the Hebrews is not written by Paul, it is not a letter, and it is not intended for the Hebrews.

This treatise was written by an anonymous author in the middle of the first century A.D. The author is a Jewish-Christian who was trying to convince a community of Jewish-Christians that they could abandon many of their old Jewish ways because Jesus was their High Priest.

The argumentation is strange to us, and is based upon Greek philosophy and Jewish Midrash argumentation. The main theme drawn from Greek philosophy is that of form and matter. A form is the ideal representation of an object, while the matter is the concrete representation of that thing. The form is perfect, for it represents all exemplars of a particular thing, while matter is imperfect for it represents only the one thing that it is (e.g., the idea of a book versus a real book).

Jesus was the "form" while all the other priests of the Old Testament were the "matter." Jesus was one and perfect. The priests of the Old Testament were imperfect, and they therefore had to be many.

The Jewish Midrash argument is that if one can say something that is true about a lesser creature, then one can say that it is much more true about a greater creature. The rabbis often spoke of how kings were this or that, and how the king of kings, Yahweh, was so much greater. The author of this treatise speaks of the worship of the Old Testament and how it was this or that, while the worship inaugurated by Jesus was far superior.

The "letter" closes with an admonition to live with greater faith and obedience to God the Father. Faith is described as being assurance about the things hoped for and conviction about the things not seen.

JAMES

The Letter of James is attributed to James, the brother (cousin) of the Lord Jesus.

The central argument of the letter is that we must live our commitment of faith in the Lord in our everyday lives. We cannot say we have faith and then treat the poor with disdain or ignore their need.

The letter speaks of the blessedness of those who undergo trials and therefore whose faith is proven real.

James warns against using the tongue to create divisions within the community. He speaks of it as a small organ in the body, yet one that can cause the greatest of difficulties.

He condemns arrogance and boasting, presumption and avarice. Toward the end of the letter he speaks of those who are ill and who should seek an anointing from the elders of the community (the scriptural basis for the Sacrament of Anointing).

FIRST PETER

Some scholars question whether First Peter was written by the prince of the apostles, but there are no convincing arguments that would make us reject Peter's authorship.

The letter speaks of the dignity that has been conferred upon us Christians through the Sacrament of Baptism. We have been made a holy race chosen by the Lord, a royal priesthood. We must live that holiness by choosing a virtuous life.

We are to live an ordered life-style, obeying the proper authorities. Our families should be examples of virtue lived out on an everyday basis.

Peter exhorts the reader not to become discouraged by suffering, for Christ himself suffered. He also says that it would be better to suffer unjustly (when we do not deserve it) than to be punished for what we have done.

In chapter 3 Peter speaks of how Jesus preached to the souls of those who had died and invited them into heaven. This is the scriptural basis for our belief that Jesus descended into the underworld after his death to invite into heaven all of those who had never heard of him.

Peter closes the letter by charging the leaders of the Church to be honest and gentle in their care of the flock. He also encourages younger men to obey their elders with humility.

SECOND PETER

While the author of this letter claims to be Peter the Apostle, it is almost surely written by an anonymous author (most probably a Hellenistic Jew). The major theme of the letter is that the delay of the parousia does not mean that it will not occur. Some heretical movements proclaimed that there would no final judgment. The author uses his claim of apostolic authority to show that both the second coming and the final judgment are revealed truth.

The letter was probably written at the end of the first century A.D. or the beginning of the second century. It was accepted into the canon at a relatively late date (the 4th century A.D.). Even in the earliest days of the Church its authorship was an open question.

FIRST JOHN

Ironically, the First Letter of John is not a letter. This becomes clear when one observes that it does not have the formal opening and closing that one would expect in a Greek letter, nor does it speak in the same manner that one would expect to see in a letter.

It is a treatise written sometime after the publication of the Gospel of John. Because that gospel portrayed Jesus as totally divine, knowing and controlling everything all throughout his ministry, it was a bit suspect by the early Christian community. They were being assailed by a heresy called Docetism, which denied the humanity of Jesus. Some thought that this gospel was suspiciously similar to the Docetist teachings.

Thus, the author of this letter emphasizes the humanity of Jesus. The prologue to the letter mirrors the prologue to the Gospel of John, but while the gospel's prologue spoke of the Word that existed forever in the presence of God, the letter's prologue speaks of the word of God that became so incarnate that we observed it, spoke with it, touched it, etc.

The other major point that this letter makes is that one must observe the commandments if one wants to be called a disciple of Jesus. The Gospel of John taught that there was really only one commandment: to believe that Jesus was the only-begotten Son of God. The theory was that if one believed this, one would live a life compatible with that belief. It was what Saint Augustine said when he taught us that we should love God and do what we would.

The problem was that some members of the community did what they wanted, which was not always moral. When they were questioned on it, they would proclaim that they were living in the freedom of the Sons of God and that they were anointed by the Holy Spirit, so no one should be questioning their conduct.

This letter calls them liars, for one cannot sin and still live in the light. By sinning, one has already chosen the darkness. Furthermore, if one loves God, one must love God's children, one's own brothers and sisters in the community.

The letter also defines God as love, and it states that if anyone wants to live in God, that person must live in love. It gives an important observation by stating that it is not that we have loved God first. God has loved us first and taught us the true meaning of love. We can only respond to this incredible generosity on the part of God.

BOOK OF REVELATION

The Book of Revelation is the only apocalyptic book to be part of the New Testament. Between 200 B.C. and 200 A.D., several apocalyptic books were written in Jewish and Christian communities. They all have certain things in common.

All apocalyptic books speak of two world eras: the present evil era and the coming age when God will reign upon the earth. This is their major difference with prophetic books. Prophetic books call people to conversion, for if they convert, God might remit their punishment. In apocalyptic books, things have progressed too far. There must be a cataclysmic change to purify the world from its perfidy.

Apocalyptic books also have extensive symbolism. Colors, numbers, animals, clothing, battles between angels and the forces of evil, etc. are all part of their symbolic matrix.

For example, numbers are important throughout most of these books. Ten stands for a fairly large amount, but seven stands for perfection (for ancient peoples believed that there were seven planets, and thus to say seven was to say the entire universe). Therefore, in their thinking, seven designated a number that was larger than ten. One thousand was considered an indefinite sum but a very large number.

Twelve symbolized both the number of the tribes of Israel and the number of the apostles. Thus, twelve times twelve times one thousand, or one hundred and forty-four thousand, stood for the Old and the New Israel, which the Lord had blessed with incredible fecundity (the meaning of the 1,000).

The Book of Revelation is not so much about when the end times will occur. Rather, it is a call to witness while one awaits the end times (remember the word witness in Greek is "martureo," for many will be called to martyrdom in order to give witness to the gospel).

The forces of evil will combat the forces of good throughout history. Jesus defeated those forces on the cross, and we share in that victory every time we take up our cross in order to die with Jesus so that we might live with him forever.

APPENDIX 2: THE RESPONSORIAL PSALM*

In his final recorded appearance to the apostles before his Ascension, Jesus spoke of what was written about him in "the Law, the Prophets, and the Psalms" (Luke 24:44). Hence, the Church has always indicated, especially through the Liturgy, that there is a history of Christ in the Psalms.

Each Sunday in the Responsorial Psalm at Mass, the liturgical assembly is invited to read a page of this history. In doing so, every one of us can discern some aspect of Jesus and hear his voice on a matter of importance to us.

However, in order for this result to be attained we must participate fully, consciously, and actively in the Responsorial Psalm, which occurs after the First Reading in the Liturgy of the Word.

Liturgists tell us that the Responsorial Psalm together with the Alleluia Acclamation before the Gospel is the most important part of the people in the Proper of the Mass for it functions as a kind of commentary on the Scriptures just proclaimed. It draws the soul to arrive at the interpretation of the Reading intended by the Church.

Indeed, the Responsorial Psalm is the only psalm used at Mass for its own sake rather than to accompany an action. It is the Word of God. That is why the Church insists that it may never be replaced by a nonbiblical text.

However, it is evident that in many cases, the people do not even know what is happening as the Responsorial Psalm goes flitting by during the celebration. This is even truer when the Responsorial Psalm is sung by the cantor with only a Refrain relegated to the people.

What is needed is to make information available to all about the function of this part of Mass, so that they will be able to take advantage of the music and the words to enter into the theme of response. The following observations may be of help in this respect.

CANTICLE OF THE COVENANT

Throughout the history of the Church, which is the people of God (in figure in the Old Testament and in fulfillment in the New), we find a pattern. God "speaks" to his people by accomplishing wondrous deeds for them. The people respond by celebrating these wondrous deeds.

God guides the people of the Exodus across the Red Sea. Miriam, following the lead of Moses her brother, celebrates the Lord who has cast horse and rider into the sea (Exodus 15:1, 21).

God delivers Hannah from her sterility by giving her a son, Samuel. Hannah responds by celebrating the Lord who enables a sterile woman to give birth (1 Samuel 2:5).

God delivers Tobit from blindness. Tobit responds by celebrating the Lord who lets his light rise over Jerusalem as well as in the hearts of his people (Tobit 13:11).

In New Testament times, God blesses Mary's virginity by letting her become the Mother of Jesus. Mary responds by glorifying the Lord and exulting in God her Savior, in Jesus whom she is bearing (Luke 1:46-55).

In accord with these examples, the Responsorial Psalm plays a similar role in the liturgical celebration. The Word proclaimed recalls God's wondrous deeds of old. The assembly celebrates these wondrous deeds and actualizes them in the celebration. It responds to the God of these wonders with the Responsorial Psalm.

The Word proclaimed is the word of the Covenant. The Responsorial Psalm is the canticle of the Covenant. It prepares for the Covenant, and asks God to keep us in it.

*Reprinted with permission from *Active Participation at Mass* by Anthony M. Buono, pp. 65-72, © 1994 by Alba House.

THE PSALTER:
THE CHRISTIAN PRAYER BOOK

In order to sing the Responsorial Psalm well, we should get to know something about the Book of Psalms or Psalter. It has become the book of Christian prayer, the compendium of the entire biblical message.

According to St. Thomas Aquinas, the Psalter—in contrast to the other biblical writings—"embraces in its universality the matter of all of theology. The reason why this biblical book is the one most used in the Church is that it contains in itself all Scripture. Its characteristic note is to restate, under the form of praise, all that the other biblical books express by way of narrative, exhortation, and discussion.

"The purpose of the Psalter is to make people pray, to elevate souls to God through contemplation of his infinite majesty, through meditation on the excellence of eternal happiness, and through communion in the holiness of God and the efficacious imitation of his perfection" *(Exposition on the Psalms of David)*.

The Psalms have been called with good reason "a school of Christian prayer." These sacred songs cover a wide range of human experiences; they bring out our strengths and weaknesses, faith and wonderment, joys and sorrows.

The Psalms also show forth the prophesied glory of Jesus: for it is only in Christ that their full significance is revealed. The noted Bible scholar Joseph Gelineau has written that Jesus "personally described himself as the Lord whom God seated at his right hand (Psalm 110 - Matthew 22:44); as the stone rejected by the builders which became the head of the corner (Psalm 118 - Matthew 21:42); as he who comes, blessed in the name of the Lord (Psalm 118 - Matthew 23:39); he personally applied to himself on the cross the appeal of the persecuted psalmist (Psalm 22 - Matthew 27:46) and his prayer of trust (Psalm 31 - Luke 23:46)."

Thus, the Psalms set forth Christ's lowly coming to earth, then his kingly and priestly power, and finally his beneficent labors and the shedding of his Blood for our redemption. So Christological are they that they have rightly been termed "the Gospel according to the Holy Spirit." It is the Holy Spirit who inserted in them indisputable references to the life of Christ.

POETIC QUALITIES OF THE PSALMS

The Psalms are among the world's best poetry. We all know "The Lord Is My Shepherd," but there are a host of others among the 150 Psalms that are just as classical.

The poetry of the Psalms contains rhythm, which is the recurrence of accented or unaccented syllables at regular intervals. But its outstanding trait is parallelism, which consists in the equal distribution or balance of thought in the various lines of each verse.

Synonymous parallelism is the repetition of the same thought with equivalent expressions:

"He who is throned in heaven laughs;
   the Lord derides them."

Antithetic parallelism expresses a thought by contrast with an opposite:

"For the Lord watches over the way of the just,
   but the way of the wicked vanishes."

Synthetic parallelism occurs when a second line completes the thought of the first by giving a comparison:

"When I call out to the Lord,
   he answers me from his holy mountain,
when I lie down in sleep,
   I wake again, for the Lord sustains me."

By paying attention to the poetic aspect of the Psalms, we will be able to recite or sing the Responsorial Psalm with more understanding and greater participation.

PRAYING THE RESPONSORIAL PSALM

The Psalms are not readings or prose prayers, even though on occasion they may be recited as readings. In Hebrew they were called "Songs of praise" and in Greek *Psalmoi,* that is, "Songs to be sung to the lyre." All the Psalms have a musical quality that dictates the correct way of delivering them.

Even when a Psalm is recited and not sung, its delivery must still be governed by its musical character. A Psalm presents a text to the minds of those singing it and listening to it, but it aims at moving their hearts.

In order to pray the Psalms with understanding, we must meditate on them verse by verse, with our hearts ready to respond in the way the Holy Spirit desires. As the one who inspired the Psalmists, the Holy Spirit is always present to those who in faith and love are ready to receive his grace.

Indeed, the singing of the Responsorial Psalm expresses the reverence that is due to God's majesty. But it should also be the expression of a joyful spirit and a loving heart, in keeping with its character as sacred poetry and inspired song and above all in keeping with the freedom of the children of God.

The Responsorial Psalm is a different prayer from one composed by the Church. The inspired Psalmist often addresses the people as he recalls the history of God's people; sometimes he addresses creation; and at other times he even introduces a dialogue between God and the people.

In praying the Psalm we should open our hearts to the different attitudes that may be expressed, which vary with the type of writing to which it belongs (Psalms of Grief or Trust or Gratitude and the like). Although the Psalms originated many centuries ago in the East, they express accurately the pain and hope, the unhappiness and trust, of every people and every age and country, and celebrate especially faith in God, revelation, and redemption.

In the words of another renowned Scripture scholar, Andre Choracqui, "We were born with this book [of Psalms] in our very bones. A small book; 150 poems; 150 steps between death and life; 150 mirrors of our rebellions and our loyalties, of our agonies and our resurrections."

The Psalms have great power to raise minds to God, to inspire devotion, to evoke gratitude in favorable times, and to bring consolation and strength in sad times. They constitute an inexhaustible treasury of prayers for every occasion and mood in a format that is true to the whole tradition of the History of Salvation.

Thus, we should strive to pray the Responsorial Psalm with the best of intentions both at home and at Mass. It will then become for us an opportunity to rediscover our own humanity, in its anguish, its rebellion, its violence, and its reconciliation as well.

It will become for us an opportunity to rediscover more broadly the whole of history, for example, those men and women who also struggle, who suffer, who cry out, who hope, and who pray in the four corners of the earth.

Finally, it will become for us an opportunity to encounter Christ mysteriously present in the heart of this humankind in which we find ourselves.

APPENDIX 3: GLOSSARY AND PRONUNCIATION GUIDE

For purposes of pronunciation, a simple system of phonetic spelling has been devised and included in parentheses for every entry defined. The **accented syllable** is indicated by **capital letters,** and the pronunciation for the letters is as follows.

uh = a, e, i, o, u unaccented (the Schwa)	**o** = odd (short)	**yoo** = use, unite (accented, long)
a = hat	**oh** = no	**uhr** = further
ah = father	**oi** = noise, joy	**ch** = church
ai = aisle, ice	**ow** = cow	**sh** = shame, wish
aw = awful, for	**oo** = boot	**zh** = vision
ay = ape, care	**u** = foot, book (accented, long)	**g** = get
e = get (short)	**uh** = culture, cut (accented, short)	**j** = judge
ee = eve	**yuh** = nature (unaccented, short)	**k** = cow, key
i = pit (short)		**kw** = quick
		w = witch

Aaron (AR-uhn; ER-uhn). Brother of Moses and the first high priest of Israel (Ex 6:20; 28:1ff).

Abba (AB-uh; ah-BAH). Aramaic word for "father" or "daddy" used by Jesus of his Father (Mk 14:36).

Abelmoholah (ay-buhl-mi-HOH-luh). A city on the Jordan river and the residence of Elisha the prophet (1 Kgs 19:16).

Abiathar (uh-BAI-uh-thuh). Son of the priest Ahimelech (1 Sm 22:20) and himself a priest of David (2 Sm 8:17). He is mentioned by Jesus in the discussion with the Pharisees concerning the apostles' picking grain on the sabbath (Mk 2:26).

Abijah (uh-BAI-juh). Son and successor of Rehoboam (1 Chr 3:10) and ancestor of Jesus (Mt 1:7).

Abilene (ab-uh-LEEN; -LEE-nee). A district ruled by Lysanias (Lk 3:1) at the time of Jesus that lay to the northwest of Damascus.

Abishai (uh-BAI-shi). A brother of Joab, he accompanied David during his flight from Saul (1 Sm 26:6ff) and from Absalom (2 Sm 16:9).

Abiud (uh-BAI-uhd). An ancestor of Jesus (Mt 1:13).

Abner (AB-nuhr). A commander of the army of Saul (1 Sm 17:55; 26:7). He first sided with a son of Saul, Ishbaal, after the death of Saul. He eventually betrayed him and furthered the cause of David among the tribes of the north.

Abraham (AY-bruh-ham). Founder of the Hebrew nation and father of the people of God (Gn 11:26ff; 17:4f, etc.). Originally called Abram (Gn 11:26), he received the name Abraham at the time of God's covenant with him (Gn 17:4).

Abram (AY-bruhm). *See* **Abraham.**

Achaia (uh-KAI-uh). Roman province comprising the central part of modern Greece (Acts 18:12, 27).

Achim (AY-kim). An ancestor of Jesus (Mt 1:14).

Acts of the Apostles (aks uhv thee uh-POS-uhlz). The Book that continues the Gospel of Luke with a history of the primitive Church.

Adam (AD-uhm). The first man (Gn 2:8), who was placed in the garden of Eden (Gn 2:15) but disobeyed God and was expelled from the garden (Gn 3:23).

Advocate (AD-vuh-kut). See Paraclete.

Ahaz (AY-haz). Son and successor of King Jotham of Judah (2 Kgs 15:38) and father of Hezekiah (2 Kgs 16:20). It was to him that Isaiah prophesied that the Messiah would be born of a virgin (Is 7:14).

Alexander (al-ig-ZAN-duhr). Son of Simon of Cyrene and brother of Rufus, mentioned during the way of the cross (Mk 15:21).

Alpha (AL-fuh). First letter of the Greek alphabet. Used with "omega," the last letter, it signifies complete-ness, as "from A to Z." God is termed the Alpha and Omega, the First and the Last, the Beginning and the End (Rv 1:8), as is also Christ (Rv 22:13).

Alphaeus (al-FEE-uhs). Father of James the Less (Mt 10:3; Acts 1:13).

Amalek (AM-uh-lek). Eponymous founder of a nomadic tribe that dwelt in the Negeb (Gn 36:12). The Amalekites fought with the Israelites during their time in the Sinai (Ex 17:8ff). They also fought various battles against Israel, often in alliance with Israel's enemies.

Amaziah (am-uh-ZAI-uh). A priest at Bethel at the time of the Prophet Amos (Am 7:12).

Amminadab (uh-MIN-uh-dab). Father of Nahshon (Nm 1:7), father-in-law of Aaron (Ex 6:23), and an ancestor of Jesus (Mt 1:4).

Amos (AY-muhs). The third of the 12 Minor Prophets of the Old Testament, who proclaimed the need for social justice in people's relationships with each other. One of the ancestors of Jesus (Mt 1:10) bears the name Amos, but—as the NAB indicates in a footnote—a better reading is "Amon."

Amoz (AY-muhz). Father of the Prophet Isaiah (Is 2:1).

Ancient One (AYN-chuhnt won). A new translation for the more traditional "Ancient of Days," it is a name of God taken from apocalyptic writings that appears three times in Daniel (7:9, 13, 22).

Andrew (AN-droo). Brother of Peter (Jn 1:40) and one of the twelve apostles (Mt 10:2).

Anna (AN-uh). The aged prophetess who spoke of the coming redemption at Jesus' presentation in the temple (Lk 2:36ff).

Annas (AN-uhs). High priest of Jerusalem (6-15 A.D.), whose office passed to his sons and his son-in-law Caiaphas (Jn 18:13). He was involved in the trials of Jesus (Jn 18:13ff).

Antioch (AN-tee-ok). Name of two cities. Antioch on the Orontes River was the capital of Syria where the disciples of Jesus were first called "Christians" (Acts 11:19-26). Antioch in Pisidia on the border with Phrygia was one of the first cities in which Paul preached (Acts 13:14ff).

Apollos (uh-POL-uhs). An educated Christian Jew from Alexandria, who preached in Ephesus and in Corinth (Acts 18:24—19:1).

Arabia (uh-RAY-bee-uh). Northern part of the peninsula between the Red Sea and the Persian Gulf (Is 21:13) or the entire peninsula (Neh 2:19).

Arabs (AR-uhbz). Inhabitants of Arabia, some of whom were in Jerusalem on the day of Pentecost (Acts 2:11).

Aramean (ar-uh-MEE-uhn). A member of a nomadic people from northern Syria and southern Babylon.

Archelaus (ar-kuh-LAY-uhs). Son of Herod the Great, who became the ruler of Judea, Samaria, and Idumea upon his father's death in 4 B.C.-6 A.D. and was deposed in 6 A.D. (Mt 2:22).

Arimathea (ar-i-muh-THEE-uh). A town in Judah that was the birthplace of Joseph of Arimathea, who buried Jesus in his own tomb (Mk 15:43).

Asaph (AY-saf). A person's name, e.g., a cantor in the temple under David and Solomon to whom Psalms 50 and 73—83 are attributed.

Asher (ASH-uhr). Name of one of the twelve tribes of Israel and of its Patriarch, who was the eighth son of Jacob (Gn 49:20). Anna was from this tribe (Lk 2:36).

Asia (AY-zhuh). The Roman province of Asia, which included only the western third of what is now Asia Minor. Ephesus was its capital and it was evangelized by Paul on his 3rd missionary journey (Acts 18—21).

Attalia (at-uh-LAI-uh). A seaport on the coast of Pamphylia (Asia Minor).

Augustus (uh-GUS-tuhs). Emperor of Rome from 31 B.C. to 14 A.D., during whose reign Jesus was born (Lk 2:1).

Azor (AY-zawr). An ancestor of Jesus (Mt 1:13f).

Baal (BAY-uhl). The chief god of the Phoenicians and Canaanites, worshiped as the god of crops, flocks, and fertility—even by some Israelites (1 Kgs 16:31-33).

Baal-shalishah (BAY-uhl SHAHL-uh-shuh). A place in Ephraim from which bread and corn were brought to Elisha when he was at Gilgal (2 Kgs 3:42-44).

Babel (BAY-buhl). The place where the ancients built a tower to the heavens in arrogance before God (Gn 11:9).

Babylon (BAB-uh-luhn). A city on the Euphrates and the capital of the Babylonian Empire to which the Israelites were exiled in 597 and 587 B.C. (2 Chr 36:20; Ps 137:1). In the New Testament, the name was used as a synonym for Rome (1 Pt 5:13; Rv 14:8; 17:5). *See* **Babylonian Exile.**

Babylonian Exile (ba-buh-LOH-nee-uhn EK-sai-uhl). The period in Jewish history from the carrying away of the people to Babylon in 597 and 587 to their return in 538 B.C. (Mt 1:11).

Barabbas (buh-RAB-uhs). A prisoner whom Pilate released in place of Jesus (Mk 15:6-15).

Barsabbas (bahr-SAB-uhs). Name of two men: (1) Joseph Barsabbas, also called Justus, who was one of the candidates to succeed Judas Iscariot as an apostle (Acts 1:23). (2) The surname of Judas, the prophet, who was sent to Antioch together with Barnabas, Paul, and Silas to communicate the decisions of the Council of Jerusalem to the community there (Acts 15:22-32).

Bartholomew (bahr-THOL-uh-myoo). One of the twelve apostles (Mk 3:18).

Bartimaeus (bahr-tuh-MEE-uhs). A blind beggar from Jericho who was cured by Jesus (Mk 10:46-52).

Baruch (BA-ruhk; buh-ROOk). The prophet Jeremiah's secretary, to whom is ascribed the third of the 18 Prophetic Books of the Old Testament.

Beelzebul (bee-EL-zee-buhl). Name of the god of Canaan, who in the New Testament is referred to as the prince of demons (Mk 3:22).

Bethany (BETH-uh-nee). A village on the eastern slope of the Mount of Olives (Lk 10:38; Jn 11:1, 18).

Bethlehem (BETH-li-hem). The birthplace of Jesus, a village 4.5 miles south of Jerusalem (Lk 2:4-7).

Bethphage (BETH-fuh-jee). A village east of Bethany mentioned in connection with Jesus' triumphal entry into Jerusalem (Mk 11:1).

Bethsaida (beth-SAY-uh-duh; -SAI-duh). A town on the northern shore of the Sea of Galilee (later called Julia) that was the home of Andrew, Peter, and Philip (Jn 1:44; 12:21).

Boaz (BOH-az). Husband of Ruth (Ru 4:13) and ancestor of Jesus (Mt 1:5f).

Caesar (SEE-zuhr). Surname of Julius Caesar, given from the 1st century onward to the Roman emperors (Lk 2:1; 3:1).

Caesarea (sez-uh-REE-uh). Name of various cities. (1) Caesarea Philippi, a town where Jesus prepared his disciples for his approaching sufferings and death and Peter made his famous confession of Christ's divinity (Mk 8:27). (2) A town where the converted Paul was sent to escape the Hellenists who tried to kill him (Acts 9:30).

Caiaphas (KAY-uh-fuhs; KAI-yuh-fuhs). High priest (18-36 A.D.) and head of the Sanhedrin during the trial of Jesus (Mt 26:57).

Cana (KAY-nuh). Village of Galilee, located north of Nazareth, and site of Jesus' first miracle (Jn 2:1-11).

Canaan (Kay-nuhn). One of the old names for Palestine, the land of the Canaanites who were dispossessed by the Israelites.

Capernaum (kuh-PUHR-nay-uhm). A town on the northwestern shore of the Sea of Galilee where Jesus made his headquarters during his Galilean ministry (Mk 2:1).

Cappadocia (kap-uh-DO-shee-uh). A province in eastern Asia Minor, whose people were Aryans (Acts 2:9).

Carbuncles (KAHR-bun-kuhlz). As used in the Bible, something bright and glittering, possibly rubies or emeralds (Is 54:12).

Carmel (KAHR-mel). A mountain chain and ancient site of worship, often lauded for its beauty (Is 35:2).

Carnelians (kahr-NEL-yuhnz). Hard sparkling reddish quartz used in jewelry (Is 54:11).

Cephas (SEE-fuhs). The name given by Jesus to the apostle Peter (Jn 1:42).

Chaldeans (kal-DEE-uhnz). Members of an Eastern Aramean tribe that beginning in 1100 B.C. invaded Babylon. They are termed ancestors of the Israelites (Jdt 5:6) as a result of the tradition that Abraham came from Ur of the Chaldees (Gn 11:28). In exile the Israelites became servants of the "king of the Chaldeans" (2 Chr 36:20).

Cherubim (CHER-uh-bim). In the Old Testament, these were superhuman beings whose nature was not made explicit. They were regarded as the porters who carry God (Ps 18:11; 80:2) and were a sign of his power, for he was enthroned on the cherubim (1 Sm 4:4; 2 Kgs 19:15). In Christian tradition, they are identified as the second of the nine choirs of angels.

Chloe (KLOH-ee). A woman whose people informed Paul of factions in the Corinthian community (1 Cor 1:11).

Chronicles (KRON-i-kulz). Fifth and sixth of the 17 Historical Books of the Old Testament.

Cilicia (suh-LISH-ee-uh). A region that lay along the southeastern coast of Asia Minor.

Cleopas (KLEE-oh-puhs). One of the disciples with whom Jesus walked on the way to Emmaus and broke bread (Lk 24:18).

Clopas (KLOH-puhs). The husband of Mary of Clopas (Jn 19:25).

Colossians (kuh-LOSH-uhnz). People of Colossae in Phrygia to whom Paul wrote one of the Letters of the New Testament.

Corinth (KOR-inth). Capital of the province of Achaia, and an extremely commercial city, which Paul made the center of his activity in Greece (Acts 18:11).

Corinthians (kuh-RIN-thee-uhnz). Christians of Corinth to whom Paul wrote two of the Letters of the New Testament.

Cornelius (kawr-NEEL-yuhs). A Roman centurion from Caesarea who was baptized by Peter (Acts 10f), showing that the Church was open to pagans as well as Jews.

Cretans (KREE-tans). Inhabitants of Crete, an island in the Mediterranean forming a natural bridge between Europe and Asia Minor, some of whom were in Jerusalem on the day of Pentecost (Acts 2:11).

Cush (koosh). Ethiopia (modern day Sudan).

Cyrene (sai-REEN). A Greek colony in northern Africa, with a large population of Greek-speaking Jews. Many of them were in Jerusalem on the day of Pentecost (Acts 2:10).

Cyrus (SAI-ruhs). Founder of the Persian world empire, who in October 539 B.C. overthrew the Babylonian king, Nabonidus, and allowed the Jews to return from their exile (2 Chr 36:22f). He is termed God's anointed by Isaiah (Is 45:1).

Daniel (DAN-yuhl). An ancient figure of widom who is attributed to be the author of the Book of Daniel (which although placed in the time of the Babylonian Exile was actually written much later during the time of the Maccabees). He is called the last of the 4 Major Prophets of the Old Testament.

David (DAY-vid). Second and greatest King of Israel and an ancestor of Jesus (Mt 1:6).

Decapolis (di-KAP-uh-lis). A federation of 10 Greek cities in Palestine mostly east of the Jordan, through which Jesus passed during his public ministry (Mk 5:20; 7:31).

Deuteronomy (doo-tuh-RON-uh-mee). Fifth and last Book of the Pentateuch.

Diadem (DAI-uh-dem). A crown or royal headband (Is 62:3).

Didymus (DID-i-muhs). Greek form of the name Thomas (the apostle), which signifies "twin" (Jn 11:16; 20:24; 21:2).

Dromedaries (DROM-uh-der-eez). Camels with unusual speed and trained for riding (Is 60:6).

Ebed-melech (ee-bid-MEE-lik). An Ethiopian eunuch who saved Jeremiah the prophet from a cistern into which he had been thrown (Jer 38:7ff).

Ecclesiastes (i-klees-ee-AS-tees). Fourth of the 7 Wisdom Books of the Old Testament.

Eden (EE-duhn). Place where God planted a garden in which he put Adam and Eve (Gn 2:8).

Egypt (EE-juhpt). A country northeast of Africa often in contact with Israel. Egyptian Jews were in Jerusalem on the day of Pentecost (Acts 2:10).

Elamites (EE-luh-maits). Inhabitants of Elam, east of Babylon (Gn 10:22; 14:1ff), some of whom were in Jerusalem on the day of Pentecost (Acts 2:9).

Eldad (EL-dad). One who prophesied in the Israelite camp in the wilderness (Nm 11:26ff).

Eleazar (el-ee-AYZ-uhr). An ancestor of Joseph, the husband of Mary (Mt 1:15).

Eli (EE-lai). A priest of Shiloh (1 Sm 1:9) who judged Israel forty years (1 Sm 4:18). He spoke to Hannah (1 Sm 1:12ff), and it was to him that the child Samuel was brought (1 Sm 1:28; 2:11; 3:1-10).

Eli, Eli [or: Eloi, Eloi], Lema Sabachthani (AY-lee, AY-lee, LAY-muh, sa-BAK-thuh-nee). The English transliteration of a Greek phrase (Mt 27:46; Mk 15:34), which is in turn the transliteration of the Hebrew (or Aramaic) version of Ps 22:1: "My God, my God, why have you abandoned me?"

Eliab (i-LEE-uhb). Eldest son of Jesse and brother of David who presented a commanding appearance (1 Sm 16:6).

Eliakim (i-LAI-uh-kim). Son of Hilkiah and successor to Shebna as King Hezekiah's majordomo (Is 22:20ff).

Elijah (i-LAI-juh). A prophet during the reigns of Ahab and Jezebel in the Northern Kingdom (1 Kgs 17:1-16).

Elisha (i-LAI-shuh). A prophet in the Northern Kingdom in the second half of the 9th century B.C. (2 Kgs 4:8-16).

Eliud (i-LAI-uhd). An ancestor of Jesus (Mt 1:14f).

Elizabeth (i-LIZ-uh-buhth). Wife of Zechariah, mother of John the Baptist, and relative of the Virgin Mary (Lk 1:5-57).

Emmanuel (i-MAN-yoo-uhl). Symbolic name meaning "God is with us" given by Isaiah to the child whose birth he foretold (Is 7:14) and which is applied to Jesus (Mt 1:23).

Emmaus (i-MAY-uhs). The town 7 miles from Jerusalem to which two disciples walked on the day of the resurrection accompanied by Jesus (Lk 24:13-35).

Ephah (EE-fuh). A measurement of weight (1 Sm 1:24); also the name of a son of Midian (Gn 25:4) and eponymous ancestor of a tribe (Is 60:6).

Ephesians (i-FEE-shuhnz). Inhabitants of Ephesus in Asia Minor to whom Paul wrote one of the Letters of the New Testament.

Ephphathah (EF-uh-thuh). An Aramaic word, meaning "Be opened," that was uttered by Jesus as he was healing a deaf man (Mk 7:34).

Ephraim (EE-free-uhm). One of the twelve tribes of Israel, which became the principal tribe of the Northern Kingdom (Jer 31:9; Zec 9:10).

Ephrathah (EF-ruh-thuh). Ancient name of Bethlehem or the district around it (Mi 5:1).

Esther (ES-tuhr). Eleventh of the 13 Historical Books of the Old Testament.

Euphrates (yoo-FRAY-teez). A large river that runs from Armenia to the Persian Gulf. It and the Tigris form the two boundaries of Mesopotamia. It also forms one of the boundaries of the widest extent of the borders of Israel.

Eve (EEV). The first woman whom God placed in the garden of Eden (Gn 2:22), but she disobeyed God and was expelled from the garden (3:23).

Exodus (EK-suh-duhs). The deliverance of the Israelites from Egypt by God's mighty hand; also, the second Book of the Pentateuch that narrates the story of this great event.

Expiation (ek-spee-AY-shuhn). A translation of the Hebrew word for pardon or suppression of sin. Jesus is called "an expiation" because he assumes pardon of all sins (Rom 3:25).

Ezekiel (i-ZEE-kee-uhl). Third of the 4 Major Prophets who prophesied in exile during the Babylonian Captivity in the 6th century B.C.

Ezra (EZ-ruh). Priest and scribe who is the main character of the seventh of the 13 Historical Books of the Old Testament.

Feast of Unleavened Bread (feest uhv uhn-LEV-uhnd bred). A feast of spring and renewal celebrating the founding event of the people of God: the deliverance from bondage by the Exodus from Egypt (Lv 23:4-8; Mk 14:1, 12). Each family reenacted the first Passover by eating the Passover meal. The feast included a day of an offering of the firstfruits from the barley harvest.

Gabriel (GAY-bree-uhl). An angel who interpreted the vision of Daniel (Dn 8:15ff) and told him of the seventy weeks (Dn 9:22ff). He also announced the birth of John the Baptist to Zechariah (Lk 1:11ff) and that of Jesus to Mary (Lk 1:26ff). In Christian tradition he is known as an archangel, the eighth of the nine choirs of angels.

Gabbatha (GAB-uh-thuh). A district in Jerusalem where Pilate's official residence was located (Jn 19:13).

Galatians (guh-LAY-shuhnz). The inhabitants of Galatia, a Roman province in central Asia, to whom Paul addressed one of the Letters of the New Testament.

Galileans (gal-uh-LEE-uhnz). Inhabitants of Galilee (Lk 13:1).

Galilee (GAL-uh-lee). The region west of the Sea of Galilee and the Jordan, where Jesus was reared and began preaching (Mk 1:14).

Gehazi (gi-HAY-zee). Servant of the prophet Elisha (2 Kgs 4:8ff).

Gehenna (gi-HEN-uh). Place of punishment after death or after the Last Judgment (Mt 10:28).

Genesis (JEN-uh-sis). First Book of the Pentateuch.

Gennasaret (gi-NES-uh-ret). *See* **Sea of Galilee.**

Gentiles (JEN-tailz). Among the Jews it meant either foreign nations (Acts 7:45) or pagans, i.e., polytheists or idolaters who did not worship Yahweh (Mt 4:15; Lk 2:32).

Gethsemane (geth-SEM-uh-nee). A garden on the Mount of Olives, which was the scene of Christ's agony and betrayal (Mt 26:36-56).

Gibeon (GIB-ee-uhn). Hivite city north of Jerusalem that was a cult center and a royal shrine until Solomon's reign (1 Kgs 3:4-15).

Gilgal (GIL-gal). A site near Jericho associated with Joshua's renewal of the covenant (Jos 4:19f) and the site of Saul's installation as king (1 Sm 10:8).

Golgotha (GOL-guh-thuh). Aramaic name ("Place of the Skull") for a little hill northwest of Jerusalem where Jesus was crucified (Mt 27:33).

Gomorrah (guh-MAWR-uh). One of the cities destroyed by God because of its immorality (Gn 19:1ff). It became a symbol for God's judgment upon the sinful.

Greeks (greekz). Name that identified the inhabitants of Greece but also referred to a specific culture: Hellenism (cf. 1 Cor 1:22).

Habakkuk (HAB-uh-kuk). Eighth of the 12 Minor Prophets of the Old Testament.

Haggai (HAG-ai). Tenth of the 12 Minor Prophets of the Old Testament.

Hannah (HAN-uh). The mother of Samuel, the last judge of Israel (1 Sm 1—2).

Hebrews (HEE-brooz). Last of the Letters of the New Testament.

Hebron (HEE-bruhn). A city in the hill country of Judah, this was the city from which David reigned for seven years before he was made king of the united kingdom of the northern and southern tribes of Israel (2 Sm 2:11).

Hellenists (HEL-uh-nists). Jews from outside Palestine who took Greek as their primary language and adopted Greek ideas and practices (Acts 6:1).

Herod (HER-uhd). The Herodian family, which though Jewish in religion was Idumean in origin. Herod "the Great" was appointed by Rome as King of Judea in 40 B.C. He slaughtered the infants at Bethlehem (Mt 2:16).

Archelaus (ahr-kuh-LAY-uhs) was ethnarch of Judea 4 B.C. to 6 A.D. **Antipas (AN-tee-pahs)** was tetrach of Galilee and Perea until 39 A.D. He married his brother's wife Herodias and beheaded John the Baptist. **Philip (FIL-uhp)**, tetrach of Trachonitis, was a mild man. His grandson, Herod **Agrippa (uh-GRIP-uh) I**, was king of all Palestine from 41 to 44 A.D. and put James to death (Acts 12:2). His son, Agrippa II, ruled in Trachonitis until 100 A.D. The latter heard Paul's defense (Acts 25:23ff).

Herodians (hi-ROH-dee-unz). Partisans and courtiers of the reigning dynasty of the Herods. Although they were Jews in religion, their spirit was Gentile. They conspired with their enemies, the Pharisees, against Jesus (Mt 22:16).

Hezekiah (hez-uh-KAI-uh). Son and successor of Ahaz as King of Judah for 29 years (2 Kgs 18—20), who reformed the worship (2 Kgs 18:4ff) and was an ancestor of Jesus (Mt 1:9f).

Hezron (HEZ-ruhn). An ancestor of Jesus (Mt 1:3).

Hilkiah (hil-KAI-uh). The father of Eliakim (Is 22:20). Name of six other persons (mostly priests) in Israel.

Holocausts (HAHL-oh-kosts). In the ancient sacrifices only the blood and certain parts of the victim were offered to God; the rest was divided among the priest and faithful who had offered it (Lv 7:11-21). A holocaust (from the Greek "wholly burnt") was a sacrifice in which an entire animal except its hide was consumed in the fire on the altar, with the primary purpose of rendering glory to God (Lv 1:1ff).

Horeb (HAWR-eb). The mountain at which Moses received his commission (Ex 3:1) and to which Elijah fled (1 Kgs 19:9).

Hosanna (hoh-ZAH-nuh). Hebrew expression signifying "May God save," used in the course of Jewish feasts (Ps 118:25f). It served as an acclamation during Christ's entrance into Jerusalem, in the sense of "Long live," and it is always chanted during the course of the Liturgy (Mt 21:9).

Hosea (hoh-ZAY-uh). Third of the 12 Minor Prophets of the Old Testament, who spoke of his difficult relationship with his wife as being parallel to the relationship between God and the people of Israel.

Hur (huhr). A contemporary of Moses who, along with Aaron, helped hold Moses' arms upright during Israel's battle with Amalek (Ex 17:10ff).

Iconium (i-KOH-nee-uhm). A city in Asia Minor visited by Paul (Acts 13:51—14:6.21).

Isaac (AI-zik). Son of Abraham (Gn 17:19), whose immolation ordered by God, then prevented, prefigures the sacrifice of Christ (Gn 22).

Isaiah (ai-SAY-uh). First of the 4 Major Prophets of the Old Testament, who prophesied especially about the Passion of our Lord. Isaiah was a great prophet of Israel from 740 to 700 B.C. Chapters 40 to 55 of the Book named after him were probably written much later during the Babylonian Exile (587-539 B.C.) and chapters 56 to 66 after the Exile.

Iscariot (is KAR-ee-uht). Surname of Judas, the apostle who betrayed Jesus (Mt 26:14).

Isles (ailz). Dry land as opposed to water (Is 42:15), but its extended meaning was one of the farthest regions of the earth (Ps 72:10; Is 41:5).

Israel (IZ-ray-uhl). Name given by God to Jacob, the son of Isaac (Gn 32:29). Also used for his descendants, the twelve tribes of the Hebrews, and later the ten northern tribes led by Ephraim, as well as of the Church (the new Israel: Gal 6:16).

Israelites (IZ-ray-uh-laits). People of Israel (Acts 10:36).

Ituraea (i-TYOO-ree-uh). A region northwest of Palestine beyond the Jordan ruled by Herod Philip (Lk 3:1).

Jaar (JAY-uhr). Another name for Kiriath-jearim, one of the Canaanite towns and a center of Baal worship, where the Ark remained for a few generations (Ps 132:6).

Jacob (JAY-kuhb). Son of Isaac and Rebekah and twin brother of Esau, whose birthright he took (Gn 25). He was renamed Israel by God (Gn 32:29). The name also refers to the father of Joseph, foster father of Jesus (Mt 1:16).

Jairus (JAI-ruhs). The synagogue-ruler whose daughter Jesus raised from the dead (Mk 5:22; 8:41).

James (jaymz). Name of three persons: (1) the apostle James ("the less"), son of Alphaeus (Mt 10:3); (2) the apostle James ("the greater"), son of Zebedee and brother of John the apostle who died as a martyr during the persecution of Herod Agrippa (Acts 12:2); (3) James, the "brother of the Lord," probably the son of Mary of Clopas, who was the first bishop of Jerusalem, martyred in 62, and presumed author of one of the Letters of the New Testament (Gal 1:19; Mt 13:55).

Javan (JAY-vuhn). A name that stands for the cities on the west coast of Asia Minor (Is 66:19; Ez 27:13).

Jechoniah (jek-uh-NAI-uh). A variant of Jehoiachin, son of Jehoiakim, grandson of Josiah (1 Chr 3:15, 17), and ancestor of Jesus (Mt 1:11f).

Jehoshaphat (ji-HOSH-uh-fat). Son and successor of Asaph as King of Judah for 25 years (1 Kgs 22:42) and ancestor of Jesus (Mt 1:8).

Jeremiah (jer-uh-MAI-uh). Second of the 4 Major Prophets, who prefigures the Messiah mainly by his personal sufferings.

Jericho (JER-uh-koh). An ancient city at the southern end of the Jordan Valley, also called the City of Palms (Dt 34:3), which was miraculously captured by Joshua as the opening wedge of his battle to take Canaan (Jos 6). It was also the site of Jesus' healing of the blind Bartimaeus (Mk 10:46).

Jerusalem (ji-ROO-suh-luhm). Capital of Israel, conquered by David (also called City of David), known as the city of God (Heb 12:22; Rv 3:12) and the Holy City (Mt 4:5; 27:53). The Church is the new Jerusalem and the image of the Heavenly Jerusalem (Gal 4:26; Rv 21:1—22:5).

Jesse (JES-ee). The Father of David (Is 11:1) and an ancestor of Jesus (Mt 1:6).

Jesu (JAY-zoo). Diminutive and familiar form of Jesus.

Jesus (JEE-zuhs). The personal name of the Son of God made man, which means: "The Lord is salvation" or "Savior," and denotes his mission: to save humans from death and sin and make them once more children of God and heirs of heaven.

Jethro (JETH-roh). The father-in-law of Moses (Ex 3:1), he is also called

Reuel (Ex 2:18) and Hobab (Nm 10:29). He was a priest of Midian.

Joanna (joh-AN-uh). A woman who helped to support Jesus and his followers (Lk 8:2) and who went to the tomb on Easter Sunday (Lk 24:10).

Job (johb). First of the 7 Wisdom Books of the Old Testament.

Joel (JOH-uhl). Second of the 12 Minor Prophets of the Old Testament.

John (jon). Son of Zebedee and brother of James the Greater who became an apostle and wrote the last of the 4 gospels; three of the Catholic Letters are also attributed to him. Another John is the author of the Book of Revelation.

John the Baptist (jon thuh BAP-tist). Son of Zechariah and Elizabeth (Lk 1:5ff), who was Christ's precursor.

Jonah (JOH-nuh). Fifth of the 12 Minor Prophets of the Old Testament, whose book serves as a parable reminding Israel that God is Lord of all peoples upon the earth.

Joram (JAWR-uhm). Son and successor of Jehoshaphat as King of Judah (1 Kgs 22:51) and an ancestor of Jesus (Mt 1:8). Also called Jehoram.

Jordan (JAWR-duhn). The largest river in Palestine, which played a large part in the history of Israel and the early public life of Christ (Mt 3:13-17).

Joseph (JOH-sif). Son of Jacob and Rachel (Gn 30:24). He is regarded by the Church as a figure of Joseph, the "just man," who was the spouse of the Virgin Mary and foster father of Christ (Mt 1:18ff).

Joses (JOH-siz). Cousin of Jesus (Mk 6:3—called Joseph in Mt 13:55). Son of Mary (Mk 15:40, 47), wife of Clopas (Jn 19:25—called Joseph in Mt 27:56).

Joshua (JOSH-yoo-uh). First of the 3 Books that follow the Pentateuch.

Josiah (joh-SAI-uh). Son and successor of Amon as King of Judah (2 Kgs 21:24), who reformed religion and repaired the temple, and was an ancestor of Jesus (Mt 1:10f).

Jotham (JOH-thuhm). King of Judah in the time of Isaiah (2 Kgs 15:32) and an ancestor of Jesus (Mt 1:9).

Judah (JOO-duh). Son of Jacob (Gn 29:35) and ancestor of the tribe of Israel whose capital was Jerusalem. After the schism of the 10 northern tribes it became the Kingdom of Judah or Judea. He was an ancestor of Jesus (Mt 1:3).

Judas (JOO-duhs). Name of five persons: (1) Judas (Jude Thaddeus) the apostle (Lk 6:16; Mt 10:3); (2) Judas, a "brother of the Lord," and presumed author of the "Letter of Jude" (Mk 6:3); (3) Judas, surnamed Barsabbas, sent by the apostles to Antioch (Acts 15:22, 32); (4) Judas Iscariot, who betrayed Jesus (Mt 10:4); (5) Judas of Damascus at whose house Paul lodged after his conversion (Acts 9:11).

Jude (jood). See Judas: 2.

Judea (joo-DEE-uh). The most southern part of the three districts of Palestine west of the Jordan. Together with Samaria and Idumea it formed the Roman province of Judea with its capital at Jerusalem.

Judean (joo-DEE-uhn). Adjectival form of Judea.

Judges (JUHJ-iz). Second of the 3 Books that follow the Pentateuch.

Judith (JOO-dith). Tenth of the 13 Historical Books of the Old Testament.

Justus (JUHS-tuhs). Surname of Joseph Barsabbas (Acts 1:23).

Kidron (KAI-druhn). Valley along the east side of Jerusalem that joins the Valley of Hinnom and extends 20 miles to the Dead Sea.

Kings (kings). Third and fourth of the 13 Historical Books of the Old Testament.

Kor (also spelled cor) (kor). An indeterminate large weight measure.

Lamb of God (lam uhv god). A title of Jesus to show that he bears the sins of mankind and offers himself as a sacrificial lamb, prefigured by the paschal lamb through whose blood the Israelites were saved from their Egyptian bondage (Jn 1:29).

Lamentations (lam-en-TAY-shuhnz). Third of the 18 Prophetic Books of the Old Testament.

Lazarus (LAZ-uhr-uhs). Brother of Martha and Mary (Jn 11:5). He was raised from the dead by Jesus (Jn 11:43ff) and was present at the supper in his honor (Jn 12:2). This is also the name of the poor man in the parable of Lazarus and the rich man who would not assist him (Lk 16:20ff).

Law (law). Primarily the ten commandments that God gave to the chosen people, which were concerned mostly with external obedience. The new law was instituted by Christ and is based on charity (which sums up the ten commandments). It requires both internal and external obedience.

Lebanon (LEB-uh-nuhn). Mountainous chain north of Palestine, heavily wooded and known especially for its cedars (Jgs 9:15; Is 35:2).

Levi (LEE-vai). Name of two persons. (1) The son of Jacob and Leah (Gn 29:34), who gave his name to a tribe of Israel (Mal 2:4). (2) The tax collector who became an apostle and is called Matthew (Mt 9:9ff), the eventual author of the first gospel.

Levites (LEE-vaits). Members of the tribe of Levi, who assisted the priests in temple worship. In the parable of the Good Samaritan the Levite failed to help his neighbor (Lk 10:32).

Leviticus (li-VIT-i-kuhs). Third Book of the Pentateuch.

Libya (LIB-ee-uh). Ancient Greek name for northern Africa west of Egypt, which has Cyrene as one of its cities (Acts 2:10).

Lord (lawrd). Originally a title that signified nothing more than "sir." From the 3rd century B.C. onward, the Jews replaced the ineffable name "Yahweh" with "Adonai" (Lord) in reading the Bible. Applied to Jesus by the first Christians, the name "Lord" was thus equivalent to an affirmation of his divinity (Acts 2:36).

Lud (luhd). The name for two separate regions, one in Asia Minor (Is 66:19; probably Lydia) and one in Africa (Jer 46:9; Ez 30:5).

Luke (look). Companion of Paul and author of the third gospel and the Acts of the Apostles.

Lyre (LAI-uhr). A string musical instrument used to praise the Lord (Ps 81:3).

Lysanias (li-SAY-nee-uhs). Tetrarch of Abilene (Lk 3:1), a small region in Lebanon.

Lystra (LIS-truh). A city in Lycaonia (Asia Minor) where Paul and Barnabas were mistaken for Zeus and Hermes (Acts 14:6-18).

Maccabees (MAK-uh-beez). Twelfth and thirteenth of the 13 Historical Books of the Old Testament.

Macedonia (mas-uh-DOH-nee-uh). A Roman province north of Greece in the Balkans that was visited by Paul (1 Thes 1:7).

Magdala (MAG-duh-luh). A town on the northwest shore of the Sea of Galilee, 3 miles north of Tiberias (Mt 15:39), home of Mary Magdalene (Jn 19:25).

Magdalene (MAG-duh-luhn). Alternate surname of Mary of Magdala, who followed the body of Jesus to the grave (Mt 27:61) and was the first to learn of the resurrection (Mt 28:1-8).

Malachi (MAL-uh-kai). Last of the 12 Minor Prophets of the Old Testament.

Malchiah (mal-KAI-uh). A prince who owned the cistern into which Jeremiah was thrown in an assassination attempt. He was rescued by Ebedmelech (Jer 38:6ff).

Malchus (MAL-kuhs). A servant of the high priest whose ear Peter cut off with a sword (Jn 18:10).

Mammon (MAM-uhn). A word derived from the Aramaic *mamona,* meaning property, both in the New Testament and in rabbinic writings.

Mamre (MAM-ree). A site near Hebron. It was marked off with an ancient oak tree and was probably a sanctuary.

Man (man). In the eyes of the Jews, a being dependent on God for his life. The Christian has two selves within him: the "old self," drawn to evil, made up of body and soul; and the "new self" created by the Holy Spirit, who must triumph over sin (Rom 6:6).

Manna (MAN-uh). Food miraculously supplied by God to the Israelites during their 40 years in the desert (Nu 11:9), a type of the Eucharist—the Bread from heaven (Jn 6:31ff).

Mark (mahrk). Companion of Paul and author of the second gospel.

Martha (MAHR-thuh). Sister of Mary (Lk 10:38) and Lazarus (Jn 11:1).

Mary (MAY-ree). The Virgin, mother of Jesus (Mt 1:18ff; Lk 2:6). Mary was also the name of the mother of James and Joses (Mt 27:56), who was present at the crucifixion and at the burial of Jesus (Mt 27:61) as well as on the morning of the resurrection (Mt 28:1). She seems to be the same as Mary the wife of Clopas (Jn 19:25). This is also the name of the sister of Martha and Lazarus (Lk 10:38; Jn 11:1) and of the woman from Magdala who was a follower of Jesus (*see* **Magadlene**).

Massah (MAS-uh). Name given to the site of the rock in Horeb from which Moses drew water for the rebellious Israelites (Ex 17:1-7; Ps 95:8f). The name is coupled with Meribah (Dt 33:8).

Matthan (MATH-an). Grandfather of Joseph, Mary's husband (Mt 1:15).

Matthew (MATH-yoo). One of the twelve apostles identified with Levi, son of Alphaeus, and a tax collector (Mt 9:9; Mk 2:14). He is regarded as the author of the gospel that bears his name.

Matthias (muh-THAI-uhs). The disciple chosen by lot to replace Judas Iscariot (Acts 1:24ff).

Medad (MEE-dad). One who prophesied in the Israelite camp in the wilderness (Nm 11:26ff).

Medes (meedz). Inhabitants of the land of Media, some of whom were in Jerusalem on the day of Pentecost (Acts 2:9).

Melchizedek (mel-KIZ-uh-dek). King of Salem and priest of God who offered bread and wine as an unbloody sacrifice in thanksgiving for Abraham's victory over the Eastern Kings (Gn 14:18-20). The Church sees therein the figure of the sacrifice of Jesus, "a priest forever according to the order of Melchizedek" (Ps 110:4; Heb 5:6, 10; 6:20; 7:11, 17).

Meribah (MER-i-buh). Hebrew word signifying "the (place of the) quarreling" that served to designate the same site as Massah (Ex 17:7).

Mesopotamia (mes-uh-puh-TAY-mee-uh). The area between the Tigris and the Euphrates rivers, some of whose inhabitants were in Jerusalem on the day of Pentecost (Acts 2:9). It is Iraq today.

Messiah (muh-SAI-uh). A Hebrew word signifying "one who has been anointed." The kings of Israel were anointed in the name of God (1 Sm 9:16). The term Messiah later was used to designate a "future king" who would make all things new (Dn 9:25-26). This son of David, expected by the Jewish nation, was the Messiah par excellence (Mk 10:47-48), a term that has been rendered in Greek by *Christos.* This was a common name that ultimately became a title for Jesus the Savior (Rm 1:1).

Micah (MAI-kuh). Sixth of the 12 Minor Prophets of the Old Testament.

Midian (MID-ee-uhn). Son of Abraham by Keturah (Gn 25:1-6), whose descendants became a tribe of nomads and merchants called Midianites (Nm 31:1-12, 32-34).

Moriah (muh-RAI-uh). The place where Abraham was told to offer up Isaac (Gn 22:2).

Moses (MOH-zis). The leader and lawgiver of the Israelites, who successfully brought them out of Egypt (Ex 12:50) through the desert (Ex 19ff), to the shores of the Jordan. On Mount Sinai he received the law, which contained the ethical teaching (Rom 5:12ff).

Mosoch (MOH-sok). An area believed to be in the vicinity of Armenia.

Mount of Olives (mount uhv OL-uhvz). A mountain with three summits east of Jerusalem. Gethsemane is on its lower slope. It is closely associated with the life of Jesus (Mk 11:1; 14:26). *See also* **Olivet.**

Myrrh (mir). An oderous resin (Mt 2:11).

Naaman (NAY-uh-muhn). A general of the king of Damascus who was healed of his leprosy by Elisha (2 Kgs 5).

Nahshon (NAH-shon). The son of Amminadab (1 Chr 2:10, 11) and ancestor of Jesus (Mt 1:4).

Nahum (NAY-huhm). Seventh of the 12 Minor Prophets of the Old Testament.

Name (naym). Identical with the person it designates. The name of God indicates God himself and all his perfections. "To act in the name" of someone means to participate in the reality (and its power) expressed by this name. Change of vocation also requires a new name (e.g., Peter).

Naphtali (NAF-tuh-lee). One of Jacob's sons (Gn 46:24), who gave his name to one of the twelve tribes (Jos 19:32-39) that later formed part of Galilee.

Nathan (NAY-thuhn). (1) Son of David by Bathsheba (2 Sm 5:13) and an ancestor of Jesus (Lk 3:31). (2) A prophet who dissuaded David from building the temple and promised him a sure succession (2 Sm 7:1ff), and who rebuked him when he sinned (2 Sm 12:1ff).

Nazarene (NAZ-uh-reen). A word derived from Nazareth, the hometown of Christ. He was often called a Nazarene (Mt 2:23). Another form of the name is "Nazorean."

Nazareth (NAZ-uh-rith). A town in low Galilee, which is the hometown of Mary and Joseph, mother and foster father of Jesus (Lk 1:26; 2:4) and where Jesus spent his early life (Mt 2:23).

Nazirite (NAZ-uh-rait). One who is set apart for service of the LORD by a vow. Nazarites were not to cut their hair, nor drink wine, nor partake of any fruit of the vine.

Nazorean (naz-uh-REE-uhn). An alternate form of "Nazarene" (Mt 2:23).

Nehemiah (nee-huh-MAI-uh). Cup-bearer of the Persian King Cyrus, who helped to reestablish the Jewish commonwealth after the Babylonian Exile and is the main character of the eighth of the 13 Historical Books of the Old Testament.

Neighbor (NAY-buhr). A word corresponding to four Hebrew terms that signify respectively: brother, country-man, fellow tribesman, and member of the same race (Ex 20:17). It is these whom the Israelite was commanded to love, not foreigners (Lv 19:33f). Jesus declares that one's neighbor is every person, even one belonging to a hostile group (Lk 10:29-37).

Ner (nuhr). The father of Abner, the commander of the army of King Saul of Israel (1 Sm 26:5).

Netherworld (NETH-uhr-wuhrld). The ancient concept of the abode of the dead (in Hebrew: "sheol"), which supposed no activity or lofty emotion among the deceased, who were pictured as surrounded by the darkness of oblivion (Ps 16:10).

Nicanor (nai-KAY-nuhr). One of the seven deacons of the Church at Jerusalem (Acts 6:5).

Nicholas (NIK-uh-luhs). A convert to Judaism from Antioch who became one of the seven deacons of the Church at Jerusalem (Acts 6:5).

Nicodemus (nik-uh-DEE-muhs). Greek name borne by an influential member of the Sanhedrin, who came to Jesus by night and later interceded for him when the plot was hatched that ended in his death (Jn 3:1-10; 7:50f).

Nineveh (NIN-uh-vuh). The later capital of Assyria, the great city on the Upper Tigris, whose inhabitants repented at the preaching of the Prophet Jonah (Jon 3:1ff).

Noah (NOH-uh). Patriarch who with his family was saved in the Ark from the Flood (Gn 6ff).

Nun (nuhn). Father of Joshua (Nm 11:28).

Obadiah (oh-buh-DAI-uh). Fourth of the 12 Minor Prophets of the Old Testament.

Obed (OH-bid). Son of Boaz and Ruth (Ru 4:17) and an ancestor of Jesus (Mt 1:5f).

Olivet (OL-i-vet). Alternative name for the Mount of Olives—a one mile long ridge with four identifiable summits, east of Jerusalem beyond the Valley of Jehoshaphat, through which flows the Kidron. Gethsemane, Bethphage, and Bethany lie along its slopes (Acts 1:12).

Omega (oh-MEG-uh). Last letter of the Greek alphabet. Used with "Alpha," it means the first and the last (Rv 1:8).

Ophir (OH-fuhr). A region on the coast of southern Arabia or eastern Africa—famous for its gold (Ps 45:10).

Pamphylia (pam-FIL-ee-uh). A small Roman province of southern Asia extending 75 miles along the Mediterranean coast and 30 miles inland to the Taurus mountains, some of whose inhabitants were in Jerusalem on the day of Pentecost (Acts 2:10).

Paraclete (PAR-uh-kleet). A word used in the Gospel of John for the Holy Spirit. It could be translated as "comforter," "consoler," "advocate," etc. The paraclete will reveal that which the disciples could not understand (Jn 14:26; 16:13). He is the Spirit of Truth (Jn 14:16).

Parapet (PAR-uh-pet). The railing that one was to build on the edge of all roofs in Israel.

Parmenas (PAHR-muh-nuhs). One of the seven deacons of the Church at Jerusalem (Acts 6:5).

Parthians (PAHR-thee-uhnz). Inhabitants of the Parthian Empire to the east, known today as Iran, some of whom were in Jerusalem on the day of Pentecost (Acts 2:9).

Paschal (PAS-kuhl). An adjective referring to the Passover of the Old Testament and the Passover of the New (i.e., Easter).

Passover (PAS-oh-vuhr). Feast instituted to commemorate the departure from Egypt with the "passing over" of the angel of death and the crossing of the Red Sea (Dt 16:1-8). At this observance (Last Supper) Jesus instituted the Eucharist (Mt 26:26ff).

Patriarchs (PAY-tree-ahrks). Name given to those who founded the Hebrew race and nation. The New Testament applies it to Abraham (Heb 7:4), the sons of Jacob (Acts 7:8, 9), and David (Acts 2:29).

Pentateuch (PENT-uh-took). The first five Books of the Old Testament.

Pentecost (PEN-ti-kost). The Jewish feast, fifty days after Passover, that recalled the giving of the law and offered in thanks the firstfruits of the wheat harvest (Lv 23:15-22). At Pentecost the Holy Spirit came upon the apostles and the others gathered in the Upper Room (Acts 2:1ff), marking the birthday of the Church and inaugurating the Christian feast of Pentecost.

People of God (PEE-puhl uhv god). Term by which Israel is designated throughout the Bible. God has gratuitously chosen her and she is his own possession (Dt 7:6). God dwells in her midst (Ex 25:8). The people is thus holy and set apart from other peoples (Lv 20:24). In its turn, Christianity is also called the People God claims for his own, but it rejects any kind of national particularism (1 Pt 2:9).

Perez (PEE-riz). Son of Judah by Tamar (Gn 28:29) and an ancestor of Jesus (Mt 1:3).

Perga (PURH-guh). A city in Pamphylia (Asia Minor). It was visited by Paul and Barnabas (Acts 13:13f).

Persians (PUHR-zhuhnz). Originally, a Median tribe that settled in Persia, east of the Persian Gulf, whose members are mentioned in 2 Chr 36:20). Scripture also mentions Cyrus the Great who released the captive Jews (Ezr 1:1); Darius, who confirmed the decree of Cyrus (Ezr 6:1), and Artaxerxes (Ezr 4:7; 7:1).

Peter (PEE-tuhr). One of the twelve apostles (Mt 10:2) and author of two of the seven Catholic Letters of the New Testament. His name was Simon, but he was surnamed Cephas (Jn 1:42) or its Greek equivalent Peter. He was made the first Pope of the Church by Jesus (Mt 16:16ff).

Phanuel (fuh-NYOO-uhl). Father of Anna (Lk 2:36).

Pharaoh (FAR-oh). Title of Egyptian rulers.

Pharisees (FAR-uh-seez). Jewish sect that sought the perfect expression of spiritual life through strict observance of the law and tradition alone. Some of its members were greatly at odds with Jesus (Jn 9:16, 22).

Philemon (fi-LEE-muhn). One of Paul's Letters of the New Testament.

Philip (FIL-ip). Name borne by the apostle from Bethsaida (Jn 1:43f), the deacon (Acts 6:5), the tetrarch, son of Herod the Great and Cleopatra (Lk 3:1), and Herod Philip, son of Herod the Great and Mariamne (Mt 14:3).

Philippi (fi-LIP-ai). City of Macedonia, named after Philip, father of Alexander the Great. It was evangelized by Paul (Acts 16:12ff).

Philippians (Fi-LIP-ee-uhnz). Inhabitants of Philippi to whom Paul wrote one of the Letters of the New Testament.

Phrygia (FRIJ-ee-uh). A province in southwest Asia Minor, where Paul preached on his 2nd and 3rd missionary journeys (Acts 16:6; 18:23), some of whose inhabitants were in Jerusalem on the day of Pentecost (Acts 2:10).

Pilate (PAI-luht). The fifth procurator or governmental representative of Rome in Palestine 26-36 A.D., who condemned Jesus to death (Jn 19:16).

Pisidia (pi-SID-ee-uh). One of the small Roman provinces in southern Asia Minor north of Pamphylia, visited by Paul on his 1st and 2nd missionary journeys (Acts 13:14-50; 14:21-24).

Pontius (PON-shuhs). First name of Pilate (Lk 3:1).

Pontus (PON-tuhs). A large province of northern Asia Minor located along the Black Sea, some of whose inhabitants were in Jerusalem on the day of Pentecost (Acts 2:9).

Poor (poor). Originally, a word with a purely economic and social meaning. Gradually, it took on the meaning of humble, modest, small, the little people often oppressed by the rich and powerful but who remained faithful to God (Am 2:6f). It was in this sense that Jesus said: "Blessed are you who are poor" (Lk 6:20).

Praetorium (pri-TAWR-ee-uhm). The residence of a Roman praetor, or his military headquarters, where he had his guard and held court. The procurators of Judea in the time of Christ had their praetorium at Caesarea, in the palace of Herod the Great (Acts 23:35). Tradition makes the fortress called Antonia the praetorium where Christ was tried (Mk 15:16).

Prochorus (PROK-uh-ruhs). One of the first seven deacons of the Church at Jerusalem (Acts 6:5).

Promise (PROM-uhs). A term of Greek origin that designates and interprets the meaning of all the previous prophetic history of the chosen people in their Messianic mission. The Old Testament gave promise of Christ, but it is in Christ that all this preparatory and figurative history finds its perfect fulfillment (Mt 5:17; Acts 13:32f; Rom 15:8; 2 Cor 1:20; Gal 3:14).

Prophets (PROF-its). Men chosen by God to speak in his name. They were the teachers and guardians of the religion of Israel, at times advisers to kings, defenders of the poor and oppressed, and heralds of the future Messiah and his kingdom.

Proverbs (PROV-uhrbs). Third of the 7 Wisdom Books of the Old Testament.

Psalms (sahmz). Second of the 7 Wisdom Books of the Old Testament.

Put (poot). A region most probably in Africa (Jer 46:9).

Qoheleth (koh-HEL-ith). The name of the author of the Book of Ecclesiastes. The name means "preacher," and this might be a symbolic name. His work is marked by cynicism and yet respect for the fact that the will of God is a mystery.

Quirinius (kwi-RIN-ee-uhs). Roman governor of Syria in 6-9 B.C., at the time of the birth of Jesus in Bethlehem (Lk 2:2).

Rabbi (RAB-ai). A title for the teachers of the law. It means "my master" (Mt 23:7-11; Jn 1:38) and was often applied to Christ.

Rahab (RAY-hab). A non-Jewish woman who played a large role in the capture of Jericho (Jos 2:1) and became the mother of Boaz, great grandmother of King David and ancestor of Jesus (Mt 1:5).

Ram (ram). An ancestor of David (Ru 4:19) and of Jesus (Mt 1:4).

Raqa (RAH-kah). An Aramaic word probably meaning "fool," "imbecile," or "blockhead"—a term of abuse (Mt 5:22).

Redemption (ree-DEMP-shuhn). Deliverance procured by payment of a ransom. It refers to the deliverance of the human race from sin, its effects and punishments, by Jesus Christ, who by shedding his blood on the cross paid the price of our salvation (Rom 3:24). It was prefigured by the deliverance of Israel from bondage in Egypt and Babylonia.

Rehoboam (ree-huh-BOH-uhm). Son and successor of King Solomon (1 Kgs 11:43) and ancestor of Jesus (Mt 1:7).

Remnant (REM-nuhnt). An expression used by the prophets designating the survivors of great catastrophes (Gn 7:1f; Is 6:13) who will remain the depositories of the promise (Mi 4:6f) and help in the restoration (Is 37:31f).

Resurrection (res-uhr-REK-shuhn). The resurrection of Jesus, which became the fundamental historical fact, the principal witness of his divinity (1 Cor 15:4, 12). It is also the divine judgment that has ordered the defeat of death and pledges salvation and resurrection to the faithful (Rom 4:25; Col 2:12ff).

Revelation (rev-uh-LAY-shuhn). The only apocalyptic book of the New Testament. It speaks about the need to give witness to one's faith while one awaits the end of time.

River (RIV-uhr). A term that standing alone refers to the Euphrates River, the longest and most important river in Western Asia (Ps 72:8; Zec 9:10).

Romans (ROH-muhnz). One of Paul's Letters of the New Testament.

Rome (rohm). Capital of the Roman Empire, which like Babylon became a symbol of organized paganism and opposition to Christianity. The city also had a small Christian community from the forties onward. Both Peter and Paul were martyred there.

Rufus (ROO-fuhs). Son of Simon of Cyrene and brother of Alexander, mentioned during the way of the cross (Mk 15:21).

Ruth (rooth). A Moabite woman who married an Israelite, was widowed, and returned to Jerusalem with her mother-in-law, and became the ancestor of David and Jesus (Mt 1:5). Also, the last of the three Books that follow the Pentateuch.

Sabbath (SAB-uhth). Seventh day of the week, consecrated to God, on which no work could be performed (Dt 5:12-15). Among Christians, the day after the sabbath gradually became the sabbath or first day in commemoration of the resurrection of Christ—hence "the Lord's day" (Jn 20:19ff; Acts 20:7).

Sadducees (SAD-joo-seez). A religious party of the Jews who were the nationalists of their day. They believed in God but rejected the oral traditions of their forefathers and denied the resurrection of human beings and the existence of angels. They opposed Jesus (Mt 22:23ff) and the apostolic Church (Acts 5:17).

Saints (saynts). A common Old Testament term to designate those who belong to God that was applied in the New Testament to those who believed in Christ. It occurs first in Acts 9:13 and is frequent in the writings of Paul. Those are saints who are separated from non-Christians, are attached to the glorious Christ, and are sanctified by the indwelling of the Holy Spirit.

Salem (SAY-luhm). The city ruled by Melchizedek (Gen 14:18), most probably a name for Jerusalem.

Salmon (SAL-muhn). Father of Boaz (called Salma in 1 Chr 2:11) and ancestor of Jesus (Mt 1:4).

Salome (suh-LOH-mee). One of the women present at the crucifixion of Jesus (Mt 15:40) and at the empty tomb (Mk 16:1).

Salvation (sal-VAY-shuhn). A term referring to the work of God on behalf of his people's deliverance (Ps 33:16f; Is 31:1; Hos 5:13—6:3) and then personal deliverance (Ps 51:14). In the New Testament it means the work of spiritual deliverance—remission from sin (Lk 17:19) and the liberation from the servitude that sin brings to human beings (Mt 1:21; Lk 1:77; Acts 5:31) and leading Christians to their highest destiny (Rom 1:16; 5:9f; 1 Cor 15:2; Jas 1:21).

Samaria (suh-MAYR-ee-uh). Capital of the kingdom of Israel after the schism of the ten tribes that was destroyed in 721 B.C. by Sargon (2 Kgs 18:9-12). It was rebuilt by Herod the Great and called Sebaste and Philip preached the gospel there (Acts 8:5-9).

Samaritans (suh-MAYR-uh-tuhnz). Inhabitants of the central region of Palestine between Judea and Galilee who were a mixed race of Israelites and Assyrian colonists, and very hostile to the Jews at the time of Christ. Our Lord passed through their country more than once, and preached and worked miracles among the people. He also spoke well of them (Lk 10:30-37), defended them (Lk 9:51-56), and commanded that the gospel be preached to them.

Samuel (SAM-yoo-uhl). The greatest of the Judges (1 Sm 7:15) and a prophet (1 Sm 9:9) instrumental in instituting the monarchy (1 Sm 9ff). The first two of the 13 Historical Books of the Old Testament are named after him.

Sanhedrin (san-HEE-druhn). Civil and religious council of the Jews, composed of 71 members and presided over by the high priest.

Sapphires (SAf-airz). Precious stones (Is 54:11).

Sarah (SAR-uh). Wife of Abraham who conceived in old age and gave him a son (Isaac) in accord with God's promise (Heb 11:11). Her name was changed by God from Sarai to Sarah (Gn 17:15).

Sarai (SAIR-ai). See **Sarah**.

Satan (SAY-tuhn). God's great adversary who seeks to destroy human beings (Mt 13:19, 28). This devil or prince of demons is a spirit completely given up to evil. By dying on the cross Christ crushed his power (Rv 20:1ff).

Saul (sawl). First King of the Israelites around 1020-1000 B.C. (1 Sm 10:17ff). This is also the Hebrew/Aramaic form of the name of the man known as Paul (the Greco/Roman version), who became a great apostle of the Good News to the Gentiles (Acts 13:9).

Scribes (skraibz). Jews devoted to the study of the law (Mt 2:4; 17:10).

Scriptures (SKRIP-chuhrs). The inspired Books of the Old Testament, the work of the Holy Spirit, comprising the law, the prophets, and the writings (Foreword to the Book of Sirach). Christianity added its own writings: the gospels and letters of the New Testament (1 Tm 5:18; 2 Tm 3:16; 2 Pt 3:14-16).

Scythian (SITH-ee-uhn). A member of a nomadic people from central Asia.

Sea (see). A term that when standing alone refers to the Mediterranean Sea (Ps 80:12).

Sea of Galilee (see uhv GAL-uh-lee). A lake only 13 miles long and 8 miles wide, 60 miles north of Jerusalem, subject to sudden violent storms (Mt 8:24). Also called the Sea of Gennesaret (Lk 5:1) and the Sea of Tiberias (Jn 6:1).

Seba (SEE-buh). An unknown territory, possibly in Africa.

Seraphim (SER-uh-fim). An angel with six wings who stands in the presence of God (Is 6). The name means the "fiery ones."

Servant (SUHR-vuhnt). An expression applied to the people of Israel within the framework of the covenant (Ex 7:16; Pss 69:37; 102:15) and the faithful in general (Ps 34:1). It became a Messianic title as the result of its use by Deutero-Isaiah in the so-called Servant of Yahweh Songs (Is 42:1-9; 49:1-13; 50:4-11; 52:13—53:12) and as such is applied to Jesus (Mt 12:18; Acts 3:13).

Shaphat (SHAY-fat). The father of Elisha the prophet (1 Kgs 19:16).

Sharon (SHAR-uhn). Coastal plain between Joppa and Mount Carmel, a plane proverbial for its fertility, pasture lands, and beauty (Is 35:2).

Shealtiel (shee-AL-tee-uhl). Father of Zerubbabel (Ezr 3:2) and an ancestor of Jesus (Mt 1:12).

Sheba (SHEE-buh). The Kingdom of the Sabeans in southern Arabia, whose people are pictured as traders in precious stones and incense (Is 60:6).

Shebna (SHEB-nuh). Majordomo of King Hezekiah (Is 22:15ff).

Shekel (SHEK-uhl). A measure of precious metal. Each vendor would measure a given shekel against one's own sample shekel.

Shema Israel (shuh-MAH iz-RAY-uhl; -REE; IZ-ruhl). Ancient Jewish confession of faith recited daily by the pious. It is composed of three passages: Dt 6:4-9; 11:12-21; and Nm 15:37-41. The name comes from *Shema Yisrael* ("Hear, O Israel": Dt 6:4), the words with which the confession begins.

Shiloh (SHAI-loh). A sanctuary town in Israel and a site where the ark of the covenant was kept (1 Sm 4).

Shinar (SHAIN-ahr). Plain of Babylonia in which were located Babel, Erech, Accad, and Calneh (Gn 10:10) and where the Tower of Babel was built (Gn 11:1-9).

Shunem (SHOO-nuhm). A place in a very rich section of Palestine (2 Kgs 4:8), north of Jezreel and belonging to the tribe of Issachar (Jos 19:18).

Sidon (SAI-duhn). Phoenician port north of Tyre, on the Mediterranean (Mt 15:21). These two pagan cities served the evangelists as symbols of a corrupt civilization (Lk 10:13-15).

Silas (SAI-luhs). *See* **Silvanus.**

Siloam (sai-LOH-ahm). Pool situated south of the city of Jerusalem to which Jesus adverted in a talk about workmen killed there (Lk 13:4).

Silvanus (sil-VAY-nuhs). Also known as Silas, a Jerusalem Christian sent with Paul to Antioch (Acts 15:22ff) who later accompanied him on his 2nd missionary journey (Acts 15:40) and was imprisoned with him in Philippi (Acts 16:19ff).

Simeon (SIM-ee-uhn). Name of three persons: (1) the old man who received the child Jesus in his arms at the temple (Lk 2:25-35); (2) an influential member of the Christian community at Antioch (Acts 13:1); (3) Peter the apostle, according to his Hebrew name (Acts 15:14). (He is also called Simon.)

Simon (SAI-muhn). Name of several persons, including: (1) the father of Judas Iscariot (Jn 13:2); (2) the prince of the apostles, later called Peter or Simon Peter (Jn 20:1-9); (3) a Pharisee who entertained Jesus (Lk 7:40) and in whose house a woman anointed Jesus' feet.

Sinai (SAI-nai). A peninsula south of the Wilderness of Paran between the Gulf of Aqabah and Suez. Also applied to a wilderness (Ex 19:1), where Israel came after they left Egypt and to the mountain (Ex 19:20) where God gave Moses the law.

Sirach (SAI-ruhk). Last of the seven Wisdom Books of the Old Testament, whose author is Jesus, the son of Sirach (Sir 50:27).

Sodom (SOD-uhm). One of the cities destroyed by God because of their immorality (Gn 19:1ff). It became a symbol for God's judgment upon the sinful.

Solomon (SOL-uh-muhn). Son and successor of David, who was a pious king (1 Kgs 3:5, 7-12) but eventually lost much of the empire David had built up (1 Kgs 11:14ff) and led to discontent in Israel (1 Kgs 11:26ff). Also, an ancestor of Jesus (Mt 1:6).

Solomon's Portico (SOL-uh-mouhnz POR-ti-koh). A protected area in the outer court of the temple (Jn 10:23).

Son of Man (son uhv man). A Messianic title found in the Prophet Daniel (7:13f) and used by Jesus, who by means of it progressively revealed himself as the Messiah to the Jews. It expresses Christ's twofold destiny of suffering (Mk 8:31) and of glory (Mk 8:38).

Song of Songs (song uhv songs). Fifth of the 7 Wisdom Books of the Old Testament.

Sosthenes (SOS-thuh-nees). An associate of Paul in the First Letter to the Corinthians (1:1).

Stephen (STEE-vuhn). One of the seven deacons of the Church at Jerusalem (Acts 6:5) and the first martyr for Christ, who—like his Master—prayed for his executioners (Acts 7:60).

Sychar (SAI-kahr). Village of Samaria located near Jacob's well, where Jesus encountered the Samaritan woman (Jn 4:5).

Synagogue (SIN-uh-gog). A place where the Jews gathered on the sabbath to listen to the explanations of the Scriptures. Each locality had one in in which Jesus prayed and studied (Lk 4:20).

Syria (SIR-ee-uh). The region between Asia Minor to the north and Palestine to the south, whose chief cities were Damascus and Antioch. A Roman province to which Palestine was subordinated (Lk 2:2).

Talitha Koum (TAHL-uh-thuh koom). An Aramaic phrase meaning "Little girl, I say to you, arise," recorded by Mark 5:41 in the episode of the raising of Jairus's daughter.

Tamar (TAY-mahr). Canaanite woman who bore Perez and Zerah to her father-in-law Judah and became an ancestor of Jesus (Mt 1:3).

Tarshish (TAHR-shish). Phoenician colony in southern Spain, whose name denotes a center of smelting metallic ore (1 Kgs 10:22; Ps 72:10).

Tarsus (TAHR-suhs). Birthplace and early residence of the apostle Paul (Acts 21:39; see also Acts 9:30). It was the capital of the Roman province of Cilicia, and located at the confluence of East and West.

Temple (TEM-puhl). House of worship that was built by Solomon, destroyed and then rebuilt after the Babylonian Exile, and finally destroyed in 70 A.D. by the Romans. The Body of Christ is the new temple built at his resurrection. The Church is the spiritual temple made up of living bricks who are the baptized Christians.

Terebinth (TER-uh-binth). A tree, possibly an oak. Trees, especially ancient trees, were highly visible in a desert area and served as landmarks and shrine sites.

Tetrarch (TE-trahrk). Originally, a ruler of the fourth of a country. In Roman times it was employed merely as a title for a ruler over part of a divided kingdom or a prince below the rank of a king (Mt 14:1).

Thaddeus (THAD-ee-uhs). One of the twelve apostles. In certain texts he is called Lebbaeus. He is identified with Judas (Jude), brother of James "the less" (Mt 10:3).

Theophilus (thee-OF-uh-luhs). The personage to whom Luke addressed both his gospel and the Acts of the Apostles (Lk 1:3; Acts 1:1).

Thessalonians (thes-uh-LOH-nee-uhnz). Two of Paul's earliest Letters written to the people of Thessalonica, capital of the province of Macedonia (Acts 17:1-9).

Thomas (TOM-uhs). One of the twelve apostles, surnamed in Greek Didymus, which means "twin" (Jn 11:16; 20:24).

Tiberius Caesar (tai-BIHR-ee-uhs SEE-zuhr). The successor of Augustus Caesar from 14 to 37 A.D. as emperor of the Roman Empire (Lk 3:1).

Timaeus (tai-MEE-uhs). Father of Bartimaeus (Mk 10:46).

Timon (TAI-muhn). One of the seven deacons of the Church at Jerusalem (Acts 6:5).

Timothy (TIM-uh-thee). Son of a Greek father and a Jewish mother, who was converted by Paul, and became one of his most devoted colleagues. Two of the Letters of the New Testament are addressed to Timothy.

Titus (TAI-tuhs). A Greek convert whom Paul calls his true child in the faith. One of the Letters of the New Testament is addressed to Titus.

Tobit (TOH-bit). Ninth of the 13 Historical Books of the Old Testament.

Twelve, The (twelv, thuh). Proper name used by the evangelists for the twelve apostles (Mt 26:14; Mk 14:10; Lk 22:47; Jn 20:24).

Trachonitis (trak-uh-NAI-tis). A territory to the east of the Jordan. The eastern portion of Bashan (Lk 3:1).

Tubal (TOO-buhl). This is the name of an individual (Gn 10:2; 1 Chr 1:5) and an area. It was probably a city on the Black Sea.

Tyre (TAI-uhr). Phoenician city located on the rocky isle facing the eastern coast of the Mediterranean Sea (Mt 11:21f).

Ur (oor). The ancestral city of Abraham. It is unclear whether it is the city of Ur in Babylon or a city in Turkey (Gn 11:28).

Uriah (yoo-RAI-uh). Bathsheba's husband, whose death David arranged (2 Sm 11:14ff). He is mentioned in the genealogy of Jesus (Mt 1:6).

Uzziah (uh-ZAI-uh). Son and successor of Amaziah as King of Judah (2 Kgs 14:21), and an ancestor of Jesus (Mt 1:8f).

Wadi (WAH-di). An often dry river bed (Gn 26:19). The Wadi of Egypt was one of the boundaries of the Davidic kingdom.

Water Gate (WAW-tuhr gayt). A gate restored by Nehemiah on the east of Jerusalem (Neh 8:1ff).

Wisdom (WIS-duhm). Sixth of the 7 Wisdom Books of the Old Testament.

Yahweh (YAH-weh). The proper personal name of the God of Israel, signifying "I am who am" (Ex 3:14f). It is commonly explained in reference to God as the absolute and necessary Being. It may be understood of God as the Source of all created beings. Out of reverence for this name, the term Adonai, "my Lord," was later used as a substitute. The word LORD in the *New American Bible* version represents this traditional usage. The word "Jehovah" arose from a false reading of this name as it is written in the current Hebrew text.

Yahweh-yireh (YAH-weh-YIR-ee). A Hebrew expression meaning "The LORD will see," which Abraham used to name the site where God had stopped him from killing his son Isaac (Gn 22:14).

Zacchaeus (za-KEE-uhs). A tax collector who entertained Jesus (Lk 19:1ff).

Zadok (ZAY-dok). One of the chief priests dung the reigns of David (2 Sm 8:17) and Solomon (1Kgs 1:8, 32ff) and also an ancestor of Jesus (Mt 1:14).

Zarephath (ZAR-uh-fath). An Old Testament town remembered chiefly because Elijah resided there during the latter half of the famine caused by the drought (1 Kgs 17:9ff), which was specifically mentioned by Jesus (Lk 4:26).

Zealot (ZEL-uht). Member of a fanatical Jewish party, strongest from 6 to 70 A.D. It sought to overthrow the Roman authority and establish a Jewish theocracy over the earth. Its members resorted to violence and assassination and provoked the Roman War, which ended with the destruction of Jerusalem in 70 A.D. It seems to have been headed by Judas of Galilee (Acts 5:37). One of Christ's disciples was a member of this party (Lk 6:15; Acts 1:13).

Zebedee (ZEB-uh-dee). Father of the apostles James "the less" and John (Mt 4:21).

Zebulun (ZEB-yuh-luhn). One of the twelve tribes of Israel springing from Zebulun, the son of Jacob and Leah (Gn 30:19f). Christ later carried on his ministry in its regions and thus fulfilled the ancient prophecy of Isaiah (Is 8:23ff; Mt 4:12-16).

Zechariah (zek-uh-RAI-uh). Name of many people, such as: (1) the son and successor of Jeroboam (2 Kgs 14:29); (2) husband of Elizabeth and father of John the Baptist (Lk 1;5ff); (3) the eleventh of the 12 Minor Prophets of the Old Testament.

Zedekiah (zed-uh-KAI-uh). Son of King Josiah, brother of King Jehoiakim, and uncle of king Jeroiachin, he was the last king of Judah (597-587 B.C.). After being warned by the prophet Jeremiah about the consequences of his policy (Jer 34:2ff), he was captured while fleeing from Jerusalem when it fell in 587 B.C. The Babylonians blinded him and carried him off into exile (2 Kgs 25:6ff).

Zephaniah (zef-uh-NAI-uh). Tenth of the 12 Minor Prophets in the Old Testament.

Zerah (ZIR-uh). Son of Judah, who is mentioned in the genealogy of Jesus (Mt 1:3).

Zerubbabel (zuh-RUHB-uh-buhl). Grandson of Jehoiachin (1 Chr 3:19), who returned from Babylon and became governor (Hg 1:1), and an ancestor of Jesus (Mt 1:12).

Zion (ZAI-uhn). Central part of the hill on which the temple of Jerusalem was built. This term is often used to designate Jerusalem as a holy city (Pss 2:6; 132:15; Zec 9:9), the Church of God (Heb 12:22), and the heavenly city (Rv 14:1).

Ziph (zif). A city of Judah, probably in the vicinity of Hebron where David spared Saul's life (1 Sm 26:2ff).

APPENDIX 4: INDEX OF BIBLICAL TEXTS

READINGS

Genesis

1:1—2:2	156
1:1, 26-31a	160
2:7-9; 3:1-7	83
3:9-15, 20	14
11:1-9	221
12:1-4a	89
22:1-2, 9a, 10-13, 15-18	165
22:1-18	162

Exodus

12:1-8, 11-14	138
14:15—15:1	167
17:3-7	92
19:2-6a	247
19:3-8a, 16-20b	222
22:20-26	334
34:4b-6, 8-9	234

Numbers

6:22-27	54

Deuteronomy

8:2-3, 14b-16a	237

1 Samuel

16:1b, 6-7, 10-13a	100

1 Kings

3:5, 7-12	274
19:9a, 11-13a	283

2 Kings

4:8-11, 14-16a	255

1 Chronicles

15:3-4, 15-16; 16:1-2	287

Proverbs

31:10-13, 19-20, 30-31	350

Wisdom

6:12-16	346
12:13, 16-19	269

Sirach

3:2-7, 12-14	49
27:30—28:9	307

Isaiah

2:1-5	10
5:1-7	321
7:10-14	27
8:23—9:3	67
9:1-6	36
11:1-10	18
22:19-23	298
25:6-10a	326
35:1-6a, 10	23
42:1-4, 6-7	61
45:1, 4-6	331
49:3, 5-6	64
50:4-7	117
52:7-10	43
52:13—53:12	143
54:5-14	170
55:1-3	279
55:1-11	172
55:6-9	312
55:10-11	263
56:1, 6-7	294
58:7-10	76
60:1-6	57
61:1-3ab, 6a, 8b-9	135
62:1-5	30
62:11-12	40

Jeremiah

20:7-9	301
20:10-13	251

Baruch

3:9-15, 32—4:4	174

Ezekiel

18:25-28	316
33:7-9	304
34:11-12, 15-17	355
36:16-17a, 18-28	176
37:1-14	223
37:12-14	108

Hosea

6:3-6	243

Joel

2:12-18	79
3:1-5	225

Zephaniah

2:3; 3:12-13	72

Zechariah

9:9-10	259

Malachi

1:14b—2:2b, 8-10	342

Matthew

1:1-25	32
1:18-24	29
1:18-25	35
2:1-12	59
2:13-15, 19-23	52
3:1-12	21
3:13-17	63
4:1-11	87
4:12-17	70
4:12-23	69
5:1-12a	74, 340
5:13-16	78
6:1-6, 16-18	81
9:9-13	246
9:36—10:8	249
10:26-33	253
10:37-42	257
11:2-11	25
11:25-30	262
13:1-9	267
13:1-23	265
13:24-30	273
13:24-43	271
13:44-46	277
13:44-52	276
14:13-21	281
14:22-33	285
15:21-28	297
16:13-20	300
16:21-27	303
17:1-9	91
18:15-20	306
18:21-35	309
20:1-16A	314
21:1-11	116
21:28-32	319
21:33-43	324
22:1-10	329
22:1-14	328
22:15-21	333
22:34-40	336
23:1-12	344
24:37-44	13
25:1-13	349
25:14-15, 19-21	354
25:14-30	352

READINGS (continued)

25:31-46 358
26:14—27:66 120
27:11-54 131
28:1-10 182
28:16-20 216

Luke

1:26-38 16
1:39-56 292
2:1-14 38
2:15-20 42
2:16-21 56
4:16-21 137
11:27-28 289
24:13-35 196

John

1:1-5, 9-14 47
1:1-18 46
1:29-34 66
3:16-18 236
4:5-15, 19b-26, 39a,
   40-42 97
4:5-42 94
6:51-58 242
7:37-39 228
9:1, 6-9, 13-17, 34-38 106
9:1-41 103
10:1-10 202
11:1-45 110
11:3-7, 17, 20-27, 33b-45 113
13:1-15 141
14:15-21 212
17:1-11a 219
18:1—19:42 147
20:1-9 187
20:19-23 233
20:19-31 191

Acts

1:1-11 213
1:12-14 217
2:1-11 229
2:14, 22-33 193
2:14a, 36-41 199
2:42-47 188
6:1-7 204
8:5-8, 14-17 209
10:34-38 62

10:34a, 37-43 183
13:16-17, 22-25 31

Romans

1:1-7 28
4:18-25 245
5:1-2, 5-8 93
5:6-11 248
5:12-15 252
5:12, 17-19 86
5:12-19 85
6:3-4, 8-11 256
6:3-11 180
8:8-11 109
8:9, 11-13 261
8:18-23 264
8:22-27 227
8:26-27 270
8:28-30 276
8:35, 37-39 280
9:1-5 284
11:13-15, 29-32 296
11:33-36 299
12:1-2 302
13:8-10 305
13:11-14 12
15:4-9 20

1 Corinthians

1:1-3 65
1:10-13, 17 68
1:26-31 73
2:1-5 77
5:6b-8 185
10:16-17 239
11:23-26 140
12:3b-7, 12-13 231
15:20-26, 28 356
15:20-27 291
15:54b-57 288

2 Corinthians

5:20—6:2 80
13:11-13 235

Galatians

4:4-7 55

Ephesians

1:3-6, 11-12 15
1:17-23 215

3:2-3a, 5-6 58
5:8-14 102

Philippians

1:20c-24, 27a 313
2:1-5 318
2:1-11 317
2:6-11 119
4:6-9 323
4:12-14, 19-20 327

Colossians

3:1-4 185
3:12-17 51
3:12-21 50

1 Thessalonians

1:1-5b 332
1:5c-10 335
2:7b-9, 13 343
4:13-14 348
4:13-18 347
5:1-6 351

2 Timothy

1:8b-10 90

Titus

2:11-14 37
3:4-7 41

Hebrews

1:1-6 44
4:14-16; 5:7-9 146

James

5:7-10 24

1 Peter

1:3-9 190
1:17-21 195
2:4-9 206
2:20b-25 201
3:15-18 211
4:13-16 218

1 John

3:1-3 340

Revelation

1:5-8 136
7:2-4, 9-14 338
11:19a; 12:1-6a, 10ab 290

RESPONSORIAL PSALMS

16:1-2, 5, 7-8, 9-10, 11 (℟.:11a)..194

16:5, 8, 9-10, 11 (℟.:1) 166

18:2-3, 3-4, 47, 51 (℟.:2) 335

19:8, 9, 10, 11 (℟.:Jn 6:68c)......................................176

22:8-9, 17-18, 19-20, 23-24 (℟.:2a) 118

23:1-2, 2-3, 5-6 (℟.:1) 356

23:1-3a, 3b-4, 5, 6 (℟.:1) 101, 200

23:1-3a, 3b-4, 5, 6 (℟.:6cd)..326

24:1-2, 3-4, 5-6 (℟.:6) 339

24:1-2, 3-4, 5-6 (℟.:7c and 10b)..................................27

25:4-5, 6-7, 8-9 (℟.:6a) 316

27:1, 4, 7-8 (℟.:13) 217

27:1, 4, 13-14 (℟.:1a)..67

29:1-2, 3-4, 3, 9-10 (℟.:11b) 62

30:2, 4, 5-6, 11-12, 13 (℟.:2a)......................................171

31:2, 6, 12-13, 15-16, 17, 25 (℟.:Lk 23:46) 145

33:1-2, 4-5, 18-19 (℟.:22)...205

33:4-5, 6-7, 12-13, 20-22 (℟.:5b) 162

33:4-5, 18-19, 20, 22 (℟.:22)..89

40:2, 4, 7-8, 8-9, 10 (℟.:8a and 9a)...............................64

42:3, 5; 43:3, 4 (℟.:42:2)...178

45:10, 11, 12, 16 (℟.:10bc)...291

47:2-3, 6-7, 8-9 (℟.:6) 214

50:1, 8, 12-13, 14-15 (℟.:23b).......................................244

51:3-4, 5-6, 12-13, 14, 17 (℟.:3)......................................80

51:3-4, 5-6, 12-13, 17 (℟.:cf. 3a)....................................84

51:12-13, 14-15, 18-19 (℟.:12a) 179

63:2, 3-4, 5-6, 7-8 (℟.:2b)..346

63:2, 3-4, 5-6, 8-9 (℟.:2b)..301

65:10, 11, 12-13, 14 (℟.:Lk 8:8) 263

66:1-3, 4-5, 6-7, 16, 20 (℟.:1) 210

67:2-3, 5, 6, 8 (℟.:2a)..54

67:2-3, 5, 6, 8 (℟.:4)...295

69:8-10, 14, 17, 33-35 (℟.:14c).....................................252

72:1-2, 7-8, 10-11, 12-13 (℟.:cf. 11) 58

72:1-2, 7-8, 12-13, 17 (℟.:cf. 7) 19

80:9, 12, 13-14, 15-16, 19-20 (℟.:Is 5:7a) 322

85:9, 10, 11-12, 13-14 (℟.:8)...283

86:5-6, 9-10, 15-16 (℟.:5a)..269

89:2-3, 16-17, 18-19 (℟.:2a)..256

89:4-5, 16-17, 27, 29 (℟.:2a)...31

89:21-22, 25, 27 (℟.:2a)...136

95:1-2, 6-7, 8-9 (℟.:8)...92, 304

96:1-2, 2-3, 11-12, 13 (℟.:Lk 2:11)................................37

96:1, 3, 4-5, 7-8, 9-10 (℟.:7b)..331

97:1, 6, 11-12 40

98:1, 2-3, 3-4 (℟.:1a)..15

98:1, 2-3, 3-4, 5-6 (℟.:3c)..43

100:1-2, 3, 5 (℟.:3c)..247

103:1-2, 3-4, 9-10, 11-12 (℟.:8)....................................308

104:1-2, 5-6, 10, 12, 13-14, 24, 35 (℟.:30)...............161

104:1-2, 24, 35, 27-28, 29, 30 (℟.:cf. 30)....................226

104:1, 24, 29-30, 31, 34 (℟.:cf 30)................................230

112:4-5, 6-7, 8-9 (℟.:4a)...76

116:12-13, 15-16bc, 17-18 (℟.:cf. 1 Cor 10:16) 139

118:1-2, 16-17, 22-23 181

118:1-2, 16-17, 22-23 (℟.:24).......................................184

118:2-4, 13-15, 22-24 (℟.:1)..189

119:57, 72, 76-77, 127-128, 129-130 (℟.:97a)............275

122:1-2, 3-4, 4-5, 6-7, 8-9 11

128:1-2, 3, 4-5 (℟.:cf. 1) 49

128:1-2, 3, 4-5 (℟.:cf. 19)...350

130:1-2, 3-4, 5-6, 7-8 (℟.:7)...108

131:1, 2, 3 343

132:6-7, 9-10, 13-14 (℟.:8)..288

138:1-2, 2-3, 6, 8 (℟.:8bc)...298

145:1-2, 8-9, 10-11, 13-14 (℟.:cf. 1) 259

145:2-3, 8-9, 17-18 (℟.:18a) 112

145:8-9, 15-16, 17-18 (℟.:cf. 16) 279

146:6-7, 8-9, 9-10 (℟.:cf. Is 35:4) 24

146:6-7, 8-9, 9-10 (℟.:Mt 5:3)...72

147:12-13, 14-15, 19-20 (℟.:12)...................................238

RESPONSORIAL CANTICLES

Ex 15:1-2, 3-4, 5-6, 17-18 (℟.:1b) 169

Is 12:2-3, 4, 5-6 (℟.:3)..173

Is 12:2-3, 4bcd, 5-6 (℟.:3)...179

Dn 3:52, 53, 54, 55 (℟.:52b) 234

ALLELUIA VERSES AND VERSES BEFORE THE GOSPEL

Ps 85:8 12	Jn 1:14a, 12a 65
Ps 95:7-8 81	Jn 4:42, 15 (cf.) 94
Ps 130:5 (cf.) 285	Jn 6:51 242
Is 61:1 (cited in Lk 4:18) 25, 137	Jn 8:12 ....78, 102
Mt 1:23 29	Jn 10:14 202
Mt 2:2 59	Jn 10:27 319
Mt 4:4b 87, 281	Jn 11:25a, 26 110
Mt 4:23 (cf.) 69, 296	Jn 13:34 ....141, 309
Mt 5:12a 74	Jn 14:6 207
Mt 11:25 (cf.) 261, 270, 276	Jn 14:18 219
Mt 11:28 340	Jn 14:23 ....211, 336
Mt 16:18 300	Jn 15:4a, 5b 352
Mt 17:5 (cf) 90	Jn 15:16 (cf.) 323
Mt 23:9b-10b 344	Jn 15:26b, 27a 253
Mt 24:42a, 44 348	Jn 20:29 191
Mt 28:19a, 20b 216	Acts 16:14b 313
Mk 1:15 249	1 Cor 5:7b-8a 186
Mk 9:7 (cf.) 63	2 Cor 5:19 306
Mk 11:9, 10 357	Eph 1:17-18 (cf.) 302, 328
Lk 1:28 (cf.) 16	Phil 2:8-9 ....119, 146
Lk 2:10-11 38	Phil 2:15d, 16a 333
Lk 2:14 41	Col 3:15a, 16a 52
Lk 3:4, 6 21	Heb 1:1-2 55
Lk 4:18 (cf.) 246	1 Pt 2:9 237
Lk 11:28 289	Rv 1:8 235
Lk 24:32 196	